COURTING DEMOCRACY IN BOSNIA AND HERZEGOVINA

The International Criminal Tribunal for the former Yugoslavia (ICTY) struggled to apprehend and try high-profile defendants such as Serbian leader Slobodan Milošević, and often received more criticism than praise. This volume argues that the underappreciated court has in fact made a substantial contribution to Bosnia and Herzegovina's transition to democracy.

Based on more than three years of field research and several hundred interviews, this study brings together multiple research methods – including surveys, ethnography, and archival materials – to show the court's impact on five segments of Bosnian society, emphasizing the role of the social setting in translating international law into domestic contexts. Much of the early rhetoric about the transformative potential of international criminal law fostered unrealistic expectations that institutions like the ICTY could not meet. Judged by more realistic standards, however, international law is seen to play a modest yet important role in postwar transitions. The findings of this study have implications for the study of international courts around the world and the role that law plays in contributing to social change.

Lara J. Nettelfield is an Assistant Professor at Simon Fraser University's School for International Studies. She is currently completing a postdoctoral fellowship at the Institut Barcelona d'Estudis Internacionals. Prior to joining Simon Fraser University, she taught at Columbia University in New York City. She has published in the *International Journal of Transitional Justice* and the Canadian International Council's *International Journal.* She has worked for the NATO Parliamentary Assembly (NATO PA) and the Organization for Security and Cooperation in Europe (OSCE), in addition to nongovernmental organizations in Bosnia and Herzegovina. Nettelfield's writing has also appeared in the *Los Angeles Times, Globe and Mail,* and *Vancouver Sun.*

Her research has been funded by Fulbright Hays, the German Marshall Fund, the Social Science Research Council (SSRC), the International Research and Exchange Board (IREX), the American Councils for International Education: ACTR/ACCELS, and Columbia University's Harriman Institute.

CAMBRIDGE STUDIES IN LAW AND SOCIETY

Cambridge Studies in Law and Society aims to publish the best scholarly work on legal discourse and practice in its social and institutional contexts, combining theoretical insights and empirical research.

The fields that it covers are: studies of law in action; the sociology of law; the anthropology of law; cultural studies of law, including the role of legal discourses in social formations; law and economics; law and politics; and studies of governance. The books consider all forms of legal discourse across societies, rather than being limited to lawyers' discourses alone.

The series editors come from a range of disciplines: academic law; socio-legal studies; sociology and anthropology. All have been actively involved in teaching and writing about law in context.

Series editors

Chris Arup
Monash University, Victoria
Martin Chanock
La Trobe University, Melbourne
Pat O'Malley
University of Sydney
Sally Engle Merry
New York University
Susan Silbey
Massachusetts Institute of Technology

Books in the Series

The World Trade Organization Knowledge Agreements
2nd Edition
Christopher Arup

Law and Nature
David Delaney

Constitutionalizing Economic Globalization:
Investment Rules and Democracy's Promise
David Schneiderman

Law, Anthropology, and the Constitution of the Social:
Making Persons and Things
Edited by Alain Pottage and Martha Mundy

Law and Globalization from Below:
Towards a Cosmopolitan Legality
Edited by Boaventura de Sousa Santos and César A. Rodríguez-Garavito

(Continued after the index)

For M.

COURTING DEMOCRACY IN BOSNIA AND HERZEGOVINA

The Hague Tribunal's Impact in a Postwar State

LARA J. NETTELFIELD

Simon Fraser University and Institut Barcelona d'Estudis Internacionals

CAMBRIDGE UNIVERSITY PRESS
Cambridge, New York, Melbourne, Madrid, Cape Town, Singapore,
São Paulo, Delhi, Dubai, Tokyo

Cambridge University Press
32 Avenue of the Americas, New York, NY 10013-2473, USA

www.cambridge.org
Information on this title: www.cambridge.org/9780521763806

First published 2010

Printed in the United States of America

A catalog record for this publication is available from the British Library.

Library of Congress Cataloging in Publication data
Nettelfield, Lara J.
  Courting democracy in Bosnia and Herzegovina: the Hague Tribunal's impact in a
  postwar state / Lara J. Nettelfield.
     p.   cm. – (Cambridge studies in law and society)
  Includes bibliographical references and index.
  ISBN 978-0-521-76380-6 (hardback)
  1. International Tribunal for the Prosecution of Persons Responsible for Serious
  Violations of International Humanitarian Law Committed in the Territory of the
  Former Yugoslavia since 1991.   2. Democratization – Bosnia and Herzegovina.
  3. Bosnia and Herzegovina – Politics and government – 1992–   I. Title.   II. Series.
  KZ1203.A12N48 2010
  949.74203–dc22   2010002815

ISBN 978-0-521-76380-6 Hardback

The author would like to thank the following publication for permission to reprint
previously published material:
International Journal of Transitional Justice, for permission to use the material
in Chapter 7, which appeared in a slightly different form as: Lara J. Nettelfield,
"From the Battlefield to the Barracks: The International Criminal Tribunal for
the Former Yugoslavia and the Armed Forces of Bosnia and Herzegovina,"
International Journal of Transitional Justice 4 No. 1, 2010
, copyright © 2010 Oxford University Press.

Contents

Figures

Tables

Acknowledgments

I first arrived in Sarajevo on an overnight bus from Zagreb in the summer of 1998. Little did I know then that Bosnia and Herzegovina would be my home for much of the next decade. That summer I started to form relationships with people all over the country who would sustain, support, and inform this study.

In Sarajevo, one of my host institutions was the Research and Documentation Center (RDC). I joined RDC employees on many journeys to the farthest corners of Bosnia and Herzegovina and beyond – events and meetings in Cazin, Bijeljina, Brčko, Sanski Most, Stolac, Bosansko Grahovo, Goražde, Belgrade, Vukovar, and Budapest come to mind. This study benefited greatly from the RDC's experience documenting violations of international humanitarian law and genocide. I spent many hours discussing the issues addressed in this book with the RDC's talented staff (past and present). They are the unsung heroes of the Center's "Human Losses in Bosnia and Herzegovina 1991–95" project and the data in many parts of this book. I especially thank Selma Korjenić, Senada Gugić, Jadranko Kurbegović, Eldar Jahić, Amela Šatrović, Lara Musulin, Mirela Vasić, Linda Popić, Božana Puljić, Safer Hukara, and Mirsad Tokača. Amela helped me set up my appointments with NGOs all over the country; Jadranko often stayed late so I could finish coding data. Selma, a talented sociologist, helped me administer the survey of the armed forces and code the data. Mirela aided the coding effort.

My second home in Sarajevo was the University of Sarajevo's Human Rights Center. Its director at the time, Dino Abazović, assisted me with many aspects of this project, including the content of the survey of the armed forces. Dino's previous research on the same topic helped me avoid reinventing the wheel. Saša Madacki gave me a refresher course on the SPSS statistics program and consulted on the survey.

Radmila Turanjanin, Ljuljeta Koshi, Sabina Pstrocki, Alma Kačar, Senada Kreso, and Leila Rachidi helped with various aspects of this project. Radmila's high standards are inspiring. Tarik Samarah, Faruk Šabanović, Peter Lippman, Tim Hughes, Charlotte Eager, Susan L. Somers, Malcolm Brabant, David Schwendiman, Raffi Gregorian, Edward Llewellyn, Nidžara Ahmetašević, Mina Vidaković, Sven Alkalaj, Ahmed Žilić, Kathryne Bomberger, Asta Zinbo, Zlatko Hurtić, Sonja Biserko, and Ivan Kuzminović also provided perspective from their fields. Lejla Pašić Ebner was always supportive. Edina Bećirević of the University of Sarajevo's Criminal Sciences

fellowship. Earlier, a Columbia University Arnold A. Saltzman Institute for War and Peace Summer (IWPS) Travel Fellowship, and a Foreign Language and Area Studies (FLAS) grant for Serbo-Croatian, helped me both to conduct preliminary research and to acquire necessary language skills. Alessandro Silj helped coordinate the SSRC grant. Jacques Rupnik facilitated my time as a visiting scholar at the Centre d'études et de recherches internationales (CERI) in Paris in 2005. Conversations there with Igor Štiks, a novelist and political scientist, influenced my thinking about the region and his hometown, Sarajevo. A follow-up travel grant, the International Research and Exchange Board (IREX) Individual Advanced Research Opportunity grant (IARO), helped me finalize my research, as did one from Simon Fraser University (SFU).

At SFU, the students of IS302, *Introduction to Humanitarian Intervention and Assistance* – especially Meghan Brown, Drew Stewart, Larissa Muir, James Haga, Eric Wright, Ivan Živković, Jelena Golubović, and Iman Gonzalez – influenced this project with their hard questions and creative thinking. I would also like to thank my SFU colleagues Andre Gerolymatos, Jeff Checkel, Mark Skinner, and Derek Congram. Every young scholar should be so lucky as to have a research assistant as talented as Sabiha Jukić.

The Institut Barcelona d'Estudis Internacionals (IBEI), where I am currently a postdoctoral Fellow, provided a wonderful home in which to finish this book. At IBEI, I thank Fred Halliday and Robert Kissack for important contributions in the final months of this project. Thanks also to former IBEI postdoctoral Fellow Gemma Colantes-Celador of City University London.

This book owes an intellectual debt to many of my colleagues and friends from UC Berkeley and Columbia University, who have all gone on to bigger and better things. Hawley Johnson was a constant companion on research trips in Southeastern Europe. I am also grateful to Sue Nahm, Shareen Hertel, Arturo Sotomayor, Katia Papagianni, Rory Finnin, Ashley Esarey, Leslie Powell, Troy McGrath, Kay Achar, Ernesto Estrella, Ruth Ferrero, Michael Struett, Nadege Ragaru, Leila Kazemi, and Douglas Greenfield, to name a few. To Tanya Domi, Elise Guiliano, Fordeen Despard, Dana Baze, Jacqueline Berman, and Sherrill Stroschein, I owe a special debt of gratitude; their undying enthusiasm and support kept me going over the years.

I must thank Rosemary Armao, Neven Andjelić, Nermin Durmo, Hariz Halilović, Barbara Krijgsman, Katherine Reyes, Mensura Hadžović, Aida Hozić, David L. Phillips, Senad Kamenica, Alma Mašić, Edin Forto, Srdjan Mandić, Marijana Kramarić Štiks, Mirsad Sabić, Elvis Selimović, Sumantra Bose, Drew Sullivan, August Stankić, Robert Stockdale, Vesna Bogojević, Alex Talmon l'Armée, Napier Collyns, and James Wilk; without them, the journey would have been even longer and more difficult. Thanks also to Carlena Gower, DJ Eldon, Jerry and Bonnie Galbreath, Nicole Kolhoff, Beverley Sutherland, Sunil Kumar, Anissa Bouziane, Rima Abd-el-Baki, Maria Fontanals Novell, Urban Ahlin, Yasmine Sherif, Tania Rzhondkovsky, Philip Anderson, Peter Sherwin, and Bill and Nancy Mullally.

Jonathan and Bettyann Nettelfield gave me a home even when I was away, making it all possible, and Jonathan inspired this project in more ways than he knows. Joanna Nettelfield helped me get organized when I returned from Bosnia. My old friend from Kyiv, Kimberly Storr, added remarkably to all aspects of this project with her wit, wisdom, and wordsmithing. Kim was also a constant source of encouragement. I fulfilled a decades-old promise to the late Mika C. Bissett to write a book; sadly, she was not able to pen hers.

Despite this wonderful group of individuals who contributed to my project, I am sure there are things that have been overlooked. Any remaining errors or omissions are my responsibility.

Finally, I wish to acknowledge the hundreds of anonymous interviewees and survey participants who generously gave their time to yet another foreigner poking around in their country. They cannot all be named here, but I am grateful for their contributions. I hope I have managed to tell a story with which they can identify.

Lara J. Nettelfield
Barcelona July 2009

Abbreviations

AAAS	American Association for the Advancement of Science
AFBiH	Armed Forces of Bosnia and Herzegovina
AP	Associated Press
ARBiH	Armija Republike Bosne i Hercegovine (Army of the Republic of Bosnia and Herzegovina)
ARK	Autonomna oblast Krajina (Autonomous Region of Krajina)
ATCA	Alien Tort Claims Act (U.S.)
BHRT	Radio televizija Bosne i Hercegovine (Radio and Television of Bosnia and Herzegovina)
BiH	Bosna i Hercegovina (Bosnia and Herzegovina)
CCI	Centar civilnih inicijativa (Center for Civic Initiatives)
BIRN	Balkan Investigative Reporting Network
CIA	Central Intelligence Agency (U.S.)
CRA	Communications and Regulatory Agency
DPA	Dayton Peace Agreement (colloquial name of the GFAP)
DPC	Democratization Policy Council
EAF	Entity Armed Forces
ECHR	European Convention on Human Rights
EU	European Union
EUFOR	European Union Force
EUPM	European Union Policing Mission
EUSR	European Union Special Representative
FBiH	Federacija Bosne i Hercegovine (Federation of Bosnia and Herzegovina)
FRY	Federal Republic of Yugoslavia
FTV	Federalna televizija Bosne i Hercegovine (Television of the Federation of Bosnia and Herzegovina)
GFAP	General Framework Agreement for Peace (formal name of the Dayton Peace Agreement)
HDZ	Hrvatska demokratska zajednica (Croat Democratic Union)
HJPC	High Judicial and Prosecutorial Council

HLC	Humanitarian Law Center
HV	Hrvatska vojska (Croatian Army)
HVO	Hrvatsko vijeće obrane (Croat Defense Council)
HRC	Human Rights Chamber
HRW	Human Rights Watch
HZHB	Hrvatska zajednica Herceg-Bosna (Croatian Community of Herceg-Bosna)
ICC	International Criminal Court
ICG	International Crisis Group
ICJ	International Court of Justice
ICMP	International Commission on Missing Persons
ICRC	International Committee of the Red Cross
ICTR	International Criminal Tribunal for Rwanda
ICTY	International Criminal Tribunal for the former Yugoslavia
ICVA	International Council of Voluntary Agencies
IEBL	Inter-Entity Boundary Line
IFOR	Implementation Force (NATO)
IHL	international humanitarian law
IJC	Independent Judicial Commission
IKV	Interkerkelijk Vredesberaad (Interchurch Peace Council)
IMC	Independent Media Commission
IPTF	International Police Task Force
IWPR	Institute for War and Peace Reporting
JMC	Joint Military Commission
JNA	Jugoslovenska narodna armija (Yugoslav People's Army)
KM	Konvertabilna marka (convertible mark; officially: Bosnia and Herzegovina Convertible Mark, BAM)
LEC	Local Election Commission
MSF	Médecins Sans Frontières
MUP	Ministarstvo unutarnjih poslova (Ministry of Internal Affairs or Ministry of Interior)
NATO	North Atlantic Treaty Organization
NIOD	Nederlands Instituut voor Oorlogsdocumentatie (Netherlands Institute for War Documentation)
NGO	non-governmental organization
OHR	Office of the High Representative
OOTW	Operations Other Than War
OSCE	Organization for Security and Cooperation in Europe
OTP	Office of the Prosecutor (ICTY)
PEC	Provisional Election Commission
PfP	Partnership for Peace (NATO)
PHR	Physicians for Human Rights
PIC	Peace Implementation Council (of Dayton Peace Agreement)

PIFWCs	Persons Indicted for War Crimes
PIP	Podrinje Identification Project
PL	Patriotska liga (Patriotic League)
PO BiH	Prosecutor's Office of Bosnia and Herzegovina
RDC	Research and Documentation Center
RS	Republika Srpska
RTRS	Radio televizija Republike Srpske (Radio and Television of Republika Srpska)
SANU	Srpska akademija nauka i umetnosti (Serbian Academy of Sciences and Arts)
SAO	Srpska autonomna oblast (Serbian Autonomous District)
SCMM	Standing Committee on Military Matters
SDA	Stranka demokratske akcije (Party of Democratic Action)
SDC	Supreme Defense Council (FRY)
SDS	Srpska demokratska stranka (Serb Democratic Party)
SENSE News Agency	South East News Service Europe Agency
SFOR	Stabilization Force (NATO)
SFRY	Socialist Federal Republic of Yugoslavia
SIPA	State Investigation and Protection Agency
TO	Teritorijalna odbrana (Territorial Defense Force)
TRC	Truth and Reconciliation Commission
UN	United Nations
UNDP	United Nations Development Programme
UNHCR	United Nations High Commissioner for Refugees
UNMIBH	United Nations Mission in Bosnia and Herzegovina
UNPA	United Nations Protected Area
UNPROFOR	United Nations Protection Force
UNSC	United Nations Security Council
USIP	United States Institute for Peace
VJ	Vojska Jugoslavije (Yugoslav Army)
VOPP	Vance-Owen Peace Plan
VRS	Vojska Republike Srpske (Army of Republika Srpska)
VSRBiH	Vojska Srpske Republike Bosne i Hercegovine (Army of the Serb Republic of Bosnia and Herzegovina)
YIHR	Youth Initiative for Human Rights
ZOBK	Zajednica opština Bosanske Krajine (Community of Municipalities of the Bosnian Krajina)

BOSNIA AND HERZEGOVINA

Source: United Nations.

1 Introduction

Assessing the Impact of the International Criminal Tribunal for the Former Yugoslavia (ICTY) in Bosnia and Herzegovina

March 8, 2004: cold rain drizzled on a group of 50 women, many of them widows, gathered outside the gates of the United Nations (UN) compound in the Sarajevo neighborhood of Nedžarići, which housed the local office of the International Criminal Tribunal for the former Yugoslavia (ICTY). Each carried an umbrella in one hand, and with the other gripped a large cloth banner bearing the names of their husbands, sons, and brothers who had perished after the fall of the Srebrenica enclave. The town had been declared a UN safe area in 1993; however, in July 1995, Bosnian Serb and Serbian forces had overrun the town, killing over 8,000 Bosniak (Bosnian Muslim) men and boys who ended up in mass graves.[1] It was the single worst atrocity of the Bosnian war. The perpetrators would later try to hide the signs of their crimes, disturbing the bodies to move them to clandestine locations.

The reason for the public protest was the news of the recently drafted United Nations Security Council (UNSC) Resolution outlining the planned closure of the ICTY.[2] But at that time, in 2004, nine years after the end of the war, many of Srebrenica's clandestine graves had not yet been discovered. Srebrenica and its inhabitants would continue to experience unspeakable human suffering long after the war's end. "We are the families of the killed and the disappeared. Because of us the Tribunal was founded. Don't close it. Don't obstruct it. Let it dispense justice and truth," said a sign carried by the huddled protesters. They saw themselves as some of the court's original constituents who were, however, rarely asked about such important matters, and who were about to be let down yet again by the international community.

---

[1] In September 1993, Bosnian Muslim leaders voted to rename their community "Bosniaks" at the Second Congress of Bosniaks in Sarajevo. See Robert J. Donia, "The New Bosniak History," *Nationalities Papers* 28, no. 2 (June 2000), 351–358; Robert J. Donia, *Sarajevo: A Biography* (Ann Arbor: University of Michigan Press, 2006), xxi.

[2] There were two UN Security Council Resolutions addressing the closure of the ICTY around the time of the protest: UNSC Resolution 1503 (2003) (S/RES/1503, August 28, 2003) and UNSC Resolution 1534 (2004) (S/RES/1534, March 26, 2004).

Figure 1.1. Members of the Mothers of the Enclaves of Srebrenica and Žepa, including Sabaheta Fejzić and Sabra Kulenović, protest the plan to close the International Criminal Tribunal for the former Yugoslavia, Sarajevo. March 8, 2004.
Photograph: Senad Gubelić, *Oslobođenje*.

Their protest illustrated the complicated and fraught relationship Bosnian citizens had with the Tribunal set up to prosecute genocide and violations of international humanitarian law in the countries of the former Yugoslavia. This and other similar groups had become increasingly critical of the court's work over the postwar years. Yet on this day, the women decided to send another message: beyond their disappointment and disillusionment, they felt this international institution had not finished its work in Bosnia and Herzegovina and should not close its doors.[3] The court, despite significant flaws, was integral to the postwar goals of this small group of Bosnian citizens who chose to fight the cold on a wet March morning.

This book tells a story largely untold, about these women and other groups in Bosnian society who have been affected by the ICTY. It addresses the role that the court played in Bosnia's ongoing transition to democracy. In doing so, this study joins the growing body of research that examines how efforts to seek accountability for mass atrocities affect domestic developments in postconflict societies.[4]

---

[3]   The formal name of the country today is Bosnia and Herzegovina; I primarily use the short version "Bosnia" throughout. The country, recognized as independent in April 1992, was called the Republic of Bosnia and Herzegovina; its name was changed to Bosnia and Herzegovina by the December 1995 Dayton Peace Agreement (formally the General Framework Agreement for Peace, or GFAP) that ended the war.

[4]   See especially Eric Stover and Harvey M. Weinstein, eds., *My Neighbor, My Enemy: Justice and Community in the Aftermath of Mass Atrocity* (Cambridge: Cambridge University Press, 2004); Kristen Cibelli and Tamy Guberek, *Justice Unknown, Justice Unsatisfied?: Bosnian NGOs*

Utilizing an interdisciplinary approach – drawing on survey research, oral histories, archival materials, and ethnography – it shows how the court has advanced Bosnia's processes of democratization in ways underappreciated by many current analysts. The court has facilitated social movements and the creation of new institutions, and has ultimately changed attitudes about accountability. While Bosnia's polity is fragile and, for many, the future is in question, this study illustrates some of the positive legacies of international justice.[5]

UN Security Council Resolution 827 created the ICTY on May 25, 1993, to address violations of international law in Southeastern Europe.[6] The resolution states that the court is intended to "contribute to the restoration and maintenance of peace."[7] The ICTY would later describe its achievements in language similar to the spirit of the Security Council Resolution that founded it: "holding leaders accountable, bringing justice to victims and giving them a voice, establishing the facts and developing international law and strengthening the rule of law."[8] The architects of the ICTY assumed that the court would have a substantial impact in the region.

Speak about the International Criminal Tribunal for the Former Yugoslavia (Boston, MA: Tufts University, 2000) <www.hrdag.org/resources/publications/justicereport.pdf> (accessed July 20, 2009); Human Rights Center and the International Human Rights Law Clinic, University of California, Berkeley, and the Human Rights Center, University of Sarajevo, "Justice, Accountability and Social Reconstruction in Bosnia and Herzegovina: An Interview Study of Bosnian Judges and Prosecutors," *Berkeley Journal of International Law* 18, no. 1 (2000):102–164; James Meernik, "Justice or Peace: How the International Criminal Tribunal Affects Societal Peace in Bosnia," *Journal of Peace Research* 42 (2005): 271–290; John Hagan and Sanja Kutnjak, "The Politics of Punishment and the Siege of Sarajevo: Toward a Conflict Theory of Perceived International (In)Justice," *Law and Society Review* 40, no. 2 (2006): 369–410. For a review of the literature, see Leslie Vinjamuri and Jack L. Snyder, "Advocacy and Scholarship in the Study of International War Crimes Tribunals and Transitional Justice," *Annual Review of Political Science* 7, no. 1 (2004): 345–362. See also Mark Osiel, *Mass Atrocity, Collective Memory and the Law* (New Brunswick, NJ: Transaction Publishers, 2000); Carlos Santiago Nino, *Radical Evil on Trial* (New Haven, CT: Yale University Press, 1996); A. James McAdams, ed., *Transitional Justice and the Rule of Law in New Democracies* (Notre Dame, IN: University of Notre Dame Press, 1997); Neil Kritz, ed., *Transitional Justice: How Emerging Democracies Reckon with Former Regimes*, 3 vols. (Washington, DC: United States Institute of Peace Press, 1995); and Naomi Roht-Arriaza and Javier Mariezcurrena, *Transitional Justice in the Twenty-First Century: Beyond Truth versus Justice* (Cambridge: Cambridge University Press, 2006).

5 See, for example, Srećko Latal, "Bosnia Heads for the Bottom, not Europe," Balkan Investigative Reporting Network (BIRN), *Balkan Insight*, July 14, 2009, <www.balkaninsight.com/en/main/blogs/21070/> (accessed July 14, 2009); and Paddy Ashdown and Richard Holbrooke, "A Bosnian Powder Keg," *The Guardian*, October 22, 2008.

6 UN Security Council Resolution 808 (1993) (S/RES/808, February 22, 1993) first set up the framework for the court, <www.un.org/Docs/scres/1993/scres93.htm> (accessed July 14, 2009).

7 The full text of UN Security Council Resolution 827 (1993) (S/RES/827, May 25, 1993) can be found at <www.un.org/Docs/scres/1993/scres93.htm> (accessed February 24, 2009).

8 International Criminal Tribunal for the former Yugoslavia, Achievements, <www.icty.org/sid/324> (accessed February 24, 2009). An early version of the ICTY's web site, now offline, listed its mission as, "to bring to justice persons allegedly responsible for serious violations of international humanitarian law; to render justice to the victims; to deter further crimes; and to contribute to the restoration of peace by promoting reconciliation in the former Yugoslavia."

4 Courting Democracy in Bosnia and Herzegovina

Extra-legal influences were as much a part of the rationale for its establishment as upholding the international rule of law.

The women in front of the UN compound on that March day, like many advocates of international justice, initially had much hope about the court's potential and promise for the region. Optimism had surrounded the ICTY and other similar judicial institutions created after the end of the Cold War. The massive geopolitical realignment that occurred at the time enabled the expansion of transitional justice instruments in countries moving toward democracy. "Transitional justice" became the umbrella term for methods to address mass atrocities and human rights violations in these changing societies, such as international tribunals, truth and reconciliation commissions, and lustration proceedings.[9] These methods, advocates argued, would help create the institutions and values necessary for democratic consolidation. The assumption by human rights activists was that such measures would have positive effects. Human Rights Watch, for example, reasoned that "reckoning with the crimes of the past does not impede the transition to democracy; it facilitates it."[10]

Over time, however, confidence in international courts eroded as arrests were not made, high-level cases were inconclusive, and legal instruments used in Iraq meted out what appeared to many as something other than justice.[11] The whole enterprise of international justice began to seem to some like a misuse of limited funds.

The first scholarly analyses of these ad hoc courts looked at their effects in the countries in which they operated, and drew pessimistic conclusions. Most found that they were counterproductive, failed to deliver their intended results, exacerbated the ethnic tensions they were designed to quell, and were disliked by the citizens in postconflict countries they were designed to serve.[12] Scholarly consensus

---

[9] The literature is vast and growing. The foundational book for most studies is Ruti G. Teitel, *Transitional Justice* (New York: Oxford University Press, 2002). For a work on truth commissions, see Priscilla B. Hayner, *Unspeakable Truths: Confronting State Terror and Atrocity* (New York: Routledge, 2001). For an overview of the various mechanisms, see Martha Minow, *Between Vengeance and Forgiveness: Facing History After Genocide and Mass Violence* (Boston: Beacon Press, 1998). On war crimes in Southeastern Europe, see Paul R. Williams and Michael P. Scharf, *Peace with Justice?: War Crimes and Accountability in the former Yugoslavia* (Lanham, MD: Rowman and Littlefield, 2002); Norman Cigar and Paul Williams, *Indictment at The Hague: The Milošević Regime and Crimes of the Balkan Wars* (New York: NYU Press, 2002); and James Gow, *The Serbian Project and Its Adversaries: A Strategy of War Crimes* (London: Hurst and Company, 2003).

[10] Kenneth Roth, "Milošević's Indictment Sets Much Needed Precedent," July 12, 2001, *Human Rights Watch*, <www.hrw.org/en/news/2001/07/12/milosevics-indictment-sets-much-needed-precedent> (accessed February 24, 2009).

[11] See, for example, Michael A. Newton and Michael P. Scharf, *Enemy of the State: The Trial and Execution of Saddam Hussein* (New York: St. Martin's Press, 2008).

[12] See Stover and Weinstein, *My Neighbor, My Enemy*; Jack L. Snyder and Leslie Vinjamuri, "Trials and Errors: Principle and Pragmatism in Strategies of International Justice," *International Security* 28, no. 3 (2003/04): 5–44; Helena Cobban, "Think Again: International Courts," *Foreign*

began to form that these experiments in international justice had largely failed. This book presents evidence that differs sharply from that gloomy conventional wisdom, and illustrates how attitudes changed over time, civil society mobilized, and domestic institutional capacity to try war crimes developed because an international tribunal had helped to put those developments in motion.

To date there have been relatively few analyses of the domestic impact of international tribunals, even in Southeastern Europe. This is surprising given the vast resources available to the ICTY and the historical significance of the proceedings: the first judgment treating rape as a war crime, the first indictment of a sitting head of state, and the court's impact on the evolution of international law. The region's wars have been the subject of wide-ranging discussion and many books.[13] Scholars have studied the founding of the ICTY and its internal politics, and journalists have described the crimes committed in the region, which included mass rape, deliberate destruction of cultural and religious institutions, and genocide.[14] Still, although interest in the subject is growing, only one scholarly book and a handful of articles have thus far directly addressed local attitudes toward and the effects of the ICTY.[15]

Policy (March–April 2006); and Tonya Putnam, "Human Rights and Sustainable Peace," in Stephen J. Stedman, et al., eds., *Ending Civil Wars: The Implementation of Peace Agreements* (Boulder, CO: Lynne Rienner Publishers, 2002), 237–272. For a critique written by a UN insider, see Ralph Zacklin, "The Failings of Ad Hoc International Tribunals," *Journal of International Criminal Justice* 2, no. 2 (2004): 541–545.

[13] Quintin Hoare and Noel Malcolm, eds., *Books on Bosnia: A Critical Bibliography of Works Relating to Bosnia-Herzegovina since 1990 in West European Languages* (London: The Bosnian Institute, 1999). This bibliography, now quite outdated, contains 379 books in the languages of Western Europe. The Bosnian Institute's "Books on Bosnia" database contains 3741 books about Bosnia and the region. See <www.bosnia.org.uk/about/bI_books/bI_pub.cfm> (accessed September 20, 2009).

[14] See Michael P. Scharf, *Balkan Justice: The Story Behind the First International War Crimes Trial Since Nuremberg* (Durham, NC: Carolina Academic Press, 1997); Gary Jonathan Bass, *Stay the Hand of Vengeance: The Politics of War Crimes Tribunals* (Princeton, NJ: Princeton University Press, 2000); John Hagan, *Justice in the Balkans: Prosecuting War Crimes in the Hague Tribunal* (Chicago, IL: University of Chicago Press, 2003); Laura Silber and Alan Little, *Yugoslavia: Death of a Nation* (New York: Penguin Books, 1997); David Rohde, *Endgame: The Betrayal and Fall of Srebrenica, Europe's Worst Massacre Since World War II* (New York: Farrar, Straus and Giroux, 1997); Alexandra Stiglmayer, ed., *Mass Rape: The War Against Women in Bosnia-Herzegovina* (Lincoln: University of Nebraska Press, 1994); Peter Maass, *Love Thy Neighbor: A Story of War* (London: Papermac, 1996); Ed Vulliamy, *Seasons in Hell: Slaughter and Betrayal in Bosnia* (New York: Simon and Schuster, 1994); and Roger Cohen, *Hearts Grown Brutal: Sagas of Sarajevo* (New York: Random House, 1998).

[15] The topic has also been addressed in one journalistic account: Elizabeth Neuffer, *The Key to My Neighbor's House: Seeking Justice in Bosnia and Rwanda* (New York: Picador, 2001). See also Stover and Weinstein, *My Neighbor, My Enemy*; Hagan and Kutnjak, *Politics of Punishment*; Cibelli and Guberek, *Justice Unknown*. On the subject of state cooperation with the ad hoc tribunals, see Victor Peskin, *International Justice in Rwanda and the Balkans: Virtual Trials and the Struggle for State Cooperation* (Cambridge: Cambridge University Press, 2008). For the experience of witnesses at the court, see Eric Stover, *The Witnesses: War Crimes and the Promise of Justice in The Hague* (Philadelphia, PA: University of Pennsylvania Press, 2007).

Analysis to Date

Analysis of impact requires deciding how to measure it, which standards to use, and how to decide whether the goals have been achieved. No agreed definition exists of what would constitute success in transitional justice efforts, or how to determine it. There are many people speaking, writing, and ruminating about international courts: victims, perpetrators, bystanders, scholars, international lawyers, diplomats, and citizens. Each of them, implicitly or explicitly, has in mind a counterfactual idea about what the region would have looked like and where the development of international justice would be today, had the court been able to meet some underspecified "ideal," or if it had never been created at all.[16] These counterfactual notions form models against which comparisons are made. The reputation of international courts is influenced by both domestic and international public opinions. Popular opinion often reflects a lack of knowledge about criminal prosecutions and their limitations. Misperceptions about the role of law in a given polity, a topic which is a source of much dispute even among experts, muddies understanding. Opinions are influenced by press reports and international head-lines that emphasize extraordinary events, such as the death of Slobodan Milošević in his cell in 2006, judges caught napping at the bench, and indictees escaping justice. Inside Bosnia, the profound sense of injustice felt by victims of the war has fueled popular perceptions that the court has failed there. A gulf exists between the often unrealistic expectations of international criminal justice and the output of the court on any given day. There is a normative component to this question as well, as one recent volume asks: "At what point, if any, is one to reasonably concede that the 'realties' of world politics require compromise from cherished principles or moral ends, and that what has been achieved is ethically justified?"[17]

That is not to say that the attitudes of the victims and other stakeholders are unimportant, or that anyone should be satisfied by less-than-ideal outcomes. However, there should be a greater appreciation of the fact that popular senti-ment would not likely have changed if more (or different) perpetrators had been tried and sentences had been longer. Victims, generally, will assess the court through comparisons to an impossible ideal, in which every perpetrator is brought before the court. This expectation imposes an impossible standard: that failure to provide such justice at the international level is disrespectful to those

---

[16] For a similar argument with a different emphasis, see Kathryn Sikkink, "The Role of Consequences, Comparison and Counterfactuals in Constructivist Ethical Thought," in Richard Price, ed., *Moral Limit and Possibility in World Politics* (Cambridge: Cambridge University Press, 2008). Sikkink contends that those who compare to the ideal argue that having no trials would have been better than the ones that have occurred. On the use of counterfactual thinking, see Philip Tetlock and Aaron Belkin, eds., *Counterfactual Thought Experiments in World Politics* (Princeton, NJ: Princeton University Press, 1996).

[17] Richard Price, "Moral Limit and Possibility in World Politics," in Price, *Moral Limit and Possibility in World Politics*, 1.

who suffered and perished. Many victims' groups are concerned only with convictions and specific charges, but not with complicated issues of evidence and due process. The approaches and emphases of different professions influence understandings of effects, too, at both the international and regional levels. For instance, some diplomats think lawyers should and could take political factors into consideration; legal professionals disagree. Most prosecutors aspire to court decisions that will hold up at the appellate level and to scrutiny over time. Defense attorneys – an often maligned group in international justice circles – want to make sure criminal liability for their clients is established according to fair standards of due process. All of these factors make for an exceptionally difficult task, especially when the crimes in question resulted from widespread and often organized political violence, yet the form of liability is individual guilt, as it was at the ICTY.

These observations are not an excuse for the shortcomings of the ICTY – many will be discussed – but arise from a desire to be explicit about the limitations that hinder the evaluation of a pioneering institution such as this court. There are no road maps. All of the social actors invested in the outcomes of international tribunals evaluate the court against ideals of their own. Some of these ideals are closer to, some farther from, the legal and extra-legal functions that courts can, in reality, perform.

International law has always been a weak instrument for dealing with widespread political violence. One scholar lamented that in some circles there is "a misguided impulse to capture ineffable human suffering within the confines of the judicial process."[18] This never has been and never will be possible. The demands and goals of the international criminal justice system are different from those of the people who suffer from violent conflict. Courts will never be able to make up for the losses people have endured from war. One informant in this study rued a youth lost to the ravages of war. A political community and a way of life were also lost: "Yugo-nostalgia" was a common postwar theme for many people interviewed for this study, who recalled the prewar years and the positive aspects of the Socialist Federal Republic of Yugoslavia (SFRY), such as relative economic stability and freedom of movement. The war caused demographic changes everywhere. A "brain drain" to Europe and beyond, and a loss of social capital, housing stock, and educational facilities, will affect future generations.[19] The judicial process could never hope to reflect more than a fraction of this collective loss in Bosnia.

The expectations gap, however, still persists. Local groups interpret international law in their own terms and translate it into their cultural contexts and, where international criminal law has proved inadequate, they have sought out

[18] Payam Akhavan, "Justice in the Hague, Peace in the Former Yugoslavia? A Commentary on the United Nations War Crimes Tribunal," *Human Rights Quarterly* 20, no. 4 (1998): 737–816.
[19] For example, a growing number of studies are starting to look at future demographic losses due to conflict.

other avenues for redress of their past and present suffering, such as other courts, cultural representations, and memorials.[20]

At the ICTY, the pursuit of individual criminal guilt has always been confounded by the perception that the wars in the region were particularly complicated. Findings of individual guilt offer an imperfect instrument for addressing criminality that involved varying levels of state involvement among different actors. It was especially difficult to tackle the sometimes dominant (but incorrect) narrative that these were wars of equal parties. Things are further complicated by the fact that any state project of violence that reorders populations based on ethnoreligious criteria means that all citizens will be affected. Members of ethno-religious categories who may have suffered relatively less in strict terms of human loss can experience other forms of loss in equal proportion. Many argue that the court does not respond to their experience, or narrative, of the war when those in the dock are primarily members of their ethnic group. The same is true for members of ethnic minorities who stay on what becomes the "other side" in times of war. Furthermore, some citizens do not see the conflict in terms of ethnic groups at all; they only see politicians using violence to achieve political goals.[21] Therefore, it is understandable that, as tools of social repair, courts are problematic. They produce narratives that do not correspond accurately to lived experience. Yet, as this study illustrates, courts helped to mobilize those affected by collective suffering to strive for better conditions; this study also shows how citizens came to change their attitudes over time.

Many academic observers of this international criminal court have underestimated the difficulty of day-to-day work in these institutions. Scholars who analyze international institutions often have the same high and unrealistic expectations as the public. They do not enter the courtroom every morning to witness the people who work there accomplishing a multitude of daunting daily tasks: creating the operating rules of the court, interpreting them, negotiating both civil and common law legal systems, and dealing with non-compliance in the region, all while fending off, or in some cases welcoming, the influence of geopolitics. This work is done by people from all over the globe who do not even share a common mother tongue. One ICTY prosecutor asked: "Would you go in for a surgery in which you had a Brazilian doctor, a Ugandan nurse, a Canadian anesthesiologist and the operation took place in a Japanese hospital?"[22] It is an apt metaphor for what happens in The Hague every day.

---

[20] On the tensions between the international law and local interpretations, see Sally Engle Merry, *Human Rights and Gender Violence: Translating International Law into Local Justice* (Chicago, IL: University of Chicago Press, 2006).

[21] On how average Bosnian citizens forged a daily existence not marked by nationalism and rooted in prewar counterdiscourse, see Torsten Kolind, *Post-War Identification: Everyday Muslim Counterdiscourse in Bosnia Herzegovina* (Aarhus, Denmark: Aarhus University Press, 2008).

[22] Geoffrey Nice, Former Principal Trial Attorney in the Office of the Prosecutor of the ICTY, presentation, Columbia University, New York, April 17, 2006.

There is another, perhaps even more limiting aspect to ivory-tower analysis which must be acknowledged. Scholars have professional incentives to overturn conventional thinking. In the social sciences, we are often taught to look for *man bites dog* and not *dog bites man*. Some research questions in the social sciences routinely produce somewhat polemical discussions across both sides of a debate because of this incentive structure. As a result, our analyses are often not as nuanced as they should be. Scholars will protest that this is a dishonest intellectual position, and one perhaps in violation of our own professional ethics. Still the inducement is there: to be overly critical is more rewarding than not. A related dilemma can be seen in Bosnia. One news agency bureau chief lamented the constant criticism of developments in postwar Bosnia, which she argued was a reaction to the inability to voice dissent in the socialist era. She felt it clouded the ability of many citizens to see positive developments.[23]

This book, too, has a counterfactual underpinning its analysis. It implicitly compares reality to a state that will never be known: a world in which the international community, having intervened in Bosnia to end the war and hoping to influence postwar Bosnian society, did not engage in international criminal prosecutions – in other words, a postwar Bosnia without the ICTY. Contrary to much contemporary analysis, I argue, such a Bosnia (and by extension, the region), would have been much worse off.

This study argues that the most effective way to address the above issue, in the absence of specific criteria agreed upon by a consensus of experts, is to be explicit about the tools and methods utilized, and about the basis for findings in the course of the evaluation. This analysis does not presume that the current popularity of international trials in some circles means that they are the only way for countries that have suffered violent conflicts to address the past.[24] It argues that, where there have been trials, we should understand fully how they have reverberated throughout society. For such analysis, Bosnia is a crucial case. This study also does not take for granted that international solutions are better than local ones; the debate, in fact, has evolved to the point where there is an understanding that local solutions are likely to be more effective. International courts should only be engaged when local ones are not an option.

So, if even scholarly evaluation can be problematically biased, the social sciences can best enlighten this issue by means of a broad inquiry. Above all, the social scientist is concerned, generally speaking, with the contributions of institutions: the role of norms; the interplay between domestic and international factors; and the ability of institutions to create openings for social movements, solve so-called collective action problems, and identify which factors contribute to greater

---

[23] Aida Cerkez-Robinson, Associated Press Bureau Chief in Bosnia and Herzegovina, discussion with author, July 25, 2008.

[24] Mark A. Drumbl, *Atrocity, Punishment, and International Law* (Cambridge: Cambridge University Press, 2007), 9, discusses the enthusiasm in some circles for international trials.

peace and security in the world. One far-reaching study, for example, argues that international intervention has contributed to an overall post–Cold War decline in worldwide violence.[25] The ICTY is an example of one such intervention. This book represents an effort to understand and evaluate its impact using the best tools available in the social sciences, and a move toward wielding those tools for the public good.[26]

Consequently, this book departs from, but builds on, the work that has come before it. Many analyses of the court to date have used the ICTY's own stated desired effects in the region as the criteria by which to measure its success. This seems like a logical approach to assessment: did the court do in the region what it said it would? However, it is important to recognize the origins of these stated legal and extra-legal goals. First, they are primarily the policy pronouncements of architects of the court, used in times of crisis to justify its creation at a point when not all of those supporting it had honorable intentions. Gary Bass describes the founding of the court as "an act of tokenism by the world community, which was largely unwilling to intervene in the ex-Yugoslavia but did not mind creating an institution that would give the *appearance* of moral concern."[27]

Furthermore, justifications for international courts are derived from knowledge of criminal law in the domestic sphere, a practice which, legal scholars have argued, leads to an under-appreciation of the differences between international and domestic jurisprudence. Scholars have identified the following six intended outcomes of international prosecutions: 1) to uncover the truth about past atrocities; 2) to punish perpetrators; 3) to provide a way to respond to the needs of victims; 4) to promote the rule of law in new democracies; 5) to promote reconciliation; and 6) to serve as a deterrent for future crimes.[28] Most of these points are consistent with the stated goals and achievements of the ICTY. Mark Drumbl, similarly, outlines the rationale for international criminal courts as: retributive, deterrent, and what legal scholars call expressivist goals. Drumbl argues that deterrence as a rationale overlooks the lack of recidivism in many perpetrators of mass atrocities. Other works on deterrence are only beginning to measure whether or not it

---

[25] Human Security Report Project, *Human Security Report 2005* (Oxford: Oxford University Press, 2005), < www.humansecurityreport.info>.

[26] See, for example, Craig Calhoun, "Toward a More Public Social Science," Social Science Research Council, <www.ssrc.org/president_office/toward_a_more/> (accessed April 28, 2008). A compilation of works that seek to inform a broader audience about war crimes can be found in Roy Gutman, David Rieff, Anthony Dworkin, and Sheryl A. Mendez, eds., *Crimes of War 2.0: What the Public Should Know* (New York: W.W. Norton, 2007). This book has been translated into 11 languages.

[27] Bass, *Stay the Hand*, 207.

[28] Laurel E. Fletcher and Harvey M. Weinstein, "Violence and Social Repair: Rethinking the Contribution of Justice to Reconciliation," *Human Rights Quarterly* 24, no. 3 (2002): 573–639. See also Richard J. Goldstone, "Advancing the Cause of Human Rights: The Need for Justice and Accountability," in Samantha Power and Graham Allison, eds., *Realizing Human Rights: Moving from Inspiration to Impact* (New York: St. Martin's Press, 2000), 195–223.

functions as an effective inhibitor to potential criminals in other conflict zones.[29] The fact that few such crimes are prosecuted, however, means that they could only function as a weak deterrent mechanism at best. Retribution – the desire to give a perpetrator his or her just deserts – is backward-looking, Drumbl argues, and neglects to examine how crimes come to be viewed as acceptable in societies in the midst of violence.[30]

Thus, deterrence and retribution may be weaker justifications than other criteria for the creation of, and consequent evaluation of, international courts. Drumbl's research has shown that using these factors as the preferred rationale means essentially forcing analysts to create a counterfactual world that comes from our understanding of domestic proceedings. They inherently represent a narrow measure, perhaps even an inappropriate one. This argument undercuts the idea that these criteria should hold primacy in our analysis and evaluation of the functions of international courts.

The forward-looking, extra-legal rationales for international tribunals are, however, more promising. What legal scholars call expressivism emerges as a justification for international prosecutions: it is "the messaging value of punishment to affirm respect for law, reinforce a moral consensus, narrate history and educate the public."[31] Some scholars see retribution as a form of expressivism, because it plays an educative role in sending the message to both the perpetrator and society that the action in question cannot be tolerated.[32]

---

[29] For the argument that the ICTY would deter further war crimes, see Theodor Meron, "The Case for War Crimes Trials in Yugoslavia," *Foreign Affairs* 72, no. 3 (Summer 1993). For the argument in the context of the International Criminal Court (ICC), by one of the ICTY's early supporters, see Cherif Bassiouni, "To Deter and Dissuade, and so Deny – Use of International Courts," *UN Chronicle* 36, no. 1 (Spring 1999).

[30] Drumbl, *Atrocity*, 11.

[31] Drumbl, *Atrocity*, 12. On expressivism see also: Mark A. Drumbl, "The Expressive Value of Prosecuting and Punishing Terrorists: Hamdan, the Geneva Conventions, and International Criminal Law," *George Washington Law Review* 75, no. 5/6 (2007). See also Drumbl, *Atrocity*; and Robert D. Sloane, "The Expressive Capacity of International Punishment: The Limits of the National Law Analogy and the Potential of International Criminal Law," *Stanford Journal of International Law* 43, no. 1 (2007). On domestic law, see Elizabeth Anderson and Richard H. Pildes, "Expressive Theories of Law: A General Restatement," *University of Pennsylvania Law Review* 148, no. 5 (2000); and Joel Feinberg, "The Expressive Function of Punishment," in Joel Feinberg, *Doing and Deserving: Essays in the Theory of Responsibility* (Princeton, NJ: Princeton University Press, 1970).

[32] Jean Hampton, "The Moral Education Theory of Punishment," *Philosophy and Public Affairs* 13, no. 3 (Summer 1984): 208–238. Hampton argues, "Thus, according to the moral education theory, punishment is not intended as a way of conditioning a human being to do what society wants her to do (in the way that an animal is conditioned by an electrified fence to stay within a pasture); rather, the theory maintains that punishment is intended as a way of teaching the wrongdoer that the action she did (or wants to do) is forbidden because it is morally wrong and should not be done for that reason. The theory also regards that lesson as public, and thus as directed to the rest of society. When the state makes its criminal law and its enforcement practices known, it conveys an educative message not only to the convicted criminal but also to anyone else in the society who might be tempted to do what she did." Ibid., 212.

Expressivist goals have greater resonance with the concerns of the social sciences, which by and large look at ideas, institutions, and attitudes. Rather than trying to define the court's broader goals precisely or put up a yardstick against which performance is measured, this study engages these broad categories. It argues that any analysis of international tribunals should encompass more than the courts' declared achievements, which are often over-stated by their architects to justify the courts' existence.

Conventional Wisdom and Motivation for This Book

The pessimistic conventional wisdom regarding the ICTY's contribution to advancements in Bosnia stems chiefly from just a handful of sources: scholarly critics of human rights institutions, insider tell-all books and, from within the region, disappointed victims as well as intransigent and manipulative politicians. This book is motivated primarily by a desire to respond to the first two groups, because they have contributed to the sentiment in some circles that no trials would have been preferable to what has occurred to date, a conclusion that this project illustrates is clearly not the case. I will briefly discuss each point in turn.

Some recent scholarly analyses have argued that war crimes trials are a threat in the sense that they can to do more harm than good, and can exacerbate tensions in the regions they address. An article by Jack Snyder and Leslie Vinjamuri argued that, "... the prosecution of perpetrators of atrocities according to universal standards – applied with insufficient attention to political circumstances risks causing more atrocities than it would prevent, because it pays insufficient attention to political realities."[33] Similarly, another article expressed this prevalent sentiment: "In a criminal trial, two sets of facts – those of the prosecution and those of the defense – do public battle with each other. Those competing facts are probed and examined and a winner and a loser are ultimately decided. When such a trial concerns events that took place in recent memory, in a society that is highly and deeply traumatized, the trial too often exacerbates existing political rifts. This was the case with the ICTY and ICTR [International Criminal Tribunal for Rwanda]."[34] While it is undeniable that, due to such immediacy, political tensions may flare as a result of trials, backlash was largely a short-term phenomenon in Bosnia.

The first volume dedicated to the effects of the ICTY and ICTR war crimes tribunals concluded that they failed to achieve many of their stated goals. Setting out to examine what they described as the "multiple layers of societal repair," the authors found that criminal trials played only a small role in an individual's conception of justice and had little impact on rebuilding processes.[35] In contrast, this

---

[33] Snyder and Vinjamuri, "Trials and Errors," 5.
[34] Cobban, "Think Again," 22. Cobban is referring to the other ad hoc tribunal, the International Criminal Tribunal for Rwanda (ICTR).
[35] Stover and Weinstein, *My Neighbor, My Enemy,* 323–325.

study identifies a more positive legacy, based on a broader discussion of the impact of law and a narrower measure of what is possible for international criminal law. In contrast with the first wave of scholarship, I argue that citizens in transitional states should expect criminal trials to be only a small part of their general understanding of justice. Trials will never be magic bullets for postconflict societies. Still, when the social setting is favorable (or even just permissive), they are powerful instruments. As one study noted: "The words of court decisions have a force that differentiates them from most other utterances."[36]

Human rights scholars have noted a general divide between analysts who use quantitative methods and those who rely on qualitative ones. Quantitative scholars conducting so-called large-N studies, which look at multiple case studies and examine the impact of trials, often find no effect, whereas those concerned with individual case studies find that trials or human rights instruments can have an impact.[37] This project uses a mix of methodological tools and finds a positive contribution across this methodological divide in scholarly research, and addresses multiple case studies in one country.

A spate of inside-the-court tell-all books also have contributed to the idea that the ICTY was a misuse of funds. The former spokeswoman for the ICTY's Office of the Prosecutor, Florence Hartmann, wrote an insider's account of her time there. She made weighty claims, among them, that there was an Anglo-American conspiracy influencing developments, and that specific charges were opposed by certain prosecutors.[38] These types of publications are valued by scholars because they open the doors to institutions that are often black boxes to them. The truth is, however, that it is hard for outsiders to evaluate such information since they lack knowledge of the sources to which such insiders have had access, and from which they draw this information. Of the individuals who reviewed Hartmann's book, many lacked such insider knowledge, but nevertheless praised the account without much real scrutiny.[39] The book confirmed prevalent popular beliefs that the court was too influenced by foreign states even to deliver a fair trial and, thus, had been a waste of resources.

[36] Peter Brooks and Paul Gewirtz, *Law's Stories: Narrative and Rhetoric in the Law* (New Haven, CT: Yale University Press, 1996), 5.
[37] See, for example, Emilie Hafner-Burton and James Ron, "Human Rights Institutions: Rhetoric and Efficacy," *Journal of Peace Research* 44, no. 4 (2007): 379–384. See also Emilie Hafner-Burton and Kiyoteru Tsutsui, "Justice Lost! The Failure of International Human Rights Law to Matter Where Needed Most," *Journal of Peace Research* 44, no. 4 (2007): 407–425. An important exception is Kathryn Sikkink and Carrie Booth Walling, "The Impact of Human Rights Trials in Latin America," *Journal of Peace Research* 44, no. 4 (2007): 427–445.
[38] Florence Hartmann, *Paix et châtiment: Les guerres secrètes de la politique et de la justice internationales* (Paris: Flammarion, 2007).
[39] Most (though not all) of the dissenting reviews were written by individuals with knowledge of both the court and the region. For example, see Marko Attila Hoare's review, <greatersurbiton.wordpress.com/2008/01/10/florence-hartmanns-peace-and-punishment/> (accessed February 25, 2009). Hoare still argued that the book "remains essential reading for several reasons."

Similarly, the publication of former Chief Prosecutor Carla Del Ponte's memoir – dramatically titled, in the Italian version, *The Hunt: The War Criminals and
I* – outlined the influence of political forces and the reluctance of world powers to
aid the work of the ICTY. These claims reverberated in the region, bringing further into question the purpose of trials.[40] This memoir, however, only thinly based
on the citation of court documents, gives little concrete insight into the functioning of the court. Still, several things can be gleaned from it, including that Del
Ponte was responsive to the requests of politicians to delay the announcement
of certain indictments; that the court's statute did not include the crime of conspiracy, which was problematic for the indictment of higher level officials; and
that investigators, in her opinion, lacked both education and knowledge, and yet
trial attorneys were quite dependent on them. Furthermore, at several points
she notes that the melding of common and civil law systems was problematic on
many levels for the prosecution. She did not address some overarching issues and
questions, for example, about her overall prosecutorial strategy, her views on the
court's extended mandate, and different decisions that could have led to alternative outcomes.[41]

These works have generally been received positively, but there is still much
we do not know about the daily operations of international courts. Critics of the
ICTY – both those opposed for political reasons, and those opposed to the idea of
international justice – held up these books as evidence of the futility of the ICTY
and similar institutions, overlooking the personal motivations for many such publications. Similarly, while scholars are often loath to admit what they do not know,
very few have a grasp of day-to-day developments in the court. It is important to
recognize we are less than perfect commentators on such works. Those insider
accounts more focused on questions relevant to international legal professionals,
predictably, did not receive much press coverage.[42] They made news only to the
small audiences they addressed, and did not influence popular opinion.

This study seeks to temper the discussion and explicitly tackle the problem of
understanding what can be concluded through various types of "evidence," at
both the international and local levels. There are things that we know about the
court through mostly anecdotal discussions – outside influence, how the judges
and prosecutors felt about specific charges, or even the extra-legal functions to
which the court aspires. However, we just do not know how widespread outside
influences are, where the greatest pressure points are, what percentage of court

[40] In Italian: Carla Del Ponte con Chuck Sudetic, *La caccia: Io e i criminali di guerra* (The hunt: The war criminals and I) (Milan, Italy: Feltrinelli, 2008). In English the title was more modest: Carla Del Ponte with Chuck Sudetic, *Madame Prosecutor: Confrontations with Humanity's Worst Criminals and the Culture of Impunity* (New York: Other Press, 2009).
[41] See also Charles Simic, "Connoisseurs of Cruelty," *New York Review of Books* 56, no. 4, March 12, 2009.
[42] See, for example, Gideon Boas, *The Milošević Trial: Lessons for the Conduct of Complex International Criminal Proceedings* (Cambridge: Cambridge University Press, 2007).

insiders reject the court's broader aspirations – and we cannot know until we have a larger body of work from inside the court to draw upon. Scholars cannot yet conclude whether politics trumped international due process so as to make the whole enterprise fruitless.

There is no denying that there are real-world policy motivations for this study. International justice has proven to be a relatively expensive undertaking. The court's budget, which averaged close to $100 million dollars per year between 1999 and 2008, was one of the first items targeted by critics of the ICTY. The costs of foreign salaries, exhumations of mass graves, and elaborate systems of documentation all contributed to this budget. In the policy community, the reigning sentiment was that, in a world of limited resources, investment in ad hoc tribunals should produce significant returns. For example, at a conference of the American Association for the Advancement of Science (AAAS), which brought together scholars working on different aspects of transitional justice, the keynote speaker, Neil Kritz, of the United States Institute for Peace, commented: "Both international tribunals are costing approximately two billion dollars. One inevitably has to ask the question: how else might those two billion dollars have been spent, and with what impact in the former Yugoslavia and Rwanda and the [African] Great Lakes region? Those are the real issues that research has to inform."[43] While the value of the ICTY's work in the region is difficult to quantify in strictly financial terms, this project will show some areas where different resource allocations could have led to greater contributions in the societies the court was created to address.

The Argument in Brief

This book argues that the ICTY contributed to positive democratic development inside Bosnia in ways overlooked by previous scholars. The court was a boon for Bosnia's transition because it played a role in the creation of new postwar political identities based on the rule of law and participation.[44] All of the case studies illustrate this finding and how it transpired, through social action, changing narratives about the past, or positive attitudes about justice and accountability. Furthermore, by creating a space in which accountability could be discussed, the ICTY facilitated the mobilization of civil society groups that lobbied for accountability, legislative changes, and financial redress. These innovations made the

---

[43] "Empirical Research Methodologies of Transitional Justice Mechanisms," conference report, meeting of the American Association for the Advancement of Science and the Center for the Study of Violence and Reconciliation, Stellenbosch, South Africa, November 18–20, 2002.

[44] Mahmood Mamdani, *When Victims Become Killers: Colonialism, Nativism, and the Genocide in Rwanda* (Princeton, NJ: Princeton University Press, 2001). Mamdani writes: "The question of political justice goes beyond holding the perpetrators of the genocide accountable. Ultimately, it is about the definition of political identities." Ibid., 274.

state (and the international community) more accountable to citizens. The court also led directly to the development of local prosecutorial capacity. Thus, this book focuses primarily on three aspects of the expressivist legacy: attitudes, ideas, and institutions.

Two chapters in this book deal with attitudes toward the court and its impact. They illustrate that members of all ethno-religious communities in Bosnia came to have positive attitudes about the court, and while there is some division along ethnic lines, it is not as pronounced as conventional wisdom would leave one to believe. Chapter 7, for example, illustrates how even soldiers in Republika Srpska (one of Bosnia's two entities), a decade after the war, were not as opposed to the court as many observers might have expected. Furthermore, attitudes have changed over time: views of the court have become more favorable, and opinions have changed about its contribution to broader goals, such as the role of prosecutions in the return of refugees.

The attitudinal preconditions of democratic states have been of interest to modern social scientists since Gabriel Almond and Sidney Verba identified the requisite political culture in such polities. They argued it was a "pluralistic culture based on communication and persuasion, a culture of consensus and diversity, a culture that permitted change but moderated it."[45] The survey data presented here gives reason to be at least cautiously optimistic that the court has contributed to the creation of such a political culture.

Furthermore, scholars have long puzzled over the question of how and under what conditions human rights norms are socialized.[46] Previous studies have identified several mechanisms that explain how international institutions lead to norm adaptation. One strand of research argues that norms are internalized based on a rational calculation of the cost-benefit ratio of adopting them; states, and by extension the elites who run them, are more likely to internalize and comply with international institutions if the costs of doing so are not perceived as higher than the benefits over an extended period of time.[47] Under this form of socialization, behavior may change but internal views may not.

Cooperation with the ICTY was required by the peace agreement that ended the war. Republika Srpska, in many cases, complied only when it was absolutely required. In certain instances, the international community had to enforce compliance by firing politicians and imposing financial penalties for nonconformity.

---

[45] Gabriel A. Almond and Sidney Verba, *The Civic Culture: Political Attitudes and Democracy in Five Nations* (Newbury Park, CA: Sage Publications, 1989), 6.

[46] For one of the first descriptions of how human rights norms are internalized, see Thomas Risse, Stephen C. Ropp, and Kathryn Sikkink, *The Power of Human Rights: International Norms and Domestic Change* (Cambridge: Cambridge University Press, 1999). The Bosnian case study largely conforms to the model presented in Chapter 1 of their book.

[47] Frank Schimmelfennig, "Strategic Calculation and International Socialization: Membership Incentives, Party Constellations, and Sustained Compliance in Central and Eastern Europe," *International Organization* 59, no. 4 (2005): 831.

Still, running parallel to these events were changes in the larger population that resulted from the promotion of the norm of accountability and, at least at the outset, public discussion regarding compliance with the court. In response to this coerced compliance, elites had little choice but to say positive things about the ICTY. A cascade effect occurred in the general population, and attitudes changed for the better. In addition, groups that initially felt ignored by the work of the ICTY started to report that they felt the court was credible, even necessary, which indicated an effect independent of the rational calculation of the country's politicians. In later years, when nationalist sentiment increased after Bosnia's 2006 general elections, rhetoric changed in ways that illustrate the complex process of norm diffusion. Some political elites did revert to their previous assertions, which included the denial of specific crimes, a strategy they employed when they were sure local international officials would not punish such behavior.

Disappointment with both the workings of the court and the broader shortcomings of the international community in Bosnia led to the formation of new social movements for accountability. In the language of social movements theory, the court created a "political opportunity structure" to facilitate collective action, which Sidney Tarrow defines as "the consistent – but not necessarily formal, permanent or national – dimensions of the political environment which either encourage or discourage people from using collective action."[48] One case study in this book illustrates, for example, how the court's documentation provided a fact base that aided the survivors of the Srebrenica massacre in their bid to expand the norm of accountability to include the international community. Scholars are just starting to appreciate the far-reaching relationship between international law and social movements. To date, the study of international law has not appreciated how, "while the international legal system continues to be organized on a global basis, it is also increasingly being revealed as inadequate, and is resisted, coopted and transformed by social movements at the local ... and ... 'glocal levels'," meaning those which work both internationally and locally.[49] Srebrenica's survivors have indeed transformed and coopted discourses of international law.

The court's exit strategy in the region lay in the creation of domestic prosecutorial and trial capacity. An extensive restructuring of the country's judicial system, and coordination of cases between the ICTY and local courts, led to prosecutions inside Bosnia, probably the court's most visible legacy for democratic development.

[48] Sidney G. Tarrow, *Power in Movement: Social Movements, Collective Action, and Politics* (Cambridge: Cambridge University Press, 1994), 18.
[49] Balakrishnan Rajagopal, *International Law from Below: Development, Social Movements and Third World Resistance* (Cambridge: Cambridge University Press, 2003), 237. For a look at how these changes affect developments within institutions, see John Hagan, Ron Levi, and Gabrielle Ferrales, "Swaying the Hand of Justice: The Internal and External Dynamics of Regime Change at the International Criminal Tribunal for the former Yugoslavia," *Law & Social Inquiry* 31, no. 3 (2006): 585–616.

Although fraught with some of the problems that surround institution building in transitional environments, the court has made significant contributions to the rule of law locally.

Critics are correct to point out that not all outcomes of the work of the ICTY were desirable. Some compromises were made, some indictments were bungled, and some judges in the courtroom seemed to overstep their roles. In the region, the court's work was appropriated by elites with less than honorable intentions. Other critics saw the strong reaction to the court's work as evidence that international trials should not be conducted in transitional environments. It should not have been surprising that any discussion of recent political violence, especially one mediated by an international body, provoked a strong reaction, especially given that wartime nationalist parties remained in power after the conflict ended. Most institutions are not perceived as legitimate by all of the people affected by their work at the time of their formation. But attitudes change over time. In the case of international courts, this was as true of Nuremberg as it was for the ICTY. [50]

The findings of this study show that, while the ICTY often inspired feelings and collective action that were, on the surface, divisive for the citizens of Bosnia, it helped to deepen political participation. Much of the negative reaction to the ICTY's work led to initiatives that were channeled through courts and institutions, a hallmark of democratic development. This book shows that transitional justice is not at odds with democratization, as some recent studies have suggested.[51] Chapter 2 outlines the scholarly literature in more depth, and argues that the literature on contentious politics can place the negative reaction to the court in a better context. Such works have much in common with domestic studies in the field of law and society that see law as a pervasive influence throughout society.[52]

The conclusion that courts could do more than simply determine the guilt or innocence of individuals charged with certain crimes is not unique to the international arena. Some observers have long thought that courts and surrounding

[50] For a recent work on both domestic and international aspects of the Nuremberg legacy, see Norbert Ehrenfreund, *The Nuremberg Legacy: How the Nazi War Crimes Trials Changed the Course of History* (New York: Palgrave Macmillan, 2007). For a different view, see Istvan Deak, "Misjudgment at Nuremberg," *The New York Review of Books* 40, no. 16 (1993). For a letter responding to this article, and a reply by Deak, see Aryeh Neier, letter to the editor, *The New York Review of Books* 40, no. 18 (1993).

[51] See also Bronwyn Leebaw, "Transitional Justice, Conflict, and Democratic Change: International Interventions and Domestic Reconciliation," conference paper, APSA Task Force on Difference and Inequality in the Developing World, University of Virginia, Charlottesville, VA, April 21–23, 2005, <www.apsanet.org/imgtest/TaskForceDiffIneqLebaw.pdf> (accessed February 25, 2009).

[52] The literature in the field of law and society is vast. For a good overview of some of the most important scholars in the field, see Bryant Garth and Austin Sarat, eds., *How Does Law Matter?: Fundamental Issues in Law and Society* (Chicago: Northwestern University Press, 1998).

institutions can double as effective tools of social change – or in the more negative formulation, as tools of social engineering. This study is a new look at an old question: Can the law change behavior?[53] If so, how?

The ICTY's effects, of course, extend beyond Southeastern Europe. The community of experts in international law has flourished, partly as a result of the court's existence. The ICTY helped craft an international identity for members of the community involved in human rights, justice, and development. Transnational advocacy networks were established before the creation of the court and, after things became operational in The Hague, continued to press for accountability in other countries experiencing violence.[54] The flow of information from transnational networks to the ICTY (and vice versa) facilitated advancements in international law and, ultimately, the creation of a permanent international body, the International Criminal Court. Though seemingly independent, these developments in the international arena had spillover influence on domestic events. International support for specific cases and initiatives kept them on the agenda in Bosnia, and new bodies of international jurisprudence were eventually consulted and referenced in domestic courts. This book highlights the domestic impact of these bodies, but events in Bosnia also influenced many international developments to follow.

While this research finds, on balance, a positive legacy of the court, the ICTY could have done more to maximize its positive domestic impact in postwar Bosnia. The court contributed to a changed atmosphere in Southeastern Europe, raised awareness and created a language for notions of accountability, individualized guilt, and amassed tremendous amounts of documentation. This project shows that the conventional wisdom that the ICTY failed in its mission is also derived from an underestimation of how factors external to the court affected its work. The most important factor was the social setting created by the Dayton Peace Agreement. The transformative potential of law will always be limited by the broader institutional context in which it is applied. Dayton undercut the liberal message sent (however imperfectly) by the court. In addition, inside Bosnia, the postwar environment and attitudes of other international actors toward the question of war crimes meant that the court had considerable local obstacles to overcome. Given the court's unfavorable institutional context, its lack of social bases in the region, and detractors on the ground, we must recognize that the

---

[53] In law and society studies focusing on the United States, the classic work, which takes a pessimistic view of the ability of the Supreme Court to bring about social change, is Gerald N. Rosenberg, *The Hollow Hope: Can Courts Bring About Social Change?* (Chicago: University of Chicago Press, 1991). For a different view of law, see Michael W. McCann, *Rights at Work: Pay Equity Reform and the Politics of Legal Mobilization* (Chicago: University of Chicago Press, 1994).

[54] On transnational advocacy networks, see Margaret E. Keck and Kathryn Sikkink, *Activists Beyond Borders: Advocacy Networks in International Politics* (Ithaca, NY: Cornell University Press, 1998).

ICTY made more progress in contributing to extra-legal goals than has been appreciated to date.

Methodology

The central question of this book is: How do international trials affect the societies they address? The Bosnian case provides an opportunity to look at the cumulative effects of the court one decade and a half after its creation. The case studies illustrate how the work of the court shaped political identities and democratic developments. Each of the chapters shows how this work affected specific places, trials, and segments of society, all of which were undergoing change in postwar Bosnia.

This book represents an extensive period of field research and an attempt to use multiple methodologies to weigh in on the central research question. Over the past decade, between 1998 and 2008, I lived in Bosnia a cumulative total of four years. This time in the country provided the opportunity to utilize a wide range of tools: formal survey methodology, ethnographic research, oral history techniques, and archival work. Where I interviewed large numbers of organizations or individuals within the same sector, every effort was made to ask a standard set of questions. Field research for this project, including interviews with court officials, civil society representatives, politicians, journalists, and the armed forces, was completed primarily between 2002 and 2005, with follow-up trips to Bosnia in 2007 and 2008. These interviews took me to places all over the country. It is important to note that most of the field research for this book was conducted during a period of positive political development in Bosnia, a point to which I return in the conclusion.

How the ICTY presented itself to the population in the region was of particular interest. I participated in numerous regional seminars and conferences in Belgrade, Budapest, Vukovar, Tuzla, Srebrenica, and Sarajevo on subjects relating to my project, observing how various groups and individuals framed the issues under discussion and how they interacted with each other. I made three research trips to the ICTY and also observed five ICTY Outreach events in Sarajevo, Bjelašnica, Brčko, Foča, and Konjic. Altogether, this project collected the input of well over 600 individuals, whose participation ranged from filling out a questionnaire, to participating in longer oral-history interviews conducted in several meetings, to ethnographic research that included participant observation over several years. All told, this book is the culmination of more than a decade of closely following developments in Bosnia and Herzegovina.

Plan of the Book

Chapter 2, "Crafting the Polity: Transitional Justice and Democratization," presents the argument that frames this project and provides background on the theoretical debates informing this study. It argues that foreign trials help to create democratic political identities and culture. The court helped foster debates about the political community in Bosnia, promoted political participation, and facilitated the creation of democratic institutions. This chapter places the study among larger debates within political science, notably the transitions literature in comparative politics, the international relations literature concerned with norm expansion, and the relatively new field of transitional justice. It also addresses several works in the law and society literature that have not yet been central in the discussion of international courts. Lastly, it argues that, despite the specificity of the structure of the Bosnian state and the role of the international community in its governance, this case study serves as a useful heuristic model for the examination of international courts.

Chapter 3, "An Unfavorable Context: War, Dayton, and the ICTY," addresses the social setting in which the court worked, and illustrates how this context was the court's biggest challenge. In addition, it emphasizes how the court's structural relationship to the country and the lack of enforcement mechanisms affected its work. As a result, much criticism of the court was in fact due to factors beyond its control. This chapter describes the international organizations that made up the postwar intervention in Bosnia and how each dealt with the subject of war crimes. It also provides a brief background of the wars of Yugoslav succession in the 1990s and outlines the current state of knowledge about the composition of the war's casualties and the implications for our understanding of the court's work.

Chapter 4, "Expanding the Norm of Accountability: Srebrenica's Survivors, Collective Action, and the ICTY," addresses how the ICTY's work has influenced and been influenced by some of the family associations representing survivors of the Srebrenica genocide – in which over 8,000 Bosniak boys and men perished after the fall of the United Nations safe area to Bosnian Serb and Serbian forces in July 1995. Based on fieldwork started in 2002, primarily with one family association, the Mothers of the Enclaves of Srebrenica and Žepa, this chapter traces the evolution of these groups and their efforts to seek accountability for the events of 1995. It argues that both the work of the court and its failings influenced the victims' advocacy and activism, and provided legitimacy to their social mobilization. While the court was not the cause of the social movement surrounding the genocide, the court's findings provided the empirical material that enabled victims to make claims of accountability and mobilize on behalf of their missing relatives. The chapter outlines how their search for accountability expanded to include not just the perpetrators of war crimes, but the international community as well. Survivors thus expanded the norm of accountability to include previously untouchable actors, at a time in which some scholars were also beginning to examine this issue. The collective action of family associations is a form of political participation important for democratizing societies. This chapter shows how the application of international criminal law can help foster mobilization.

The research for this chapter was enriched by numerous international and domestic trips with members of the Mothers of the Enclaves of Srebrenica and Žepa, including a bus journey with the group to the Netherlands in 2004. In The Hague, association lawyers presented the Dutch government with their case for reparations for the fall of the UN enclave. That same year, association representatives organized a trip for Srebrenica orphans to Ulcinj, Montenegro, where they met with local civil society leaders. In 2005, meetings in Paris provided a perspective from another European country. In Bosnia, attendance at five of the annual memorial ceremonies in Potočari, and many months in the Srebrenica municipality itself, informed research on developments there. In 2002, numerous local and international officials at the International Commission on Missing Persons (ICMP) explained the process related to the identification of the enclave's missing. Interviews with seven other organizations related to Srebrenica, and numerous seminars and roundtables in Bosnia and the United States on the genocide, provided additional background for this chapter.

Chapter 5, "Making Progress with Few Resources: Civil Society and the ICTY," looks at the attitudes toward the court of non-governmental organizations (NGOs), the segment of the Bosnian population that has often been the first line of contact for victims of the war. It summarizes the results of interviews with 53 randomly selected non-governmental organizations, replicating a study published in 2000 by Kristen Cibelli and Tamy Guberek, *Justice Unknown, Justice Unsatisfied?: Bosnian NGOs Speak about the International Criminal Tribunal for the former Yugoslavia*.[55] In the interest of having longitudinal quasi-panel data, this chapter was written in close collaboration with those authors, and includes a replication of their initial methods and similar sample size. This chapter demonstrates that attitudes toward international institutions do change over time. It also shows that, while attitudes toward the ICTY have generally improved over the years, knowledge about its purpose and structure has not. This chapter illustrates that, even if the ICTY missed some opportunities to have civil society help get its message out, civil society nevertheless registered a change in its attitudes, which increased levels of legitimacy for the court. Respondents also felt the court had achieved some aspects of its extra-legal aspirations in greater levels than were found in the previous study.

Chapter 6, "Narrative and Counter-Narrative: The Case of the Čelebići Trial," examines attitudes toward the ICTY through discussions with local residents of Konjic, a town an hour's drive from Sarajevo. The trial addressed crimes that took place in the Čelebići prison camp, a Bosnian government military warehouse where approximately 700 Bosnian Serb soldiers and civilians were held. Four men were accused of crimes there. It was the first collective trial for violations

---

[55] Cibelli and Guberek, *Justice Unknown, Justice Unsatisfied?*

of international law since World War II. It was the court's first case dealing with crimes committed against ethnic Serbs. This trial was one of the court's earliest efforts; it began in the spring of 1997, only two years after the war ended. This chapter is based on oral histories and in-depth interviews conducted with residents of Konjic, as well as observation of an ICTY outreach event there. It shows that, while different stories about the causes of the war were one of the ICTY's underappreciated obstacles, the narrative produced by the trial prompted valuable debates in Konjic and across Bosnia, notably among Bosniak elites, who previously had been hesitant to discuss the crimes of those who reported to the wartime Bosnian government.

Chapter 7, "From the Battlefield to the Barracks: The ICTY and the Armed Forces," addresses attitudes toward the ICTY among soldiers in the now-united army, many of whom stood on opposing sides only fifteen years ago. It shows that views of the pursuit of justice are positive, generally speaking, among all ethnicities. It also illustrates that soldiers believe the court has made contributions toward its extra-legal aspirations. The basis for this chapter is an anonymous qualitative survey of 463 soldiers conducted in the five Bosnian cities of Sarajevo, Mostar, Tuzla, Banja Luka, and Bijeljina, in addition to oral histories of a handful of soldiers. This chapter is significant because it addresses a segment of society – members of the military – not often given a voice in scholarly studies of transitional justice mechanisms.

Chapter 8, "Localizing War Crimes Prosecutions: The Hague to Sarajevo and Beyond," addresses the question of the ICTY's contribution to the rule of law in Bosnia through a discussion of local prosecutions of war crimes. It outlines the process the international community took to reconstitute the country's judicial system through the reappointment of all prosecutors and judges and a downsizing of their number, the creation of a War Crimes Chamber at the Court of Bosnia and Herzegovina, and the search for a strategy to guide prosecutions. This chapter argues that the localization of prosecutions is probably the clearest example of the court's contribution to Bosnia's democratic development.

Chapter 9 presents the conclusions and reaffirms the book's central message that the court's legacy should be viewed in broad terms not previously central to many analyses. It suggests that the study of the impact of international tribunals would benefit from some of the insights of legal anthropology and law and society studies that have addressed the issue, even if these scholars have cast the debate in different terms. This chapter emphasizes the court's contributions, despite an unfavorable environment, to Bosnia's ongoing transition. In addition, it analyzes several factors within the court, such as a lack of effective internal governance mechanisms, that have impeded its ability to realize its expressivist aspirations. It calls for a discussion of what is reasonable to expect of international criminal law, and urges that discussion of international trials be returned to a modest place in debates about postwar transitions.

2 Crafting the Polity

Transitional Justice and Democratization

On March 11, 2006, former Serbian President Slobodan Milošević was found dead in his cell at Scheveningen, the seaside district in The Hague that houses the prison used by the International Criminal Tribunal for the former Yugoslavia (ICTY). The untimely passing of the first indicted sitting head of state renewed international discussion about the ICTY and its impact in the region. Press reports called this a "crushing blow" for the Tribunal, and stated that "justice had been cheated."[1] Reactions from citizens in Bosnia, and the region in general, ranged from celebration, to lack of interest, to the conspiratorial: accusations from a loud minority that the court itself had murdered its highest-level indictee. This latest development seemed to confirm conventional wisdom in scholarly circles, leaving many feeling that international courts were having a difficult time realizing their extended mandates and could do little to help transitional states.

Conventional wisdom, of course, is a moving target; it changes in response to developments over time. As mentioned in Chapter 1, in the case of the Tribunal, popular conventional wisdom was mostly negative in part because most international reporting on the court was done only when extraordinary things happened. Positive news about courts is not particularly newsworthy, except for specialists. Furthermore, developments which are not newsworthy are not always strictly positive: decisions based on the scrupulous collection of evidence and arguments made in the courtroom, changes in rules of procedure that improve the administration of the court, and decisions at the appellate level that show a court is willing to overturn first-instance judgments – these are examples to which editors may not be willing to devote column inches, especially at a time of shrinking budgets for international reporting. Additionally, the ability of a handful of

---

[1] Peter Beaumont, "Slobodan Milošević Dies Alone with History Still Demanding Justice," *The Guardian*, March 12, 2006, <www.guardian.co.uk/world/2006/mar/12/warcrimes.milosevictrial> (accessed July 14, 2009); Vesna Peric Zimonjic, "'Justice Cheated' as Milošević Found Dead in His Prison Cell," *The Independent*, March 12, 2006, <www.independent.co.uk/news/world/europe/justice-cheated-as-milosevic-is-found-dead-in-his-prison-cell-469602.html> (accessed July 14, 2009).

indictees – including Milošević himself, Vojislav Šešelj, and others – to use the court as a platform to reach their domestic constituencies, fuels these beliefs about international justice. Light sentences in a number of cases were perceived by many as an insult to the victims' suffering, and contributed to a low opinion of the court's usefulness.

Where does such negative scholarly conventional wisdom come from? To some extent, it is the result of the cumulative findings of multiple studies. Sometimes the source of those studies matters. Scholars have professional incentives to be overly critical; there is no particular professional incentive for a scholar to laud an institution for a job well done. More troubling in the case of the ICTY, however, is the fact that many empirical studies failed to find positive impact. Why?

In this chapter, I argue that the scholarly conventional wisdom has in part resulted from the over-emphasis on the application of positivist frameworks and tools of measurement to the question of ICTY impact. In contrast, studies in the fields of law and society and legal anthropology can provide important insights about how we should understand the influence of international criminal law; in each of these fields, a growing body of work looks at international courts, although few of these works have, to our intellectual peril, framed their inquiry in the terms used by the policy world. Integrating these fields into the discussion offers important additional tools to capture international law's pervasive influence in transitioning societies and how what legal scholars call *expressivism* works in local contexts. This broader discussion should help researchers return international law to a modest place in the study of postwar transitions, which encompasses broad societal needs and social processes. However, international law is deeply concerned with those very needs and processes.

Apart from political science, the scholarly fields that examine the impact of courts (including international ones) have been primarily those of law and society, and anthropology. The types of questions these fields ask differ slightly, but their common focus is on how courts influence social change in societies. Anthropologists focus more on the translation of international principles into local cultural contexts. Much of the new and pioneering work in this field has focused on questions about the role of international law in the everyday lives of individuals who are typically not consulted or captured in legal scholarship. One recent volume, for example, argues: "the paths to and from international justice take many forms ... . The institutions of justice exist at the intersection of multiple and often contradictory processes, involving different and sometimes irreconcilable senses of justice."[2] In political science, some scholars have sought to explain under what conditions tribunals are formed.[3] Other studies have looked at whether the presence of a transitional justice mechanism has influenced the consolidation of democracy. The field

---

[2] Marie Benedict Dembour and Tobias Kelly, eds., *Paths to International Justice: Social and Legal Perspectives* (Cambridge: Cambridge University Press, 2007), 9.

[3] Gary Jonathan Bass, *Stay the Hand of Vengeance: The Politics of War Crimes Tribunals* (Princeton, NJ: Princeton University Press, 2000).

of international law and society has frequently focused on the former "third world" and, along with legal anthropology, has addressed how international principles work locally. This interdisciplinary interest in the role of international criminal law in transitional periods has enriched our knowledge tremendously. However, it has shortcomings. There are, for instance, no common criteria about what outcomes to look for when international criminal law is applied in times of transition. Furthermore, the fact that international law does not always lead to precise and predictable outcomes has often been interpreted as evidence that transitional institutions are bad or "failing." In fact, international courts often serve the functions that most other institutions do, both international and domestic: they channel contention and mediate interests about issues of concern.

In the following pages, this chapter articulates some of the ICTY's effects, using insights from studies of contentious politics, and what is known as the *constitutive* branch of law and society. Understanding the court as a site of *social contention*, where "wars about the war" are waged through the context of law, can inform our understanding of the role of international tribunals in post-conflict societies. With this literature as a backdrop, this chapter explains how the ICTY has advanced social, attitudinal, and institutional changes. It outlines the contributions and limits of previous studies of democratic transitions, transitional justice, and attitudinal research. It concludes that international trials which, as the case studies illustrate, are fraught with contradictory demands, are favorable for democratization processes. This sets the stage for the following chapter, which introduces a note of caution: Chapter 3 outlines some of the events leading up to the formation of the ICTY and the context in which the court worked in Bosnia. The liberal values upheld in international law may not be furthered much by an institutional structure that does little as a practical matter to uphold those values.

Contributions of This Study: Ideas, Attitudes, and Institutions

Mobilization around Ideas of Accountability

Scholars of social movements have explored what ideas, events, and institutions inspire collective action. Movements are commonly defined as "collective challenges by people with common purposes and solidarity in sustained interaction with elites, opponents, and authorities."[4] Collective action is often prompted by what has been called a "political opportunity structure"; that is, when certain changes create openings for mobilization.[5] Scholars have pointed to changes in political leadership (e.g., from conservative to liberal forces) as one type of opening;

---

[4]   Sidney Tarrow, *Power in Movement: Social Movements, Collective Action and Politics* (Cambridge: Cambridge University Press, 1994), 3–4.

[5]   Ibid. 18.

the creation of new institutions, such as tribunals, serve this purpose as well. The structure of opportunities can help explain why groups with considerable griev-ances but no opportunities may not organize.[6] In Bosnia, the ICTY provided an opening for collective action because it created a space for discussion about atroci-ties, legitimacy for others to follow suit, and a flow of information about the war.

The first (and most obvious) groups to organize comprised the victims of war who were directly affected by ongoing proceedings. However, those who felt as if they had been overlooked by the work of the court also lobbied for redress, moti-vated to organize around what they perceived as a failure by the Tribunal to act on their behalf. Once mobilized, some challenged the ICTY itself, questioning its rules of procedure, choice of indictees, and so on. The court provided a com-mon language inspired by law, familiar to (if not always understood by) citizens in the region.

Mobilization thus had multiple motivations; some responses were politically inspired and prompted by forces opposed to the court, some facilitated by the lack of legal response to specific crimes, and some inspired by particular cases. Not all mobilization looks "democratic"; forces that were opposed to international justice mobilized because they wished to suppress the truth about past atroci-ties and to protect individuals wanted for crimes. While obviously not desired by any proponent of law and order, this mobilization and even dissent were positive insofar as they kept within the democratic arena. It also represented a new understanding by less progressive forces that activism must be restricted to circumscribed institutions and forms, even if, as in this case, compliance was enforced by foreign troops. As scholars of democratic transitions have noted, the containment of political activity within the confines of institutional structures is an important sign of democratization.[7] When violence is no longer an option, and dissenting forces channel their demands through courts, democratization is occurring. In short, the *judicialization* of issues surrounding war crimes is a desirable thing.[8]

The ICTY helped mediate the accuracy of claims by both civil society and politi-cal forces, both for and against the court. Admittedly, the mechanism of indi-vidual accountability complicated this task somewhat. In an environment where there is no singular and coherent narrative about the causes and events of a war,

[6]   Ibid., 17–18.

[7]   Juan J. Linz and Alfred Stepan, *Problems of Democratic Transition and Consolidation: Southern Europe, South America and Post-Communist Europe* (Baltimore, MD: John Hopkins University Press, 1996), 5–6.

[8]   The relationship between democratization and social movements is complex. Not all movements contribute to democratizing processes. Charles Tilly argues that social movements can be democratizing when they "broaden the range of participation in public politics, equalize the weight of participants in public politics, erect barriers to the direct translation of categorical inequalities into public politics and/or integrate previously segmented trust networks into public politics." Charles Tilly, *Social Movements 1768–2004* (Boulder, CO: Paradigm Publishers, 2008), 143.

competing claims flourish (a point developed in Chapter 6). Trials bring these disagreements to light and clarify the major axis of contention. They make it possible to understand which facts are contested and why. Legal proceedings bring what may have remained private discussions into the public realm. Those claims are then endorsed (or not) by court decisions.

The court's documentation, created through lengthy investigative processes and expert testimonies, while not a complete history of the war, provided a source against which claims about the extent and nature of crimes could be evaluated. In Bosnia, even the very nature of the war was contested. The ICTY ruled on these questions and declared that the war had an international character; in other words, that it was not a civil war. While, in the short term, it did not change opinions for many who were partial to the civil war thesis, it made some of the more extreme versions of this thesis harder to maintain. Cycles of activism and protest changed in form, content, and intensity over the years, responding to the realization that certain claims could not hold up under scrutiny. The ICTY's presence thus shaped the formation of activism and social mobilization.

The presence of the ICTY also made it easier for other civil society groups to pursue initiatives related to the court's mandate. Various local educational and documentation initiatives benefited from having an international body committed to prosecuting violations of international law, working as a reference, impetus, or partner.

Furthermore, it is generally underappreciated that courts themselves may be sites and objects of contentious politics.[9] Judicial activism has been part of a repertoire of social movements, a strategy as important as public protest, shaming, or claims made on state resources.[10] Scholars who think that courts can and should provide definitive answers to fundamental questions and concerns of constituents may view contention as detrimental to democratization.[11] Some assume that legal interventions are based on, and produce consensus about, the particular issues under consideration in any given case, and that "prosecutors – as spokesmen for 'the people' – tell stories through which [moral] sentiments are elicited and membership [in a community] is consolidated."[12] They can provide relatively complete accounts of specific crimes in specific places.

However, decisions resulting from different trials, even when concerning the same crime base, will produce differing narratives depending on the witnesses and experts called. Criminal trials for systematic violations of human rights rarely

---

[9] See Charles Tilly and Sidney Tarrow, *Contentious Politics* (Boulder, CO: Paradigm Publishers, 2007).

[10] On repertoires, see Charles Tilly, *Contentious Performances* (Cambridge: Cambridge University Press, 2008).

[11] The most common metaphor is one of closure for the victims. For a critique of this metaphor, see Jose E. Alvarez, "Rush to Closure: Lessons of the Tadić Judgment," *Michigan Law Review* 96, no. 7 (June 1998): 2031–2112.

[12] Mark Osiel, *Mass Atrocity, Collective Memory and the Law* (New Brunswick, NJ: Transaction Publishers, 2000), 29.

produce agreement.[13] Mark Osiel argues that legal proceedings are in fact founded on *civil dissensus*. They produce the "kind of solidarity embodied in the increasingly respectful way that citizens can come to acknowledge the differing views of their fellows."[14] The disagreement produced by trials represents a development common to and important for democratizing states, he argues. During a trial for mass atrocities, differing views about the crimes being discussed are the subject of deliberation for the first time. This deliberation represents a form of communication and questioning that, until the trial, had no reason to take place and most likely never would have.

The importance of exchanges based on defined rules is that they enable parties to a trial to agree on how to disagree. Osiel argues that individuals can hold differences of opinion about the atrocities under consideration and under what circumstances they were committed, as long as there are rules that govern exchanges between parties. "We form our attachments to our adversaries not only through procedures establishing agreement on how to disagree, but through the actual human experience of the resulting exchanges, provided they conform to these civility rules. Through such exchanges, we need not transcend our differences on matters of ultimate concern."[15] That is not to say that all of the exchanges at the ICTY conformed to the rules of engagement one hoped for, but the majority did.

This argument has important implications for how we think about the role of law in post-conflict societies. Osiel is reacting to observers who have argued that the narratives exchanged in the courtroom and, later, the narrative that prevails with the judges, could form the basis for a shared collective memory of a nation. The recognition that trials can serve a much different function is a pointed reminder of the role of principled and rule-based disagreement in democracies. This insight is also addressed in the democratization literature, which has emphasized the role of channeling disagreement through institutions.[16]

In an international trial, this process is more complicated, as the main axis of communication between the defense and prosecution takes place under sponsorship of an international entity. Nevertheless, international trials do start their deliberations among differing groups in a foreign land, and eventually this process – both the trials and the exchange – moves to the countries affected by the proceedings.

There may never be broad-based agreement about recent history in a given state. However, smaller steps may be made toward a better understanding of how certain circumstances could have led to human rights violations. The rules of engagement that governed interaction in an international court may eventually be adopted in the local setting. Osiel describes this process of creation of a social

[13] Ibid., 32–33.
[14] Ibid., 22–23. Jose E. Alvarez also uses the concept of *civil dissensus* in support of the work of the ICTY. See Alvarez, "Rush to Closure."
[15] Osiel, *Mass Atrocity*, 43.
[16] See Linz and Stepan, *Problems of Democratic Transition*.

trust and unity based on disagreement. Individuals must, at a minimum, respect each other, in order to communicate disagreement. This is an important aspect of democratization. In the case of the ICTY, the concept of civil dissensus provides an important corrective to much of the common wisdom about the roles of international trials.

Furthermore, the communication of disagreement followed a different axis in Bosnia: between the survivor population and the international community. The ICTY also helped foster civil dissensus in other arenas, and facilitated the efforts of local citizens to push the limits of who and what would be included in the trials for wartime atrocities. The ICTY targeted specific crimes and individuals within a defined period of time, but had positive derivative effects that extended beyond the mandate of the original institution. Leslie Vinjamuri argues, "the creation of weak institutions has unintended consequences … . By lending additional power to proponents of liberal values, weak institutions enable strong and committed individuals to support the expansion of these norms."[17] Chapter 4 illustrates how some civil society groups expanded the norm of accountability to include the international community at a time when scholars, observing the explosion of international intervention in the post–Cold War period, were also raising the issue of the accountability gap of international organizations.

This development on the ground was concurrent with new research that sought to understand the potential role of international actors in the international order. International forces have been taking up the roles and functions of states, administering territory, and making promises to stateless persons and those in conflict situations. These new roles have prompted discussion about their formal legal responsibilities. For example, Frédéric Mégret and Florian Hoffmann ask whether the United Nations (UN) might be violating human rights. They examined how "the transformation of the UN from a traditional intergovernmental organization into a more supra-governmental one involved in occasional direct tasks of governance is potentially reshaping its human rights mission."[18] This rhetorical question, posed academically, was actively addressed inside Bosnia (with the help of local and foreign lawyers) to examine the role and failings of the UN and its member states, as discussed in Chapters 3 and 4.

Scholars have thought mostly about the impact of international norms on domestic populations, but this study makes the case that the role of domestic forces in the construction and expansion of international norms should not be

---

[17] Leslie Vinjamuri, "Trading Order for Justice? Prosecuting War Criminals in the Aftermath of Conflict" (Ph.D. dissertation, Columbia University, 2001), 8.

[18] Frédéric Mégret and Florian Hoffmann, "The UN as a Human Rights Violator? Some Reflections on the United Nations' Changing Human Rights Responsibilities," *Human Rights Quarterly* 25, no. 2 (2003): 315. On this theme, see also Anthony Lang, Jr., "The United Nations and the Fall of Srebrenica: Meaningful Responsibility and International Society," in Toni Erskine, ed., *Can Institutions Have Duties? Collective Moral Agency and International Relations* (New York: Palgrave Macmillan, 2004); and Adam LeBor, *Complicity with Evil: The United Nations in the Age of Modern Genocide* (New Haven, CT: Yale University Press, 2007).

overlooked. The court was a conduit for ideas about accountability and human rights, and interacted with domestic elements, such as civil society groups, that considered it appropriate to hold international actors accountable for failing to protect local citizens. There is a healthy body of literature in international relations that acknowledges the interplay between domestic and international forces, but the role of these domestic forces does not get a lot of attention in scholarly literature on the diffusion of human rights norms.[19]

Understanding Norm Change

The ICTY has no enforcement mechanisms of its own and the states that support its work have rather weak ones at best (such as the prevention of membership in certain institutions or the threat of withheld aid). This project therefore addresses the literature that examines whether ideas influence political outcomes and have causal value in the political world. Much scholarship has been concerned with how principled ideas become norms, wherein norms are "collective expectations about proper behavior for a given identity."[20] The means by which ideas become norms is described as a process of socialization, or the "induction of new members ... into the ways of behavior that are preferred in a society."[21] In Bosnia, the word induction risks sounding condescending; re-induction would probably describe the situation more accurately, as the war was a clear rupture from historical societal relations.

The case studies show that, over time, those opposed to the Tribunal in postwar Bosnia who were forced to comply with the norms of the ICTY began to utilize the language of human rights, giving at least the appearance of being in line with new universal norms about accountability. This process of socialization occurred precisely in the way existing paradigms would predict. Thomas Risse, Stephen Ropp, and Kathryn Sikkink, for example, developed a model that illustrates the diffusion of human rights norms. Unwilling elites first adopt those norms for strategic purposes, to avert punishment by the international community.[22] Even if the espousal of support for accountability and transparency is accompanied by weak compliance and begrudging cooperation, those elites begin to employ the language of human rights, in what Risse, Ropp, and Sikkink call a new "discursive

---

[19] See, for example, Peter B. Evans, Harold K. Jacobson, and Robert D. Putnam, *Double-Edged Diplomacy: International Bargaining and Domestic Politics* (Berkeley, CA: University of California Press, 1993); Robert Putnam "Diplomacy and Domestic Politics: The Logic of Two-Level Games," *International Organization* 42, no. 3 (1988): 427–460.

[20] Peter J. Katzenstein, ed., *The Culture of National Security: Norms and Identity in World Politics* (New York: Columbia University Press, 1996), 54.

[21] Ibid., 11.

[22] They refer to this as instrumental adaptation. See Thomas Risse, Stephen C. Ropp, and Kathryn Sikkink, *The Power of Human Rights: International Norms and Domestic Change* (Cambridge: Cambridge University Press, 1999), 15–16.

practice."[23] Often this new vocabulary is utilized for reasons having nothing to do with justice: actors instead may seek legitimacy, money, recognition, or membership in specific institutions. This was as true for Bosnia as for many other post-conflict states.

In the short term, this makes it seem as if political opposition to international justice made a mockery of attempts to bring perpetrators to justice. When political forces close to or associated with wartime atrocities start to espouse human rights, while harboring criminals and concealing information, it is tempting to denounce judicial institutions as entirely ineffective or weak. However, the model developed by Risse, Ropp, and Sikkink suggests that this phase does not last and that elites will begin to internalize pro-human rights rhetoric and live up to their commitments. In postwar Bosnia, some elites opposed to the ICTY cooperated inconsistently and strategically, and only when the costs of *not* cooperating were too high. In this light, it is not so surprising that the pursuit of justice could often look like a farce, especially when some politicians who acted the part of rule-abiding citizens were at the same time harboring international criminals.[24]

This new discursive practice, however, has positive spin-off effects when other groups, like civil society leaders, alter their attitudes and rhetoric to fall in line with views voiced by those elites, as the case studies here illustrate. Even if commitment is insincere in the strategic adoption phase, this lesser form of internationalization has an effect that is measurable, for example, in survey data, which is analyzed in the chapters to follow. Norms indicate what proper behavior is, and attitudinal research measures individuals' perceptions and beliefs about institutions, as well as the effects of institutions that purport to embody certain norms. Attitudes are always evolving. Positive changes can represent a positive step to developing necessary attitudes that are important for the development of a democratic political culture. The authors of this original concept, Sidney Verba and Gabriel Almond, argue that there is no single formula for the creation of a democratic political culture. Still, they identify certain "channels of political socialization" that help shape attitudes. At the domestic level, education is one such example they identify. But in international society, international courts, like the ICTY, could also be considered an example.[25]

Attitudes, however, are influenced by the type and quality of information received and the perceived benefits. One of the problems that all international organizations face is the difficulty of informing the populations affected by their work about the purpose, structure, and goals of their institutions. In this regard, the International Criminal Tribunal for the former Yugoslavia was no different from many other international bodies. The empirical case studies that follow

---

[23] Ibid., 14.

[24] However, as noted below, this study raises the question of what happens when the commitment to enforce compliance (in this case by international forces) weakens.

[25] Gabriel A. Almond and Sidney Verba, *The Civic Culture: Political Attitudes and Democracy in Five Nations* (Newbury Park, CA: Sage Publications, 1989), 371.

show how attitudes changed over time: as individuals in the region watched trials and saw the consistency of the court's work, some, but certainly not all, stopped viewing it as an instrument created to try a particular ethnic group. The quality of information likely affects this process. However, increased information and better sources are not enough on their own. A study outlined in Chapter 9 found that attitudes about basic facts changed for the worse in Serbia, an occurrence that took place after the so-called October Revolution of 2000. That this study charts more positive findings may be related to enforced compliance with the court, and the fact that during the period under consideration, international officials made an effort to punish non-conformity.

The Bosnian case study demonstrates that efforts to educate citizens have several obstacles to overcome. Outreach requires substantial institutional support as well as help from international organizations present on the ground. Local knowledge is key. The ICTY did not employ enough people from the region with knowledge of local affairs, practices, and customs, and this inhibited their ability to frame issues and direct messages. This empirical observation finds support in the scholarly literature. James Scott attributes the absence of this knowledge, or *metis*, as the primary reason for the failure of large-scale efforts to improve human affairs.[26] He defines *metis* as the "wide array of practical skills and acquired intelligence in responding to a constantly changing and human environment."[27] The court employed a multinational mix of judges and prosecutors from small and large countries, but better local *metis* would have enabled the court's representatives to share its results more effectively with local populations. The application of universal norms must be done with local contexts in mind.[28] It is impossible to measure the overall societal impact of court outreach, as the program was too small for widespread societal change, but this study finds significant changes in those groups that had direct contact with the court.

The question of local knowledge brings up the issue of whether the international justice project is a Western liberal model being exported to new territories. Indeed, the model of international forces imparting desired values has a ring of civilizational superiority. Many scholars have interpreted the imposition of the court as a form of Western hegemony or "imperialism," part of a liberal project not entirely appropriate for the countries of the region.[29] The Socialist Federal Republic of

[26] James C. Scott, *Seeing Like a State: How Certain Schemes to Improve the Human Condition Have Failed* (New Haven, CT: Yale University Press, 1998).

[27] Ibid., 313.

[28] To be sure, however, many of the complaints lodged about those who dealt with the court in the postwar years had nothing to do with local contexts or culture, but rather with simple institutional arrogance and insensitivity. For example, officials did not return documentation or materials as promised.

[29] Balakrishnan Rajagopal, *International Law from Below: Development, Social Movements and Third World Resistance* (Cambridge: Cambridge University Press, 2003), 18. Rajagopal describes how the hegemony and force of Western ideas about humanitarian intervention was "[u]ntil recently ... unshakeable."

Yugoslavia (SFRY), however, had a long history and experience of international law, which was written into its domestic criminal code.[30] Despite a tendency of some to view the creation of the court as part of a Western "hegemonic" project, the application of international law to the Bosnian case (and in the region) was in keeping with the country's own legal traditions. Much of this debate is misplaced. In general, the struggle the court has faced to increase its social bases of support in the region has had more to do with the fact that the international forces which, on the one hand, wielded the liberal project of international law, had on the other hand failed to successfully denounce the social forces in the region that did not believe in the universal norms of human dignity upheld in that law. In short, the international community upheld the work of the ICTY, but failed to eliminate the social project that produced those very violations of international law. The groups whose representatives proclaim a "Western" conspiracy at the ICTY are often those who support division, intolerance, and even deny mass atrocities.

Institutional Change: Local Judicial Capacity

International trials led to the creation of local judicial capacity, through the transfer of cases instituted by the court and handed to local jurisdictions, the approval of local cases at the ICTY, and locally, the growing realization that improvements in the security sector (meaning judicial, military, and police reform) would be integral to efforts to promote both Euro-Atlantic integration and citizens' feelings of safety. Chapter 8 shows that although judicial reform was slow to get off the ground, ultimately this was one of the strongest contributions of the ICTY to local democratization.

Most scholarly work about the impact of international trials on local justice has focused on regions in which the international community did not have a large presence on the ground. Understanding of the relationship between international networks and local capacity started in the context of transitions from authoritarian rule in Latin America. Having observed local trials there, Ellen Lutz and Kathryn Sikkink argue that a *justice cascade* (their term) occurred as the "result of the concerted efforts of a transnational justice advocacy network, made up of connected groups of activist lawyers with expertise in international and domestic human rights law."[31] This cascade resulted in the local prosecution

---

[30] An English copy of the criminal code of the Socialist Federal Republic of Yugoslavia (SFRY) is available online at: <pbosnia.kentlaw.edu/resources/legal/bosnia/criminalcode_fry.htm> (accessed July 20, 2009). See Chapter 16, "Criminal Acts Against Humanity and International Law."

[31] Ellen Lutz and Kathryn Sikkink, "The Justice Cascade: The Evolution and Impact of Foreign Human Rights Trials in Latin America," *Chicago Journal of International Law* 2, no. 1 (2001), 17.

of persons suspected of violations of international law in Argentina and other countries. This network enabled beleaguered human rights advocates in the region to reach outside of their own states to align themselves with foreign justice advocates, and later to use foreign courts to pursue cases they could not address at home. Sikkink and Lutz showed that this resulted in an attitudinal and institutional change that led to the adoption of legislation and the ratification of international agreements on human rights, thus facilitating domestic trials.

The parallel to events in Bosnia, however, is not exact, even if the idea of a "justice cascade" is an apt metaphor for understanding events in Southeastern Europe. This case does not exactly represent an example of Lutz and Sikkink's justice cascade strictly speaking, because local prosecutions were part of the Tribunal's exit strategy. Also, the role of the advocacy network was less important. International officials in the country, aided by the ICTY, largely spearheaded the process to create the conditions for local trials. Tribunal officials always envisioned handing off their cases to local authorities when the time was right; thus the development of local capacity was always a goal.

Nevertheless, some of the general insights of Lutz and Sikkink's research could be seen at work in Bosnia: international trials did affect local developments. Legal professionals who had cut their teeth in The Hague and knew the difficulties associated with crafting new institutions greatly aided in this process. They brought with them lessons learned in the international arena. Moreover, investigations conducted at the international level were later useful in local courtrooms. The ICTY analyzed institutions such as the police and armed forces in order to establish chains of command and command responsibility. Evidence collected by the ICTY also contained many names of perpetrators it did not have time to address, who were later pursued in local courts.

There were other lessons learned from the work in The Hague. For example, journalists covering the process understood what they wanted from the court, and what other members of civil society needed, even if they were not entirely able to prevent the inflation of expectations that plagued the ICTY. In addition, advocacy networks that kept a spotlight on Bosnia – groups such as Amnesty International and Human Rights Watch – made sure that the flaws in the overall process and the lack of progress in specific cases did not disappear from public view.

Bosnia's justice cascade was more than just the initiation of local trials. There was also the creation of institutional expectations beyond the ICTY's formal capacity to mediate that process. It slowly became unacceptable to not prosecute locally. Thus, the institutional legacy of trials in The Hague extended beyond the handoff of specific cases. There was also the expectation that arrests would occur, awareness in the media that solid press coverage of the trials was important, and increasing public demand for information about cases, not to mention demand for a seat in the courtroom. The transition process was far from seamless, however, as Chapter 8 outlines.

Scholars of transitional justice often argue that a weak institutional environment means that prosecutions following universal norms will be divisive, or even provoke violence. This school of thought argues that transitional states should wait until strong institutions can be built and the rule of law established without threat from the powerful actors that are targeted by prosecutions.[32] In short, they assert, one needs a strong state before addressing the crimes of the former regime.

This study, alternatively, supports the understanding that the promotion of the rule of law over the course of the transition itself helps craft stronger institutions, especially in situations where members of the former regime are left in power. Prosecutorial targeting of members of parties in power, or with strong ties to those in power, will obviously be a source of contention, but even partial prosecutions can reveal the criminality of the former regime. This was of course somewhat easier in Bosnia because the transition was taking place under the administration of the international community. Spoilers were contained because the enforcers were armed. Chapter 9, however, illustrates some of the limits associated with having members of the former regime in the government.

The methods often used to study democratic transitions, primarily from the field of political science, have obscured some important observations about the role of both international and local justice initiatives, as the next section explains.

Theories of Democratic Transition

The fields that advanced the study of transitional justice mechanisms have helped to shape current conventional wisdom by producing a body of scholarship that failed to capture the contributions of these mechanisms. The so-called transitions literature, primarily in the field of political science, grew from the examples of numerous countries in Latin America and Southern Europe that spurned authoritarian regimes in favor of democracies in the late 1970s and 1980s. Scholarly works addressing these case studies focused on how and whether authoritarian regimes might break down, the ingredients necessary for the eventual consolidation of democracy, and how democracy might be improved.[33] These early works also inspired activists "in the field" who were working to change regimes.[34] The label

---

[32] Jack L. Snyder and Leslie Vinjamuri, "Trials and Errors: Principle and Pragmatism in Strategies of International Justice," *International Security* 28, no. 3 (2003/04): 5–44.

[33] Terry Lynn Karl, "From Democracy to Democratization and Back: Before *Transitions from Authoritarian Rule*" (Working Paper 45, Center on Democracy, Development and the Rule of Law, Stanford Institute on International Studies, September 2005). The first major study was Guillermo O'Donnell and Philippe C. Schmitter, *Transitions from Authoritarian Rule: Tentative Conclusions about Uncertain Democracies* (Baltimore, MD: John Hopkins University Press, 1986).

[34] Karl, "From Democracy," 4.

"transitions" implied that the countries in question were moving to another type of government, and it was assumed that the eventual outcome would be a "consolidated" democracy, usually defined as a democracy under no risk of a return to non-democratic forms of government.

Examining what was required in the process of consolidation of democracy, Juan Linz and Alfred Stepan argued that there were certain behavioral, attitudinal, and constitutional prerequisites for democracy to be considered "the only game in town."[35] They argued that it was crucial that significant actors no longer utilize violence to realize their goals, that the public believe that democratic institutions should govern public life, and that democratic institutions mediate conflict in public life. Linz and Stepan also concurred with Dankwart Rustow, who argued in a now-famous 1970 essay – as these transitions were just beginning – that the most important prerequisite for democracy was that the citizens of a given territory agree on the contours of their nation-state. As Rustow put it: "There must be a sense of national unity."[36] Linz and Stepan referred to this as the problem of "stateness." This foundational requisite may have posed the greatest problem for ICTY impact in Bosnia: the country lacks a sense of national unity and the Dayton Peace Agreement did not provide the basis for the development of a civic national identity, a point developed in Chapter 3.

In their landmark study, Linz and Stepan identified another five components, aside from stateness, necessary for democracy's consolidation: civil society, political society, economic society, the rule of law, and a state bureaucracy.[37] However, consolidation, as discussed in transitions literature, emphasized a model in which *all* of these conditions would be fulfilled and countries would be considered safe from slippage. Transitional justice mechanisms, in this view, were viewed as largely irrelevant. Furthermore, scholars of transitions faced methodological pressures from their more positivist colleagues. Large-N studies illustrated that countries could ignore their past and make the transition quite successfully.

After the fall of the Berlin Wall in 1989, the "transitologists" were faced with a different kind of transformation: the transition from communism to democracy and from command economies to free (or freer) ones. Immediately, there were questions about the relevance of Latin American transitions to the experiences of the post-socialist states of Eastern Europe and the former Soviet Union. Some scholars argued against the utility of comparing the transitions in Eastern Europe with those in Latin America, claiming the nature of the systems in place in each region precluded successful comparisons.[38] Similarly, some earlier studies, which addressed the

---

[35] Linz and Stepan, *Problems of Democratic Transition*, 5.

[36] Dankwart Rustow, "Transitions to Democracy: Toward a Dynamic Model," *Comparative Politics* 2, no. 3 (1970): 337–363. See also Karl, "From Democracy," 12.

[37] Linz and Stepan, *Problems of Democratic Transition*, 245–253.

[38] For the "pro" comparison view, see Philippe C. Schmitter, "The Conceptual Travels of Transitologists and Consolidationists: How Far to the East Should They Attempt to Go?" *Slavic Review* 53, no. 1 (Spring 1994): 173–185; and for the opposing view, see Valerie Bunce, "Should Transitologists Be Grounded?" *Slavic Review* 54, no. 1 (Spring 1995): 111–127.

transitions occurring in Eastern Europe, argued that it was presumptuous to say that the transitions occurring were to democracy, and that it was doubtful in some cases that the label *post-communism* was even appropriate. As time went on, the term *post-communism* fell out of favor as some argued that the vast differences in the outcomes in the region had rendered it obsolete.[39] The entire transitions paradigm was later called into question. Thomas Carothers argued that many of those countries supposedly captured by the model are not, in fact, transitioning to democracy as it suggests, while other countries are failing to conform to certain built-in assumptions.[40] Bosnia is sometimes considered such a case; some refer to it as a frozen conflict.

The early transitions and consolidation literature suffered from an inflexible assumption that once countries became consolidated democracies, they would not revert to prior forms of governance. It was, in essence, a very deterministic way of looking at transitions. The role of transitional justice in this analytic scheme was uncertain. While it was clear that countries could become democratic without addressing atrocities of past regimes, the quality and inclusiveness of those regimes were overlooked. Later studies of democratization revealed a more nuanced understanding that countries are constantly experiencing democratization and de-democratization. Charles Tilly writes that, "a regime is democratic to the degree that political relations between the state and its citizens feature broad, equal, protected and more binding consultation. Democratization means net movement toward broader, more equal, more protected, and more binding consultation. De-democratization, obviously, then means net movement toward narrower, more unequal, less protected, and less binding consultation."[41] Acknowledgment of the importance of consultation created a theoretical space for engagement between victims *as citizens* of the former regime (and therefore important constituents) and the state. Perhaps most importantly, Tilly emphasized the importance of the *quality* of democracy for all citizens.

Generally speaking, however, the countries of Southeastern Europe were somewhat outside this discussion of transitions. They presented a dilemma for analytical studies of the region because they were not only experiencing a double transition from conflict and from communism, but were also the subject of heavy international intervention and administration. Still, several volumes on postwar Bosnia attempted to make sense of its unique situation. David Chandler argued that Bosnia was "faking democracy," and that the international intervention "undermined autonomy and self government on the assumption that external assistance is necessary for building an alternative that will more effectively bridge segmented political divisions."[42] Sumantra Bose addressed the state of the democratization effort in Bosnia and, while suggesting that the country must be

---

[39] Jacques Rupnik, "The Post-Communist Divide," *Journal of Democracy* 10, no. 1 (1999): 57–62.

[40] Thomas Carothers, "The End of the Transition Paradigm," *Journal of Democracy* 13, no. 1 (2002): 5–21.

[41] Charles Tilly, *Democracy* (Cambridge: Cambridge University Press, 2007), 13–14.

[42] David Chandler, *Bosnia: Faking Democracy after Dayton* (London: Pluto Press, 1999), 194.

understood at the local and regional levels, argued that the axis of conflict in post-war Bosnia was, contrary to popular opinion, not between the formerly warring parties but between the former parties to the conflict and the international community.[43] This was true in the early postwar years, and in the realm of justice, but would change over time.[44] Most of this work was rightfully critical of the pace and form of international intervention but the implicit counterfactual of this study – a Bosnia in which the international community had not intervened in the area of war crimes trials – was never considered.

Given its status as a quasi-protectorate unlike almost any other in the world, the Bosnian case study was somewhat difficult to theorize about. Consequently, many postwar analyses of countries in the region were conducted by organizations with a distinct focus on policy objectives, such as the International Crisis Group. Bosnia was best suited to studies of states with large international administrations, such as Kosovo and East Timor, or of places that had experienced mass atrocities, such as Rwanda or Chechnya.[45] These advocacy organizations often pointed out the vast scope of reforms yet to be completed.

Still, some things were measured systematically. The importance of democratic development to U.S. foreign policy goals meant that the constant measurement of progress in various aspects of development was taken up by non-governmental organizations such as Freedom House. So-called policy metrics rose with contributions from some of the scholarly world's top observers of democratic transitions in both Latin America and the former socialist world.[46] With the help of experts on various regions, Freedom House started measuring progress in areas such as civil society, corruption, electoral competition, and judicial framework and independence.[47]

Freedom House's reports on *Freedom in the World* and *Nations in Transit* are found in the offices of both policymakers and scholars alike. The numeric progress added a more scientific flavor to the understanding of transitions. It also showed the process of de-democratization articulated by Charles Tilly and others, and captured the backward steps inevitably made by countries in transition. Progress was neither inevitable, nor was it linear.

---

[43] Sumantra Bose, *Bosnia after Dayton: Nationalist Partition and International Intervention* (Oxford: Oxford University Press, 2002), 6.

[44] Several dissertations have also attempted to assess various aspects of the international intervention; for example, Dana Susan Burde, "Creating community? PTAs in (post) conflict zones" (Ph.D. dissertation, Columbia University, 2001); Gemma Collantes Celador, "The Role of Police Reform in Peacebuilding Missions: Lessons from Post-Dayton Bosnia and Herzegovina" (Ph.D. dissertation, University of Wales, Aberystwyth, 2006).

[45] On state building with an international presence, see Simon Chesterman, *You, the People: The United Nations, Transitional Administration, and State-Building* (New York: Oxford University Press, 2005).

[46] Adrian Karanytsky, Freedom House, "Human Rights in Post-Communist Eurasia," presentation at graduate seminar, Columbia University, February 7, 2007.

[47] See <www.freedomhouse.org/template.cfm?page=42&year=2008> (accessed July 20, 2009).

In Freedom House's measure of judicial independence, Bosnia advanced from 4.25 in 2006 to 4.0 in 2008 (on a scale of 1 to 7, where 7 is the lowest); the opening of Bosnia's War Crimes Chamber in 2005 surely contributed to this rating. While the rule of law was included under the rubric of judicial independence, the metric mostly captures quantifiable indicators such as the passing of laws and the building of institutions. This study identifies, in addition, other legacies influenced by The Hague, such as social mobilization and the development of a legal consciousness, that are not easily captured in such important exercises in quantification.

Origins of the Field of Transitional Justice

The academic study of transitional justice responded to the proliferation of truth commissions, lustration (disqualifying from office or other public roles those associated with the abuses of the prior regime), and war crimes tribunals at the end of the Cold War.[48] Much early writing on transitional justice was descriptive or journalistic, detailing the events, people, and places where tribunals or truth commissions, or processes of lustration, were implemented. But it did not address the overall role of these institutions in the transition to democracy – a question important to political scientists interested in the elements that lead to a consolidated democracy, to legal scholars interested in the role of judicial institutions, and to policy makers who argued for these mechanisms.

Scholarly works on transitional justice followed. The United States Institute for Peace (USIP) published a three-volume series on the topic, with a collection of articles by prominent academics outlining the experiences of different countries and the different mechanisms employed.[49] The series drew attention to the increasing concentration on transitional justice and provided impetus for further scholarly inquiry into the emerging field.

In political science, early work on transitional justice focused on explaining why certain transitional justice mechanisms were chosen and others ignored. Many scholars showed how the political circumstances of a transition influenced the nature of justice pursued. Samuel Huntington argued that decisions about whether authoritarian leaders were punished for human rights violations that occurred under their regimes were "shaped almost exclusively by politics, the nature of the democratization process, and the distribution of political power during and after the transition."[50] He outlined the common rationales for and against

---

[48] For what is probably the largest transitional justice bibliography, see the transitional justice database project, University of Wisconsin, Madison, available online at: <users.polisci.wisc.edu/tjdb/bib.htm> (accessed October 14, 2009).

[49] Neil J. Kritz, ed., *Transitional Justice: How Emerging Democracies Reckon with Former Regimes*, 3 vols. (Washington, DC: United States Institute of Peace, 1995).

[50] Samuel P. Huntington, *The Third Wave: Democratization in the Late Twentieth Century* (London: University of Oklahoma Press, 1993), 215.

such prosecutions, reflecting expressivist, retributive, and deterrence rationales. Arguments for prosecution identified by Huntington include: 1) "truth and justice require it"; 2) "prosecution is a moral obligation"; 3) "democracy is based on law" and no one is above the law; 4) "prosecution is necessary to deter future violations"; 5) "prosecution is essential to establish the viability of the democratic system"; 6) "prosecution will assert the supremacy of democratic norms and values and encourage the public to believe in them"; and 7) prosecution brings "into the open the extent of the crimes and the identity of those responsible" and "establish[es] a full and public record." Arguments against include: 1) "democracy has to be based on reconciliation," which means setting aside the past; 2) "the process of democratization" requires understanding that there will not be retribution; 3) in many cases both sides were guilty of crimes and "a general amnesty for all provides a far stronger base for democracy"; 4) crimes were justified by the need to "suppress terrorism ... and restore law and order to society"; 5) many "people and groups shared in the guilt for the crimes committed"; and 6) amnesty is necessary "to establish the new democracy on a solid basis."[51]

Similarly, Luc Huyse showed how the mode of transition and the international context both affect the choices available to elites of successor regimes, and several dissertations have drawn from this theoretical framing.[52] One study examined the case of Poland and asked why elites would choose to pass lustration legislation that would adversely affect them. The research found they passed measures in order to avoid the risk of what a succeeding regime (which might not include them in a governing coalition) might otherwise impose.[53]

It was the field of law, however, that produced an understanding of the partial and limited, yet important, role of most transitional justice mechanisms. Ruti Teitel's *Transitional Justice* acknowledges the limitations and partiality of transitional initiatives, but argues that: "the turn to legalism, however contingent, is emblematic of the liberal state, with transitional justice reconstructing the political identity on a juridical basis by deploying the discourse of rights and responsibilities."[54] The book's underpinning assumption, that the fields of politics and law are not bounded entities to be studied separately, created an opening for more empirical studies that looked at the influence of law on daily political and social life. Teitel set out to "understand the meaning of the rule of law for societies undergoing massive political change."[55] Through extensive reference to historical

[51] Ibid., 213–214.
[52] Luc Huyse, "On the Choices Successor Elites Make in Dealing with the Past," *Law and Social Inquiry* 20, no. 1 (1995): 51–78.
[53] Monika Nalepa, "The Power of Secret Information: Transitional Justice after Communism" (Ph.D. dissertation, Columbia University, 2005). For a look at outcomes in three cases in Africa, see Michelle Sieff, "Reconciling order and justice? Dealing with the past in post-conflict states" (Ph.D. dissertation, Columbia University, 2002).
[54] Ruti Teitel, *Transitional Justice* (Oxford: Oxford University Press, 2000), 225.
[55] Ibid., 12.

cases ranging from the Bible to the post–World War II trials, her research imparts an understanding of not only how enduring the question of the relationship between law and politics is, but also what the role of law is specifically in transitional periods. She argues:

> In modern political transformation, it is through legal practices that successor societies making liberalizing political change, for, in mediating the normative hiatus and shift characterizing transition, the turn to law comprises important functional, conceptual, operative and symbolic dimensions. ... In the liberal society, rather than resignation to historical repetition, the hope of change is put in the air. Even by their engagement in transitional justice debates, successor societies signal the rational imagining of the possibility of a more liberal political order.[56]

Teitel's exposition of what the shift to law means reflects a concern for the broader legacy of international tribunals and other methods of dealing with mass atrocity. [57]

Studying the Region: Some Works Addressing the ICTY

Early works on the ICTY focused on the politics of its formation and its internal dynamics. Most notably, in *Stay the Hand of Vengeance*, Gary Bass addressed the question of why states support the creation of such courts. Looking at a wide range of cases, he argued that leaders set up tribunals when they are in the pursuit of a principled idea he called *legalism*. Bass contended that legalism comes from a "particular kind of liberal domestic polity" because tribunals are extensions of the rule of law from the domestic sphere to the international one, and an example of states projecting their liberal beliefs onto the international arena.[58] Bass's work followed the discipline's desire to explain why states choose to pursue certain transitional justice instruments, or none at all.[59] Like this study, implicit counterfactuals played a role in many of these studies.[60] Kathryn Sikkink observes that Bass's argument that the ICTY was set up to create the appearance of concern was "an

---

[56] Ibid., 221.
[57] For another important overview of various transitional justice mechanisms, see Martha Minow, *Between Vengeance and Forgiveness: Facing History after Genocide and Mass Violence* (Boston, MA: Beacon Press, 1998).
[58] Bass, *Stay the Hand*, 7–8.
[59] For a work that asks what facilitates or hinders accountability for past abuses in countries that still face serious resistance from elements of the old regime, see Chandra Lekha Sriram, *Confronting Past Human Rights Violations: Justice vs. Peace in Times of Transition* (London: Frank Cass, 2004).
[60] On counterfactuals, see Philip E. Tetlock and Aaron Belkin, eds., *Counterfactual Thought Experiments in World Politics: Logical, Methodological, and Psychological Perspectives* (Princeton, NJ: Princeton University Press, 1996).

example of comparison to an ideal. The ideal is that wealthy states should intervene to stop human rights violations in other states."[61]

Stay the Hand of Vengeance set the stage for others to consider the inner workings of the ICTY itself, as well as the people who created the institution, and who developed many of its rules as they went along.[62] John Hagan's *Justice in the Balkans* opens with a list of the "key characters" in the story of the ICTY. Bass himself even ranks among the 100-odd names listed: as one of the early observers, he had become part of the intellectual history of the court itself. Hagan tells the story of a group of committed individuals who crafted the institution. Affected by geopolitics outside of the courtroom and access to key witnesses inside it, the work of the ICTY was undertaken by a multinational assembly of legal professionals. Hagan gave scant mention, however, to what the people of Southeastern Europe thought about the proceedings and whether considerations about local impact weighed on ICTY officials.

That was an issue first taken up by journalists, initially by veteran *Boston Globe* reporter Elizabeth Neuffer, who examined both the Yugoslav and Rwandan tribunals in *The Key to My Neighbor's House*. She described the court, five years after the war, struggling to prove itself relevant to the people in Bosnia, where basic information about its proceedings was absent from the daily news, and thousands of crimes remained unpunished. Although even then there were dashed hopes about what the court could do in the region, its positive contributions were reflected in Neuffer's recounting of stories told by victims of all ethnicities rebuilding their lives and homes. Neuffer found that legal judgments removed the idea of collective guilt, and court transcripts kept the war's actions out of the realm of myth or propaganda. Additionally, even back then, trials were facilitating refugee returns. Still, she acknowledged the limits to international legalism, commenting, "neither tribunal's justice is all it could be."[63] At the time the book was written, the ICTY was trying to address one of what she viewed as its main shortcomings: a lack of contact with victims. The court's Outreach Program was just getting off the ground.

Some non-scholarly works on the ICTY came from the perspective of the courtroom visitor and hinted at the court's expressivist legacy. Novelist and journalist Slavenka Drakulić sketched the lives of several indictees, contrasting her observations with the experiences of her father – who never spoke of his years as a soldier

---

[61] Kathryn Sikkink, "The Role of Consequences, Comparison and Counterfactuals in Constructivist Ethical Thought," in Richard Price, ed., *Moral Limit and Possibility in World Politics* (Cambridge: Cambridge University Press, 2008), 105.

[62] On the early years at the ICTY, see Richard J. Goldstone, *For Humanity: Reflections of a War Crimes Investigator* (New Haven, CT: Yale University Press, 2000).

[63] Elizabeth Neuffer, *The Key to My Neighbor's House: Seeking Justice in Bosnia and Rwanda* (New York: Picador, 2001), 391.

in World War II – and lessons from her childhood history books, colored by the perspective of Yugoslavia's Communist Party. She observed:

Only now can I understand how easy it is to start a war in the absence of facts. War does not come from nowhere; I saw in Yugoslavia that it must be prepared. It is easy for political leaders to use images like the ones I remember, to use people's emotional memory and build hatred upon it. Because in totalitarian societies, where there is no true history, each person has in his own memory a collection of such images, and it becomes dangerous if he has nothing more than that. ... Yet if the truth is not established about the war for the homeland, the next generation will one day find itself in exactly the same situation as my post–Second World War generation. All they will have to rely on will be dusty images and bloody stories. These will vary, depending on which side their parents were on, but they will be left with only memory, not history.[64]

A keen longtime observer of postwar developments in the region, Drakulić acknowledged that the "war is still with us," a fact evidenced by the intense emotions provoked by the ICTY. Though her account is partly autobiographical, she examined the institution's importance from the perspective of a generation that suffered the silence promoted by the Party, and asserting that one of the ICTY's main contributions is uncovering the real history of the war.

Other studies on transitional justice sought to assess the impact of specific instruments. This new research area was partly motivated by the calls of policy makers to evaluate the success or failure of these institutions, many of which they were funding. It was a logical progression from research that had focused on how conditions present in the transition shaped whether the past had been addressed or not. Early analyses, however, often held institutions up to impossibly high standards. The ICTY and the South African Truth and Reconciliation Commission, were the first subjects of inquiry.[65]

Early studies emphasized the lack of public knowledge about the court. The first work addressing local attitudes toward the ICTY found that there was generally little knowledge about the court and little impact in the region. The first major publication was a study of Bosnian judges' and prosecutors' attitudes toward the court. It found that local legal experts were poorly informed about the ICTY and that they viewed its sporadic contact with them as a sign of disrespect – these were, after all, professionals who were proud to be part of a developed Western legal tradition.[66]

---

[64] Slavenka Drakulić, *They Would Never Hurt a Fly: War Criminals on Trial in The Hague* (London: Viking, 2004), 11–12.

[65] See James L. Gibson, *Overcoming Apartheid: Can Truth Reconcile a Divided Nation?* (New York: Russell Sage Foundation, 2004); Richard A. Wilson, *The Politics of Truth and Reconciliation in South Africa: Legitimizing the Post-Apartheid State* (Cambridge: Cambridge University Press, 2001).

[66] Human Rights Center and the International Human Rights Law Clinic, University of California, Berkeley, and the Human Rights Center, University of Sarajevo, "Justice, Accountability and Social Reconstruction in Bosnia and Herzegovina: An Interview Study of Bosnian Judges and

In research with similar findings, in 2000, two Tufts undergraduates published an analysis of Bosnian civil society's attitudes, finding that local organizations knew very little about the court's purpose or mission.[67] A replication of this study is presented in Chapter 5.

The first book on the topic of local attitudes found international criminal trials falling short of their stated goals. *My Neighbor, My Enemy*, published in 2004, represented four years of field research during which the editors, Eric Stover and Harvey Weinstein, sent teams of scholars, of many ethnicities and backgrounds, on short trips into selected cities across Southeastern Europe and in Rwanda.[68] At the end of their data collection, they assembled an impressive and provocative edited volume with chapters ranging in subjects from teachers and artists, to the attitudes of residents of divided towns toward justice, accountability, and the international ad-hoc tribunals. The driving research question was: "How do societies torn apart by war and mass atrocity pursue justice for past crimes and, at the same time, rebuild their shattered communities?" The editors added that they "particularly wanted to know what effect the international community's preoccupation with criminal trials of suspected war criminals was having on the process of rebuilding after war." Setting out to examine what they described as the "multiple layers of societal repair," they found that criminal trials played only a small role in an individual's conception of justice and had little impact on rebuilding processes. The book covered both the Yugoslav and Rwandan tribunals, and contained some of the first large-scale survey data on the subject. The editors concluded that, "our studies suggest that there is no direct link between criminal trials (international, national, and local/traditional) and reconciliation, although this could change over time. In fact, we found that criminal trials – especially those of local perpetrators – often divided small communities by causing further suspicion and fear."[69] They continued, "the idea of 'justice' encompasses more than criminal trials and the ex cathedra pronouncements of foreign judges in The Hague."[70] *My Neighbor, My Enemy* argued for a holistic approach to social repair. The authors defined social reconstruction as "a process

---

Prosecutors," *Berkeley Journal of International Law* 18, no. 1 (2000): 102–164. Interestingly, these legal officials were asked to name "the supreme law of the land." Most of the officials in Republika Srpska (RS) named the RS Constitution. The Croat respondents listed the Constitution of the Federation and the Constitution of Bosnia and Herzegovina. All of the Bosniak respondents mentioned only the state-level Constitution of Bosnia and Herzegovina.
[67] Kristen Cibelli and Tamy Guberek, "Justice Unknown, Justice Unsatisfied?: Bosnian NGOs Speak about the International Criminal Tribunal for the Former Yugoslavia," (Boston, MA: Tufts University, 2000), <www.hrdag.org/resources/publications/justicereport.pdf> (accessed July 29, 2009).
[68] Eric Stover and Harvey M. Weinstein, eds., *My Neighbor, My Enemy: Justice and Community in the Aftermath of Mass Atrocity* (Cambridge: Cambridge University Press, 2004).
[69] Eric Stover and Harvey M. Weinstein, "Conclusion: A Common Objective, a Universe of Alternatives," in Stover and Weinstein, *My Neighbor, My Enemy*, 323.
[70] Ibid.

that affirms and develops a society and its institutions based on shared values and human rights."[71] They argued these processes occur at all levels.[72] However, in trying to measure the role of trials using a holistic approach that took into consideration much broader economic, social and cultural factors, it was inevitable the authors found that trials fell short when they asked only whether courts contributed to their formal stated goals.

This framing overlooked many positive aspects of the court's expressivist legacy not listed among the court's objectives, including the broader political, developmental, and institution-building processes with which tribunals are connected. Stover and Weinstein's book pointed to a research trajectory for empirical examination of the court's effects in the region, but it also left room for further inquiry into what the appropriate measures and yardsticks should be. It was to be expected, for example, that criminal trials in The Hague would do little to alleviate the sense of injustice, political disillusionment, and poverty experienced by most of the region's citizens. No court ever could. And even though the (foreign) editors employed teams of local scholars, *My Neighbor, My Enemy* contains little mention of everyday politics on the ground in the places under examination; there are scant local-language citations. This suggests that, despite attempts to mobilize local knowledge, collaborative partners in the region did not impart their wisdom about the changing local political context. While opinions were still divided over the war and the court, the day-to-day dialogue of elites was infused with the language of law and accountability, in part because the work of the ICTY had caused attitudes to change over time. In addition, the court's extended legacy, as discussed below, was to be found in advancements with which the court was connected, but for which it was not necessarily credited.

Consequently, the study by Stover and Weinstein lent scholarly support to new conventional wisdom about the court: that the ad-hoc tribunals had failed both in their mission to get their message out and in serving the domestic populations they were meant to aid. This buttressed the impression of a number of more conservative critics that the 2 billion dollars spent on these tribunals was an unwise investment. In addition, it should be acknowledged that this study was conducted very early after the end of the war, and that it overlooked the indirect impact that this book outlines.

Two other recent studies had similar relatively gloomy conclusions about the court, which resulted primarily from their particular focus of inquiry. In *Hijacked Justice: Dealing with the Past in the Balkans,* Jelena Subotić uses the case studies of Serbia, Croatia, and Bosnia to illustrate how local political actors often appropriate

---

[71] Ibid, 5.

[72] A small body of writing that looks at peacekeeping "from below" has developed alongside these more empirical studies of transitional justice. See, for example: Paula M. Pickering, *Peacebuilding in the Balkans: The View from the Ground Floor* (Ithaca, NY: Cornell University Press, 2007); Beatrice Pouligny, *Peace Operations Seen from Below: UN Missions and Local People* (Bloomfield, CT: Kumarian Press, 2006).

mechanisms for domestic goals. She argues that the "domestic misuse of transitional justice norms," which she calls " 'hijacked' justice is tremendously problematic and significant in that it greatly reduces the effectiveness of transitional justice initiatives, jeopardizes their legitimacy, and does not bring about the profound social transformation that countries coming out of violent conflict require."[73] All mechanisms of international justice will, she argues, be appropriated by local actors with various goals; however, the case studies in this volume illustrate what is, by definition, not captured in research focused on the hijacking of transitional justice norms by "insincere" political actors. Instead, this study emphasizes how, over time, other actors may use the knowledge produced by the ICTY to weaken the claims of those "insincere" political actors in support of democratizing goals. This volume finds more utility in the diffusion model of norms outlined but shares an emphasis with Subotić about how the social setting constrains international justice initiatives.

A study with substantial regional content, Victor Peskin's *International Justice in Rwanda and the Balkans: Virtual Trials and the Struggle for State Cooperation*, outlines the conditions under which states cooperate with tribunals.[74] One core argument is that "the ICTY has been able to exercise its soft power more effectively than the ICTR because of the ICTY's great success in completing trials, maintaining professionalism in court operations, and obtaining frequent and favorable international press coverage."[75] Still, in keeping with most conventional wisdom about the court in the region, Peskin argues his book "challenges the inspiring Kantian vision of international law associated with human rights advocacy by highlighting the ways in which international tribunals may generate domestic crises and threaten political stability."[76] The insights of this thoroughly researched manuscript are numerous and it offers an important caution against the exuberance of activists. However, the focus of the book on state cooperation – an area in which ad-hoc tribunals have no enforcement powers – was a topic chosen precisely because it was one of the biggest challenges facing these institutions.[77]

In contrast, this volume picks up areas of inquiry those previous works did not explore: the role of civil society and local forces that used the ICTY's work toward democratizing ends. I find support for the conclusion that domestic political crises stem not so much from the mechanism itself (that is, the ICTY), but from the denial of crimes, and behavior surrounding that denial. Elites' admission of wrong-doing often paved the way for further social reconstruction.

---

[73] Jelena Subotić, *Hijacked Justice: Dealing with the Past in the Balkans* (Ithaca, NY: Cornell University Press, 2009), 6.

[74] Victor Peskin, *International Justice in Rwanda and the Balkans: Virtual Trials and the Struggle for State Cooperation* (Cambridge: Cambridge University Press, 2008.)

[75] Ibid., 7.

[76] Ibid., 9.

[77] Ibid., xi.

Cross-national Comparisons of Transitional Justice

Cross-national comparisons, dominant in fields such as political science, have generally found tribunals coming up short. Jack Snyder and Leslie Vinjamuri, in an oft-quoted study of transitional justice mechanisms in 32 cases between 1989 and 2003, argued that, "... the prosecution of perpetrators of atrocities according to universal standards – applied with insufficient attention to political circumstances, risks causing more atrocities than it would prevent, because it pays insufficient attention to political realities."[78] They continued: "a norm-governed political order must be based on a political bargain among contending groups and on the creation of robust administrative institutions that can predictably enforce the law."[79] Therefore, they see transitional justice as more appropriate after the development of institutions that support the rule of law.[80] However, this argument, that justice should be pursued after institutions are created, overlooks how the pursuit of justice itself helps to establish such institutions in the first place – institutions that are unlikely to come to fruition when based on political bargains.

Snyder and Vinjamuri questioned the advocacy of transitional-justice tools, including tribunals, in situations where domestic institutions are too weak to support them. Critics of tribunals who favor the "wait to punish" approach sometimes advocate the use of amnesties to address the problem of human rights violators present after the conclusion of a conflict.[81] Another similar study about human rights treaties using cross-national comparisons argues that those treaties do not make a difference in the countries where they matter most.[82] These studies might give pause to some activists, but the shortcomings of large-N research for a question as delicate as this should be acknowledged. Many of the Tribunal's benefits outlined in this book would not be captured in these efforts at quantification.

A notable exception was a study by Kathryn Sikkink and Carrie Booth Walling. These authors compiled a database of truth commissions and trials at all levels, outlining the dramatic growth in the use of both in Latin America. They argued that the empirical claims by critics – that trials undermine the rule of

---

[78] Jack L. Snyder and Leslie Vinjamuri, "Trials and Errors: Principle and Pragmatism in Strategies of International Justice," *International Security* 28, no. 3 (2003/04): 5.

[79] Ibid.

[80] Several works in political science argue for the development of institutions before undertaking liberalizing measures. See Roland Paris, *At War's End: Building Peace after Civil Conflict* (New York: Cambridge University Press, 2004).

[81] Jack Snyder and Leslie Vinjamuri, "A Midwife for Peace," *International Herald Tribune*, September 26, 2006, <www.iht.com/articles/2006/09/26/opinion/edsnyder.php> (accessed July 20, 2009).

[82] Emilie M. Hafner-Burton and Kiyoteru Tsutsui, "Justice Lost! The Failure of International Human Rights Law to Matter Where Needed Most," *Journal of Peace Research* 44, no. 4 (2007): 407–425.

law, happen early or not at all, and threaten young democracies – do not stand up under scrutiny.[83]

A working paper giving an overview of all recent studies of transitional justice – both large-N and small-N research – found that, overall, scholars finding negative impacts were in the minority. The authors emphasized that the research program is still young. They argue persuasively that:

Most studies find that [transitional justice] makes either moderately positive or no contribution at all. Only a few studies find harmful effects. However, our primary conclusion is that existing empirical knowledge about the impacts of transitional justice is still very limited, and does not support strong claims about the positive or negative effects of [transitional justice] across cases. Research on this subject is still nascent, and many of its early findings are questionable and contradictory.[84]

Law and Society

The study of international criminal tribunals, as interdisciplinary as it is, has curiously overlooked the potential of the field of law and society for a broader understanding of their impact. This research has focused mostly on U.S. courts, but is increasingly international, and provides a broad theoretical base to understand courts more generally. The *constitutive* school of law and society has much in common with social movement scholars who look at international organizations as sites of social contention. Rather than look at procedural aspects of the law, law and society scholars recognize the role of law in everyday life, as a strategy and mobilizing tool, and as a catalyst. As one recent overview modestly notes: "The claim here is simple and unremarkable: it is that law is a social formation having characteristic features which affect and influence the attitudes and actions of officials and citizens, and which are not reducible without loss into other categories. It follows that the study of law in society has two main parts, the first to understand the law, the second to understand its interaction with other social actions."[85]

Within the field there are two basic approaches. The instrumental approach argues that "social results can be attributed to law or legal reforms"; while the constitutive approach sees "law more as a pervasive influence in structuring society than as a variable whose occasional impact can be measured."[86] Both approaches weigh in on the question of how law impacts societies, but the constitutive

---

[83] Kathryn Sikkink and Carrie Booth Walling, "The Impact of Human Rights Trials in Latin America," *Journal of Peace Research* 44, no. 4 (2007): 427–445.

[84] Oskar Thoms, James Ron, and Roland Paris, "The Effects of Transitional Justice Mechanisms," Working paper, Centre for International Policy Studies, University of Ottawa, April 2008.

[85] Denis J. Galligan, *Law in Modern Society* (Oxford: Oxford University Press, 2007), 6.

[86] Bryant G. Garth and Austin Sarat, "Studying How Law Matters: An Introduction," in Bryant G. Garth and Austin Sarat, eds., *How Does Law Matter?* (Evanston, Il: Northwestern University Press, 1998), 2.

approach also views law as forming a part of economics, politics, and society in ways that may defy some types of social-science measurement.[87] This book is concerned with trying to measure social change and uses some of the tools common in the instrumental approach, but argues that the court's legacy is best understood in ways laid out by adherents of the later constitutive school.

In doing so, it joins the growing scholarship focused on *international* law and society.[88] International legal research largely deals with questions of jurisprudence, but international legal scholars are starting to appreciate the role that international law can play as a catalyst for social movements, institutional reform, and activism. The research produced to date generally represents law as a catalyst for other forms of collective action, often prompted by a negative response to legal processes. In this view, international law, as in the domestic realm, cannot be measured simply by numbers of specific trials or legal precedents, since it is intimately connected to other events occurring in the countries of concern. One of the leading scholars in this growing field asks:

How does one write resistance into international law and make it recognize subaltern voices? In particular, international law has been crucially shaped during the twentieth century by the nature and forms of Third World resistance to development. ... By showing that the central aspects of modern international law cannot be understood without taking due account of the impact of development and Third World social movements, this work challenges traditional narratives of how international legal change has come about and how one might understand the place of law in progressive social praxis.[89]

Although that volume places itself within much of the literature dealing with development, it amounted to one of the first systematic attempts to understand international law's relationship with the less developed world, and how law itself can both aid struggles and be co-opted by those subject to it – in line with research that looks at how norms can be expanded and adapted.

In addition, two seminal law and society studies in the domestic field can inform how we understand the impact of international courts. *The Hollow Hope*

---

[87] Ibid., 4–5.

[88] There is a growing body of literature on judicial politics in foreign countries. See, for example, Lisa Hilbink, *Judges beyond Politics in Democracy and Dictatorship: Lessons from Chile* (Cambridge: Cambridge University Press, 2007); Tamir Moustafa, *The Struggle for Constitutional Power: Law, Politics, and Economic Development in Egypt* (Cambridge: Cambridge University Press, 2007). One recent volume notes the origins of this movement: "Two decades ago, Martin Shapiro urged public law scholars to expand their horizons and begin studying 'any public law other than constitutional law, any court other than the Supreme Court, any public lawmaker other than the judge, and any country other than the United States.'" See Tamir Moustafa and Tom Ginsberg, "Introduction: The Functions of Courts in Authoritarian Politics," in Tom Ginsberg and Tamir Moustafa, eds., *Rule by Law: The Politics of Courts in Authoritarian Regimes* (Cambridge: Cambridge University Press, 2008), 1.

[89] Rajagopal, *International Law from Below*, 1. See also Richard Falk, Jacqueline Stevens, and Balakrishnan Rajagopal, eds., *International Law and the Third World* (New York: Routledge, 2008).

tried to measure rigorously the impact of the celebrated U.S. Supreme Court decision in *Brown v. the Board of Education*. In this book, legal scholar Gerald Rosenberg argues that the 1954 *Brown* decision did not, in fact, succeed in desegregating American schools, and that movement was not seen on this issue until the 1964 Civil Rights Act. Through an exhaustive accounting, Rosenberg tries to measure change strictly, specifically counting the desegregation of schools throughout the United States. He concludes from his study that courts are poor tools of social change. The measures he applies have much in common with the early scholarship about the ICTY: positivist tools of measurement that, however, fail to capture tertiary and spill-over effects, or changes in attitudes resulting from the pronouncements of the court.[90]

The questions of how to measure the effectiveness of courts (domestic or international), which measures to use, and how to derive them still persist. However, this study, in keeping with the constitutive branch of the law and society scholarship exemplified in the work of Michael McCann, whose important book, *Rights at Work: Pay Equity Reforms and the Politics of Legal Mobilization*, places law within a broader social context. McCann argues for acknowledging legacies in understanding legal reform efforts. He argues that "legal reform efforts thus should not be judged only by their initial goals, local scale of conflict, or immediate outcomes. ... Rather we should distinguish among reform efforts according to their lasting impacts on subsequent struggles – i.e. whether they are successfully contained or potentially expansionist in character."[91] This expressivist legacy of international tribunals is outlined in the case studies that follow.

Attitudinal Research

Another tool commonly used to measure court impact is attitudinal research, a methodology used in two cases studies in this book. Surveys, however, are limited tools for understanding the influence of the law. We currently have no real benchmarks for understanding how to interpret the great numbers of surveys about international justice, accountability, and the contribution of various transitional justice mechanisms to specific improvements in postwar settings, or to the extended mandates of tribunals in postconflict countries.

Attitudinal research conducted at both the international and domestic levels, however, provides a base to which similar studies about the ICTY can be compared

---

[90] Gerald N. Rosenberg, *The Hollow Hope: Can Courts Bring About Social Change?* (Chicago: University of Chicago Press, 1991).

[91] Michael W. McCann, *Rights at Work: Pay Equity Reform and the Politics of Legal Mobilization* (Chicago, IL: University of Chicago Press, 1994), 307. See the interesting exchange between these two authors in Gerald N. Rosenberg, "Positivism, Interpretivism and the Study of the Law," in Michael McCann, ed., *Law and Social Movements* (Aldershot, UK: Ashgate, 2006); and Michael McCann "Causal vs. Constitute Explanations (Or on the Difficulty of Being So Positive ...)," in ibid.

and it can help provide context. Most studies of international courts do not refer to attitudinal research about domestic courts, sentencing practices, or police forces, but such studies can inform our understanding about research at the international level. Generally, levels of overall support for the judicial system, even in the Western world, are quite low. Take, for example, a recent study of attitudes toward Canada's criminal justice system. It found that only 20 percent of respondents believed the courts were "doing a good job helping the victim" and that just 15 percent "felt the courts provide justice quickly"; 44 percent felt the "courts were doing a good job at providing a fair trial for the accused." The courts and the correctional system were viewed less favorably than the police.[92] This study emphasized the finding that the more removed individuals are from the justice system, the more their attitudes are influenced by media accounts (an argument for continued support of media training at the international level, to be sure). If support is relatively low for judicial institutions in a Western democracy, what is reasonable to expect of international efforts, which are rather removed and focused, by definition, on only a handful of cases? One analyst in Sarajevo, for example, lamented the expectation of extremely high levels of knowledge about issues that are not priorities for Bosnian citizens.[93] The case studies that follow find that Bosnian citizens generally viewed the court as having realized some of its extra-legal goals. The surveys did not seek opinions about international criminal law's more pervasive influence, but some of the responses indicate knowledge of that effect, which extends beyond the court's stated extra-legal objectives.

At the international level, only one major study, *The People on War Report: ICRC Worldwide Consultation on the Rules of War*, published in 1999, has addressed attitudes about international law and international tribunals in a comprehensive manner. Over 12,860 people in twelve war-torn territories, in addition to citizens in four of the five UN Security Council Members, plus Switzerland, were surveyed.[94] Attitudes about trials and international accountability showed strikingly little regional variation. In response to the question of how, after a conflict, to deal with

---

92 Maire Gannon, Karen Mihorean, Karen Beattie, Andrea Taylor-Butts and Rebecca Kong, eds., *Criminal Justice Indicators 2005* (Ottawa: Statistics Canada, 2005), available online at: <www. statcan.gc.ca/pub/85-227-x/85-227-x2002000-eng.pdf> (accessed September 24, 2009).

93 Reuf Bajrović, Independent Analyst, Sarajevo, "Beyond Statebuilding: NATO and EU Conditionality in Bosnia and Herzegovina," presentation at workshop organized by the University of Kent, Sarajevo, December 19, 2008.

94 Greenberg Research, Inc., *The People on War Report: ICRC Worldwide Consultation on the Rules of War* (Geneva: ICRC, October 1999) <www.icrc.org/web/eng/siteeng0.nsf/html/p0758> (accessed July 8, 2009). The Security Council members surveyed were the United States, United Kingdom, France, and the Russian Federation (but not China). Switzerland, although not on the Security Council, was among the countries surveyed. The war-torn countries, places, and peoples surveyed were: Colombia, El Salvador, Philippines, Georgia, Abkhazia (not internationally recognized), Afghanistan, Cambodia, Bosnia and Herzegovina, Lebanon, Israel, Palestinians, Somalia, South Africa, and Nigeria.

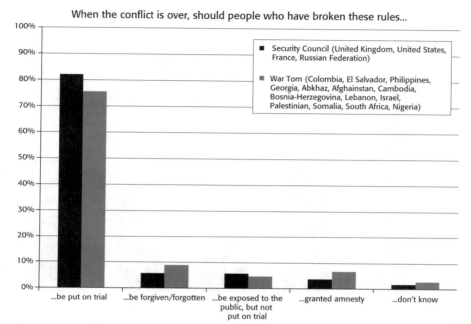

Figure 2.1. International attitudes towards war crimes.
Source: People on War Report: ICRC Worldwide Consultation on the Rules of War, ICRC, 2000.

"people who have broken [the] rules" of international law, 76 percent of those surveyed in war-torn territories and 82 percent in Security Council nations answered that these people should "be put on trial," confirming popular support for trials.[95] In a follow-up question, 36 percent of individuals in war-torn areas believed that the wrongdoers should be punished by an international criminal court, followed by their own government (24 percent); support was slightly higher in Security Council nations for international justice, at 42 percent and 22 percent, respectively. Figures 2.1 and 2.2 present these findings.

This research defied prevailing assumptions in literature that international institutions and solutions lacked legitimacy or that other mechanisms would be preferable. Even though this study is now rather dated, it still provides a valuable overview of attitudes, and indicates levels of support across diverse settings both for the existence of international courts and for trials to deal with the crimes of the past.

---

[95] Interestingly, the percentage of respondents who answered that those who violate international law should "be forgiven" is 16 percent among war-torn respondents but only 4 percent among Security Council respondents.

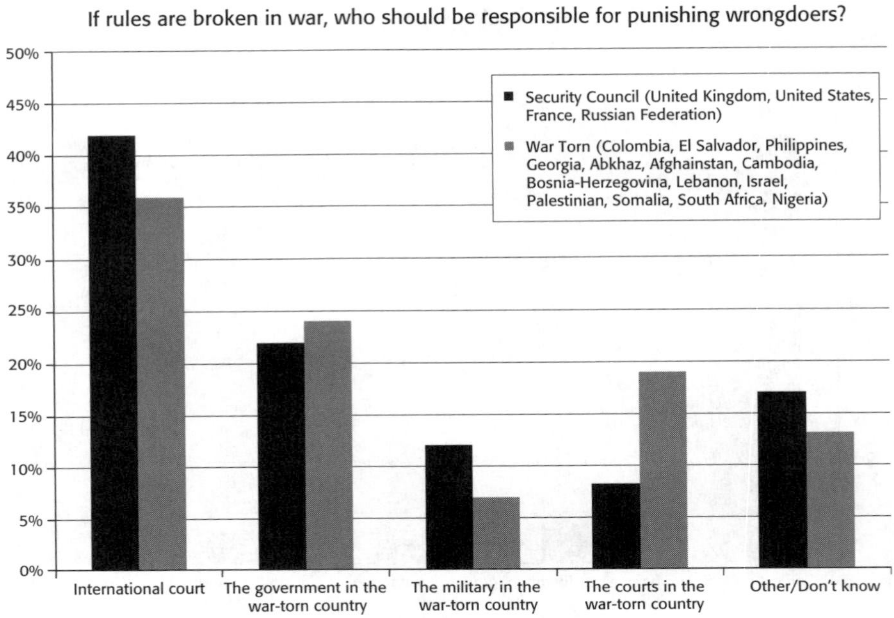

If rules are broken in war, who should be responsible for punishing wrongdoers?

Figure 2.2. International attitudes towards bodies responsible for punishing war crimes. *Source:* People on War Report: ICRC Worldwide Consultation on the Rules of War, ICRC, 2000.

Locating the Case

It is reasonable to ask whether, given the specificity of the Bosnian case study and the uniqueness of the state reshaped by international forces at the signing of the Dayton Peace Agreement, there is any reason to believe that this study does anything more than describe the state of affairs in postwar Bosnia, even if it uses some of the tools of social science inquiry to do so. I believe the answer to that question is yes. Its empirical support for the assertion that international trials helped shape the polity in postwar Bosnia has implications for all transitions. While identifying many problems and obstacles, this study identifies, on balance, a positive long-term legacy of the ICTY in Bosnia. This study asks the reader to look forward and wonder, as Martha Minow put it: "What can be imagined and built, even in the face of critiques and limitations?"[96]

In contrast to the opinions of many who have defined success and failure by the very lofty expectations of the court's architects, I argue that the ICTY had positive influences in shaping Bosnia's nascent democratic identity and institutional

---

[96] Minow, *Between Vengeance and Forgiveness*, 29.

structure. These case studies show how the ICTY created space for political participation, changed attitudes, and facilitated the growth of democratic institutions,
illustrating the court's expressivist legacy and confirming the aspirations of several more theoretical works on transitional justice. The following chapters provide
empirical examples, informed by theoretical insights found in international relations, comparative politics, and law and society, to derive a deeper understanding
of the role of law in modern political transitions. It argues that a strictly positivist method of social science may overlook important contributions to processes
of democratization. It asks the reader to place understanding of the ICTY within
studies of contentious politics and law and society scholarship, and to see law as a
pervasive influence throughout society.

This approach shares an affinity with research that tries to analyze complexity
in social life. Judicial institutions are connected to many other social processes. As
one important study noted, "In a system, chains of consequence extend over time
and many areas: The effects of action are always multiple ... . Although the language is misleading, there is no criterion other than our desires which determines
which effects are main and which effects are side."[97] The expressivist legacy of the
ICTY in Bosnia, therefore, is difficult to pinpoint precisely. The case studies, however, hint at a larger legacy than has previously been recognized: that international
law can facilitate the emergence of social movements, help constitute domestic
institutions, and prompt the difficult discussions about the past that transitional
states should debate. Citizens appropriate international law for their own needs
and thus, I argue, it plays a role in larger processes of postwar reconstruction. That
pervasive influence of international norms is, however, translated into a particular institutional setting in the region. In the case of Bosnia, the liberal project that
espoused the application of international law met an "illiberal" state transitioning to democracy in which, although elections were guaranteed, other basic rights
and freedoms were not. Citizens were limited by the fact that ethnicity was the
defining feature of the postwar polity, and the political project that had produced
the mass atrocities of the war continued to thrive. This situation resulted in part
from the state structure that was negotiated with the help of international forces.
These issues are taken up in Chapter 3.[98]

---

[97] Robert Jervis, *System Effects: Complexity in Political and Social Life* (Princeton, NJ: Princeton
University Press, 1998), 10.

[98] On illiberal democracies, see Fareed Zakaria, "The Rise of Illiberal Democracy," *Foreign
Affairs* 76, no. 6 (November/December 1997): 22–43. Zakaria notes the problem of "illiberal
democracies," his term for states that have regular elections but lack civil liberties: "On the eve
of the 1996 elections in Bosnia, the architect of the Dayton peace accords, American diplomat
Richard Holbrooke, fretted: 'Suppose the election was declared free and fair and those elected
are racists, fascists, separatists, who are publicly opposed to [peace and reintegration]. That is
the dilemma.'" Ibid., 22.

3 An Unfavorable Context
War, Dayton, and the ICTY

The contributions of the International Criminal Tribunal for the former Yugoslavia (ICTY) to Bosnia's democratic development must be understood within the context of the hostile and complex political circumstances the institution faced. Created in the midst of a war largely misunderstood by most of the foreigners claiming to act on the country's behalf, the court's local obstacles changed only in form once the violence came to an end. With the signing of the General Framework Agreement for Peace (GFAP), known colloquially as the Dayton Peace Agreement (DPA), court representatives had to contend with a lack of cooperation in Bosnia due to the continued presence of wartime leaders in political life. Additionally, in the immediate postwar years, international officials in the region were reluctant to actively address the proceedings in The Hague or how the lack of redress for war crimes affected social reconstruction. The subjects of violations of international humanitarian law and the genocide convention were confined to the ICTY, leaving many members of the international community able to ignore complicated issues involving the horrors of the recent war that were still very present in the lives of Bosnia's citizens.

This chapter outlines the environment in which the court operated both during and after the war, and argues that factors beyond the ICTY's control were its biggest challenge to realizing its extended mandate. In essence, the liberal interventionist project of the application of international criminal law was projected into what was fundamentally an illiberal environment. The ICTY's problems stemmed more from that contradiction than from the problems within its own walls, even if there were many.

In addition, the creation of the court by the UN Security Council in 1993, well over a year into the Bosnian war, came after much other international engagement in the region addressing the breakup of Socialist Federal Republic of Yugoslavia (SFRY). Attitudes toward the court were influenced by the international community's other interventions, which sent conflicting messages to citizens across Southeastern Europe. The court struggled to project liberal values in an environment in which foreign powers actively worked with those who had started the war. Furthermore, lacking real social bases of support in the region, the court attempted to realize its extended mandate over time with no real strategies for how to do so.

The story of the ICTY in Bosnia is one of an institution that developed over time and slowly implemented steps within key target populations to increase domestic impact. It did so in what is arguably the world's most complicated polity, which at the end of the war had multiple and overlapping layers of governments, three (de facto) military forces on the ground, a patchwork of legal systems, and most (but not all) of the tools afforded to protectorates of the colonial era, all overseen by security guarantees of a foreign peacekeeping operation. It would be fair to say that if ever the cards were stacked against the success of an international institution from the beginning, such is the case of the ICTY.

This chapter provides background on the war and major developments in Bosnia's and the region's recent history to inform the case studies that follow and to flag some of the key individuals targeted by the court's indictments.

Why War?

The causes of the Yugoslav wars of succession have been the subject of numerous scholarly works. The violence in Southeastern Europe has commonly been attributed to just a handful of factors: ancient ethnic hatreds, purely economic causes, and rational elites who wielded the nationalism card in order to create mono-ethnic states under their control.[1] It was even rumored that one scholar called the Bosnian war "a religious war waged by people who were not very religious." Perceptions of the causes of violence have implications for prosecutorial strategy and, ultimately, affect the likelihood that criminal justice effectively penalizes violations of international law and contributes to postwar developments.

Any discussion of the history of the region with respect to the wars of succession in the 1990s would begin at a time that will be unsatisfactory to someone. For most foreign observers of the conflict, conventional wisdom holds that the 1980 death of Josip Broz Tito, the lifetime President of the SFRY, marked the beginning of serious tensions among the republics. When the wars of succession started, foreign journalists generally repeated the convenient (but incorrect) metaphor that Tito had managed to keep a lid on ethnic grievances, which "burst" onto the scene when he died. In reality, the federalist structure of SFRY from its inception faced

---

[1] On ancient ethnic hatreds, see Robert Kaplan, *Balkan Ghosts: A Journey Through History* (New York: Picador, 2005). On economic causes, see Susan L. Woodward, *Balkan Tragedy: Chaos and Dissolution After the Cold War* (Washington D.C.: Brookings Institution Press, 1995). For an overview of various explanations, see Jasna Dragović-Soso, "Why Did Yugoslavia Disintegrate? An Overview of Contending Explanations," in Lenard J. Cohen and Jasna Dragović-Soso, eds., *State Collapse in South-Eastern Europe: New Perspectives on Yugoslavia's Disintegration* (West Lafayette, IN: Purdue University Press, 2007), 1–39.

many crises regarding the contours of the state and the distribution of resources to the various republics. Significant grievances dated to the 1960s, and there were numerous crises in the 1960s and 1970s.[2] International intervention, in the form of foreign loans, also affected later political developments. After Tito's death, financial pressures on the country exacerbated the existing tensions among the republics. The country's privileged position as an ally of the West had enabled it to receive loans and financial guarantees that gave it the means to create an unsustainably high standard of living, which aggravated relations within the ethnofederal state.[3] Economics played a role in the conflict, but political factors were necessary to precipitate bloodshed. Recent scholarship has illustrated how these factors combined, producing a tragic outcome.

One of the most incisive studies on the wars in the region argues that both economic factors and the role of elites mattered, and uses extensive survey data from the region to effectively dismiss the ancient-hatred thesis – the idea that people in the region could never get along – so popular in some journalistic accounts. V. P. Gagnon Jr. shows how, in the 1960s and again in the 1980s, economic crises prompted the development of a new cadre of Communist Party reformers interested in restructuring the political and economic system to face new challenges in the SFRY. The conservatives in the party, he argues, who stood to lose out if reforms were implemented, responded to threats to their diminishing position in society. "Conservatives provoked, created and fueled conflict along ethnic lines in order to demobilize and marginalize those pushing for change, thereby silencing and marginalizing them, as well as their supporters, both in the party and in the wider society," he argues.[4] Eventually, they had to resort to a strategy of violence to do so, one "which would redefine and reconstruct political space."[5] Only political violence could effectively disentangle the ethnic map of the Yugoslav state. Gagnon's contribution debunked the notion that the conflict was provoked by nationalist politicians simply wielding the ethnic card to willing citizens who responded to their latent nationalistic tendencies. His account was more counterintuitive: it was the harmony in relations that necessitated a strategy of violence for the dissolution of the country, a task that was especially tragic for Bosnia. Other scholarly studies, too, have outlined a history of harmonious relations.[6]

Prior to the wars in the region, interethnic relations were strong. Gagnon cites surveys conducted on the eve of the war showing that 80 percent of Bosnians felt

---

[2] See Sabrina P. Ramet, *Nationalism and Federalism in Yugoslavia, 1962–1991* (Bloomington, IN: Indiana University Press, 1992). On crises in Bosnia and Herzegovina, see Neven Andjelic, *Bosnia-Herzegovina: The End of a Legacy* (London: Frank Cass, 2003).

[3] Woodward, *Balkan Tragedy*, especially Chapter 3.

[4] V. P. Gagnon, Jr., *The Myth of Ethnic War: Serbia and Croatia in the 1990s* (Ithaca, NY: Cornell University Press, 2004), 52–53.

[5] Ibid., 29.

[6] See also Robert J. Donia and John V.A. Fine, Jr., *Bosnia and Hercegovina: A Tradition Betrayed* (New York: Columbia University Press, 1994).

relations were positive where they lived.[7] Furthermore, Bosnia ranked the lowest (behind only Vojvodina) in surveys that measured ethnic distance in SFRY.[8] However, the use of an ethnic lens in staffing key government posts meant, ironically, that nationalism thrived in the Bosnian League of Communists, in contrast with the rest of the country.[9]

Other research suggested the ethnic consciousness commonly attributed to people in the region was not found even in wartime. An ethnographic study conducted during the siege of Sarajevo found that the division into ethno-national groups was the result, not the cause, of the war in Bosnia.[10] Most analysts were shocked by the country's demise and descent into violence given its high level of development, and the comparative absence of conflict in the Soviet successor states, which many experts had assumed would be the likely candidates for bloodshed.[11] As one journalist put it: "Many of the ethnic cleansers in Bosnia were lawyers and engineers who, in peacetime, wore ties to work and had Sony television sets in their living rooms."[12] Still, even the best scholarship on the conflict failed to explain why, when faced with a choice, some people chose violence, accepted the guns offered to them, and turned on their neighbors despite harmonious prewar relations. The ICTY would indict both individuals who maintained strict ideas about the need for ethnically "clean" or "pure" states and those who, on the stand, portrayed themselves as victims of circumstances unfolding around them. From the perspective of criminal liability, however, the mental state of the perpetrator, or *mens rea* (literally "guilty mind" – the malicious intent to commit a wrongful act), could be present even in the absence of strong ethnic affinities, even when the crimes for which the perpetrator was charged contained elements of discrimination based

---

[7] Ibid., 40. Other research posed the question of why of all the indicators in support of an overarching and common identity failed in the face of rising nationalism: see Dusko Sekulic, Garth Massey, and Randy Hodson, "Who Were the Yugoslavs? Failed Sources of a Common Identity in the Former Yugoslavia," *American Sociological Review* 59, no. 1 (February 1994): 83–97.

[8] Gagnon, *Myth of Ethnic War*, 40.

[9] Ibid. The study sites a rate of nationalist feelings of 29 percent in the Bosnia League of Communists, compared to 8 percent in the general population in Bosnia. Gagnon is citing a newspaper report of a survey undertaken by Ibrahim Bakić and Ratko Dunđerović, Institute for the Study of National Relations in Bosnia-Herzegovina, "Građani Bosne i Hercegovine o međunacionalnim odnosima" (Citizens of Bosnia and Herzegovina on inter-ethnic relations), *Oslobođenje*, March 22, 1990, 2.

[10] See Ivana Maček, *Sarajevo Under Siege: Anthropology in Wartime* (Philadelphia, PA: University of Pennsylvania Press, 2009).

[11] This is because of the common association of level of development with conflict. Some other scholars focused on the role of the military in conflict. See, for example, Valerie Bunce, *Subversive Institutions: The Design and Destruction of Socialism and the State* (Cambridge: Cambridge University Press, 1999). Bunce asks why all of the socialist regimes fell at roughly the same time, and why only some ended in bloodshed.

[12] Peter Maass, *Love Thy Neighbor: A Story of War* (London: Papermac, 1996), 14.

on identity.[13] Put simply, one may be convicted of genocide despite not agreeing with the architects of the crime.

The Milošević Trial

From the standpoint of the Office of the Prosecutor (OTP) at the ICTY, most prosecutorial energy and institutional resources were invested into the trial of Slobodan Milošević, President, from 1989 to 1997, of the Republic of Serbia, Bosnia's neighbor to the east in the SFRY. The Milošević trial (Case IT-02-54) was billed as the "trial of the century."[14] The rise to power of the man who would become known in the international public imagination as the "butcher of the Balkans" captured much attention. In Gagnon's narrative, Milošević, a member of the Socialist Party, stood to lose out in the tide of sweeping reforms being proposed by individuals such as Ante Marković, the last Yugoslav prime minister.[15] Marković would later tell the ICTY that Milošević and Croatian President Franjo Tuđman had made a deal to get him out of power in a meeting at Karađođevo in Serbia, in March 1991. That was also the meeting in which the two discussed the partition of Bosnia, splitting the Bosnian Republic between greater Serbia and Croatia.[16]

Milošević's political ambitions reached the interest of international lawyers once his forces crossed into other republics over what were soon to become foreign borders.[17] The Milošević indictment addressed crimes in Croatia, Bosnia, and Kosovo. The three-part document laid out a plan of criminality that extended across three states and over almost a decade. This trial and others would show that the wars started under his leadership featured a military strategy in which violations of international law were integral, including the forced expulsion of non-Serb populations, the targeting of civilians, and mass rapes. The question of when normal political activity becomes criminal activity under international law was

---

[13] See for example, the trial transcripts in the case of Goran Jelisić (IT-95-10), a convicted war criminal who, before the war, never expressed strong ethnic sentiment. His pre-war criminal record was limited to a few bad checks. ICTY outreach event, Brčko, May 8, 2004, author's notes.

[14] This chapter identifies the ICTY's case number where indicted persons are mentioned, so that the reader can easily access documents related to specific cases.

[15] Milošević's ascent to power included the assassination of his erstwhile mentor, former Serbian President Ivan Stambolić; a Belgrade court later found him guilty of the crime of ordering the killing.

[16] Marković testified: "I had received information about the topic discussed in Karađođevo, that is, the division of Bosnia and Herzegovina between Serbia and Croatia, and that Milošević and Tuđman had agreed to carry out this division, and also there was talk of the dismissal of the Prime Minister, Ante Marković, because he was in the way of both of them in implementing this division of Bosnia and Herzegovina." See trial transcript page number 28026, *Prosecutor v. Milošević* (IT-02-54), Thursday, October 23, 2003.

[17] On Milošević, see Lenard J. Cohen, *Serpent in the Bosom: The Rise and Fall of Slobodan Milošević* (New York: Basic Books, 2002); Judith Armatta, *Twilight of Impunity: The War Crimes Trial of Slobodan Milošević* (Durham, North Carolina: Duke University Press, 2010).

what the prosecutors at the ICTY would need to decide.[18] The prosecution argued that it started when the accused placed paramilitary forces on what was soon to become foreign soil. The "Kula camp video," introduced during the prosecution phase of the trial, shows Milošević celebrating the anniversary of the creation of the Red Berets, a paramilitary unit with state support in Serbia then active in Croatia.[19]

The video is significant because it identifies the creation date of the unit: May 1991.[20] Such dates are important because they mark the relationship between political developments and what could be classified as international crime. In June 1991, Croatia and Slovenia both declared their independence from the SFRY. In Slovenia, a brief conflict ensued and lasted only 10 days. Croatia's declaration, however, led to a four-year war with the rump Yugoslavia after troops of the Yugoslav People's Army (Jugoslovenska narodna armija or JNA) entered Croatia in what was claimed as a bid to keep federal Yugoslavia united. As ICTY Prosecutor Geoffrey Nice explained:

The value of the Kula camp video ... cannot be overstated. It showed knowledge by Milošević of what was done in his name but more important was what it showed of his criminal mind for the very purposes of the prosecution. Setting up a paramilitary unit to operate in another's republic is to make a conscious decision to disturb the peace of that state otherwise maintained by the proper and lawful operation within that state of its legitimate "monopoly of violence" – the army and the police. By taking the steps he did in 1991, with the Red Berets, Milošević provided irresistible evidence of the *mens rea* required for the indictment.[21]

The Red Berets were one of many paramilitary forces connected to the Federal Republic of Yugoslavia and had the full support of the state security services in Belgrade. Two other officials in the video, Jovica Stanišić, head of the State Security Service in Serbia, and Franko Simatović, Commander of Special Operations of the State Security Service, would both be subject of ICTY indictments in 2003 (IT-03-69). The Red Berets were part of a larger overall effort by Milošević to mobilize ethnic Serbs outside of Serbia, establishing separate spheres of political organization. Those Serbs were encouraged to support the JNA, and not form separate armies.

There were other trials for violations in Croatia that established state involvement in the crimes of the region. The JNA's siege of Vukovar, for example, in Eastern

[18] Geoffrey Nice, Former Principal Trial Attorney in the Office of the Prosecutor of the ICTY, presentation, Columbia University, New York, April 17, 2006.

[19] See for example, *Prosecutor v. Milošević* (IT-02-54-T), Surrogate sheet for exhibit number: P390 Tab 1, Description: "Video showing an awards ceremony with members of Red Berets, political leaders and military leaders including: Slobodan Milošević, Franko Simatović, Jovica Stanišić, Mihalj Kertes, political leaders and military leaders giving and receiving awards." Kula camp video ERN V000-3533-V000-3533. Most of the ICTY documents cited can be found at the newly released "ICTY Court Records" database, which can be accessed after registration at <www.icty.org>.

[20] Ibid.

[21] Geoffrey Nice, "Panel: Legacy of Milošević Trial," March 31, 2007; <www.helsinki.org.yu/doc/GN_bgdspeech.doc> (accessed July 15, 2009).

Croatia, foreshadowed many similar crimes that were to take place in the Bosnian war. In one heinous act, four hundred non-Serb civilian patients at a local hospital were removed and tortured. Later, several hundred were executed and placed in a mass grave.[22] These crimes were the subject of the indictments against three members of the JNA: Mile Mrkšić, Veselin Šljivančanin, and Miroslav Radić (IT-95-13/1). In the trial, the prosecution focused on the crimes in the hospital and not the siege of the city. However, the trial transcripts would reveal the horrific conditions in the town and the targeting of civilian populations there.[23] The siege lasted for 87 days, from August to November 1991, and resulted in the total destruction of the city. Radić was found not guilty at the first instance and, while the other two indictees were found guilty, several significant counts were not upheld. The Vukovar hospital crimes were an early sign of the intentions of state agents, including the JNA, to remove non-Serb populations from the region in order to later unite a newly created, "cleansed" Serbian territory. To this aim, a third of the Croatian territory was under Serb control by the end of 1991.

The ICTY did focus some of its prosecutorial energy on the leaders of the JNA, although critics would argue that many key officers remained untouched by the court. As two former republics became new states, the JNA had 138,000 troops on active duty and 400,000 troops in reserves.[24] In addition to the three officers indicted for the Vukovar hospital crimes, the ICTY indicted the following JNA Generals: Momčilo Perišic (IT-04-81), Dragoljub Ojdanić, Nebojša Pavković, and Vladimir Lazarević (IT-05-87). Many leaders of the Army of Republika Srpska (VRS) would be indicted as well. Given that Serbia provided the material support and institutional structure for that army in Bosnia – and later, shelter, pensions, and apartments for retiring officers – the formal distinction between the two armies was misleading for an international audience given the impression that the conflict in Bosnia was a civil war.[25]

---

[22] See Eric Stover and Gilles Peress, *The Graves: Srebrenica and Vukovar* (Zurich: Scalo Publishers, 1998).

[23] Court witnesses pointed to incidents that started before the siege and the conditions during the siege. Witness Zvezdana Polovina, a journalist with Radio Vukovar, described the beginning of the siege of the city in court on November 30, 2005. Trial transcript starts on page 2567. She remembers an incident in May 1991: "People no longer trusted each other. Here first and foremost I mean along the ethnic lines. They went back to their houses and tended not to leave their houses much. After the killing of those Croatian police officers in Borovo Selo, nothing was ever the same again. For me the war began when the first victims fell" (page 2569), <www.icty.org/x/cases/mrksic/trans/en/051130IT.htm> (accessed July 15, 2009).

[24] Sabrina P. Ramet, *Balkan Babel: The Disintegration of Yugoslavia from the Death of Tito to Ethnic War* (Boulder, CO: Westview Press, 1996), 51.

[25] The family of General Radislav Krstić, who is serving a sentence for aiding and abetting genocide, received an apartment in a desirable part of Belgrade in 2005. See "Čijim generalima stanovi Vojske SCG" (Which generals get the apartments of the Army of Serbia and Montenegro), B92, August 1, 2005, <www.b92.net/info/vesti/index.php?yyyy=2005&mm=08&dd=01&nav_id=173774&nav_category=12> (accessed July 15, 2009).

Despite the considerable manpower which existed in the JNA, the wars in Croatia and Slovenia prompted a draft of military-age men in the rump Yugoslavia, but met resistance by thousands of reservists refusing to fight in Croatia. In the fall of 1991, the official number of those who had evaded service was 20,000, but analysts argued that the real figure was three to four times higher.[26] The JNA mobilized reservists in Bosnia as well; most Serbs responded, but most Croats and Bosniaks, with the encouragement of the Presidency of Bosnia and Herzegovina, declined. The army struggled to find recruits who would staff the war effort.

The media focus on Milošević, as an individual who was charged with criminal liability for the wars in the region, stole attention from other important precipitating events and criminal structures that facilitated the political violence. However, for the close observer, the trial record would clearly show, for example, that Milošević's territorial ambitions had deep intellectual roots in Serbia, a fact about which much has been written.[27] One of the most important documents in setting out the intellectual framework for the wars in the region was the Memorandum of the Serbian Academy of Sciences and Arts (Srpska akademija nauka i umetnosti, or SANU), of September 1986, which critiqued the problems in Yugoslav society from a Serb nationalist perspective and portrayed Serbs as historical victims of ever-increasing discrimination, even noting in one point that "the physical, political, legal and cultural genocide perpetrated against the Serbian population of Kosovo and Metohija is the greatest defeat suffered by Serbia in the wars of liberational fights that were led by Serbia from Orasac in 1804 till the rebellion of 1941."[28] The use of the word genocide, directed initially toward this smaller audience, would later be used by politicians to recast the Serbs as victims, and would help prepare the public for the commission of mass atrocities on their behalf. The ideological origins of the project to create a greater Serbia were nurtured not only by written documentation that outlined the goals, but by specific acts that required the participation of citizens of Serb ethnicity and helped mobilize the public in support of ethnically homogeneous territories. For example, in the years before the war started, there were many reburial ceremonies of Serb victims of World War II. Bette Denich argues that these ceremonies served as a "powerful emotional trigger."[29]

The question of how much history to include in court proceedings loomed large during the trials. Historians were part of a cadre of experts who provided

[26] Alan Ferguson, "Young Serbs Flee to Avoid Battle," *Toronto Star*, November 14, 1991.
[27] See, for example, Jasna Dragović-Soso, *Saviours of the Nation: Serbia's Intellectual Opposition and the Revival of Nationalism* (London: Hurst & Company, 2002) on nationalism of the pre-Milošević period.
[28] The SANU memorandum was submitted by the prosecution in the trial. Exhibit No. P446.28, ICTY, submitted May 19, 2003.
[29] Bette Denich, "Dismembering Yugoslavia: Nationalist Ideologies and the Symbolic Revival of Genocide," *American Ethnologist* 21, no. 2 (1994): 382. An extensive archive of photographs of these ceremonies exists at the Mostar-based Center for Peace and Multi-Ethnic Cooperation.

the context that helped determine the difference between the political and the criminal.[30] Historian Robert Donia, for one, has testified on behalf of the Office of the Prosecutor (OTP) in 12 ICTY trials, with more scheduled in the future.[31] Another historian, Audrey Budding, gave a sweeping overview of the history of Serb nationalism in the twentieth century at the Milošević trial.[32]

The International Community and Bosnia and Herzegovina

The involvement of the international community in the region, primarily of Western governments, predated the onset of the war in Bosnia and influenced postwar attitudes toward both the ICTY and the international institutions set up within the country to implement peace. The first significant intervention was the European Community's (EC) referral of the issue of the dissolution of the SFRY to what was known colloquially as the Badinter Arbitration Committee, set up to "advise [the EC] on legal questions arising within the context of the EC's peace negotiations."[33] The Committee handed down 15 decisions. International forces remained an active presence after the conflict began: the United Nations deployed a peacekeeping force, the United Nations Protection Force (UNPROFOR), initially formed to monitor demilitarization of the United Nations Protected Areas (UNPAs) and the creation of conditions for a durable solution for peace.[34] UNPROFOR's role was later expanded under a separate UN Security Council Resolution to cover Bosnia, and its forces were tasked with overseeing the delivery of humanitarian

---

[30]   Richard A. Wilson, "A Window on the Past: Historians and Social Scientists as Expert Witnesses at the ICTY," paper presented at the annual meeting of the International Studies Association, New York, February 16, 2009.

[31]   Donia testified in the following cases: *Prosecutor v. Tihomir Blaškić*, June–July 1997; *Prosecutor v. Dario Kordić and Mario Čerkez*, July 1999; *Prosecutor v. Miroslav Kvočka et al.* ("Omarska"), Submission of March 2001; *Prosecutor v. Blagoje Simić et al.* ("Bosanski Šamac"), September 2001; *Prosecutor v. Radislav Brdjanin and Momir Talić* ("Autonomous Region of Krajina"), March 2002; *Prosecutor v. Stanislav Galić* ("Sarajevo"), April 2002; *Prosecutor v. Milomir Stakić* ("Prijedor"), April 2002; *Prosecutor v. Slobodan Milošević*, September and November 2003; *Prosecutor v. Momčilo Krajišnik*, July 2005; *Prosecutor v. Jadranko Prlić et al.*, May 2006; *Prosecutor v. Dragomir Milošević*, March 2007; and *Prosecutor v. Momčilo Perišić*, November 2008.

[32]   See, for example, the Expert Report of Audrey Budding, "Serbian Nationalism in the Twentieth Century," submitted May 29, 2002 in *Prosecutor v. Slobodan Milošević*, ICTY.

[33]   Richard Kaplan, *Europe and the Recognition of New States in Yugoslavia* (Cambridge: Cambridge University Press, 2005), 16. See also James Gow, *Triumph of the Lack of Will: International Diplomacy and the Yugoslav War* (New York: Columbia University Press, 1997), 63.

[34]   See United Nations Security Council Resolution 743 (1992) (S/RES/743, February 21, 1992). See also UNSC Resolution 761 (1992) (S/RES/761, June 29, 1992) which authorized UNPROFOR to secure the Sarajevo airport and oversee the delivery of humanitarian aid. Both resolutions are available online at: <www.un.org/documents/sc/res/1992/scres92.htm> (accessed March 18, 2009).

aid, protecting convoys of civilians, and monitoring the Sarajevo airport.[35] Sent into the country with a limited mandate and restricted rules of engagement, the blue-helmeted peacekeepers were viewed by many as emblematic of the international community's blind resolve to remain neutral in the face of continued violence in the region and sometimes even worse. In one significant (but underreported) event of the war, French UN peacekeepers transporting Bosnian Deputy Prime Minister Hakija Turalić from the Sarajevo airport opened the door of the armored vehicle in which he sat and watched as a soldier of the Army of Republika Srpska (VRS) shot him dead.[36]

UN representatives on the ground displayed their misunderstanding of the nature of the war in correspondence with the Secretariat. Many early reports by UN officials portrayed all sides as equally guilty and created the impression that a civil war of equal parties was occurring.[37] Some, like Canadian UNPROFOR Commander Lewis MacKenzie, actively displayed affinities with Bosnian Serb leaders.[38] In addition, the Secretariat lacked leadership on the Bosnian war from the very top of the organization. Even though the UN Secretary General at the time, Boutros Boutros-Ghali, ultimately understood the real situation on the ground, he did not make the war a priority, nor did he think it deserved to be. He told an already largely indifferent Security Council that if he "expressed himself more forcefully on Bosnia he would lose its [sic] neutrality, and therefore the efficacy of the UN," and that "he did not have the luxury of personal feelings on these issues."[39] Boutros-Ghali also (in)famously told Sarajevans, then under siege, "I understand your frustration. But you have a situation that is better than 10 other places in the world I can give you. I can give you a list."[40] This struck many in the country as condescension, as they feared for their lives, and instilled a skepticism toward pronouncements of foreign officials that would last into the postwar years. The situation in the region was internationalized even before war broke out in Bosnia, and long before the ICTY was formed.

---

[35] United Nations Security Council Resolution *United Nations Protection Force (UNPROFOR) Profile*, August 31, 1996, United Nations Department of Public Information, <www.un.org/Depts/dpko/dpko/co_mission/unprof_p.htm> (accessed March 18, 2009).

[36] Steven A. Holmes, "Word of Bosnian's Killing Cuts Clinton Briefing Short," *New York Times*, January 9, 1993; Craig R. Whitney, "More than Ever, U.N. Policing is an American Show," *New York Times*, January 17, 1993.

[37] For example, Brigadier General Vere Hayes of the United Kingdom, chief of staff of the UN Military Commander, said that there was no "humanitarian siege of Sarajevo," infuriating the Bosnian government. See John F. Burns, "A Siege by Any Other Name Would Be as Painful," *New York Times*, April 17, 1993; "U.N. Chief of Staff Assailed," *Reuters*, August 17, 1993.

[38] See Carol Off, *The Lion, the Fox and the Eagle* (Toronto: Vintage Canada, 2001).

[39] Diego Enrique Arria, Witness Statement, *Prosecutor v. Slobodan Milošević*, ICTY, p. 5. Copy on file with the author. The statement was not formally admitted into evidence.

[40] John F. Burns, "Sarajevans Jeer as U.N. Leader Urges Restraint," *New York Times*, January 1, 1993. Boutros-Ghali also told Bosnians "to have patience." See Alan Riding, "FILM: Bosnia Revisited, with an Eye on the Future," *New York Times*, November 23, 1997.

The War in the Republic of Bosnia and Herzegovina, 1992–1995

With war raging in Croatia, focus shifted to the question of the future of the Socialist Republic of Bosnia and Herzegovina, the subject of Milošević and Tuđman's Karađođevo discussions. The war in Bosnia would follow similar patterns, however, with respect to the formation of separate political spheres governing citizens of Serb descent. Even before war broke out in Croatia, Serb nationalists in northwestern Bosnia formed the Community of Municipalities of the Bosnian Krajina (Zajednica opština Bosanske Krajine or ZOBK) in April 1991, which, in September 1991, was renamed the Autonomous Region of Krajina (Autonomna oblast Krajina or ARK). This move further spurred Bosnia's desire for international recognition.[41]

The next month, debates continued in the republic-level parliament about Bosnia's future, with members of the main Bosniak nationalist party, the Party of Democratic Action (Stranka demokratske akcije or SDA), and its Croat counterpart, the Croat Democratic Union (Hrvatska demokratska zajednica or HDZ), supporting resolutions that proclaimed independence. Bosnian Serb leader Radovan Karadžić (later indicted by the ICTY for, among other things, acts of genocide committed in Bosnia in both 1992 and 1995 [IT-95-5/18]) ominously threatened that the Bosniak nation would "go into extinction" if war broke out in Bosnia.[42] In a now infamous October speech in Parliament, he said: "This is the same highway to hell and misery taken by Slovenia and Croatia. Beware. Don't think that you will not drive Bosnia-Herzegovina to hell, and the Muslim people into extinction (*nestanak*). The Muslim people can't defend themselves if there is war."[43] That highway, however, was already being actively paved by members of his party. ICTY records would later reveal that many Serb civilians across the country had been armed surreptitiously up to one year before the formal onset of the war.[44] After Serb deputies walked out of the parliamentary debate, the Croat and Bosniak deputies approved a memorandum on Bosnian sovereignty, triggering the full-scale plans of Karadžić's Serb Democratic Party (Srpska demokratska stranka or SDS) to oppose it.[45]

---

[41] See *Prosecutor v. Radoslav Brđanin*, Appeals Chamber Judgement, ICTY, April 3, 2007 (IT-99-36-A), especially pages 16–18; <www.icty.org/x/cases/brdanin/acjug/en/brd-aj070403-e.pdf> (accessed July 15, 2009).

[42] See "Karadžić in a public statement to the assembly of Bosnia-Herzegovina on 14/15 October made from the podium of the assembly during an address regarding moves toward independence by the Socialist Republic of Bosnian [sic] and Herzegovina (SR BH), provided an insight into the awareness of the probable outcome of the process SDS was setting in motion," Exhibit P29, (Case IT-95-5-R61: Karadžić and Mladić), ICTY, June 28, 1996.

[43] Ibid. NB: The statement was made in 1991. See also Tone Bringa, "Averted Gaze: Genocide in Bosnia-Herzegovina," in A.L. Hinton, ed., *Annihilating Difference* (Berkeley: University of California Press, 2002).

[44] See also Chapter 6 of this volume.

[45] For a detailed discussion of these events, see Steven L. Burg and Paul Shoup, *The War in Bosnia-Herzegovina* (Armonk, NY: M.E. Sharpe, 1999), 76–79.

This walk-out occurred during a series of events in which Serb nationalists, led by the SDS, were actively establishing parallel institutions. First, after the creation of the ARK, the establishment of Serbian Autonomous Districts (Srpska autonomna oblasts or SAOs) by SDS leaders in late 1991 and early 1992 further illustrated attempts to craft a mono-ethnic political space governing only Serbs in Bosnia. Second, on October 24, 1991, SDS leaders formed the Assembly of the Serb People of Bosnia and Herzegovina. That Assembly sponsored a plebiscite on independence in November 1991 in which primarily Bosnian Serbs participated, and Croats and Bosniaks stayed home. The Serbs voted to remain a part of the rump Yugoslavia. The Bosnian Serb Assembly, a self-styled legislative body of Bosnian Serbs, declared the existence of a "Republic of the Serb People of Bosnia and Herzegovina" in January 1992. The Bosnian government declared their referendum unconstitutional and the "Serb Republic" was never recognized by any international body.

Prior to this declaration, in November, the Serb Democratic Party drafted "Instructions for the Organization and Activities of the Organs of the Serbian People in Bosnia and Herzegovina in Emergency Conditions," which instructed SDS officials in each municipality that was inhabited by Serbs (whether a majority or not) to create a Serb Municipal Assembly and a Crisis Staff, a provision of supplies for ethnic Serbs, and the establishment of extensive communication networks.[46] The Instructions envisioned that SDS crisis staff would have responsibility for assessing developments in the municipalities where Serbs lived, and be the source of direction for future action.

Against the backdrop of the continuing war in neighboring Croatia and increased tensions, a referendum was held in Bosnia on February 28 and March 1, 1992. In this referendum, 99 percent of those who cast a ballot voted for independence. Ethnic Serbs in the republic, however, largely boycotted the referendum, instructed by SDS leaders not to vote. On April 7, the European Community and the United States recognized the Republic of Bosnia and Herzegovina.[47] Immediately thereafter, Bosnian Serb and Serbian forces began a comprehensive aggression on Bosnia, including a three and a half year siege of Sarajevo, orchestrated and financed by Belgrade.[48] The war in the Republic of Bosnia and Herzegovina formally began at that time, although there had already been killings in the city of Ravno (in the region of Herzegovina) and in Bratunac (in Eastern Bosnia) in the fall of 1991.

[46] See "Instructions for the Organization and Activities of Organs of the Serbian People in Bosnia and Herzegovina in Emergency Conditions," Serb Democratic Party, Bosnia and Herzegovina, December 19, 1991. ICTY document number: 0025-2738-0025-2747-ET/Translation. *Prosecutor v. Momčilo Krajišnik* (IT-00-39).

[47] Most scholars erroneously reported that the Bosnian parliament declared independence, which is untrue. Even the U.S. State Department's web site reports this. For a discussion of this issue by a former Research Officer at the ICTY, see Andrew R. Corin, *"Union of Citizens"* or *"Union of Constituent Communities?"* unpublished manuscript, 153–156.

[48] The siege of Sarajevo, the longest siege of a city in modern history, was the main subject of the trials of Stanislav Galić (IT-98-29) and Dragomir Milošević (IT-98-29/1), both commanders in the Army of Republika Srpska.

The United Nations admitted the Republic of Bosnia and Herzegovina formally on May 22, 1992. Just before that, on May 12, the Bosnian Serb Assembly adopted the "Six Strategic Goals of the Serbian Nation":

1. State delineation from the other two national communities.
2. Corridor between Semberia and Krajina.
3. Establishment of a corridor in the valley of the Drina river, meaning the elimination of the Drina as a border between two Serb states.
4. Establishment of a border on the rivers of the Una and Neretva.
5. Division of the city of Sarajevo into Serb and Muslim parts, and the establishment of state authority in each part.
6. Outlet for Republika Srpska to the sea.[49]

Karadžić explained the first strategic goal at the 16th Session of the Bosnian Serb Assembly on that day: "The first such goal is separation from the two national communities – separation of states, separation from those who are our enemies and who have used every opportunity, especially in this century, to attack us, and who would continue with such practices if we were to continue to stay together in the same state."[50] These goals clearly outlined the political objectives that informed the military strategy of the next few years. The Six Strategic Goals were not published in the official gazette until November 1993, 18 months after they were adopted.

The war that followed is also inextricably tied to the presence of the international community, which recognized the young republic but strangled the country's ability to defend itself when it placed an arms embargo on the region that primarily affected the Republic of Bosnia and Herzegovina.[51] United Nations Security Council Resolution 713 established an arms embargo against all of the countries of the former Yugoslavia, thereby solidifying Belgrade's military advantage.[52] The inviolability of sovereign borders has long been one of the chief underwriting principles of the United Nations system; however, although Bosnia's statehood was recognized formally, in practice the international community did not afford Bosnia the rights given to other nations. Later, it created a judicial institution – the ICTY – to handle the violations of international law that took place while the Bosnian government scrambled to establish a system of defense.

---

[49] See "Expert report entitled the Origins of Republika Srpska 1990–1992, A Background Report by Robert J. Donia," Exhibit number P.934, *Prosecutor v. Momčilo Krajišnik*. The original document was: Broj 02-130/92. 12 Maja 1992 godine. Predsjednik Narodne skupštine, Mr. Momčilo Krajišnik, s.r. "Odluka o strateškim ciljevima srpskog naroda u BiH" (Decision about the strategic goals of the Serb people in Bosnia and Herzegovina), *Službeni Glasnik Republike Srpske*, Petak, November 26, 1993, str. 866, broj 22.

[50] Ibid.

[51] It also caused the Bosnian government to seek arms from other sources including Iran. See Cees Wiebes, *Intelligence and the War in Bosnia 1992–1995* (Munster, Germany: Lit Verlag, 2003).

[52] United Nations Security Council Resolution 713 (1991) (S/RES/713, September 25, 1991); <www.un.org/Docs/scres/1991/scres91.htm> (accessed July 14, 2009).

Armed Forces on Bosnian Soil

The Army of Republika Srpska

The patchwork of armed forces on Bosnian soil also hindered foreign understand-ing of wartime developments. Members of all of the armies involved in the conflict would be the subject of ICTY indictments, which eventually produced a clearer picture of the differing levels of command responsibility and culpability for vio-lations of international humanitarian law. The Bosnian government struggled to assemble an effective armed force. Many resources of the Territorial Defense Forces (*Teritorijalna odbrana* or TOs), the republic-level system of defense, were co-opted by the parties that controlled each municipality. In some areas where the TOs were mixed, the soldiers tended to join the armies dominated by their ethnic groups – which meant that TOs in Serb-dominated municipalities were absorbed by the JNA, and later the Army of Republika Srpska (Vojska Republike Srpske or VRS), and Bosniak and Croat forces by the Bosnian Army. In 1991–1992, the Bosnian TO was the subject of a power struggle, and the Bosnian government even endorsed an order to surrender TO weapons to the JNA.[53] This further solidi-fied the Serb military advantage, especially as weapons had been distributed to the SDS, militia forces, and Serb civilians all over Bosnia beginning in the spring of 1991.[54]

The Bosnian Serb component of the JNA formed what later became the VRS, led by General Ratko Mladić (IT-95-5/18).[55] The forces of Serbia and Montenegro became the Yugoslav Army (Vojska Jugoslavije or VJ). The VRS inherited units, commanders, weapons, munitions, and personnel from the JNA. It was a new army in name only, and the JNA and VRS were closely connected throughout the war. The VRS received financial and material support from the JNA and operated with the same ranks and protocol. Formally, the JNA was on Bosnian soil until May 19, 1992, when a direc-tive ordered all soldiers to return to Belgrade and the law that created the Army of the Serb Republic of Bosnia and Herzegovina (Vojska Srpske Republike Bosne i Hercegovine or VSRBiH, later VRS, Army of Republika Srpska), was enacted by the so-called Serb Republic of Bosnia and Herzegovina.[56] This directive was dated a week after the adoption of the Six Strategic Goals. The JNA had previously returned all Bosnian Serb soldiers to take up active duty in Bosnia. While ICTY indictees such as Milošević would claim ignorance about military developments in Bosnia, in reality the VRS and JNA remained undeniably linked on many levels. Telephone

---

[53] Marko Attila Hoare, *How Bosnia Armed* (London: Saqi Books, 2004), 22–23.
[54] The arming intensified in the spring of 1992. See *Prosecutor v. Momčilo Krajišnik*, Judgement, September 27, 2006 (IT-00-39-T), pp. 19–20, 45–46.
[55] Hoare, *How Bosnia Armed*, 31.
[56] See "Document regarding the agreement of withdrawal of JNA from BiH chaired by Colm Doyle," *Prosecutor v. Slobodan Milošević*, Exhibit Number P503.18, submitted July 15, 2003.

intercepts would show Milošević had extensive contact with the Bosnian Serb political leadership.[57] In addition, the VRS remained a budget line item in Belgrade until long after the signing of the Dayton Peace Agreement.

Although thousands of documents introduced at the ICTY would outline this relationship, not until a videotape of a Serbian paramilitary unit executing Bosniak males after the fall of the Srebrenica enclave was shown in the court would this relationship be brought into the public consciousness in the region.[58] The court noted, "The images of Serbian soldiers tormenting and then shooting the Bosnian Muslim prisoners, whose hands were tied behind their backs and who offered no resistance before being shot, broke through the wall of silence and denial about the subject of Srebrenica in Serbia and Montenegro. The Serbian Government condemned the killings, and the Serbian War Crimes Prosecutor acted swiftly to detain a number of suspects allegedly complicit in the murders of these six men."[59]

The relationship between the JNA, the VRS, and associated paramilitary forces was most evident in places where the largest number of violations of international law took place on Bosnian soil. These paramilitary forces had considerable state support and material resources from Serbia. They recruited hardened criminals and the unemployed. Some paramilitary leaders, like Željko Ražnatović – known as Arkan – head of the Serbian Volunteer Guard, later known as the "Tigers" (*Tigrovi*), also found recruits among nationalist soccer hooligans.[60] Arkan's men became known internationally through a picture taken by American photographer Ron Haviv of a "Tiger" kicking a Bosniak civilian recently shot by his forces in the streets of the Eastern Bosnian city of Bijeljina in March 1992.[61] The individuals in the photograph, two women and one man, were some of the war's first victims. Ražnatović was indicted by the court, but was murdered before his arrest. The ICTY also indicted Milan Lukić, Sredoje Lukić (IT-98-32-1) and Mitar Vasiljević (IT-98-32) for crimes that they committed while members of a paramilitary group in Višegrad. In July 2009, the trial chamber sentenced Milan Lukić to life and Sredoje Lukić to 30 years in prison, some of the longest terms given by the court. Milan Lukić was found guilty of some of the war's most notorious crimes: the June 14, 1992 murder of 59 Bosniak civilians who were locked into the room of a house on Višegrad's Pionirska Street, which was set on fire. Milan Lukić placed the explosive device in the house that ignited the fire;

(OTP Reference Number 89246: Page number: 00340742.) It later became known simply as the VRS and that acronym is used throughout the book.

[57] For intercepts in the period leading up to and immediately after the start of the war, see, for example, "Chart of Intercepts Reviewed by the Witness," July 15, 2003. ICTY Exhibit P503.2a. The witness in question is Stjepan Kljuić.

[58] The tape was introduced in court in June 2005. This paramilitary unit was part of the Serbian Ministry of Interior.

[59] ICTY Outreach Document, "Facts About Srebrenica," <www.icty.org/x/file/Outreach/view_from_hague/jit_srebrenica_En.pdf> (accessed July 15, 2009).

[60] See Peter Andreas, "The Clandestine Political Economy of the War and Peace in Bosnia," *International Studies Quarterly* 48 (2004): 35.

[61] On Arkan, see Christopher S. Stewart, *Hunting the Tiger: The Fast Life and Violent Death of the Balkans' Most Dangerous Man* (New York: Thomas Dunne Books, 2008).

Sredoje Lukić was found guilty of aiding and abetting the crime. A second similar event in which 70 people died also took place in 1992.[62]

These irregular forces were integral to Belgrade's overall military strategy. Frequent ICTY expert witness and scholar James Gow argues, "The organization of 'volunteer' paramilitary units served the purpose of strategic deception and ambiguity, whereby supposedly independent forces could be blamed for atrocities, the appearance of chaos could be maintained in the field and the army's professional reputation could, in contrast, be bolstered."[63] In some cities, a strategy based on creating panic in local residents by killing a handful of key elite families in the community resulted in the flight of the entire population.[64] While the intensity of crimes varied in Bosnia, Gow illustrates how the overall strategy was one in which violations of international humanitarian law were a central part of Serb military strategy.

The Army of the Republic of Bosnia and Herzegovina

The Army of the Republic of Bosnia and Herzegovina (Armija Republike Bosne i Herzegovine or ARBiH) had various institutional components that complicated the assembly of an effective system of defense for the newly independent state. At its core, the ARBiH had its origins in the TO forces. Forces were also drawn from two paramilitary organizations, the Patriotic League (Patriotska liga or PL) and the Green Berets, which were created in June 1991 by representatives of the SDA.[65] The Patriotic League started arming Muslims in Herzegovina during the summer of 1991 and conducted training exercises.[66] It grew to over 100,000 members before the war started.[67] In June 1991, the PL became the military wing of the Council for National Defense of the Muslim People.[68] In December 1991, when JNA artillery emplacements overlooking Sarajevo had already been in place for two months, proposals to create an army were drafted.[69] Initial plans to defend the territory of Bosnia and Herzegovina and maintain its territorial integrity and multiethnic character envisioned a conflict that would last only 13 weeks.[70] On April 15, 1992, after the Bosnian government was recognized by the international community,

[62] See the Case Information Sheet of Milan Lukić and Sredoje Lukić "Višegrad" (IT-98-32/1), ICTY. This decision has been appealed by both the defense and prosecution.
[63] James Gow, *The Serbian Project and its Adversaries: A Strategy of War Crimes* (London: Hurst and Company, 2003), 79.
[64] For a study on *elitocide* in Bosnia, see Dennis Gratz, "Elitocide in Bosnia and Hercegovina 1992–1995," Ph.D. diss., University of Hamburg, 2007.
[65] Robert J. Donia, *Sarajevo: A Biography* (Ann Arbor, MI: University of Michigan Press, 2006) 276.
[66] *Prosecutor v. Momčilo Krajišnik*, Judgement, September 27, 2006 (IT-00-39-T) p. 20, <www.icty.org/x/cases/krajisnik/tjug/en/kra-jud060927e.pdf> (accessed July 20, 2009).
[67] Ibid.
[68] Donia, *Sarajevo*, 276.
[69] Hoare, *How Bosnia Armed*, 35.
[70] Hoare, *How Bosnia Armed*, 30–31.

it unified the armed forces in the country, including the PL, the TO, the Ministry of Internal Affairs (Ministarstvo unutarnjih poslove or MUP) forces, the Croat Defense Council (HVO), and other Croat militias.[71] But the government was unaware of the extent of Serb preparations for war, and efforts to set up a viable defense confronted difficulties. In the capital, the fledgling Bosnian Army was derived from various groups, the consolidation of which "proceeded unevenly over many months."[72] Some citizens, who previously would never have imagined becoming soldiers, organized in the hallways of Sarajevo's housing settlements: "When I saw that it all had already gone too far and the situation was such that there was nowhere to go, then I got involved in the army with my colleagues from the hallways in the [communist] housing blocks," one remembered.[73]

The UN arms embargo inhibited the Bosnian government's acquisition of arms, leaving its army on an uneven playing field. "I hate sending my boys to the front lines with one magazine [of bullets] and then asking them to conserve their fire," one officer told a foreign journalist during the war.[74] Furthermore, the lack of cohesion in the ARBiH structure and, in the early years, the fact that among the soldiers there were criminal gangs, meant there were thefts, crimes against civilians, and disciplinary problems.[75] At certain times during the war, primarily at its beginning, criminal elements wielded considerable power in parts of Sarajevo, leaving many residents, particularly Serbs and Croats, terrified to move about in those areas.[76] The Bosnian Army and police forces later undertook significant efforts to pursue those unruly soldiers in Operations Trebević 1 and 2.[77]

Another source of manpower for the Bosnian war effort would later be the subject of ICTY indictments. Unable to acquire arms and lacking a professional army, the Bosnian government allowed an influx of foreign fighters to enter the country, and reached out to the Middle East, notably Iran, for arms. In mid-1992, a component of foreign mujahedin was integrated into the Third Corps of the ARBiH in Central Bosnia, to the surprise of many Bosnian soldiers (and citizens).[78] These foreign fighters operated in cities such as Travnik and Zenica

[71] Donia, *Sarajevo*, 292. Bosnian President Alija Izetbegović ordered all forces to submit to his authority or withdraw from the country. See Blaine Harden, "2 Republics Reconstitute Yugoslavia; Serbia, Montenegro Unite in New State," *Washington Post*, April 28, 1992.

[72] Donia, *Sarajevo*, 292. Donia argues that even though this is the date celebrated as the birth of the ARBiH, the process was not really completed until the end of the war.

[73] Interview with officer of the Armed Forces of Bosnia and Herzegovina (AFBiH), Sarajevo, December 13, 2005.

[74] Anthony Loyd, *My War Gone By, I Miss it So* (New York: Penguin Books, 2001).

[75] See Peter Andreas, *Blue Helmets and Black Markets: The Business of Survival in the Siege of Sarajevo* (Ithaca, NY: Cornell University Press, 2008).

[76] John F. Burns, "Gangs in Sarajevo Spread Terror, Unchecked by the Cowed Leaders," *New York Times*, October 22, 1993.

[77] See, for example, the testimony of ICTY witness Murat Softić in *Prosecutor v. Rasim Delić* (IT-04-83-T), pp. 1897–1899, August 29, 2007, <www.icty.org/x/cases/delic/trans/en/070829IT.htm> (accessed July 30, 2009).

[78] Interviews with Bosnian soldiers, September–October 2005.

and were to blame for many atrocities there.[79] The foreign mujahedin were the subject of ICTY inquiry in the cases against Rasim Delić, Commander of the Main Staff of the Army of the Republic of Bosnia and Herzegovina (IT-04-83), and Enver Hadžihasanović and Amir Kubura (IT-01-47), two Bosnian Army officers. Delić was charged, among other things, with command responsibility for crimes committed by the El Mujahed unit of the 7th Muslim Mountain Brigade of the ARBiH 3rd Corps (known as the El Mujahed Detachment [EMD]) and was sentenced to three years.[80] Ultimately, the court found that Delić had "failed to take the necessary and reasonable measures to prevent and punish" crimes committed by members of the EMD against VRS soldiers in the Livade and Kamenica camps in July 1995.[81] The ICTY also indicted other high-ranking officers of the Bosnian Army; for example, Sefer Halilović (IT-01-48) was charged with command authority for the crimes against Croat civilians that took place in the village of Grabovica while he was Chief of the Main Staff and Deputy Commander of the ARBiH (however, he was acquitted in November 2005).

In the end, the presence of mujahedin damaged the country's reputation much more than it bolstered the army's military position. Their arrival paralleled other changes in the army; over the course of the war the Bosnian Army was transformed from a multiethnic force to an almost entirely Bosniak one, under the heavy influence of the SDA.[82] This was a source of disappointment for many Bosnian citizens who supported a multiethnic Bosnia (and supporting institutions) as recognized in 1992. This ethnic division also stemmed from the fact that most of the Croat members of the Bosnian Army withdrew and launched their own offensive against it in 1993.

Many observers assumed that Bosnian government leaders were not the focus of ICTY inquiry. The court, however, announced that it was investigating former Bosnian President Alija Izetbegović on the day of his burial, as over 100,000 mourners braved heavy rains in Sarajevo to pay their respects.[83] The decision to reveal the existence of the inquiry was the source of much disagreement inside the court.[84]

The Bosnian Army versus the Croat Defense Council

During the first year of the war, the Bosnian Army, comprised largely of Croats and Bosniaks, was pitted against the JNA (which was transformed into the VRS). The Bosnian Army, however, lacked a unified structure and its de facto dissolution

[79] For one of the few books that addresses the topic of foreign fighters, see Wiebes, *Intelligence and the War*, esp. Ch. 4.
[80] *Prosecutor v. Rasim Delić*, no. IT-04-83-T, Judgement, ICTY, September 15, 2008.
[81] Ibid.
[82] Hoare, *How Bosnia Armed*, 128.
[83] "Dead Bosnia Hero Focus of War Crimes Inquiry," *New York Times*, October 23, 2003.
[84] Discussions with former ICTY staff, 2007–2008.

would produce another violent chapter of the Bosnian war. Croat forces operating in Herzegovina and Central Bosnia were known as the Croat Defense Council (Hrvatsko vijeće obrane or HVO) and had financial and material aid from the neighboring Croatian Army (Hrvatska vojska or HV). The HVO was nominally under the authority of the Bosnian government, after command structures were unified in April 1992, but in practice commanders never recognized the leadership of the Bosnian government. The November 1991 creation of the Croatian Community of Herceg-Bosna (Hrvatska zajednica Herceg-Bosna or HZHB) by Croat nationalists, an effort spearheaded by the HDZ, complicated this relationship as nationalist HZHB leaders played a tricky game: publicly, they maintained that they were an integral part of the Bosnian state, but in working for a separate polity, their implicit goal was integration with neighboring Croatia.[85] Less than a year into the war, Bosnian Croat forces pulled away from joint institutions and started their own offensive against the Bosnian Army, with the support of neighboring Croatia; sometimes they allied with the VRS.

In 1992 and 1993, HVO forces expelled Bosniaks from their homes and governmental positions in Herzegovina and Central Bosnia, seizing their civil, political, and military posts. The drafting of the Vance-Owen peace plan (VOPP) in 1993 exacerbated the conflict. The plan, named for its sponsors Cyrus Vance and Lord David Owen, proposed to divide the country along ethnic lines, which created an incentive for Croat forces to seize territory in advance of its signing. The conflict between the ARBiH and HVO was finally ended in March 1994 with the signing of the Washington Agreement, which established the Federation of Bosnia and Herzegovina (Federacija Bosne i Hercegovine or FBiH). One foreign correspondent reported that Croats and Bosniaks enjoyed a spring day together, basking in the sun under an old Yugoslav flag after the signing. "Imagine. Two men signed something in Washington, and here we are," a former combatant said.[86]

The ICTY would address the crimes committed by HVO forces against Bosniaks during the trial of Tihomir Blaškić (IT-95-14), arguably the most publicized trial of the Bosnian Croat military leadership. Blaškić was a colonel at the time of the crimes listed in his indictment. The court initially found Blaškić guilty and sentenced him to 45 years in jail for the massacre of over 100 Bosniak civilians in the village of Ahmići, in the Lašva Valley. On appeal he was found guilty of only a few of the original charges. His sentence was reduced to nine years, including time served, and he was released from prison after eight years and just over five months. Blaškić's offer to visit the village of Ahmići was rejected by victims in Central Bosnia who were not yet ready for such a gesture.[87] The trial of Dario Kordić, a member of the Presidency of the Croatian Community of Herceg-Bosna (HZHB), and Mario Čerkez, a former HVO member (IT-95-14/2), also addressed crimes in Bosnia's Lašva Valley.

[85] I am grateful to Robert Donia for this insight.
[86] Bruno Beloff, "Truce Stories from a Theater of War," *The Scotsman,* April 5, 1994.
[87] Ivo Šćepanović, Zvonimir Čilić, "Blaškić odustao od odlaska u Ahmiće" (Blaškić cancels departure to Ahmići), *Slobodna Dalmacija,* June 8, 2004.

A collective trial for Bosnian Croat political leaders was ongoing in 2009: Jadranko Prlić, Bruno Stojić, Slobodan Praljak, Milivoj Petković, Valentin Ćorić, and Berislav Pušić (IT-04-74) were charged with crimes committed during their leadership in the Croat mini-state "Herceg Bosna" and for plans to form a "Greater Croatia."[88] The most famous crime in this area of the country for which Bosnian Croat military leaders were charged was the destruction of the Ottoman-era bridge in Mostar. Slobodan Praljak was indicted for overseeing this; Praljak had callously said in postwar interviews "it's just an old bridge."[89]

The Bosnian Army increased its military prowess over the course of the war. Due in part to an alliance made with the Croatian Army in the summer of 1995, the ARBiH made significant territorial gains in the final months of the war, but was warned by the international community not to go too far. The army was on the verge of taking back Banja Luka, an important step to winning the war all-out on military grounds.[90] However, with the future structure of Bosnia already quietly settled (i.e., the creation of highly autonomous entities), international powers thwarted this campaign, even going so far as to threaten military action against the Bosnian government.[91] Thus, the war was brought to an end just as the Bosnian Army approached victory. In a Faustian bargain from the outset, international officials would spend much of the postwar period undoing what the international community had established in negotiations to appease the Serb aggressors. This compromise would complicate the ICTY's work.

Srebrenica

Not long before the war ended, Bosnian Serb and Serbian forces would commit the largest single crime on European soil since World War II. Testimonies at the ICTY clearly established that, from the start of the war, the expulsion of the Bosniak population from Eastern Bosnia was a strategic goal of Bosnian Serb forces, funded and aided by their counterparts in Belgrade. They sought an "ethnically pure" territory,

---

[88] The second amended indictment can be found at: http://www.icty.org/x/cases/prlic/ind/en/080611.pdf (accessed July 15, 2009). See also Richard Bernstein, "Bridge Is Restored in Bosnia, and with It Hope of Peace," *New York Times*, July 24, 2004.

[89] Praljak also created his own web site to discuss his version of the destruction of the bridge. See Slobodan Praljak, "How the Old Bridge Was Destroyed: Facts," <www.slobodanpraljak.com/english/knjiga_most_eng.htm> (accessed July 15, 2009). On the destruction of cultural and religious sites in Bosnia, see András J. Riedlmayer, "From the Ashes: The Past and the Future of Bosnia's Cultural Heritage," in Maya Shatzmiller, ed., *Islam and Bosnia: Conflict Resolution and Foreign Policy in Multi-Ethnic States* (Montreal: McGill-Queen's University Press, 2002); András J. Riedlmayer, "Crimes of War, Crimes of Peace: Destruction of Libraries during and after the Balkan Wars of the 1990s," *Library Trends* 56, no. 1 (Summer 2007): 107–132.

[90] Hoare, *How Bosnia Armed*, 121–127.

[91] On negotiations regarding the entities, see, for example, Sylvie Matton, *Un génocide annoncé* (Srebrenica: a genocide foretold) (Paris: Flammarion, 2005).

bordering on what was then the Federal Republic of Yugoslavia (now Serbia and Montenegro). Testifying for the prosecution, former Bosnian Army General Sefer Halilović noted that the Serb forces' goal of eliminating the Drina River as a border between "Serb states" made the eastern municipality of Srebrenica strategically important.[92] On this point, both the prosecution and defense agreed. The ICTY military expert for the defense in the Radislav Krstić trial, Radovan Radinović, argued that Eastern Bosnia was strategically important for the integrity of ethnic Serb territories.[93] Testimony of this sort was evidence that Serb leaders were actively implementing the first and third of the Six Strategic goals.

This was confirmed in interviews with Bosnians all over the region: one displaced person reported being told during her expulsion from the Srebrenica enclave, "No one who isn't Serb will live within 30 kilometers on either side of the Drina River!"[94] The Drina River winds down Eastern Bosnia and in some places forms the border with Serbia. This region posed a particular demographic problem for the nationalist project to create Serb states because Bosniaks populated it predominantly before the war. In the Srebrenica municipality, for example, the 1991 census listed almost 37,000 people, 75 percent of whom were Bosniak and 23 percent Serb.

The pattern of atrocities in Eastern Bosnia demonstrates a policy of violations of international law perpetrated systematically by the VRS, JNA, and associated paramilitaries throughout the war, culminating in their most heinous crime in 1995.[95] As early as 1992, when JNA forces swept the region, patterns in the numbers of missing and killed persons in four different municipalities suggested coordination at some level. Graphs for the neighboring municipalities of Srebrenica, Bratunac, Vlasenica, and Zvornik, for example, all reveal spikes in killings and disappearances during the same period.[96]

The area in and around the Srebrenica municipality was a microcosm of events in this part of the country. The precedent set in 1992 made eastern Bosnia a site of intensive fighting throughout the war, as Bosnian government forces responded to this systematic aggression. Bosnian Serb and Serbian forces took over Srebrenica for several weeks in 1992; the Bosnian Army, under the leadership of Naser Orić, then reclaimed and expanded the boundaries of the enclave to 900 square kilometers, but those gains were pushed back shortly thereafter by the continued Serb offensive.[97]

During fighting in the region, civilians swelled the town of Srebrenica, fleeing hostilities in other parts of eastern Bosnia. As the municipality was cut off from

---

[92] *Prosecutor v. Radislav Krstić* (IT-98-33-T), Judgement, ICTY, August 2, 2001: 5, <www.icty. org/x/cases/krstic/tjug/en/krs-tj010802e.pdf> (accessed July 15, 2009).

[93] Ibid.

[94] Interview with internally displaced person from the Srebrenica enclave, Tuzla, January 9, 2004.

[95] Mirsad Tokača, President, Research and Documentation Center, presentation, International Conference on the Genocide against Bosniaks of the UN Safe Area Srebrenica: Lessons for the Future," Sarajevo, July 12, 2005.

[96] Data from the Research and Documentation Center, 2005.

[97] *Prosecutor v. Krstić*, 5.

food, water, and medical treatment, many in the enclave were on the verge of starvation. In an effort to acquire food, civilians followed the Bosnian Army on attacks
in Serb villages surrounding Srebrenica. These residents became known as the
"bag holders" (*torbari*). One such attack, encouraged by civilians, took place on
Orthodox Christmas, January 7, 1993. Bosnian Army forces attacked the Serb village of Kravica, and were followed by hundreds of hungry residents of the enclave
who had heard early that morning of plans to attack.[98] Some estimates are that 30
Serb civilians were killed in the offensive. Several other similar raids conducted
from the enclave into neighboring villages, in which Serb civilians perished, created a perilous dynamic in the region. The ICTY examined Orić's role in the Kravica
killings (IT-03-68) (although he was found not guilty).

The VRS responded to the events in Kravica with a counter-offensive that
reduced the Srebrenica enclave to 150 square kilometers.[99] In March and April of
1993, between 8,000 and 9,000 Bosniaks were evacuated from the enclave, a move
contested by the Bosnian government because it contributed to the ethnic cleansing that was occurring all over the country.[100] It looked as if the VRS would not let
up until they had taken the town; the army threatened to attack unless the ARBiH
surrendered.[101]

The UN Security Council responded to the violence with Resolution 819. On
April 16, it declared Srebrenica a "safe area," instructing that "all parties and
others concerned treat Srebrenica and its surroundings as a safe area that should
be free from armed attack or any other hostile act."[102] It also demanded the "ces-
sation of armed attacks by Bosnian Serb paramilitary units against Srebrenica."[103]
Canadian UNPROFOR troops were dispatched to the enclave days later. Operation
Deny Flight, in which NATO enforced a no-fly zone over the country, took effect
that month as well.[104] The no-fly zone was another response to confrontations with
the VRS.

The passage of Resolution 819 was followed by the first post–Cold War field
mission of the UN Security Council, a fact-finding initiative undertaken to investigate the true state of affairs in Bosnia. Mission coordinator and Venezuela's
Ambassador to the UN, Diego Arria, then head of the Non-Aligned Movement in
the United Nations, later reported that UN officials on the ground did not wish
to reveal the true extent of the suffering in the enclave, which further confirmed

[98] "Fighters under Pressure from Civilians," *South East News Service Europe (SENSE)*, August 25, 2005, <www.sense-agency.com/en/stream.php?sta=3&pid=6879&kat=3> (accessed July 7, 2009).
[99] *Prosecutor v. Krstić*, 5.
[100] Ibid., 6.
[101] Ibid.
[102] Ibid. United Nations Security Council Resolution 819 (1993) (S/RES/819, 16 April 1993) <www.un.org/Docs/scres/1993/scres93.htm> (accessed July 16, 2009).
[103] Ibid.
[104] Operation Deny Flight, Fact Sheet, North Atlantic Treaty Organization, Regional Headquarters Allied Forces Southern Europe, July 18, 2003, <www.afsouth.nato.int/operations/denyflight/DenyFlightFactSheet.htm> (accessed May 19, 2008).

the complicated relationship between UN forces, both on the ground and at the Secretariat, and the parties to conflict.[105] The creation of the safe area was the first paragraph of what would become a shameful chapter in the UN's history, later undermining the ICTY's credibility in the region, as the court was also a UN body.

On the eve of the mission's departure for Bosnia (and unbeknownst to the mission members), the Bosnian government signed an agreement which called for demilitarization of the Srebrenica enclave.[106] Weapons in Srebrenica were to be handed over under the supervision of the United Nations. The ICTY's documentation later showed that General Halilović, of the Bosnian Army's 28th division, ordered his troops to pull armed personnel and military equipment out of the enclave, but not to hand over serviceable weapons.[107] Halilović issued the directive even though the Bosnian Army (ARBiH) did not have a significant amount of arms and its forces lacked a solid command structure in Srebrenica. At the same time, up to 2,000 soldiers from the Drina Corps – the VRS division active in the area – continued their stranglehold on the enclave.[108]

The final trip report of the UN Mission revealed the startling truth about circumstances in Srebrenica, and carried an ominous forecast. Drafted by Arria, and signed by all of the mission members including Russia, it observed that the enclave held 70,000 people living in an "open jail" in which people lacked food, medical care, and meaningful employment.[109] It argued that the VRS's refusal to allow a surgeon to stay in the enclave in order to help the wounded amounted to a "crime of genocide." The report continued: "This action together with the cutting off of the water supply and electricity, have put into effect a *slow motion process of genocide.*"[110] Unfortunately, this prediction was accurate, as the ICTY's judgment in the trial against Radislav Krstić later confirmed. The world did not heed this early warning, though, and despite public and ominous forecasts that should have drawn international attention to the enclave, conditions there worsened after the mission's departure.

Only two countries on the Security Council acknowledged that the UN was creating an impossible situation in the region with the creation of the safe area. After his return from the enclave, Ambassador Arria of Venezuela, along with his colleague Jamsheed Marker of Pakistan, abstained from voting for the creation

---

[105] Interview with Diego Arria, February 10, 2004.
[106] Ibid. The UNSC Mission report noted that the agreement likely prevented a large-scale massacre at the time.
[107] *Prosecutor v. Krstić*, 8.
[108] Ibid., 7.
[109] Report of the Security Council Mission Established Pursuant to Resolution 819 (1993), no. S/25700, United Nations Security Council, April 30, 1993. In addition to Venezuela, representatives of the Russian Federation, France, Pakistan, Hungary, and New Zealand were present on the mission and signed the final report. This disparate group of nations, though known for strong disagreements in the Security Council, all concurred on the state of affairs they witnessed in the Srebrenica enclave.
[110] Ibid.(emphasis added). Arria's testimony to the ICTY is addressed in Chapter 4.

of other safe areas that would give Bosnian Serb forces more opportunity to leverage their influence on civilian populations.[111] Other diplomats on the Security Council were not as bold, and Resolution 824 passed in May 1993, establishing Sarajevo, Tuzla, Žepa, Goražde, and Bihać as additional safe areas. Further guarantees were offered to the residents of these safe areas by yet another resolution in June.[112]

From 1993 to 1995 the Srebrenica enclave swelled with displaced persons from all over Eastern Bosnia, seeking shelter and the promise of safety they assumed the UN would offer. Other Bosnians moved to the new safe areas with similar hopes of finding respite from the war. The same month that the Security Council expanded its list of safe areas, the ICTY was created. One UN creation – the Srebrenica safe area – would, in a short amount of time, provide the largest body of work for its other creation.

In March 1995, the President of Republika Srpska (RS), Radovan Karadžić, signed a directive to the VRS, whereby he instructed the military to isolate Srebrenica and Žepa. Known as Directive 7, it ordered them to: "complete the physical separation of Srebrenica from Žepa as soon as possible, preventing even communication between individuals in the two enclaves. By planned and well-thought out combat operations, create an unbearable situation of total insecurity with no hope of further survival or life for the inhabitants of Srebrenica."[113] In the spring of 1995, conditions in the enclave continued to worsen, and fewer and fewer humanitarian aid convoys made it through.[114] During the opening of the Karadžić trial, ICTY prosecutor Alan Tieger quoted the accused speaking about the directive: "The time had come ... and I signed Directive 7 to capture Teočak, Srebrenica, Žepa, and Goražde. The directive was signed and we embarked on it. I was in favor of all the decisions that we made and I support them. All the decisions are recorded in the Supreme Command. I ordered in verbal and written form to attack Žepa and Srebrenica. The time had come."[115]

That same month, a U.S. government report suggested why most of the ICTY's indictees would turn out to be ethnic Serbs. The March 1995 report, issued by the Central Intelligence Agency (CIA), indicated that "90 percent of the acts of 'ethnic cleansing' were carried out by Serbs and ... leading Serbian politicians almost certainly played a role in the crimes."[116] The CIA report debunked the idea then

---

[111] Interview with Diego Arria, February 10, 2004.
[112] UN Security Council Resolution 824 (1993) (S/RES/824, 6 May 1993) created the additional safe areas of Sarajevo, Tuzla, Žepa, Goražde, and Bihać. UN Security Council Resolution 836 (1993) (S/RES/836, 4 June 1993) provided additional guarantees to the safe areas, including authorizing UN forces on the ground to deter attacks, <www.un.org/Docs/scres/1993/scres93.htm> (accessed July 15, 2009).
[113] *Prosecutor v. Krstić*, 10.
[114] Ibid.
[115] *Prosecutor v. Radovan Karadžić*, trial transcript, ICTY. October 27, 2009.
[116] Roger Cohen, "C.I.A. Report on Bosnia Blames Serbs for 90% of the War Crimes," *New York Times*, March 9, 1995.

prevalent in Western foreign policy circles that the war in Bosnia was a civil war of equal parties. It did acknowledge, however, that all sides had committed war crimes.[117] Directive 7 demonstrated the foresight and calculation of RS leaders that CIA intelligence had identified.

A year prior to this directive, in February 1994, Dutch peacekeeping forces took over from Canadian peacekeepers that had been stationed in the enclave. Against the backdrop of RS resolve to create an environment of "no hope of further survival" for safe-area residents, high UN officials expressed the opinion that UN troops should be pulled out of the enclave, leaving many to conclude that the enclave was allowed to fall on purpose. Six weeks before the fall of the enclave, Lieutenant-General Bernard Janvier, the commander of all UN forces in Bosnia and Croatia, asked Security Council members and troop-contributing nations to be realistic about the abilities of the lightly armed soldiers in the enclave and to keep their safety in mind. "We have little time ahead of us. We must take measures which allow us to limit the risks incurred by our forces," he said.[118]

Events that occurred after the enclave fell have been well documented by the ICTY and other international initiatives. It was on the basis of Karadžić's directive that the Drina Corps was ordered to conduct "active combat operations" around the enclave.[119] In July 1995, their takeover of the safe area began with the gradual capture of UN watch posts. ICTY documentation shows that the offensive began "in earnest" on July 6, and that several days later, the enclave fell to the Army of Republika Srpska. NATO briefly bombed the advancing tanks of the VRS on July 11, but further air strikes were halted due to a lack of authorization and threats by VRS forces that Dutch peacekeepers would be murdered if strikes were carried out. Video footage submitted to the court shows General Mladić proudly walking through Srebrenica saying: "Here we are on July 11th, 1995. On the eve of yet another great Serbian holiday, we present this city to the Serbian people as a gift. Finally, after the rebellion against the Dahijas, the time has come to take revenge on the Turks in this region."[120] That same day, up to 25,000 displaced persons were gathered at the headquarters of Dutchbat – short for Dutch Battalion, the nickname of UN forces in nearby Potočari – seeking protection from the UN against the unfolding chaos.

The following day, aided by Dutch peacekeeping forces, the VRS, led by Mladić, separated the men and boys from the women. ICTY witnesses reported that mass killings and rapes had already started. Over 25,000 women and children were

---

[117] Ibid.

[118] Robert Block, "UN Left 8,000 to Die in Bosnia; Confidential Document Reveals Plan to Abandon Srebrenica Six Weeks before Fall," *The Independent*, October 30, 1995.

[119] *Prosecutor v. Krstić*, 10.

[120] "Turks" was a derogatory reference to Bosniaks. Dahijas refers to the first Serb uprising in 1804 in the Ottoman Empire and subsequent slaughter of Serbian officers. "Transcript of Rule 61 Hearing Held on 3 July 1996," Witness Jean René Ruez, 537. *Prosecutor v. Radovan Karadžić and Ratko Mladić* (IT-95-18-R61; IT-95-5-R61).

bussed to Tuzla in extreme heat, without food or water; VRS forces stopped them along the way searching for so-called war criminals on the premise that they might have been overlooked during the separation. The males were rounded up and taken to several execution sites. Between 10,000 and 15,000 males (including many minors) tried to escape the enclave through the forest; of these, several thousand were intercepted at a number of points by the VRS and later transported to their death. Surviving males described the horrific conditions they endured during their escape, forced to step over the bodies of their fallen colleagues and relatives. Some did not make it to Bosnian government territory until weeks or months later.[121] By July 17, 1995, the largest massacre since World War II had occurred in Bosnia, with the complicity of the United Nations.[122]

Prosecution witnesses later told the ICTY that the Srebrenica massacre, while not only "an unspeakable human evil," defied all strategic and military logic. Richard Butler, military expert for the Prosecution, testified that:

... it is hard to envision a better bargaining chip in dealing with the political authorities of certainly the BiH government and of the International Community than having 10,000 to 15,000 Muslim men in the middle of Potočari in a legitimate prisoner of war facility under the control or under the supervision of certainly the UN troops that were there and the ICRC [International Committee of the Red Cross] at a point in time. This is the ultimate bargaining chip, to be able to get significant political leverage from people, one would think, and this chip was thrown away for another reason.[123]

ICTY investigator Jean René Ruez arrived in Tuzla on July 21, 1995.[124] Over the following years, he led the investigative team that systematically identified major crime sites and exhumed mass graves for the ICTY. This documentary effort would be crucial to establishing that genocide had been committed in and around the Srebrenica enclave. As a witness for the prosecution in the trial of Radislav Krstić, Ruez "listed all the locations in Srebrenica where the crimes were committed, from the UN base at Potočari where the first victims were shot, through Bratunac, the Sandići meadow, the Kravica village storehouse, the Glogovo district, the Konjevići intersection, Nova Kasaba, Čerska, the Jadar river, Lazete, the school and dam in Petkovći, on to the village of Pilića and a military pig farm in Branjevo."[125]

---

[121] The fall of the enclave has also been covered in several documentary films. See Maria Fuglevaag Warsinki, "Crimes and Punishment"; Federal Commission for Missing Persons, "Marš Smrta" (March of death); and BBC, "A Cry from the Grave."

[122] See Rohde, *Endgame*. See also Hasan Nuhanović, *Pod zastavom UN-a: međunarodna zajednica i zločin u Srebrenici* (Under the flag of the UN: International community and crime in Srebrenica) (Sarajevo: Preporod, 2005).

[123] *Prosecutor v. Krstić*, 21.

[124] "Krstić Stands Alone," Institute for War and Peace Reporting (IWPR), *Tribunal Update*, No. 168, March 13–18, 2000, <www.iwpr.net/?p=tri&s=f&o=166412&apc_state=hsritri2000> (accessed July 15, 2009).

[125] Ibid.

Discussion of the crimes began at the UN as early as August, but they occurred behind closed doors. U.S. Secretary of State Madeline Albright made the first allegations of mass executions in the area on August 10, 1995, when she displayed CIA spy satellite photos of the area of Novo Kasaba in a closed session of the UN Security Council. The "before" photos showed the prisoners lined up and huddled together in a field, while the "after" photos showed moved earth, evidence of mass graves, and no prisoners.[126] In that meeting Albright claimed that as many as 2,700 Bosniak males might have been executed. At the time, the UN said there were between 4,000 and 6,000 persons missing from the enclave.[127] A lack of effort to communicate these findings to the families of men and boys murdered, however, influenced future protest targets by the survivors and instilled in them a distrust of the motives of most international institutions.

The Srebrenica massacre, later ruled a genocide at the ICTY, is one of the most documented atrocities in modern history. The crimes were so horrific that it took time for the information to reach the rest of the world; many could not believe the extent of the killings. Additionally, many news organizations have thorough procedures in place, especially when dealing with controversial material, which can slow down the process by which news is distributed to the world. One Associated Press (AP) report drafted by a Bosnian reporter, for example, was stalled for weeks as AP editors (and also, the journalist would learn, lawyers) pored over the text of the article seeking to ensure accuracy.[128] This report would in all likelihood have been the first report of the events in Srebrenica, but it was not published until much later.

In August 1995, a correspondent for the Christian Science Monitor, David Rohde, was one of the first Western journalists to bring the story to the world stage. His reporting quashed any doubts that the war's worst atrocity had occurred after the fall of the eastern enclave.[129] Rohde was arrested by Bosnian Serb authorities after taking pictures of massacre sites in October 1995 and released only after high-level U.S. government intervention.[130] Around the same time, in the autumn of 1995, Bosnian Serb forces disrupted and moved gravesites in a coordinated effort to mask the crimes. Rohde later chronicled the tragedy in his book *Endgame,* which documented the cover-up and remains one of the most complete accounts of the events in Srebrenica.[131]

---

[126] David Rohde, "Evidence Indicates Bosnia Massacre," *The Christian Science Monitor,* August 18, 1995.

[127] Ibid.

[128] Correspondence with Aida Cerkez-Robinson, Associated Press bureau chief in Bosnia and Herzegovina, July 21, 2009. The article is Aida Cerkez, "Survivors tell of massacre following fall of Srebrenica. Only three escaped as 3,000 were systematically mowed down," *The Independent,* October 5, 1995.

[129] Rohde, "Evidence Indicates Bosnia Massacre."

[130] See Tom Gjelten, "Reviving Historical Hatred," *Washington Post,* July 6, 1997.

[131] Rohde, *Endgame.*

After the fall of the Srebrenica enclave in July 1995, Serb nationalists invited families of victims in Kravica and similar attacks to exact their revenge on captured Bosniak civilians.[132] It was common in postwar years in RS to hear that the Srebrenica massacre was justified retribution for the raids by the "torbari."

In the neighboring Federal Republic of Yugoslavia (FRY), just following the signing of the DPA, the former Foreign Minister of FRY and UN representative, Vladislav Jovanović, contended in a three-page letter to the UN Security Council that other Bosnian Muslims were in fact responsible for the killings in Srebrenica.[133] The letter would foreshadow a state-supported strategy of denial. It was this denial, not the presence of the ICTY, as many analysts argued, that would destabilize relations in the region for many years to come.

Many trials at the ICTY would later deal with crimes in the Srebrenica area, the most notable being the indictments against Slobodan Milošević, Radovan Karadžić, and Bosnian Serb General Ratko Mladić. By late 2009 the trial against Radislav Krstić yielded the court's only decision ruling that genocide had occurred in Bosnia.[134] Meanwhile, just after the VRS used heavy machinery to move the bodies of Srebrenica's victims, a peace agreement was being negotiated under U.S. auspices in Dayton, Ohio.

Ending the War: The Peace Agreement and the ICTY

The court was part of a patchwork of institutions created with the intent to establish peace and stability in Bosnia and worked within the context of the agreement that was drafted to end the war. The DPA, signed in December 1995, did little to provide a strong foundation for the ICTY's work, a fact that would hinder the court's efficacy throughout the first decade after the war. Dayton established a *sui generis* state comprising two entities: the Federation of Bosnia and Herzegovina, consisting largely of areas under Bosniak and Croat control, and Republika Srpska. The country's entities are highly autonomous and connected by a weak central administration. The agreement also outlined that the state of Bosnia and Herzegovina had legal continuity with the Republic of Bosnia and Herzegovina.[135]

---

[132] Robert Block, "Mass Slaughter in a Bosnian Field Knee-Deep in Blood," *The Independent*, July 21, 1995. This was one of the earliest press reports that mass atrocities had taken place.

[133] "Balkans: Serbs at UN Claim Muslims Committed Srebrenica Killings," *Ottawa Citizen*, December 20, 1995.

[134] First instance judgment: *Prosecutor v. Radislav Krstić* (IT-98-33-T), Judgement, ICTY, August 2, 2001, <www.icty.org/x/cases/krstic/tjug/en/krs-tj010802e.pdf> (accessed July 15, 2009). The appellate level judgment can be found here: *Prosecutor v. Radislav Krstić* (IT-98-33-A), Judgement, ICTY, April 19, 2004, <www.icty.org/x/cases/krstic/acjug/en/krs-aj040419e.pdf> (accessed July 15, 2009).

[135] See "Constitution of Bosnia and Herzegovina", Dayton Peace Agreement, Annex IV, article 1; <www.ohr.int/dpa/default.asp?content_id=380> (accessed July 19, 2009).

Technically, it was not one, but two peace agreements that ended the war in Bosnia, leading to its confusing political configuration: the Washington Agreement and Dayton. In 1994, the Washington Agreement had created the Federation of Bosnia and Herzegovina. Per Dayton, the Federation occupies 51 percent of the territory of Bosnia while RS occupies 49 percent; the state maintained the borders it had while a republic within the SFRY. Most notably for the work of the court, the entity structure left the security sector (military, police, and judicial system) in the hands of each entity, which, in the case of RS, stymied the ability to make arrests due to the intransigence of RS police forces. The entities were marked by what was referred to as the Inter-Entity Boundary Line (IEBL) in the immediate postwar years.

In addition to creating two entities in the country, Dayton established a tripartite (rotating) Presidency occupied in turn by an ethnic Serb, Croat, and Bosniak. Dayton included the provisions set out in the Washington Agreement and conferred the status of entity on RS. Republika Srpska was a continuation of the Republic of the Serb People of Bosnia and Herzegovina created in January 1992, which had never been recognized by any international body.[136] The name Republic of Serb People was changed to "Republika Srpska" in August 1992. In Dayton, the name of the state was changed from Republic of Bosnia and Herzegovina to simply Bosnia and Herzegovina.

Formally, the agreement contained little mention of wartime atrocities and the court. Where war crimes were mentioned at all, emphasis on cooperation with the ICTY was not matched with robust enforcement mechanisms. Annex Six of Dayton, dedicated to human rights, implores the Bosnian authorities to cooperate with the court.[137] Similarly, the Bosnian Constitution obligates the country to cooperate.[138] In what was at best an exercise in wishful thinking on the part of the negotiators, all parties to the agreement, including Croatia and the Federal Republic of Yugoslavia (FRY), were expected to comply on their own accord with not only the arrest and transfer of indictees, but also in allowing access to and the transfer of documentation vital to the Office of the Prosecutor.[139] In practice, this meant that trials were

---

[136] As a result, the structure of the country differs between the two entities. In the Federation, there are 10 cantons that have considerable authority over local developments. The RS lacks cantons and has a centralized system of government.

[137] The text reads: "All competent authorities in Bosnia and Herzegovina shall cooperate with and provide unrestricted access to the organizations established in this Agreement ... [including] the International Tribunal for the Former Yugoslavia." See The General Framework Agreement for Peace in Bosnia and Herzegovina, The Dayton Peace Agreement, 14 December 1995, Office of the High Representative and EU Special Representative, <www.ohr.int/dpa/default.asp?content_id=374> (accessed March 21, 2009).

[138] The Bosnian Constitution was incorporated as Annex IV of the peace agreement. The provision is contained in Article 2.

[139] Annex 1A, on Military Aspects of the Peace Settlement, states: "Notwithstanding the above provisions, each Party shall comply with any order or request of the International Tribunal

hostages of the political situation in the countries of the region, as politicians with-held self-incriminating information fearing (in many cases rightfully) that they would appear next on the docket.[140] The sole exception was the (primarily) Bosniak authorities of the Federation government, which complied with arrest warrants and handed over requested documentation. This condition improved slightly over the postwar period as the international community increased its abilities to force compliance and wield its powers of conditionality and, during elections, struck candidates for issues related to non-compliance.

In the early years, however, it seemed that continuity with wartime institutions would make cooperation impossible. Until the armed forces were formally unified, the military also posed a problem. RS government cooperation with the ICTY and, by extension, that of the VRS, was nonexistent in the immediate postwar period. This hindered other areas targeted for reform. In addition, VRS military intelli-gence frequently interfered with international community efforts, including spy-ing on NATO-led peacekeeping forces in defiance of the peace agreement. ICTY investigators also faced many breaches of their private communication while in the field.[141] RS political and military leaders, who feared arrests, accused ICTY offi-cials of utilizing arbitrary criteria for indictments and claimed that NATO forces were detaining people at their whim.

After the arrest of one general, Momir Talić (IT-99-36/1), detained by Austrian police while he was attending an OSCE-sponsored defense policy seminar in Vienna, RS Defense Minister, General Manojlo Milovanović, told a Belgrade-based paper: "The way in which Lt-Gen Momir Talić, chief of the General Staff of the [Bosnian] Serb Republic Army, was arrested shows that any Serb can be arrested upon the orders of the Hague Tribunal, regardless of whether he has been for-mally indicted or not."[142] The ICTY issued both sealed and unsealed indictments; Talić's indictment had been sealed and therefore was not public knowledge. When asked whether Talić's arrest could be part of a plan to unite the different forces, Milovanović told the press:

There is nothing official, no documents or anything else, that states that we should be creating a unified Bosnia-Herzegovina Army. That is perhaps just wishful thinking on the part of people in the Federation of Bosnia-Herzegovina. Even in the materials for

for the Former Yugoslavia for the arrest, detention, surrender of or access to persons who would otherwise be released and transferred under this Article, but who are accused of vio-lations within the jurisdiction of the Tribunal. Each Party must detain persons reasonably suspected of such violations for a period of time sufficient to permit appropriate consultation with Tribunal authorities."

[140] On state cooperation and the ad hoc tribunals, see Peskin, *International Justice*.

[141] Discussions with ICTY staff, May–June 2004.

[142] "Bosnian Serb officers fearful after arrest of war crimes suspect," *BBC Summary of World Broadcasts*, September 1, 1999, Justice Watch Listserv, <listserv.buffalo.edu/ archives/just-watch-l.html (accessed March 22, 2009), (original Source: *Večernje Novosti*, Belgrade, August 29,1999, 2).

the meeting in Vienna which was never held, under item one it said that there was no need to pursue any theories about a unified, single army, joint exercises, a joint command ... [newspaper's ellipsis] The international community has apparently decided to respect the Dayton agreement, but for how long, that is the question.[143]

This attitude changed over the years, as it became clear that unification of the armed forces was necessary for Bosnia to integrate into European institutions and join NATO's Partnership for Peace (PfP), and eventually NATO.

As war crimes were not a primary focus of either the peace agreement or postwar development plans, the international community appeared indifferent to the arrest of war criminals and the presence of perpetrators in Bosnia. Consequently, many Bosnians were cynical about its real commitment to punish those responsible for atrocities. In addition, the ICTY's inability to control the flow of indicted persons to The Hague was one of its main obstacles, not only in its day-to-day work, but also in its efforts to change attitudes about the court. Confusion about whose responsibility it was to ensure that indicted persons reached The Hague affected the institution's credibility. Many Bosnians doubted that such a well-funded and powerful foreign presence could fail to know the location of persons sought by the court.

Criticism of the DPA has been frequent and wide reaching.[144] The unwieldy structure created by the agreement is often considered responsible for the slow pace of Bosnia's transition, chiefly because it created a state with more layers of government than a country of four million inhabitants could reasonably support. Second, the DPA also left wartime political parties in power, allowing influential individuals to go unpunished for their wartime actions. In addition, it is criticized for its application of an ethnic key "whereby all positions from the top down were carefully allocated across ethnicites"[145] to all facets of political life, coloring the international community's approach to every aspect of Bosnian society. Donors to postwar projects and programs in Bosnia often showed preference to those organizations that accounted for members of all ethnic groups in their proposals. Such an insistence on ethnic parity inhibited the creation of a national Bosnian identity, forcing quotas that raised the importance of ethnicity above community needs, and ignoring the reality that ethno-religious identity was not always the most critical issue.

Other Dayton critics argued that, by giving 49 percent of Bosnia's territory to Republika Srpska, the agreement awarded the architects of genocide a territory won through consistent and strategic violations of international law. Ten years after the war, it was common to hear many Bosnians ruefully admit that the

---

[143] Ibid.
[144] See, for example, Nerzuk Ćurak, *Dejtonski nacionalizam* (Dayton's nationalism) (Sarajevo: Buy Book, 2004).
[145] Gagnon, *Myth of Ethnic War*, 73. Gagnon is referring to the use of an ethnic key in the SFRY, however.

"genocide worked." Slovenian philosopher Slavoj Žižek captured the contradiction of the postwar situation after RS leader Radovan Karadžić was transferred to The Hague in 2008: "The true tragedy is that Karadžić basically succeeded" in obtaining a territory free of any non-Serbs. "This is the hypocrisy. You condemn the guy, but the project succeeded."[146] In short, there were vectors of influence emanating from Dayton in the postwar period and not all of them supported the liberal democratic values that the international community purported to uphold. The ICTY's efforts to redress the wartime violence were but one current in the mix. Still, many grudgingly acknowledged that even an unjust peace was better than continued bloodshed.[147]

Postwar Peacekeeping

The peacekeepers on the ground had, at best, an ambiguous relationship with the ICTY, which desired to have NATO forces capture indicted persons. The DPA placed a 60,000-strong peacekeeping mission on the ground, under the aegis of NATO. Troop numbers in Bosnia decreased steadily over the postwar years and, in December 2004, the European Union (EU) took over the whole operation with its first-ever peacekeeping mission of 7,000 soldiers. By 2009, that number had been reduced to 2,500 soldiers. Technically, NATO forces were not obligated to apprehend or arrest war criminals if they came across them in the course of their peacekeeping duties, but in practice they conducted a number of such operations.[148] NATO commanders and Pentagon officials were opposed to expanding the mandate of troops on the ground to include specific obligations vis-à-vis war criminals, in large part because of fears about expected casualties and a resulting loss of support for the peace operation among taxpayers at home. Soldiers on the

---

[146] See "Euronews Talks with Slavoj Žižek" (interview during the 2008 Sarajevo Film Festival), September 13, 2008, <www.youtube.com/watch?v=EzM8tqjmCU8 (accessed July 21, 2009).

[147] In reality, the DPA did not differ much from earlier proposals to end the war. The first proposal, the Vance Owen Peace Plan (VOPP), divided Bosnia into 10 semi-autonomous provinces, splitting control among each of the three ethnic groups. Created by Cyrus R. Vance, former U.S. Secretary of State under President Jimmy Carter, and Lord David Owen (a career politician in the United Kingdom), the plan exacerbated tensions between Bosnian Croat forces (HVO) and the ARBiH, as the Croat forces tried to unilaterally implement the agreement in three provinces. The next agreement put on the table, the Owen Stoltenberg Peace Plan, proposed carving up Bosnia into three mini-statelets, one each dominated by Bosniaks, Croats or Serbs. Some analysts argued that while politicians continued to quibble over similar proposals, each dividing Bosnia along ethnic lines, the number of casualties increased. See Peter Maass, "Warfare, Genocide Reemerge in Face of Bosnian Peace Plan," *Washington Post*, February 9, 1992, 2; and Hoare, *How Bosnia Armed*, 85–86. Croat and Bosniak representatives signed the VOPP, but the Serbs refused. (There were two other peace plans in addition to these.)

[148] Annex 1A: "authorize[d] the IFOR [Implementation Force] to take such actions as required, including the use of necessary force, to ensure compliance with this Annex, and to ensure its own protection." There was no explicit mention of the apprehension, arrest, or transfer of indictees.

ground, all over the country, would say that they were discouraged from inquiring about operations to search for war criminals, known in international community jargon as PIFWCs (Persons Indicted for War Crimes).[149] There were also open struggles between the chief prosecutor of the ICTY and NATO representatives on the ground, with the prosecutor often scolding NATO officials for failing to make arrests. When European Union troops took over the task of maintaining a safe and secure environment in Bosnia, the leading advisory role for the arrest of war criminals remained with the NATO HQ in Sarajevo, but the primary responsibility for arrests still fell to local authorities. The relationship between NATO and the ICTY varied over the course of the postwar period, often depending upon the rapport between military commanders and the ICTY's chief prosecutor. Still, both local and international news reports were filled with stories of searches and sweeps conducted in the houses of family members of the indicted, usually to no avail. These extensive operations seemed to many merely *pro forma*, meant to appear as if an effort was being made in the absence of any real international political will to do so.

Other International Institutions

Other international organizations present in Bosnia dealt with the issue of war crimes tangentially, trying to insure that indicted persons did not run for office and unseating obstructionist politicians for non-compliance with the peace agreement, which included non-compliance with the court. The early strategy of avoidance by the international community proved to be an impossible course to sustain. Perpetrators often personified the proverbial elephant in the room, and internationals eventually gave themselves new powers to vet institutions, close bank accounts, and the like, to solve issues arising from non-cooperation with the ICTY. There could be no real political progress while skirting the issue of accountability. They realized that lack of attention to the country's violent past was inhibiting its goals for democratic development. The authority to deal with difficult questions regarding crimes committed during the war was added incrementally by international forces over the postwar period as recognition grew that international intervention could not remain toothless. This realization was in part aided by the ICTY, which, even with the imperfect mechanism of individual criminal liability, uncovered the extent of the criminality committed primarily by the wartime VRS forces and their counterparts in Serbia. The court's documentation made it abundantly clear that the effort of many in the international community to imply a moral equivalency between the parties to the Bosnian war was a fiction that would prevent them from reaching their long-term goals. This

---

[149] Conversation with U.S. soldier, Brčko, May 9, 2004. This was only one of many similar conversations held with U.S. peacekeepers.

ill-founded notion of moral equivalency was even reflected in the indictments that came down from The Hague, especially under the leadership of Chief Prosecutor Carla del Ponte. Nevertheless, the judgments of the court, with few exceptions, showed this to be a flawed prosecutorial strategy as well.

In addition, the DPA meant that many foreign donors threw their support behind people with wartime pasts connected to mass atrocities, in part because they were considered more "moderate." To cite but one example, the election of RS President Biljana Plavšić in 1997 was welcomed by many foreign donors. U.S. Secretary of State Madeleine Albright signaled clear support for her in a visit the following year.[150] Plavšić would later be charged with numerous violations of international humanitarian law and genocide (IT-00-39 and IT-00-40/1). In a plea agreement with the court, the charge of genocide was dropped.[151] She was later sentenced to 11 years in prison. She also issued an apology for her crimes, which was negotiated as part of the agreement – a gesture that initially received much attention and offered hope that it, and other such apologies, would have a beneficial impact on relations in the region.[152] However, the gesture was made insincerely, for the sake of her plea agreement, and she later recanted. In a memoir written from her Swedish prison cell, she continued to espouse the intolerant and nationalist views that she promoted during the war.[153] Other members of the Bosnian Serb political leadership would find themselves in The Hague, too, including a former Serb member of the rotating Bosnian Presidency, the wartime right-hand man of Karadžić, Momčilo Krajišnik (IT-00-39).

The DPA had given the then-nascent Organization for Security and Cooperation in Europe (OSCE) the task of running postwar elections, a job the OSCE handed over to Bosnian authorities in 2002.[154] Responsibility for coordinating the implementation of civilian aspects of the agreement was delegated to a unique institution called the Office of the High Representative (OHR). A High Representative was appointed by the steering board of the Peace Implementation Council (PIC), which

---

[150] "Albright Urges Refugee Return," *BBC News*, August 31, 1998, <news.bbc.co.uk/2/hi/europe/161970.stm> (accessed July 10, 2009).

[151] See *Prosecutor v. Momčilo Krajinik* (sic), Biljana Plavšić, Plea Agreement, ICTY, September 30, 2002, <www.icty.org/x/cases/plavsic/custom4/en/020930plea_en.pdf> (accessed July 10, 2009).

[152] See, for example, Alex Boraine and Paul van Zyl, "Moving On Requires Looking Back," *International Herald Tribune*, August 1, 2003, <www.ictj.org/en/news/coverage/article/425.html> (accessed July 10, 2009). The authors optimistically argued that, "By accepting punishment and expressing remorse, Plavšić has opened the door to real reconciliation in the region."

[153] See Biljana Plavšić, *Svedočim – knjiga pisana u zatvoru* (I testify – A book written in prison) (Banja Luka: Trioprint, 2005); and Edina Bećirević, "Bosnian Court Should Try Plavšić: Regional War Crimes Prosecutors Must Learn from Hague Tribunal's Mistakes," Institute of War and Peace Reporting (IWPR), *Tribunal Update*, no. 560, July 18, 2008.

[154] See Kimberley Coles, *Democratic Designs: International Intervention and Electoral Practices in Postwar Bosnia-Herzegovina* (Ann Arbor, MI: University of Michigan Press, 2007).

is made up of 55 countries and organizations that direct peace implementation in Bosnia. The UN Security Council then endorses the PIC's nomination for High Representative.

Postwar Bosnia is not a protectorate in the classic sense, but the PIC increased the High Representative's powers during successive Council meetings, when obstructionism became an obstacle to keeping peace. Most notably, the December 1997 PIC meeting in Bonn gave the High Representative the ability to remove officials from office and to implement legislation; these were known locally as the "Bonn powers." In other words, politicians who did not cooperate with the ICTY, among other things, could lose their jobs.

The DPA made no mention of whether indicted individuals could hold public office. The international community had to monitor the presence of suspected persons on the electoral rolls and create incentives for specific individuals to leave office or give up important posts. The first major figure to be targeted was Radovan Karadžić, former RS President, who was pressured in 1996 to resign from the position he had held since 1990 as leader of the Serb Democratic Party (SDS). The ICTY first indicted him in 1995. His public appearances and even any re-airing of his wartime speeches were banned. In exchange, the OSCE allowed his party, SDS, to participate in the first postwar general elections in 1996. This targeted approach was buoyed in a decision by the Provisional Election Commission (PEC) (Article 46), which banned ICTY indictees from running for office.[155] The OSCE's ambassador at the time, Robert Frowick, represented the international community's line: "Any political parties who keep indicted war criminals in office shall be ineligible to participate" in the elections. In the run-up to elections, Local Elections Committees (LEC), charged with organizing the vote at the local level, vetted candidates' names with the ICTY.[156] Analysts have long since argued that these elections were held far too soon after the war's end.[157]

Still, even if some perpetrators were out of public life, they were not necessarily out of political life altogether. From behind the scenes, these figures continued to direct politics, influence policy, and build financial empires through their administration of illicit businesses – most of which were started during the war by controlling arms supplies, food distribution, and human trafficking. The High Representative attempted to crack down on the financial networks of individuals

---

[155] See Provisional Election Commission Decisions, Organization for Security and Cooperation in Europe Mission to Bosnia and Herzegovina, July 16, 1996. Copy on file with the author.

[156] The ban did not include those who had served their time; although he lost the race, one of the individuals the court found guilty, Simo Zarić, later ran for the municipal assembly after serving his sentence.

[157] For an early call to postpone elections, see "Why the Bosnian Elections Must Be Postponed," August 14, 1996, *Europe Report*, No. 14, International Crisis Group, <www.crisisgroup.org/home/index.cfm?id=1504&l=1> (accessed March 21, 2009).

thought to be supporting fugitives from law.[158] Nonetheless, the administrative ban on indictees still produced some embarrassing moments for the international community. During the 1996 elections, for example, the OSCE was found to be financing the party of paramilitary leader Željko Ražnatović (who would be an ICTY indictee only the following year). His party was still considered the "opposition" and the international community had offered it support in an attempt to weaken the influence of nationalist parties that were blamed for igniting the war.[159]

The international community implemented various vetting efforts in the postwar years, somewhat resembling similar initiatives which had been implemented all over Eastern Europe. Many individuals were removed from their jobs for their wartime behavior. Some who obstructed the implementation of the DPA were also subjected to the High Representative's use of the "Bonn powers." The first notable removal was of RS Prime Minister Nikola Poplašen in March 1999.[160] The OHR removed approximately 200 officials from public office in total, including 75 under High Representative Paddy Ashdown.[161] Under the auspices of the UN Mission in Bosnia and Herzegovina (UNMIBH), police officers underwent a recertification process that included a vetting through the ICTY's database.[162] Lastly, after parliament passed a criminal code in 2003, an independent commission vetted all judges and prosecutors in the country through a reappointment process that ended in April 2004. In other sectors, though, little was done in this vein. In the military, for instance, only those holding the rank of general had their wartime backgrounds checked. Ultimately, the numbers of individuals targeted by international prosecutions and international community-sponsored vetting paled in comparison with other countries in Eastern Europe, where domestically-initiated lustration programs to vet former secret police and Communist Party members affected tens of thousands of people.

The international community acquired considerable means to address the presence of perpetrators of mass atrocities in postwar Bosnia, but the sheer number of war criminals, along with lack of attention to the issue inside Bosnia, meant that many slipped through the cracks. Dayton left the wartime political class relatively

---

[158] For but one of the relevant headlines, see "Auditor Says Embezzlement Investigation Implicates Leaders of Ruling Bosnian Serb Party," *Associated Press*, September 20, 2005.

[159] There were also anecdotal accounts of the task faced by international forces trying to implement peace. Many international workers tell the story of the OSCE voter registration field worker who unknowingly registered fugitive Radovan Karadžić for the upcoming elections, a tragic example of how many people literally did not know with whom they were dealing.

[160] "Removal from Office of Nikola Poplašen," Office of High Representative, Sarajevo, Press Release, May 3, 1999, <www.ohr.int/ohr-dept/presso/pressr/default.asp?content_id=4706>, accessed March 24, 2009).

[161] Conversation with an advisor at the Political Department of the Office of the High Representative, September 21, 2005. Others at the OHR say that an exact number is not known due to the lack of an internal record.

[162] Decertified police officers later protested their decisions but found little redress, as the UN Mission had closed. Several officers committed suicide. The ban on reapplication to their

untouched and the international community was not eager to explore the wartime records of those in power.

Occasionally, a study or white paper would illustrate the consequences of having constructed a peace agreement with the architects of genocide in Bosnia. One of the first of these was the International Crisis Group's report, "War Criminals in Bosnia's Republika Srpska: Who are the People in Your Neighborhood?," published on November 2, 2000, as international monitors fanned out across the country to observe the nation's second general elections.[163] The report named individuals in 18 municipalities in Republika Srpska who were alleged to have committed war crimes or to have supervised people who did. Many of those listed still enjoyed positions of influence in their communities. The report noted that the OSCE had certified many of the election results that kept these criminals in power. In 2004, another study claimed that as many as one out of every 389 persons in Bosnia could be indicted for violations of international humanitarian law, although this was later judged an overestimate.[164] In 2005, the Srebrenica Commission, set up by the RS government, claimed that over 25,000 individuals were involved in the Srebrenica massacre, many of whom were still employed by that same government. Carrying out mass atrocities requires organization and material resources, which generally only belong to states or state-like institutions. Many initial estimates were overly high, but this does not diminish the fact that the presence of criminal elements in public life affected the pace of the transition and made the ICTY's work difficult.

Refugee Return

The extent of the forcible displacement of Bosnian citizens outlined in ICTY documents was one of the international community's largest postwar challenges. Over two million Bosnian citizens were displaced between 1992 and 1995. Forced expulsion left the country essentially separated along ethnic lines. Large numbers of international institutions in Bosnia were employed to work on the issues of return and reconstruction of homes. They sought to "remix" the ethnic map with "minority" returns. Dayton guaranteed displaced persons and refugees the right to return to their pre-war residences and reclaim their pre-war property.

International attention to the return of refugees and internally displaced persons in Bosnia represented the longest sustained effort on the issue in any postwar

posts was finally lifted in 2007. See Nidžara Ahmetašević, "Sacked Police Hope for Justice at Last in Bosnia," Balkan Investigative Reporting Network (BIRN), *Justice Report*, May 9, 2007.

[163] "War Criminals in Bosnia's Republika Srpska: Who are the People in Your Neighborhood?" International Crisis Group, *Europe Report*, No. 103, November 2, 2000, <www.crisisgroup. org/home/index.cfm?l=1&id=1518> (accessed March 21, 2009).

[164] Robert M. Beecroft, "Comment: Parting Thoughts on Bosnia's Paralysis," IWPR, *Balkan Crisis Report*, No. 506, July 8, 2004, <iwpr.gn.apc.org/?p=bcr&s=f&o=156504&apc_ state=henibcr2004> (accessed March 21, 2009).

state, representing another form of international intervention in the country.[165] As of December 2008, there were just over one million returnees, including both those from within Bosnia and those from abroad.[166] Just under half of all returnees moved back to their pre-war residence. International officials claimed these statistics to be evidence of success, although in practice returns were difficult to count. Many who registered in their pre-war municipalities chose to live elsewhere, where the political climate and job opportunities were more favorable to them.[167] Distribution of pensions, administration of health care, and access to education all affected decisions not to return permanently. Many individuals reclaimed and maintained their property, but were reluctant to resume residence on a permanent basis.

Many returnees stated that prosecution of war criminals did positively influence their attitudes about return, even if the ICTY processed only a small fraction of the perpetrators. Still, the obstacles to return were overwhelming. In Republika Srpska, only an estimated 5 percent of the population was comprised of so-called "minority" returns. For many, the selectivity of prosecutions meant that, upon returning, they found themselves living literally next door to the same people who raped, murdered, and forcibly expelled their family members from their homes. According to ICTY judgments, the VRS had expelled Bosniak and Croat populations in almost every major city in Republika Srpska.[168]

Over time, interest and funding by international donors waned. It was not uncommon to hear of widows who were given no more than bags of cement with which to rebuild their homes. After donor agencies working on reconstruction left the country, a few motivated returnees learned to mix concrete and rebuild, but the system did not help everyone who lost a home. Many were left to figure out how to rebuild on their own.

---

[165] See Elazar Barkan and Howard Adelman, "Rites of Return," unpublished manuscript. This manuscript places the Bosnian experience in context with other global efforts to return refugees and displaced persons.

[166] Statistics Package, December 31, 2008, United Nations High Commissioner for Refugees, <www.unhcr.ba/updatedec08/SP_12_2008.pdf> (accessed July 20, 2009). Following the definitions set out in international treaties on this topic, the term *refugee* is used to refer to displaced persons outside of the territory of Bosnia-Herzegovina, while the term *internally displaced person* (IDP) refers to those displaced within the country.

[167] See for example: "The Continuing Challenge of Refugee Return," International Crisis Group, *Europe Report*, No. 137, December 13, 2002, <www.crisisgroup.org/home/index. cfm?id=1473&I=1> (accessed March 22, 2009). The term municipality may be confusing for some. It is a direct translation of the term opština, the fundamental unit of local government in the former Yugoslavia. An opština often contained a town or city of the same name and the surrounding villages.

[168] To name only one: the indictment of Radovan Karadžić charges him for persecutions in the municipalities of Banja Luka, Bijeljina, Bosanska Krupa, Bosanski Novi, Bosanski Petrovac, Bratunac, Brčko, Čajnice, Donji Vakuf, Foča, Hadžići, Ilidža, Ilijaš, Kalinovik, Ključ, Kotor Varoš, Novi Grad, Novo Sarajevo, Pale, Prijedor, Rogatica, Sanski Most, Sokolac, Višegrad, Vlasenica, Vogošća, Zvornik, and Srebrenica. See *Prosecutor v. Radovan Karadžić* (IT-95-5/18-PT), Third Amended Indictment, February 29, 2007, Count 3, "Persecutions."

The Court and the Crime Base

Thousands of miles away in The Hague, against this difficult backdrop, the International Tribunal for the Prosecution of Persons Responsible for Serious Violations of International Humanitarian Law Committed in the Territory of the former Yugoslavia since 1991, the ICTY, indicted 161 persons. As of November 2009, it had concluded proceedings against 120 of them in 85 cases.[169] With only two of the indictees still at large in 2009 – Gordon Hadžić and Ratko Mladić – the court has almost succeeded in finishing the task set out for it in 1993.

The environment the court faced in Bosnia was formidable, but the signals it broadcast to the region did not help to form a clear narrative of the wars of succession or of its prosecutorial strategy. While there was never real resolution about these big-picture questions at the ICTY, the court's findings spoke for themselves in answering overarching questions about the war. The documentation created by the ICTY was sometimes at odds with the decisions of the various chief prosecutors of the court, especially the longest serving one, Carla del Ponte, who seemed to follow a prosecutorial strategy that leaders of all ethnicities should be indicted in equal proportions, even though the crimes in the region were not committed by all in equal proportions. In her memoir, commenting on violations of international humanitarian law committed in Kosovo, she argued, "A war crimes tribunal that tries the accused from only one side of a given conflict is dispensing only a victor's justice. This alone cannot help end the culture of impunity."[170] While it is true that accountability of only one ethnicity would not contribute to the court's extended mandate, the theory of moral equivalency in prosecution strategy also kept some myths about the wars of succession alive. What seemed like ethnic parity in indictments to some, and imbalance to others, fueled confusion about war crimes in Bosnia.

This also resulted from the fact that the court's contact started late with its constituents in the region, the ones who were to be directly affected by its extra-legal goals. The ICTY, which uses French and English as its working languages, initially did not have a strategy to address citizens in the countries of the former Yugoslavia, nor were its indictments or judgments issued in the languages

[169] Updated figures can be found online at: <www.icty.org/sections/TheCases/KeyFigures> (accessed November 1, 2009). The court is divided into the Registry, its administrative arm; the Office of the Prosecutor, responsible for drafting indictments and conducting investigations; and the Chambers, where judges decide on problems of procedure and evidence. ICTY judges serve a four-year term. UN-contributing nations send experts from around the world to staff the court, located in a building formerly occupied by an insurance conglomerate. The courts budget, which was just $276,000 in 1993, grew to $342,332,300 in 2008–09. For breakdown by year, see <www.icty.org/sid/325> (accessed July 21, 2009).

[170] Carla del Ponte, with Chuck Sudetic, *Madame Prosecutor: Confrontations With Humanity's Worst Criminals and the Culture of Impunity* (New York: Other Press, 2009); in Italian published as Carla del Ponte (con Chuck Sudetic), *La caccia: Io e i criminali di guerra* (The Hunt: The war criminals and I) (Milan, Italy: Feltrinelli, 2008).

of the region. Outreach started only in 1999, six years after the founding of the institution and with inadequate sources of funding; even so, it managed to make much progress in bringing the court closer to Bosnians. The local outreach office in the country explained the purpose, findings, and limitations of its work, notably through events which started in 2004 called, "Bridging the Gap Between the ICTY and Communities in Bosnia and Herzegovina." In addition, more media coverage enabled greater public awareness. The success of outreach was largely due to the commitment of a handful of individuals in the field who juggled many demanding tasks in coordination with their office in The Hague.

The court's biggest challenge, however, was its inability to control the transfer of indictees to The Hague. The court claimed to look only for those who had committed the most serious violations of international humanitarian law, but in practice the lack of enforcement powers meant that the trials of perpetrators of lesser crimes were earliest on the docket. The first trial was of Duško Tadić (IT-94-1), a café owner in Prijedor before the war who was a relatively low-level perpetrator. He was charged with attacks in the Kozarac area and the torture and murder of civilians held prisoner in camps in the Prijedor area, particularly in the Omarska camp, in which Bosniak civilians from the area were detained. This camp was the site of some of the war's most unspeakable crimes.[171] Significant numbers of mass rapes also occurred in the camps.[172] While the most common label of Tadić was that he was a "little fish," the trial chamber outlined his substantial participation in the political project espoused by the Serb Democratic Party (SDS), and his blatantly intolerant views.[173] The crimes committed in Bosnia could not have occurred without the willing participation of other individuals like Dusko Tadić around the country. In the Prijedor area, the trial of Milomir Stakić (IT-97-24) revealed the accused's role in the establishment of the camps of Omarska, Keraterm, and Trnopolje. The trial of Radoslav Brđanin (IT-99-36) also dealt with crimes that took place in that region.

Prijedor captured the attention of the international public prior to that of ICTY's prosecutors. The first major revelation that the war was being conducted primarily against Bosniak civilians followed the publication of pictures of emaciated Bosniak men and boys detained in the Omarska camp in August 1992, conjuring up memories of World War II. Their publication was the result of the work of investigative reporters Roy Gutman and Ed Vulliamy.[174] These images led to the first public outcries against inaction in the region. The power of these photographs

---

[171] See *Prosecutor v. Dusko Tadić a/k/a "Dule"*, Opinion and Judgement, ICTY, May 7, 1997. His trial was also significant for the court as it addressed many jurisdictional issues.

[172] See the documentary film "Calling the Ghosts: A Story about Rape, War and Women," directed by Mandy Jacobsen and Karmen Jelinčić (New York: Bowery Productions, 1996).

[173] See *Prosecutor v. Tadić*, Judgement.

[174] See Roy Gutman, *A Witness to Genocide: First Inside Account of the Horrors of Ethnic Cleansing in Bosnia* (Rockport, MA: Element Books, 1993); Ed Vulliamy, *Seasons in Hell: Slaughter and Betrayal in Bosnia* (New York: Simon and Schuster, 1994).

was crucial. Extensive reports published before August 1992, by organizations such as the International Committee of the Red Cross (ICRC), had not elicited as much response. Tadeusz Mazowiecki, United Nations Special Rapporteur, also drafted a report on the situation in the region, which helped raise awareness in Europe and among those in power on both sides of the Atlantic.[175]

Wartime Deaths in Bosnia

Most of the ICTY's attention was devoted to the crimes that took place in Bosnia. As the site of the largest number of wartime deaths, it also experienced the largest number of violations of international humanitarian law, in addition to genocide. The scale of the crimes in Bosnia is evident on the court's recently redesigned web site, which lists crime scenes in the region accompanied by an interactive guide. Fifty-five crime scenes are listed in Bosnia, twice as many as in any other country in the region; there are 18 crimes scenes in Croatia, 16 in Kosovo, 1 in Serbia.[176]

In addition, today there is a record of almost every single individual who perished in the Bosnian war. Recent research has documented the total number of direct casualties of the war. The demographic breakdown of wartime human losses provides much clarity. From the early days of the fighting, international media reports had cited figures of 200,000 to 250,000 dead, numbers based on early and inflated Bosnian government estimates.[177] This figure turned out to be incorrect. In 2003, the State Commission for Gathering Facts on War Crimes (a governmental body which became the non-governmental Research and Documentation Center (RDC) in 2004), set out to gather information from newspapers, government and military records, international sources, witness statements, and other archives. Its project, "Human Losses in Bosnia and Herzegovina 1991–95," also known as the "Bosnian Book of the Dead," documents each individual lost.[178] As of late 2009, the

---

[175] See the Report on the situation of human rights in the territory of the former Yugoslavia, submitted by Tadeusz Mazowiecki, Special Rapporteur of the Commission on Human Rights, pursuant to paragraph 14 of Commission resolution 1992/S-1/1 of August 14, 1992, August 28, 1992 (E/CN.4/1992/S-1/9).

[176] See the interactive map available online at: <www.icty.org> (accessed July 20, 2009).

[177] See Bakir Hadžiomerović, "Pet Minuta" (Five minutes), *Start*, no. 223, June 26, 2007.

[178] See the Research and Documentation Center's Web site outlining the project: "Human Losses in Bosnia and Herzegovina 1991–95" (hereafter "Human Losses 1991–1995"), Research and Documentation Center, Sarajevo, <www.idc.org.ba> (accessed July 20, 2009). For a detailed analysis of the project and local reactions see Lara J. Nettelfield, "Research and Repercussions of Death Tolls: The Case of the Bosnian Book of the Dead," in Peter Andreas and Kelly M. Greenhill, eds., *Sex, Drugs and Body Counts: The Politics of Numbers in Global Crime and Conflict* (Ithaca, NY: Cornell University Press, 2010). For a study with similar findings conducted by ICTY demographers, see Ewa Tabeau and Jacub Bijak, "War-Related Deaths in the 1992–1995 Armed Conflicts in Bosnia and Herzegovina: A Critique of Previous Estimates and Recent Results," *European Journal of Population/Revue Européenne de Démographie*, 21, nos. 2–3 (June 2005), 187–215.

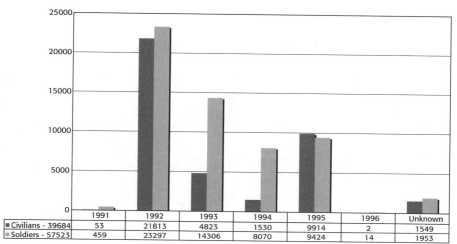

	1991	1992	1993	1994	1995	1996	Unknown
■ Civilians - 39684	53	21813	4823	1530	9914	2	1549
■ Soldiers - 57523	459	23297	14306	8070	9424	14	1953

Figure 3.1. Killed and missing persons in Bosnia and Herzegovina by status and year. *Source*: Research and Documentation Center, Sarajevo, 2007.

Center's database had records of just over 97,000 victims of the war, most linked to prewar identification card numbers *(lične karte)* and the Bosnian equivalent of U.S. Social Security numbers *(matični brojevi)*.

The Norwegian government financed a similar endeavor at the Demography Department in the Office of the Prosecutor at the ICTY. Presenting its work at a conference of experts in 2003, the ICTY research team revealed that their estimate was approximately 102,000 deaths.[179] While these figures are not final, and the RDC project will remain open for additional sources and names, experts expect that the total is unlikely to exceed 105,000.[180] While the number of deaths was considerably lower than the Bosnian government's estimates (see Figures 3.1 and 3.2), the demographic breakdown of those losses confirm the horror of what was primarily a Serbian strategy of war crimes in which the overwhelming majority of civilian victims, 83 percent, were Bosniaks.[181]

---

[179] Tabeau and Bijak, "War-Related Deaths in the 1992–1995 Armed Conflicts in Bosnia and Herzegovina; Kjell Arild Nilsen, "The number of people killed in the war in Bosnia-Herzegovina was around 102,000 ...," *NTB (Norwegian News Agency)* November 14, 2004, <www.freerepublic.com/focus/f-news/1291965/posts> (accessed March 19, 2009).

[180] For an assessment of the RDC database, see Patrick Ball, Ewa Tabeau and Philip Verwimp, "The Bosnian Book of Dead: Assessment of the Database," *HiCN Research Design Note* 5, June 17, 2007, <www.hicn.org/research_design/rdn5.pdf>.

[181] Military losses comprised slightly more than half of all deaths. However, these numbers should be treated with caution: a considerable number of people, for financial reasons, declared their family members military victims of the war.

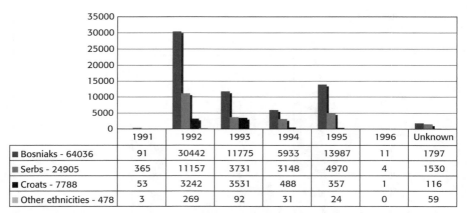

	1991	1992	1993	1994	1995	1996	Unknown
■ Bosniaks - 64036	91	30442	11775	5933	13987	11	1797
■ Serbs - 24905	365	11157	3731	3148	4970	4	1530
■ Croats - 7788	53	3242	3531	488	357	1	116
■ Other ethnicities - 478	3	269	92	31	24	0	59

Figure 3.2. Killed and missing persons in Bosnia and Herzegovina by ethnicity and year. *Source*: Research and Documentation Center, Sarajevo, 2007.

Conclusion

In postwar Bosnia, the thorny subject of the war was relegated initially to The Hague. This implicit division of labor among international forces became untenable when those in Sarajevo realized this unspoken policy was hindering long-term goals: the presence of war criminals in Bosnia stifled plans to integrate the country and the whole region, into Euro-Atlantic structures. The presence of perpetrators in Bosnian society, and especially in its public life, led to decreased trust in the government and in the country's emerging institutions. It also slowed returns of refugees and displaced persons, as many feared for the security of their prewar residences amid this culture of impunity. The Dayton structure reflected the compromises that had been made by the international forces who were eager to establish some kind of peace in Bosnia. Later, changes in international strategy to address war crimes more directly occurred in parallel with the court's effort to educate citizens in the region. New policies vindicated many local and international human rights groups, but the court, which one scholar described as "built to flounder," still struggled to project international norms of accountability in Bosnia.[182] Despite the odds, however, as the following case studies illustrate, the ICTY made progress toward realizing its extended mandate, and had other positive effects in a challenging environment.

---

[182] Bass, *Hand of Vengeance*, 207.

4 Expanding the Norm of Accountability

Srebrenica's Survivors, Collective Action,
and the ICTY

In June 2007, the survivors of the Srebrenica massacre of July 1995 started formal legal proceedings in a Hague-based court against the United Nations (UN) and the government of the Netherlands. They sought reparations for the fall of the UN enclave in which over 8,000 Bosniak men and boys perished at the hands of Bosnian Serb and Serbian aggressors. Some 200 women, experienced in the art of public protest, marched to the Dutch Prime Minister's office to deliver the legal documents related to their case.[1] Munira Subašić, president of the Mothers of the Enclaves of Srebrenica and Žepa, an association of the families of missing persons, told the press, "I have waited for 12 years for this, this could be another injustice if it is going to take a long time again."[2] The survivors' trip to The Hague was the result of years of grassroots organizing and what some scholars refer to as *legal mobilization* to seek redress for the surviving victims.[3] The significance of their case was to be found in the claims of both the plaintiffs and the defendants. An international institution and a troop-contributing state to a peacekeeping mission would have to answer to the victims of genocide in a court of law. This group of women, enabled by a group of lawyers, had expanded the norm of accountability

---

[1] "Srebrenica Families Sue Dutch State, U.N.," *Reuters*, June 4, 2007; Aldijana Omeragić, "Srebreničanke jučer u Hagu predale tužbu: Holandija spriječila zračnu podršku trupama UN!" (Srebrenica women submitted their lawsuit in The Hague yesterday: Holland prevented air support for UN troops), *Oslobođenje*, June 5, 2007.

[2] "Srebrenica Families Sue Dutch State, U.N."

[3] Frances Kahn Zemans emphasizes the role of legal mobilization as a form of political participation. "The legal system, limited as it is to real cases or controversies involving directly injured or interested parties, provides a uniquely democratic ... mechanism for individuals to invoke public authority on their own and for their benefit. The bulk of this activity takes place among private individuals who, in the process of involving legal norms, employ the power of the state and so become state actors themselves." Frances Kahn Zemans, "Legal Mobilization: The Neglected Role of Law in the Political System," *American Political Science Review* 77, no. 3 (1983): 692. She argues that Lempert provides a useful definition of legal mobilization as: "the process by which legal norms are invoked to regulate behavior." Ibid. 694. Lempert's definition can be found in Richard O. Lempert, "Mobilizing Private Law: An Introductory Essay," *Law and Society Review* 11, no. 2 (1976): 173.

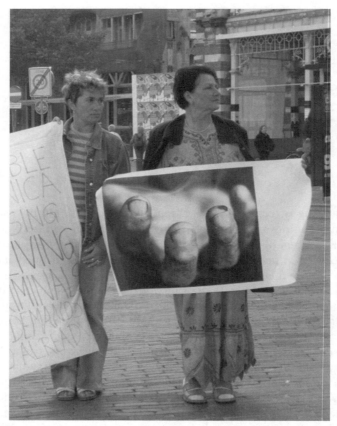

Members of the Mothers of the Enclaves of Srebrenica and Žepa, Sabra Kulenović and Kada Hotić, protest in front of the Anne Frank House in Amsterdam, July 2004. Photograph by the author.

to include the international community, which was present during the fall of the UN enclave but did not prevent the crimes that followed.[4]

A Dutch judge later ruled that the UN enjoyed absolute immunity, a decision the women – the plaintiffs in the case – said they would appeal.[5] Another

---

[4]   The plaintiffs in the case, the Foundation of the Mothers of Srebrenica and ten individuals, eight of whom are named, are represented by the Dutch law firm Van Diepen Van der Kroef Advocaten. Documents pertaining to the case can be found in English at <www.vandiepen.com/en/international/srebrenica/proceedings-the-hague.html> (accessed February 10, 2009). Semir Guzin and his partner, Miro Kebo, of the Mostar-based Law Office of Kebo and Guzin, initially started the case, spending years collecting affidavits and statements from the survivors.

[5]   "Mothers of Srebrenica shall appeal and deny absolute immunity of the UN," Press Release, Van Diepen Van der Kroef Advocaten, July 10, 2008, <www.vandiepen.com/en/internationaal/srebrenica/press-releases/140-Press-release-July-10,-2008:-Mothers-of-Srebrenica-shall-appeal-and-deny-absolute-immunity-of-the-UN.html> (accessed February 10, 2009). In

similar case, brought by two surviving family members, was also thrown out in September of 2008.[6] Even if the victims were disappointed by these outcomes, the proceedings were significant. There were few similar precedents in international affairs. How did these Srebrenica survivors manage to find themselves in a Hague courtroom? What was the role of the International Criminal Tribunal for former Yugoslavia (ICTY), created to prosecute individuals for violations of international humanitarian law in the region? By this time, the ICTY had left the survivors largely disappointed and frustrated. Too few cases had addressed Srebrenica, the largest single crime of the war, which the ICTY had declared to be an act of genocide. Public statements by Srebrenica's family associations contributed to the new conventional wisdom about the court: that it had little impact in Bosnia, and that it failed to transform the postwar state in the manner its architects intended.

However, this case study upends popular misconceptions about the court's impact in the region through a discussion of developments around the Srebrenica massacre, placing the issue of the impact of the court within the broader framework of positive unintended consequences that resulted from its work. It illustrates how the strategies of the survivors and the family associations they founded evolved parallel to and were bolstered by the court's judgments, findings, and – indeed – failings. The *judicialization* of accountability for the Srebrenica massacre meant that the international community, which had initiated inquiry into the events of July 1995, would be asked to examine its own role in the tragedy in other courts of law. The ICTY helped foster a social movement around the issue by acting as a resource that the survivors utilized in their mobilization.

This chapter argues that the work of the ICTY influenced developments on the Srebrenica question and the people affected by the tragedy in numerous ways. The court gave family associations and activists the legitimacy they would otherwise have lacked in the climate of denial that was persistent at the end of the war. This legitimacy shaped their strategies of collective action, which in part focused on the use of courts to achieve outcomes, inside Bosnia and beyond. It also provided an empirical basis with which they expanded the norm of accountability upheld by the court and enabled civil society groups to broaden the discussion of who (and what) should be brought to justice, to include actors previously thought by many to be beyond the reach of the law. This chapter points to a larger legacy of the court,

---

November 2007, the court had ruled they could proceed. See "Dutch court rules Srebrenica families can sue U.N.," *Reuters*, November 27, 2007; "Court Upholds Srebrenica Victims' Right To Sue UN: Report," *Agence France Presse*, November 27, 2007; and "Bosnian women may sue UN over Srebrenica, Hague court rules," *BH Radio 1*, November 27, 2007.

[6] A second similar case (although with different legal arguments) was brought by Hasan Nuhanović and relatives of Rizo Mustafić. Nuhanović lost his parents and brother in the massacre, and Mustafić was an electrician in the UN Dutch forces who also perished. They are represented by Liesbeth Zegveld at the Amsterdam-based law firm Böhler Franken Koppe Wijngaarden. Both cases have been appealed.

which includes its impact on the role of citizens in fostering a legal consciousness. It outlines how the court helped Bosnian citizens claim their rights.

Early Organizers – The Family Associations

The organization of Srebrenica's surviving family members began essentially at the same time as the ICTY's work on crimes committed after the fall of the safe area, but their activism was later significantly influenced by developments in The Hague. After occupying the enclave in July 1995, Mladić's forces expelled over 25,000 women and children to Tuzla with the help of Dutch peacekeepers. When their male relatives did not turn up, the displaced women started organizing in the camps. This led to their first protest, 72 days after the fall of the enclave.[7] Their demands then were not very different from what they continued to seek over a decade after the war: to determine the fates of their loved ones.

At the time, rumors abounded that the males had been transported en masse to work in labor camps and mines in Serbia. It was not without reason that these reports spread like wildfire, fostering hopes that families would be reunited. All over the country, the Army of Republika Srpska (VRS) and police forces (MUP) had used Bosniak civilians as forced labor, demanding they dig trenches and, in some cases, the graves of their neighbors. The real fate of the enclave's males was even more sinister, but there were no agents to break the devastating news to the hopeful women and children. No international organization in Bosnia had the mandate – or the will – to tell the women in the camps that their relatives had perished in a series of executions, most of which occurred between the 10th and 19th of July. One of the main points of contact for the women, the International Committee of the Red Cross (ICRC), could not have informed them about what had occurred without violating its institutional policy of remaining neutral in the field.[8] The organization's passivity in the face of the tragedy had consequences, however. In January 1996, Srebrenica's victims stormed the ICRC headquarters in Tuzla demanding information about the fate of their missing family members.[9] Many of the victims still thought that their loved ones had been arrested and were being held against their will.[10] Today, many still have bitter feelings toward the ICRC for unwittingly fostering their hopes.

The organizing effort that began in the Tuzla camps reinvented itself in the post-war period as surviving family members moved to Sarajevo and eventually started

---

[7] Interview with Zumra Šehomerović, Sarajevo, August 2, 2002. Šehomerović is a member of the Mothers of Enclaves of Srebrenica and Žepa.

[8] For a discussion written less than a year after the fall of the enclave, see Denise Plattner, "ICRC Neutrality and Neutrality in Humanitarian Assistance, International Review of the Red Cross," April 30, 1996, <www.icrc.org/web/eng/siteeng0.nsf/htmlall/57jn2z?opendocumentRC> (accessed February 9, 2009).

[9] Mark Rice-Oxley, "Srebrenica Refugees Protest Lack of Information," *Agence France Presse*, January 30, 1996.

[10] Ibid.

to return to the Srebrenica municipality itself. In 1996, many of Srebrenica's displaced moved from Tuzla to the outskirts of Sarajevo, to places like Vogošća, Ilidža, and Ilijaš, where Serbs had lived before the war but had since left for places in Eastern Bosnia, now part of Republika Srpska (RS). As the situation in the Srebrenica municipality improved, however slightly, civil society organizations opened up branch offices and sometimes headquarters there. As of 2009, there were four main family associations, and many other nongovernmental organizations (NGOs) working in the name of Srebrenica's survivors, primarily located in Sarajevo, Tuzla, and Srebrenica.[11] Some of these organizations are able to sustain their existence in part because international patrons finance their offices and travel, even though their work is sometimes critical of these donors.[12] Over time, the Bosnian government has also donated more resources to the groups.

The Mothers of the Enclaves of Srebrenica and Žepa (Udruženje "Pokret majki enklava Srebrenica i Žepa") is one of the two most prominent NGOs representing the families (mostly women) who lost their husbands, sons, and brothers in the massacre.[13] Located in Sarajevo, the office is run primarily by five women who spend their days handling requests from other surviving family members, processing forms, organizing conferences, and participating in the coordination of a now-annual memorial event in Potočari, at the former site of the UN base. The Mothers' main goal is to find their loved ones, although in practice their offices act as a support network, a processing center, and sometimes a conference facility. Before they were formally registered as an NGO in 1998, the Mothers of Srebrenica were helped by the local branch of the Luxembourg-based Society for Threatened People, run by a Bosnian historian, Fadila Memišević, who spent many years at the organization's German chapter.[14]

The other most visible group, the Women of Srebrenica (Udruženje građana "Žene Srebrenice"), is based in Tuzla and represents the population there, including the group of internally displaced persons still housed in temporary shelters in nearby Mihatovići, and many recent returnees to the municipality.[15] The two

---

[11] In the United States, a large group of Srebrenica refugees settled in St. Louis, Missouri. St. Louis is estimated to have a Bosnian diaspora population of 35,000 to 40,000 people; of those, between 4,000 and 5,000 are from Srebrenica, the largest concentration outside of Bosnia. See Philip O'Connor, "Bosnians here head home to remember Srebrenica," *www.SLToday.com*, June 25, 2005, <www.stltoday.com/stltoday/news/special/bosnia.nsf/0/4033FC1F147BEAC4 862570320076577A?OpenDocument> (accessed February 9, 2009).

[12] The groups, for example, lobby extensively for the cause of missing persons and have received considerable support from the ICMP.

[13] Most of my research was conducted with the Sarajevo-based group, Mothers of the Enclaves of Srebrenica and Žepa.

[14] Memišević is a prominent activist in Bosnia. She was selected to be part of the 1,000 Women for the Nobel Peace Prize Campaign 2005, which collectively nominated 1,000 women for the prize and resulted in the creation of PeaceWomen around the Globe. See <www.1000peacewomen. org> (accessed February 9, 2009).

[15] For an in-depth discussion of the Tuzla group, see Sarah E. Wagner, *To Know Where He Lies: DNA Technology and the Search for Srebrenica's Missing* (Berkeley: University of California Press, 2008), 66–81.

groups distribute press releases together and participate in joint events, although their cooperation has its highs and lows. While there are other groups, the Tuzla and Sarajevo family associations are the most active groups overall and are covered most frequently in the Bosnian press. The Sarajevo group receives slightly more press coverage, mostly as a result of being in the nation's capital.

A third important family association, the Mothers of Srebrenica and Podrinje (Udruženje građana "Majke Srebrenice i Podrinja"), has a more controversial reputation in the landscape of Bosnian family associations. It is headed by Ibran Mustafić, a politician in Srebrenica during the war. Along with running this NGO, Mustafić formed his own political party in the run-up to the 2002 general elections and ran for mayor of Srebrenica in 2004. Mustafić's organization often takes much stronger positions than the other two groups. For example, when the organizing committee announced that former President Bill Clinton would open the Memorial Center in Potočari, Mustafić called on all Bosnians to strongly oppose this decision. He told the local press, "As a President of a country that has world superiority, this gentleman silently watched the internationally-recognized Republic of Bosnia and Herzegovina and its citizens being killed and by not doing anything, or by his direct doing where Srebrenica is concerned, he was an accomplice in our having the Memorial Center in Potočari today – Potočari is situated in a genocidal, Nazi and criminal RS."[16] The Tuzla and Sarajevo groups did not concur with this position and issued statements of support for Clinton's imminent arrival. The groups, however, share a common strategy of legal mobilization: all three organizations have appealed to various courts for redress, armed with facts uncovered by the ICTY.[17]

Since the fall of the enclave, there has been an internationalization of the problem of postwar Srebrenica. The family associations have formed a transnational advocacy network, that is, a "network of activists, distinguishable largely by the centrality of principled ideas or values motivating their formation."[18] With other NGOs in Amsterdam, Paris, Geneva, Istanbul, and elsewhere, Srebrenica's family associations have coordinated their appeals to foreign governments and the UN. Within their network is a heterogeneous mix of organizations formed by members of the diaspora, local human rights groups, and women's organizations. The norm of justice motivates their work as they seek accountability from the perpetrators, knowledge about the location of their missing relatives, legal processes to establish the truth about the fall of the enclave, and economic justice for surviving family members. Over time, family associations have increased the intensity of

---

[16] *Oslobođenje*, August 5, 2003. Mustafić later authored a book critical of Bosniaks in the enclave during the war. See Ibran Mustafić, *Planirani Haos 1990–1996* (Planned chaos 1990–1996) (Sarajevo: UG Majke Srebrenice i Podrinja, 2008).

[17] The fourth organization, Srebrenica Mothers (Udruženje građana "Srebreničke Majke"), located in the Srebrenica municipality itself, is led by Hatidža Mehmedović. See <srebrenickemajke.org/> (accessed February 9, 2009). This organization has become more active in recent years.

[18] Margaret E. Keck and Kathryn Sikkink, *Activists Beyond Borders: Advocacy Networks in International Politics* (Ithaca, NY: Cornell University Press, 1998), 1.

their efforts to hold the international community responsible for failing to prevent the tragedy.

Strategies of Collective Action

Given the postwar silence on the part of Bosnian Serb and Serbian politicians, and other elites, about the events of July 1995, the first protests by the family associations targeted the international community instead. In doing so, they expanded the existing norm of accountability espoused by the ICTY to include the international officials they felt were also responsible for their loved ones' fates. In this way, these associations and some of the individuals who worked with them acted as "norm entrepreneurs," that is, people who use organizational platforms to convince a critical mass to embrace new norms.[19] Norms are "actively built by agents having strong notions about appropriate or desirable behavior in their community."[20] The new norm in this case was that international bodies should be held responsible when they allow political violence to occur, a novel idea given that such bodies are generally viewed as having immunity.

One of the family associations' first major demonstrations illustrated that their collective action would target both local and international forces. On October 11, 1997, women gathered in front of the Office of the High Representative (OHR), the Organization for Security and Cooperation in Europe (OSCE), the Red Cross, and various embassies, displaying banners of their protest theme "We Want the Truth" ("Hoćemo istinu"). Over the postwar period, the sight of these women in the streets, carrying signs and often pillowcases bearing the names of their loved ones, gained something of an iconic status in Bosnia and beyond. In both Tuzla and Sarajevo, their symbolic protests were a constant reminder that there was still too little information about the tragedy, and that they felt the world had betrayed them.[21] The family associations raised awareness that the international community had to account for its own role in the fall of the enclave. They also sought cooperation from international forces in pressing local Bosnian Serb elites to provide information about their missing relatives. Over time, their strategy took a legalistic turn, as they turned to the courts to achieve their goals. The evolution of this activism was bolstered by the increasing amounts of documentation at the ICTY that outlined the role of international forces in the fall of the enclave.

---

[19] See Martha Finnemore and Kathryn Sikkink, "International Norm Dynamics and Political Change," *International Organization* 52, no. 4 (1998): 887–917.

[20] Ibid.

[21] Well over a decade after the war, the Tuzla group would sponsor protests on the 11th of every month, at which protestors carried pillowcases embroidered with the names of their missing relatives.

The judicialization of the questions surrounding Srebrenica was notable for what it meant for Bosnia's nascent postwar democratic transition. In the absence of a strong Bosnian state to provide for the needs of the tragedy's survivors, a vulnerable segment of the population, collective action was channeled through the courts. This meant that the actions of institutions were examined on a case-by-case basis. The facts provided by the ICTY, however, helped establish the events that occurred in the enclave and, ultimately, shaped citizens' claims to their rights within the nascent Bosnian state. That international institutions would be the first and most prominent focus of protest was predictable; these were the only bodies that were plausible targets for the family associations in the immediate postwar period.

Exhuming and Identifying the Victims

The ICTY was the first institution to oversee the exhumation of mass graves in Eastern Bosnia. From 1996 to 2000, the Tribunal exhumed 21 gravesites – 14 primary and 7 secondary. Forensic experts who testified for the ICTY confirmed that most victims found were killed in mass executions, evidenced by the blindfolds and ligatures discovered at the sites. Experts also linked the primary and secondary gravesites, testifying that many graves were dug up and bodies moved, in the fall of 1995, in order to hide traces of the crimes.[22] While there were differences between exhumations conducted for the court's trials and those conducted for the family members of missing persons, these initial criminal investigations set the stage for the family associations to see their primary goal met: the return of the remains of their loved ones.[23]

After the ICTY completed its case-related exhumations of Srebrenica victims, the task was carried on by different organizations. Eventually, the job of exhumation and identification was handed over to the International Commission on Missing Persons (ICMP), which set up the Podrinje Identification Project (PIP) to focus on Srebrenica's missing.[24] One of the few international organizations to show sustained

---

[22] NATO peacekeeping forces (SFOR) regularly provided security for exhumations.

[23] The relationship between "forensic" exhumations and "humanitarian" exhumations (for family members) is complex. See Eric Stover and Rachel Shigekane, "The Missing in the Aftermath of War: When do the Needs of Victims' Families and International War Crimes Tribunals Clash?" *International Review of the Red Cross*, no. 848 (2002): 845–866. This divide is also addressed in Mark Skinner and Jon Sterenberg, "Turf Wars: Authority and Responsibility for the Investigation of Mass Graves," *Forensic Science Journal* 151, nos. 2–3 (2005): 221–232; Derek Congram and John Sterenberg, "Grave Challenges in Iraq," in S. Blau and D. Ubelaker, eds., *Handbook of Forensic Anthropology and Archaeology* (Walnut Creek, CA: Leftcoast Press, 2008); Erin D. Williams and John D. Crews, "From Dust to Dust: Ethical and Practical Issues Involved in the Location, Exhumation and Identification of Bodies from Mass Graves," *Croatian Medical Journal* 44, no. 3 (2003): 251–258.

[24] In the immediate postwar years, exhumations had been conducted by Physicians for Human Rights (PHR).

support for the survivors, ICMP was created by the Contact Group in 1996 and was tasked with identification of remains.[25] ICMP was aided by two Commissions on Missing Persons, one for the Federation of Bosnia and Herzegovina and one for Republika Srpska (RS), the two entities that comprise the postwar state. In 1996, the two entity governments signed a Memorandum of Understanding and agreed that the Federation's Commission would conduct exhumations in RS and vice-versa.[26] The ICTY used traditional identification techniques, asking family members to identify clothing and personal effects. In the summer of 2001, ICMP opened a new laboratory that introduced DNA identification techniques never previously used on such a scale in a postwar environment. The first DNA-assisted identification, of a 15-year-old Bosniak boy from Srebrenica, was completed in November 2001.[27] ICMP is among the small number of international organizations that have come directly to the aid of those who lost family in the massacre and interacts with them on a regular basis. At different times, ICMP has paid for the office space of both the Women of Srebrenica (in Tuzla) and the Mothers of the Enclaves of Srebrenica and Žepa (the Sarajevo-based group). Both groups admit that, were it not for this support, they would have been forced to close their doors years ago. ICMP has a civil society initiatives program which works with family associations all over the country.

The question of missing persons and the work of exhumations, facilitated by the ICTY, has greater social significance beyond the courtroom. It also has a direct impact on the socioeconomic status of victims and illustrates how processes which begin with courts are linked to postwar democratic development. For example, in the Federation, a household that lost its primary male income generator during the war is called a "Šehidska porodica" ("family of the martyr"); these households receive slightly higher benefits than a normal state pension.[28] Survivors' families,

[25] Interview with Sanela Tunović, Sarajevo, July 20, 2002. Tunović was a representative of the Public Information Office of the ICMP. The Contact Group was a gathering of influential nations – the U.S., U.K., Russian Federation, France, Germany and Italy – which formed in 1994 to help mediate an end to the war.

[26] ICMP launched a state-level Missing Persons Institute of Bosnia-Herzegovina in 2005. Created back in 2000, it was to take over the functions of the entity-level commissions. "Missing Persons Institute Launched on International Day of the Disappeared," Press Release, ICMP, August 30, 1995, <www.ic-mp.org/press-releases/missing-persons-institute-launched-on-international-day-of-the-disappeared> (accessed February 4, 2009).

[27] See "Identification of Srebrenica Victims Passes 2,000," Press Release, ICMP, June 10, 2005, <www.ic-mp.org/press-releases/identification-of-srebrenica-victims-passes-2000>(accessed February 4, 2009). The identification process seeks to take away any possible political or ethnic bias. ICMP's 11 mobile teams travel the country, visit victims' families, and take blood samples. The laboratory assigns a code to each sample and sends it to a lab in Sarajevo for analysis. Similarly, a bone sample is taken from the remains and sent with a bar code to the laboratory. The results are placed in a central database and once a day the computer runs a program that searches for DNA matches. ICMP reports that between 10 and 15 matches are made per day. Interview with Tunović.

[28] Jasmila Žbanić's, *Grbavica: The Land of My Dreams* (Strand Releasing, 2006) is a film that deals with the "Šehidska porodica" and the dire financial situation of women who suddenly became heads of their households (although the women in the film are not from Srebrenica).

however, cannot receive benefits as a "Šehidska porodica" without a death certificate issued by the appropriate authorities. Women whose husbands had not yet been found were "punished" by this regulation; if surviving family members did not have their missing loved ones declared dead before an exhumation and identification took place, they would not be able to receive benefits. This was often a difficult decision to make, as it forced the women, some of whom held on to the hope that their relative was still alive, to declare them dead in the absence of a physical body. The Law on Missing Persons, adopted in 2004, addressed this problem, but it was written after many women in the interim period went without benefits.[29] This hardship has a particularly gendered lens, as women who lost their sons and husbands in the conflict were forced to become heads of household and primary income generators after the war.

Thus, the ICTY's search for evidence was part of a larger chain of events, important to many Bosnian citizens. The demands of the international criminal justice system had positive spillover effects in other areas of Bosnian society. As Sarah Wagner argues, identification efforts address the troubling absence of physical remains and marked graves, a concern often overlooked by the international community bent on rebuilding homes and infrastructure in the immediate postwar years.[30] Identification can actually be more meaningful for survivors than seemingly more functional interventions; it directly affects their financial status – an important prerequisite for long-term political stability in Bosnia – and provides them with both individual and social recognition of their loss.

Getting Back to Potočari

The survivors' focus in the postwar years was on lobbying for a memorial complex in Potočari, the former site of the UN headquarters in the Srebrenica enclave. They were unrelenting in their desire to hold a yearly memorial service on the 11th of July, the anniversary of the fall of the enclave. With the passing of each postwar year, small steps were taken. In July 1996 an event was organized in Tuzla, attended by Jordan's Queen Noor. The following year, the former American ambassador to Austria, Swanee Hunt, and human rights advocate Bianca Jagger attended a similar event in Tuzla. However, in the same year, RS authorities prevented the women from visiting a mass grave near Zvornik. In 1998 and 1999, there were memorial services in Starec, near Kladanj. The site was chosen because it was still too difficult to organize travel to Potočari. But the goal was to get back to Potočari, both for the refugees and for internally displaced persons who wanted to return to the municipality and visit the remains of those who perished not far from the former UN compound. In 1999, the Sarajevo-based Mothers of the Enclaves of Srebrenica and Žepa

---

[29] The text in English of the Law on the Missing Persons can be found at: <www.ic-mp.org/wp-content/uploads/2007/11/lawmp_en.pdf> (accessed February 10, 2009).

[30] Wagner, *To Know Where He Lies*, 4–5.

Coffins of Srebrenica victims awaiting burial, July 9, 2007. Photograph by the author.

surveyed 12,000 individuals affected by the tragedy, both their own members and other people from the region not affiliated with their group, and asked them where they wanted their loved ones buried. Over 83 percent chose Potočari.[31]

By 2000, conditions started to improve. For the first time, the survivors were able to have a memorial service in Potočari. Some 50 buses brought 3,000 people from all over Bosnia to commemorate the massacre in Srebrenica. As soon as the buses crossed into RS, police lined the roads. Residents threw stones and flashed the three-finger "salute" that had been a provocative war-time symbol, and remains a sign of intolerance. RS authorities consistently told the press that the events would increase tensions there, and in the short term they did, but every year thereafter brought slight progress. After the 2000 event, and drawing on the results of the Mothers' survey, High Representative Wolfgang Petritsch declared in October 2000 that the land in Potočari would be a cemetery for the victims of the massacre.[32] In May of the following year a foundation was established to oversee and finance construction of the memorial, and an executive board and advisory working group were formed.[33] In July 2001, a foundation stone was

[31] Interview with Sabaheta Fejzić, Sarajevo, June 15, 2003. Fejzić is a member of the Mothers of Enclaves of Srebrenica and Žepa.

[32] *OBN News Review*, October 25, 2000, Office of the High Representative and EU Special Representative, <www.ohr.int/ohr-dept/presso/bh-media-rep/summaries-tv/obn/default.asp?content_id=1905> (accessed February 1, 2009).

[33] Decision establishing and registering the Foundation of the Srebrenica-Potočari Memorial and Cemetery, May 10, 2001, Office of the High Representative and EU Special Representative, <www.ohr.int/decisions/plipdec/default.asp?content_id=125> (accessed January 27, 2009).

Shovels at Srebrenica-Potočari Memorial and Cemetery, July 9, 2007. Photograph by the author.

laid for the memorial in front of a crowd of up to 15,000. Several months earlier, Bosniak returns to the Srebrenica municipality had begun to pick up. By 2002, RS authorities could do nothing to stop the event, even if RS police did manage to turn back several delegations from Belgrade that year – including the prominent group, Women in Black, a women's antiwar movement with an active chapter in Serbia.[34] In July 2002, between 15,000 and 20,000 people attended the memorial event. That year a campaign was held to raise funds for the memorial, using phone

[34] Author's notes, July 2002.

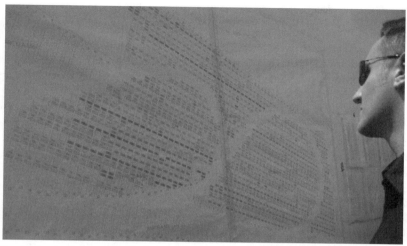

Relative looks for grave plot, Srebrenica-Potočari Memorial and Cemetery, July 11, 2004. Photograph by the author.

calls that charged small additional sums to the caller's phone bill; the effort raised over 300,000 KM, approximately 153,000 euros.[35]

In March 2003, the first 600 victims were buried in the Potočari memorial, an event attended by over 25,000 people from all over Bosnia. Another 282 were buried in July of the same year when, for the first time, a representative of RS, Prime Minister Dragan Mikerević, attended the ceremony in Potočari, even as he told the press that a formal apology would not be forthcoming from his government. Only a few months later, in September, former U.S. President Bill Clinton formally opened the memorial complex to a crowd of 25,000 to 30,000. Most of the family associations were supportive of the decision to invite Clinton to open the memorial, since he was thought to have played an important role in ending the war, if not in stopping the massacre. After the opening, the next major memorial event was in July 2004 and was attended by 20,000 people. Even vendors appeared alongside the road on the day of the event, selling cold drinks and snacks to weary travelers, a development resented by many survivors. Activists from Belgrade attended, including representatives of the Youth Initiative for Human Rights (YIHR), the Helsinski Committee for Human Rights in Serbia, and the Humanitarian Law Center (HLC), three prominent human rights organizations in Serbia. These ceremonies were all connected to a chain of events that had started with the ICTY's initial investigatory efforts.

[35] This fundraising campaign was publicized by a television spot created by Sarajevo-based artist Faruk Šabanović, which aired all over the country.

Demanding International Accountability

Developments initiated by international officials inside Bosnia also facilitated the survivors' demands for international accountability. The first High Representative to publicly acknowledge that genocide had occurred in Srebrenica was Wolfgang Petritsch, who held office from 1999 to 2002.[36] This public admission gave the survivors even more legitimacy to continue lobbying for the memorial center, which needed the support of the High Representative. Coming from the chief international community representative in Sarajevo, Petritsch's acknowledgment opened the door for the demands of family associations, and those who cooperated with them, that international institutions and governments involved with the fall of the enclave should accept some responsibility for the massacre. Survivors and family associations targeted several different actors: the UN, the Dutch government, and even the ICTY, in an effort to establish that they had erred in creating a safe area whose inhabitants they were, in the end, unwilling to protect.

One of the first appeals was to the Tribunal itself. The court's promotion of international accountability facilitated a call for recognition of the criminal liability of international officials who did not prevent the fall of the enclave. On February 4, 2000, the Mothers of Srebrenica and Podrinje (the Vogošća-based group) filed a criminal complaint against members of the international community, including the Secretary General's Special Representatives Yasushi Akashi, Kofi Annan, Carl Bildt, Boutros Boutros-Ghali, and others, charging them with "deliberately and maliciously refusing to help the UN [do] anything to prevent the massacre in Srebrenica," and having a "common criminal purpose to carve up Bosnia, a UN member organization."[37] The complaint demanded that ICTY prosecutors prepare appropriate indictments against the officials, issue warrants for their arrest, and freeze their financial assets. Professor Francis Boyle, a professor of law at the University of Illinois College of Law in Champaign, submitted the complaint, which was later endorsed by the Tuzla-based family association.[38] The Mothers of Srebrenica and Podrinje (the Vogošća-based group) had approached Boyle and asked him to represent them; he took on the case pro bono. Carla Del Ponte, ICTY Chief Prosecutor at the time, asked Boyle to put together witness statements about the UN role in Srebrenica. Boyle had also planned to file a complaint in the Belgian courts, but the Belgian statute was diluted as a result of developments related to

[36] See for example: "Speech by the High Representative for Bosnia and Herzegovina, Wolfgang Petritsch, at the EU's Summit on the Balkans," Office of High Representative, November 24, 2000, <www.ohr.int/ohr-dept/presso/bh-media-rep/summaries-tv/rtrs/default.asp?content_id=3254> (accessed July 11, 2009), in which he refers to genocide charges against two ICTY indictees related to Srebrenica.
[37] The Mothers of Srebrenica and Podrinje, letter to Carla Del Ponte, February 4, 2000, <194.109.160.107/francisboyle/complaint.html> (accessed February 1, 2005).
[38] "Hoće li Brisel osuditi Galija, Anana ..." (Will Brussels try Ghali, Annan ...), *Oslobođenje*, March 5, 2002.

a claim filed against Ariel Sharon.[39] Although no charges ultimately resulted, Del Ponte held meetings with the authors of the complaint and listened to their concerns.

Family associations later lobbied the highest office of the UN directly. When UN Secretary General Kofi Annan paid a visit to Bosnia and to the Sarajevo-based Mothers of the Enclaves of Srebrenica and Žepa on the eve of the UN mission's closure in 2002, representatives asked him for financial compensation from the organization they felt was designated to protect them.[40] One survivor told Annan, "We will not just swallow the fact that we were protected by the UN and were betrayed anyway. We really believed the United Nations. And what happened? They deceived us."[41] The argument that the UN should pay survivors some sort of reparations was a long time in the making; the group had discussed the idea of UN accountability in the Bosnian press for several years.[42]

In 2000, a team of lawyers from Mostar who had been following these developments showed up at the offices of the Mothers of the Enclaves of Srebrenica and Žepa and the Women of Srebrenica, offering to file their claims. Work collecting documentation began in January 2001. The Sarajevo and Tuzla associations, working with the Mostar legal team, collected over 10,000 powers of attorney, and documentation proving that family members went missing during the period from April 1993 to July 1995. In December 2002, the Mostar lawyers sent the Secretary General himself a letter that read:

Induced by the tragedy which has not been remembered in recent world and European history, horrified at its largeness, staggered by testimonies of its survivors, inspired by an intention to contribute to seeking justice and setting a fair compensation to the survivors – [residents of Srebrenica], we have entered, as a team of lawyers, into realization of this project.

After one year of work, collecting the facts, analyzing … everything which has been done, told and written in regard to Srebrenica and elaboration of the subject from [a] legal point of view, we address [y]ou, for the time being, on behalf of 6,586 survivors of killed [residents of Srebrenica], with the following request:

We consider the United Nations, whose Representative you are, [to] bear responsibility for the fall of the safe areas of Srebrenica and Žepa, and, [therefore], you should take over responsibility of setting a payment of a fair compensation to the survivors of the tragedy, i.e., relatives of killed and missing persons.[43]

[39] Professor Francis Boyle, e-mail to the author, July 24, 2002.

[40] See, for example, Daria Sito-Sucic, "Bosnians Seek Compensation from UN for Srebrenica," *Reuters*, December 19, 2002; Philip Gourevitch, "The Optimist," *The New Yorker*, March 3, 2003.

[41] Gourevitch, "The Optimist."

[42] See Isnam Taljić, "Srebrenica protiv Ujedinjenih Nacija" (Srebrenica against the United Nations), *Ljiljan*, July 19–26, 1999.

[43] Faruk Ćupina, Mensud Džonko, Semir Guzin and Miro Kebo, letter to Kofi Annan, December 18, 2002. In the ten-page letter, the four Mostar-based attorneys cite all of the relevant UN Security Council Resolutions. Copy on file with the author. NB: Some members of the Women of Srebrenica later withdrew their support for this case.

The UN did not reply. The legal team still hoped the developing case would strip the international organization of its immunity. They also hoped it would help prevent the UN from making similar (fatal) decisions in the future.[44] The Bosnian public was on their side: in a random poll of 300 residents in Sarajevo, Tuzla, and Zenica, conducted by the daily paper *Dnevni Avaz* (Daily Voice), 89 percent said the UN should pay reparations. Only 1 percent of those surveyed opposed the idea.[45]

Annan was less sure. In his visit with the Sarajevo group, he told the Sarajevo Mothers group he doubted "the [UN] would entertain the thought" of financial compensation.[46] Still, the Mothers continued their efforts, even criticizing him. Previously, they publicly protested the award of the Nobel Prize to Annan (and the UN) in 2001, pointing to his position as head of the Department of Peacekeeping when the enclave fell.[47]

The Mostar team was confronted with the problem of how to penetrate the opaque UN system. There was discussion that they would seek the same amount of compensation (50,000 USD) that the UN gives to families of peacekeepers lost in field operations. Initially, they were heartened by the fact that there was an apparent precedent: the UN had paid reparations to families in the Congo in the 1960s.[48] It proved a difficult task, however, and the lawyers turned their focus to the government represented by troops on the ground when the enclave fell, the Netherlands. Dutch soldiers had replaced the Canadian battalion based in Potočari in February 1994. The legal team argued that, while the UN was the organization that should have protected civilians in the enclave, it was the Dutch soldiers who had facilitated the transfer of innocent people to their deaths.[49] Furthermore, they claimed to have damning evidence: documentation that showed that the troops on the ground acted on the basis of orders from their Defense Ministry, counter to the instructions of the UN.[50]

The Dutch role in the fall of Srebrenica had been examined in a report commissioned by the Netherlands Institute for War Documentation (Nederlands Instituut voor Oorlogsdocumentatie or NIOD). The 7,000-page report, issued in April 2002,

---

[44] Interview with Semir Guzin, Mostar, August 8, 2003. Guzin is a lawyer representing the Mothers of the Enclaves of Srebrenica and Žepa.

[45] The question was: "Smatrate li da bi preživjele žrtve genocida u Srebrenici, zaštićenoj zoni UN, trebale biti obeštećene od strane UN?" (Do you think that the survivors of the genocide in the Srebrenica safe area should be compensated by the UN?), Istraživanje javnog mnijenja (Public Opinion Research), *Dnevni Avaz*, 2004. Ten percent responded "don't know."

[46] Gourevitch, "The Optimist."

[47] The Mothers found that they were not alone; many Bosnian intellectuals agreed. One commented, "The UN certainly didn't get an award for Srebrenica." See E. Kamenica, "Zbog čega je Kofi Anan dobio Nobelovu nagradu?" (Why did Kofi Annan get the Nobel Prize?), *Oslobođenje*, October 15, 2001.

[48] Interview with Semir Guzin, Mostar, August 2, 2004.

[49] See Hasan Nuhanović, *Pod zastavom UN-a: međunarodna zajednica i zločin u Srebrenici* (Under the flag of the UN: the international community and crime in Srebrenica) (Sarajevo: Preporod, 2005).

[50] Interview with Semir Guzin, Mostar, August 2, 2004.

was commissioned by the Dutch Defense Department and had been six years in the making.[51] The purpose of the report was to outline the events leading to the fall of the enclave. The research concluded that foremost responsibility for the massacre should be assigned to General Ratko Mladić, adding later that Radovan Karadžić's responsibility for the crimes committed in Srebrenica was difficult to evaluate given the poor relations between him and Mladić. It also found no evidence that Slobodan Milošević played a direct role. In addition, it did not find evidence for the accusation that General Bernard Janvier, then UNPROFOR's commander, had signed a secret agreement with Mladić by which Mladić agreed to release French UNPROFOR hostages in exchange for a denial of new support to the Dutch battalion.[52] It laid equal blame on the UN and on the Dutch forces stationed there for failure to prevent the fall of the enclave. The report drew upon hundreds of thousands of pages of documentation, including documents later used in the Krstić case at the ICTY (discussed below); the Bassiouni report, which provided some of the foundational evidence for the ICTY's creation; and over 900 interviews.[53]

After the report was presented, survivors held peaceful demonstrations in Tuzla, Sarajevo, and in front of the Dutch parliament to express their disappointment with the findings. They had hoped the Dutch government would directly assume some responsibility for the tragedy. Representatives of both the Tuzla and Sarajevo groups traveled to the Netherlands for the presentation of the report.[54] A former Dutchbat translator, Hasan Nuhanović,[55] whose whole family had been turned over to the VRS during the fall of the enclave, argued that the report excused even Ratko Mladić.[56] Nuhanović had previously stated in a hearing in the U.S. House of Representatives:

The UNPROFOR Dutch battalion forced around 6,000 men, women and children right to the hands of their executioners. In this way they assisted the war criminals

---

[51] See "Srebrenica – a 'safe' area. Reconstruction, background, consequences and analyses of the fall of a Safe Area," Netherlands Institute on War Documentation (NIOD), English version at <srebrenica.brightside.nl/srebrenica> (accessed February 10, 2009).

[52] See Part III "The Fall of Srebrenica; No Air Actions on release of the hostages: A Deal Between Janvier and Mladić?" Chapter 3, <srebrenica.brightside.nl/srebrenica/toc/p3_c03_s009_b01. html>; "Nemoguća mirovna misija" (Impossible peace mission), *Oslobođenje*, April 11, 2002.

[53] UN Security Council Resolution 780 (1992) (S/RES/780, 6 October 1992) created the United Nations Commission of Experts to Investigate Violations of International Humanitarian Law in the former Yugoslavia. The Commission, was chaired by M. Cherif Bassiouni, a law professor and specialist in international law.

[54] See also "Protesti ispred holandskog parlamenta: Ubijeni Srebrenčani u izvještaju proglašeni muslimanskom vojskom" (Protest in front of the Dutch parliament: The Report declares people killed in Srebrenica members of the Muslim army), *Dnevni Avaz*, April 12, 2002. Another survivor said, "We seek only the truth about what happened in 1995 and what will be with us for the rest of our lives. We came here because of the untruths that were announced the day before yesterday in The Hague." Quoted in: "U Hagu će protestovati 20,000 ljudi" (20,000 people to protest in The Hague), *Nezavisne Novine*, April 12, 2002.

[55] Nuhanović works with the Tuzla and Sarajevo family associations.

[56] Mensur Čamo, "Den Haag: Majke Srebrenice nezadovoljne izvještajem NIOD-a" (The Hague: Mothers of Srebrenica unsatisfied with NIOD report), *Radio Slobodna Evropa*, April 10, 2002.

in their plan to exterminate the entire male population of Srebrenica. They did not have to do that. They considered the 6,000 civilians on the base to be a burden and handed them over to the Serbs only for one reason – to speed up their own departure from Srebrenica. I should point out that this was in contravention of the written order dated 11 July 1995 from the UNPROFOR Commander Major General Gobilliard to the Dutchbat Commander Lt. Colonel Karremans.[57]

All of the family associations were unhappy with the report's findings. They were particularly disturbed by its identification of all of the males who tried to escape through the forest as members of the Bosnian Army, which was not the case. The survivors also felt that the report failed to link forces on the ground to those responsible up the chain of command, namely Ratko Mladić and Serbian President Slobodan Milošević, and other high ranking officers of the Yugoslav Army (VJ).[58]

This disappointment was exacerbated by the fact that NIOD did not plan to explain its findings to victims in the region. One former NIOD employee told a meeting of regional activists that their budget had been cut as soon as the report was finished and, furthermore, that they did not know whom to contact in the region in order to schedule a presentation.[59] As a result, the purpose (and therefore some of the findings) of the report was seen by victims to be something different from the institute's mandate. Many survivors thought that the purpose was specifically to assess the accountability of the Dutch for the massacre, and did not recognize the bigger-picture aims of the report. Without an outreach effort to explain the difference, many felt as if the Dutch had shirked their obligations yet again. In 2004, the Sarajevo-based Mothers of the Enclaves of Srebrenica and Žepa said they had never received even one translated page of NIOD's findings.

Inside the Netherlands, the report had a tremendous effect: months before general elections in 2002 the entire cabinet resigned. While some argued that the resignation cut off meaningful discussion inside the parliament about the report, others said that it was a sign that the political elite did not take the Dutch role in the fall of the enclave lightly. Civil society groups inside the Netherlands, many working with Bosnian groups, made sure the issue did not disappear from public view. The loudest voice was that of the Interchurch Peace Council (Interkerkelijk Vredesberaad or IKV) in the Netherlands, a Dutch religious organization with many years of experience working with Srebrenica's survivors. IKV representative Dion van den Berg said the report was "more comprehensive and more shameful

---

[57] See the statement of Hasan Nuhanović, Former Translator for the United Nations Protection Force (UNPROFOR) in Srebrenica: U.S. House of Representatives, Subcommittee on International Operations and Human Rights of the Committee on International Relations, Hearing on United Nations Peacekeeping, 106th Congress, 2nd session (Washington D.C.: GPO, 2000), <bulk.resource.org/gpo.gov/hearings/106h/69536.txt> (accessed February 6, 2009).

[58] "Nemoguća mirovna misija" (Impossible peace mission), *Oslobođenje*, April 11, 2002.

[59] Bob de Graaff, presentation, Conference of the Humanitarian Law Center, Budapest, January 16, 2004. De Graaff had been a member of the NIOD research team.

than I expected. It was shameful for the international community, the Dutch government, Dutchbat, and politicians in The Hague."[60] After the release of the report, IKV issued its own report in which it argued that the tragedy could have been much smaller had the Dutch reacted differently in several key moments.[61] They also demanded that the Dutch parliament form a parliamentary inquiry to find a definitive answer to the question of why the population of the enclave was not protected.[62] An inquiry was held, but IKV's request that survivors' representatives be included was not heeded. IKV continued to keep the Srebrenica issue alive. Inside Bosnia, its presence was strong within the family associations since, along with ICMP, it was one of the few groups that showed sustained concern for Srebrenica and its citizens. The report helped keep interest focused on Srebrenica, and was complemented by important decisions coming out of the ICTY around the same time.

The NIOD report was followed by further inquiry from the family associations into the Dutch government's actions. Shortly after its publication, the Women of Srebrenica asked the Dutch Embassy for a detailed accounting of all donations made in the name of Srebrenica since the end of the war. Between 1996 and 2002, the Dutch spent 592 million euros in Bosnia.[63] Total assistance to Srebrenica-related projects was 33,769,733 euros. On the list they provided, the Women of Srebrenica appeared twice, with 38,000 and 37,000 euro donations respectively, both in 1999. The Dutch were also large donors to the memorial center in Potočari and to the ICMP. Some observers commented that donations for things related to the survivors' concerns, like identification and the memorial, were sometimes underappreciated by the groups because those were not directly distributed to them. The desperate economic status of the survivors, however, was difficult to deny: most did not have enough money to make ends meet. Little effort was made by the international community as a whole to examine the plight of this population from a broad perspective, or to ensure that they were the direct beneficiaries of aid donations made in their name.

---

[60] Dion van den Berg, comments, Tuzla, July 8, 2003. "The whole discussion remained a Dutch discussion because the victims were not included," said van den Berg, a representative of IKV, during the presentation of a new book about Srebrenica: Hasan Nuhanović, *Uloga Medunarodnih elementa u Srebrenici "zaštićenoj zoni" – hronologia, analiza i komentari* (Role of international elements in the Srebrenica "protected area" – chronology, analysis, commentary) (Tuzla, 2003).

[61] Specifically, they argued that Karremans' answer to Mladić – that UNPROFOR could not provide buses to move people from Potočari to Tuzla – was a key mistake: had the UN provided this transport, the men would likely have been saved. A. Hadžić, "Holandski vojnici su mogli učiniti da tragedija u Srebrenici bude manja" (Dutch soldiers could have made the tragedy in Srebrenica smaller), *Dnevni Avaz*, April 2, 2002.

[62] Out of this inquiry, it was hoped that potential criminal cases could be brought before Dutch courts. See Nagorka Idrizović, "Istina o zločinu tražiće se od holandskog Parlamenta" (Truth about crime will be sought from Dutch parliament), *Oslobođenje*, April 22, 2002.

[63] "Compilation of Netherlands development assistance related to Srebrenica from 1995 till 2002," Embassy of the Netherlands, Sarajevo, no date. Copy on file with the author.

There had long been similar discussions about the misuse by Bosnian authorities of funds meant for Srebrenica's survivors, especially in the Tuzla canton, where a large group of them lived. It was alleged, for example, that money intended for them was spent on the water system for the canton, and even that the canton overestimated the number of survivors in its jurisdiction in order to get additional funds in their name.[64] The family associations, however, focused their demands for financial accountability at the international level, where actors were perceived to be (and likely were) more accountable and responsive. When the head of the Women of Srebrenica was asked why she had not asked local authorities for a similar accounting of funds spent in the name of Srebrenica, she responded, "they probably wouldn't reply to the request."[65]

Even if they were seen as more likely to answer, international actors were viewed with a dose of skepticism. Distrust of the Dutch, and sometimes generalized distrust of the European Union, permeated comments of association members, despite the fact that many international actors had helped them advance their cause. When European Union Force (EUFOR) was scheduled to take over from SFOR in late 2004, a member of the Mothers of the Enclaves of Srebrenica and Žepa argued, "I really don't know what to expect from their arrival. When we needed their help, they didn't want to offer it. They watched what happened and didn't react. And again, those troops, only under a different name are coming to Bosnia. After all that happened to us in 1995, nothing more can surprise us."[66] Their wartime experience continued to shape their opinions about any solution presented by European powers. Yet still they solicited answers and financial assistance from them, and cooperated with NGOs all over Europe.

Furthermore, even though Srebrenica's survivors distrusted the Dutch government, they treated it as a serious negotiating partner in legal affairs. In July 2004, the Mostar lawyers, accompanied by a bus filled with 50 Srebrenica widows and orphans, traveled to the Netherlands to present their case for reparations to the government. The lawyers' meetings with government representatives ran parallel to three protests by the Mothers of the Enclaves of Srebrenica and Žepa. Carrying signs and sheets with the names of their loved ones, the women protested in front of the Dutch parliament and Defense Ministry, on the square in front of the Anne Frank House, and on the Leidseplein, one of Amsterdam's biggest gathering spots.[67] The women leading the organization were keenly aware of

---

[64] "Hafizović: Donacije za Srebrenicu su usmjerene za projekte u Tuzlanskom kantonu" (Hafizović: Donations for Srebrenica were misdirected for projects in Tuzla canton), interview, *Ljiljan*, July 8–15, 2002.

[65] Interview with Hajra Ćatić, Tuzla, October 3, 2003. Ćatić is President of the Women of Srebrenica in Tuzla.

[66] S. Rožajac, "Srebreničani zabrinuti zbog odlaska NATO-a iz naše zemlje: EUFOR neće biti neutralan u BiH?" (People of Srebrenica worried about NATO's departure from our country: EUFOR will not be neutral in Bosnia-Herzegovina?), *Oslobođenje*, August 11, 2004.

[67] I accompanied the group on the bus trip to the Netherlands and observed the subsequent events and protests.

how important it was for them to be visible inside the Netherlands and on international news wires. Press coverage of the events was plentiful and the protests appeared on page three of the *International Herald Tribune*.[68] Nine years after the fall of the enclave, Srebrenica was still newsworthy, in part because survivors were still waiting for justice. In the Netherlands, the group renewed contact with diaspora organizations and also continued their long-standing relationship with IKV, which helped with the logistics of the visit.

The Dutch government promised a reply to the Mostar lawyers within six months. The lawyers sought 2 billion euros in compensation for the survivors and offered to negotiate in an out-of-court settlement.[69] The deal, the lawyers reasoned, would help the Netherlands save face as well.[70] A full court hearing would mean that, once filed, their 300-plus page brief about the Dutch role would become a public document, open to all the world's journalists and researchers. Months came and went and the lawyers did not receive a reply from the Dutch government. The Sarajevo Mothers group reported that they had been told informally that the Dutch would be willing to offer money, but not accept criminal responsibility.[71] By the end of 2006, the Dutch government had refused to entertain the allegations in the case; the legal team therefore opted to file in court, which produced another trip to the Netherlands in June 2007. The Mostar lawyers had paired up with a Dutch firm, Van Diepen Van der Kroef, which, as a legal firm registered in the country, served as the main representation in court. The Foundation of the Mothers of Srebrenica also registered offices in the Netherlands. The second main case, which started in June 2008, was filed by Hasan Nuhanović, the Dutchbat translator, and relatives of Dutchbat electrician Rizo Mustafić. The cases had slightly different legal strategies. The case brought by Nuhanović and the family of Mustafić, for example, focused on the rights of those who had been inside the UN compound and were handed over to Bosnian Serb forces. Both cases cited the ICTY's jurisprudence in their filings.

[68] *International Herald Tribune*, July 1, 2004, 3.

[69] See "Srebrenica Women Demand Massacre Compensation from Netherlands," *Agence France Press*, July 1, 2004; S. Rožajac, "Umjesto tužbe međunarodni advokatski tim najavljuje: Holandskom ministarstvu odbrane biće ponuđen sporazum" (Instead of suit, international legal team announces: Dutch Defense Ministry will be offered agreement), *Oslobođenje*, July 2, 2004; "Protesti i ispred kuće Anne Frank" (Protest also in front of Anne Frank House), *Dnevni Avaz*, July 2, 2004.

[70] The head of the third largest association, Ibran Mustafić, did not support the decision to file a suit against the Dutch. He called it an "absurd move," adding that the Netherlands was not the only party responsible for what happened in Srebrenica, and that reparations should also come from Bosnia, Serbia and Montenegro, France, Great Britain, and the United States. His organization filed a suit in the Strasbourg-based European Court of Human Rights against the countries it felt was responsible for the genocide. See S. Rožajac, "I država BiH na optuženičkoj klupi" (And the state of Bosnia and Herzegovina is accused of crimes), *Oslobođenje*, February 25, 2004. The court later informed the group that it would not be able to consider the charge against the United States as it fell outside of the court's jurisdiction. "Evropski sud odbio tužbu protiv SAD" (European court rejected suit against U.S.A.), *Oslobođenje*, June 18, 2004.

[71] "Holanđani nude pare, ali ne priznaju krivicu" (Dutch offer money but do not acknowledge guilt), *Oslobođenje*, October 14, 2004, 7.

United Nations and French Accountability

At the urging of civil society activists, France also explored its role in the tragedy as the nation that held the commanding positions in UNPROFOR when the enclave fell. A French parliamentary inquiry was set up to ascertain the nation's role. In July 2000, French NGO Médecins Sans Frontières (MSF) started lobbying for a commission of inquiry "to establish the extent to which the political and military actions of France were responsible for the paralysis of the UN and NATO during the attack on Srebrenica."[72] MSF lost 22 members of its local staff in the tragedy. This inquiry also addressed the long-standing rumors that the French had halted air strikes in exchange for the return of UN hostages, in a deal between French General Bernard Janvier, commander of UNPROFOR troops in the former Yugoslavia, and Mladić. During the inquiry's hearings, Janvier denied negotiating with the Serbs.[73] The commission also heard the testimony of ICTY investigator Jean René Ruez.[74] The final report, released in November 2001, argued that Britain, France, and the United States were all liable for the massacre.[75] The report stated that Srebrenica was a failure for France, but rejected allegations that a deal had been reached between Janvier and members of the VRS and RS leadership.[76] It stated, however, that Janvier made a "manifest error of judgment" by not allowing air strikes.[77] A delegation of Srebrenica's women traveled to France for the presentation of the report. They were not, however, asked to provide evidence during the inquiry. The issue of international accountability was broached with scholars, policy makers, and survivors, all calling attention to the importance of the issue. But these different discussions were not yet linked. Survivors were often left out of the process.

Even if the UN refused to entertain allegations of criminal liability in the fall of the enclave, it was difficult for the organization to ignore its role in the tragedy. The former head of UN Peacekeeping, Kofi Annan, had been promoted to Secretary

---

[72] "Srebrenica, Five Years Later: MSF Pushes for French Parliamentary Inquiry into the Fall of the Enclave," 2001 International Activity Report, Médecins Sans Frontières, <www.doctorswithoutborders.org/publications/ar/report.cfm?id=1208&cat=activity-report> (accessed February 4, 2009).

[73] The French inquiry was followed by a similar one in the Netherlands, the Dutch Parliamentary Commission of Inquiry into the Srebrenica massacre of July 1995, which published its final report in January 2003. MSF continued to insist that the question of why General Janvier refused air strikes remained unclear. See "Vital questions unanswered by Dutch inquiry into Srebrenica massacre," press release, Médecins Sans Frontières, January 30, 2003, <www.reliefweb.int/rw/rwb.nsf/AllDocsByUNID/7a57cce8b15d75eac1256cbf004ef8e7> (accessed February 5, 2005).

[74] "Srebrenica Massacres were Methodical, French Police Officer Says," *Agence France Presse*, February 23, 2001.

[75] James Burnet, "French Insist Britain Must Share Blame," *The Scotsman*, November 30, 2001.

[76] See *Rapport d'information déposé en application de l'article 145 du réglement par la mission d'information commune sur les événements de Srebrenica*, Assemblée nationale, 11e législature, président François Loncle, rapporteurs René André et François Lamy (Paris: Assemblée Nationale, 2001).

[77] James Burnet, "French Insist Britain ..."

General in 1997. The fall of the enclave and the genocide in Rwanda shadowed his new leadership. In November 1999, the General Assembly published "Report of the Secretary General Pursuant to General Assembly Resolution 53/35: The Fall of Srebrenica," which became known as the "UN Srebrenica Report." UN officials, former UNPROFOR representatives, Hasan Nuhanović, and current (unnamed) residents of Srebrenica were interviewed for the report, which also relied on forensic evidence of the ICTY that had been presented in various decisions and indictments. In 113 pages, the report outlined the details surrounding the fall of the Srebrenica enclave, as well as the UN's actions related to the country and the enclave. It concluded, "The United Nations experience in Bosnia was one of the most difficult in our history ... . Through error, misjudgment and an inability to recognize the scope of evil confronting us, we failed to do our part to save the people of Srebrenica from the Serb campaign of mass murder ... . Srebrenica crystallized a truth understood only too late by the United Nations and the world at large: that Bosnia was as much a moral cause as a military conflict. The tragedy will haunt our history forever."[78] Among those close to the UN, it was well known that a more damning version of the report was heavily edited before publication.[79]

The Sarajevo-based Mothers of the Enclaves of Srebrenica and Žepa were disappointed with the results of the report, a copy of which was not provided to them by the UN. They continued their demands for the criminal accountability of high UN officials. The Dutch were apparently pleased, as they escaped harsh criticism in the report, which laid blame for the fall of the enclave mostly on the UN itself.[80] On the eve of the closure of the UN mission in Bosnia, the UN announced a development project in Srebrenica worth 12 million dollars, to be run by the United Nations Development Programme (UNDP). The goal of the project was to foster economic and civil society development in the area. At its announcement, some labeled this a hollow act prompted by the UN's guilt for its role in the tragedy. It was, nonetheless, an unprecedented gesture by an international institution.

Outside of Bosnia, in parallel to the demands of Srebrenica's survivors, the idea that international institutions should be held responsible for their actions was gaining support in both scholarly and policy circles. This meant that the family associations' claims resonated with many international lawyers and experts, some of whom came to their aid. Much discussion centered on bringing parliaments into more frequent contact with international bodies through parliamentary assemblies and their increased participation in international summits.[81] Others began to scrutinize the postconflict state-building projects of the UN. As the UN

---

[78] Report of the Secretary General Pursuant to General Assembly Resolution 53/ 35: The Fall of Srebrenica, no. A/53/ 549, United Nations, November 15, 1999: 108.

[79] Interviews with former United Nations employees, 2004–2005.

[80] Othon Zimmerman, "Mixed Reaction to Srebrenica Report," Institute for War and Peace Reporting (IWPR), *Balkan Crisis Report*, No. 95, November 22, 1999, <www.iwpr.net/index.pl?archive/bcr/bcr_19991122_2_eng.txt> (accessed February 12, 2005).

[81] See for example: "Bridging the democracy gap in international relations: A stronger role for parliaments," Declaration adopted by consensus, Second World Conference of Speakers of

took up more and more functions of the state, delivering services and securing the rights of those within a given territory, the question of international accountability seemed even more relevant. The UN had become a different kind of human rights actor. In an article in *Human Rights Quarterly*, two scholars pondered a previously unthinkable question: "What if the UN could commit human rights violations in the fullest sense of the expression?"[82] The authors posited that, because the UN had taken on state-like functions in places such as Kosovo and East Timor, the organization could now become a perpetrator of human rights violations, a role traditionally assigned to states. While the focus of their argument was primarily these new missions, they noted that the peacekeeping missions of the 1990s in Bosnia and Somalia "raised concerns of the possibility of international humanitarian law violations in the context of 'Chapter six-and-a-half,' 'quasi-enforcement,' 'peacemaking' operations."[83] A generous read of this argument could make a case for UN accountability during peace operations, exactly what the family associations (and their team of lawyers) sought. Thus, the expanded norm of accountability had become a subject of interest in academia as well.

The Srebrenica Commission

The decisions coming out of the ICTY illustrated the extent of the Srebrenica tragedy and the extent of the cover-up that followed the crimes. Srebrenica's survivors looked toward other legal bodies to address their grievances. They found a receptive audience in a special institution created by the Dayton Peace Agreement to monitor violations of the European Convention on Human Rights (ECHR): the Human Rights Chamber (HRC). The Human Rights Chamber was a unique institution established under Annex 6 of the peace agreement and seen as necessary to address the country's numerous human rights violations. Unlike in The Hague Tribunal, victims could initiate proceedings at the HRC. The victims of Srebrenica were encouraged by one important precedent, which indicated to them that legal procedures could eventually yield desired information. A decision of the Human Rights Chamber addressed the claims of the widow of Bosnian Army General Avdo Palić, who was forcefully taken by the VRS from UNPROFOR forces in Žepa, another safe area, in July 1995. The decision ordered the RS government to investigate his disappearance and pay reparations to the widow for her mental suffering.[84] The RS

Parliament, UN Headquarters, New York, September 7–9 2005, <www.ipu.org/splz-e/sp-conf05/declaration.htm> (accessed February 4, 2009).

[82] Frédéric Mégret and Florian Hoffmann, "The UN as a Human Rights Violator? Some Reflections on the United Nations' Changing Human Rights Responsibilities," *Human Rights Quarterly* 25, no. 2 (2003): 315.

[83] Ibid., 326. On this theme, see also Lang, "United Nations and the Fall of Srebrenica"; and LeBor, *Complicity with Evil*.

[84] As one of his parting decisions, after the RS government failed to investigate the disappearance of Colonel Palić, High Representative Paddy Ashdown ordered the creation of a commission

government paid reparations at the end of 2001, but failed to investigate the disappearance. (Palić was identified in 2009. His remains were found in a mass grave in the Rogatica municipality.)

After following the Palić case, over 1,800 people representing families of the missing in Srebrenica filed a motion with the Human Rights Chamber, asking Republika Srpska "for the fate and whereabouts of their missing loved ones."[85] The initial applications to the Chamber were filed between November 2001 and March 2002. The Chamber was mandated to handle postwar violations of the ECHR, and not wartime violations per se, so the cases were considered in connection with the families' right to be informed about the location of their missing loved ones.[86]

On March 7, 2003, the Chamber ruled in favor of the applicants and demanded that the RS government immediately reveal the locations of the missing persons. It also ordered that RS pay 2 million KM in reparations. Amnesty International hailed the decision as the "first step toward providing justice to the relatives of the disappeared in Srebrenica."[87] The ICTY had laid the groundwork for the judgment in several ways. The Chamber referenced the Tribunal statute in its decision, which allows for the concurrent jurisdiction of the Tribunal and domestic courts for prosecution of violations of international humanitarian law, and which also used the "historical data and underlying facts" outlined in the Krstić case to provide background for the applications it received.[88] Without the fact base provided by the ICTY, the Chamber would have needed to conduct more investigations.

Rather than giving the reparations money directly to the families, the decision earmarked it for the Srebrenica-Potočari Memorial Foundation, which oversees the construction of the memorial facility in Potočari. Representatives of the Mothers of the Enclaves of Srebrenica and Žepa protested the judgment. Some international legal experts commented that the award of collective reparations was unprecedented in history. The Chamber had not finished its case in the minds of these survivors; it had only considered the first 49 applicants in the historic decision and had not ruled on over 1,800 others. In 2003, however, on the eve of the anniversary of the fall of the enclave, the Chamber ruled that the original judgment had "addressed" the other applicants. The Sarajevo group felt snubbed by

to reveal the fate of Esma Palić's husband. See Transcript of the OHR-OSCE Press Conference on Colonel Palić Case, January 20, 2006, OHR Press Office, <www.ohr.int/ohr-dept/presso/pressb/default.asp?content_id=36410> (accessed February 4, 2009). This story is also told in Bosnian filmmaker Alen Drljević's film "Esma" (Bosnia and Herzegovina: 2007).
[85] The Srebrenica Cases, Selimović (CH01-8365) and 48 Others, Decision on Admissibility and Merits, Human Rights Chamber for Bosnia and Herzegovina, March 7, 2003, <www.hrc.ba> (accessed February 4, 2009).
[86] The Chamber noted that the applicants raised issues covered in Articles 3, 8, and 13 of the ECHR. The Srebrenica Cases, 7.
[87] "Bosnia-Herzegovina: Human Rights Chamber decision on Srebrenica – a first step to justice," press release, EUR 63/007/2003, Amnesty International, March 7, 2003, <web.amnesty.org/library/Index/ENGEUR630072003?open&of=ENG-BIH> (accessed February 4, 2009).
[88] See The Srebrenica Cases, sections IV–VII.

the international community again. "It's all high politics," said Munira Subašić of the Association of Mothers of the Enclaves of Srebrenica and Žepa. "Why weren't all the cases considered individually? We're very disappointed."[89] She also argued that the dismissal diminished the seriousness of the crime.

There was, in fact, a touch of local politics at play in this particular case. The original applicants had worked more closely with the Women of Srebrenica and their representatives had negotiated with OHR about how funds would be distributed.[90] The Sarajevo group had been occupied with their lawsuit in the Netherlands and was not following the Chamber's case closely. Representatives of the Women of Srebrenica and other individual applicants reasoned that funds could not be distributed directly to the families lest it start a war among the survivors. They were also prepared for the dismissal of the other applicants. The RS government made its first donation to the fund for the memorial in July 2003, with a payment which many noted was precisely the amount the OHR had said was needed for completion of the facility.[91]

The RS government made an initial attempt to explain the events of July 1995 in a report published in September 2002. Published by the Documentation Center, Bureau of the Government of Republika Srpska for Relations with the ICTY, the report was submitted to the Chamber only in English and was not distributed to the public.[92] The Human Rights Chamber quoted it at length in its decision. Replying to the initial assertion that between 6,000 and 8,000 Bosniak men were executed, the first RS report described the figure as "evidently inflated," citing "invalid tracing requests, soldiers killed during combat, persons who died of physical conditions while fleeing, persons given asylum abroad, and men transferred to Muslim front lines immediately upon their arrival in Zenica or Tuzla."[93] The report maintained that "the number of Bosnian Muslim soldiers who were executed by Bosnian Serb forces for personal revenge or for simple ignorance of international law ... would probably stand at less than 100."[94] The report also stated that the existence of "mass graves does not always mean mass execution" and that the "exhumation site of the ICTY is to be considered one of the examples of mass graves created for hygienic reasons."[95]

The Chamber ordered RS to draft a second report by fall 2003. Republika Srpska delivered a second draft, but again did not distribute it to the public; the OHR and the Chamber felt the result of this effort too was unsatisfactory. High

[89] Nick Hawton, "Bosniak Compensation Bid Fails," IWPR, *Tribunal Update*, No. 320, July 11–18, 2003, <www.iwpr.net/?p=tri&s=f&o=164737&apc_state=henitri2003> (accessed February 4, 2009).
[90] Interview with Hajra Ćatić, President, Women of Srebrenica, Srebrenica, July 22, 2004.
[91] Hawton, "Bosniak Compensation Bid Fails."
[92] The Srebrenica Cases, 3–4.
[93] Ibid., 18.
[94] Ibid., 18.
[95] Ibid., 18.

Representative Paddy Ashdown said, "It is simply unacceptable that getting the truth from the [RS] government is like extracting rotten teeth."[96] He added that the report represented a "marked change of tone," but not a "change in substance."[97] The Chamber's decision ordered a commission to be set up to investigate events in Srebrenica under the auspices of the RS government. The report was later leaked to an independent TV station in Banja Luka, which revealed that it contained the first admissions by the RS government that massacres had taken place.[98]

In response to the pressure of the OHR, in December 2003 the RS government established a temporary working body called "The Commission for Investigation of the Events in and around Srebrenica between 10 and 19 July 1995." The Commission was composed of six members, including a representative of the survivors' community, Smail Čekić, a professor of history at the University of Sarajevo and director of the Institute for Research of Crimes Against Humanity and International Law; and a representative of the international community, Sir Francis Bacon, the director of the Missing Persons Institute. In addition, the OHR and the ICTY were given observer status. Several commission members were replaced at the beginning and there was some initial confusion about its mandate, but work went relatively smoothly after the appropriate team was formed. With the survivors mobilized domestically around an issue that the ICTY's documentation had established, the ability to manipulate facts decreased. It took a concerted local effort by international forces to get movement on the issue, aided by the fact that the OHR's Bonn Powers gave it the ability to remove uncooperative politicians, but the Tribunal's documentation was crucial to the process.

The Commission's interim report was published in June 2004 and was the first public admission by the RS government that a massacre had taken place.[99] The press reported that it contained the locations of 33 previously unknown mass graves. RS President Dragan Čavić, stopping short of apologizing for the massacre, said that it was a "black page in the history of the Serb people." Čavić was the first RS politician to make any such acknowledgement. He later told the Bosnian press, "I am completely aware of the international norms which dominate the world today. We must not be blind to them in detriment to the interests of our own people."[100] The norm of accountability put forth by The Hague was affecting the behavior of RS elite.[101] Čavić indicated that he understood and was at least somewhat sensitive to the global context of his actions.

---

[96] Anes Alic, "Srebrenica Denial Continues," *Transitions Online (Prague)*, October 23, 2003.

[97] Ibid.

[98] Vesna Peric Zimonjic, "Bosnian Serbs finally admit truth of Srebrenica deaths," *The Independent,* November 5, 2003, <www.independent.co.uk/news/world/europe/bosnian-serbs-finally-admit-truth-of-srebrenica-deaths-734602.html> (accessed February 5, 2009).

[99] Samir Krilic, "Bosnian Serbs Admit to Massacre," *Washington Post,* June 12, 2004.

[100] Izjave Dana, "Ne smijem biti slijepac prema svijetu," (I should not be blind to the world), *Oslobodenje,* July 25, 2004.

[101] Later, when the political climate changed, Čavić would tell a Bosnian magazine that it seemed like he had spoken in 2024, not 2004. See Dragan Čavić: "Dodik ima absolutnu vlast

The family associations were openly critical of the Commission, but quietly conceded among themselves that it represented progress, however small. They knew that the Commission was forced on the RS government, but suddenly they had RS officials contacting them on a regular basis, asking for information. Members acknowledged that it was "good to hear the words roll off [RS officials'] lips, even if under pressure."[102]

Many human rights advocates, however, would not concede even that much to the Commission. The lines of argument followed several threads. First, they argued that if the OHR was going to force the RS government to take part in a commission, it should be honest enough to set it up under the auspices of the OHR, not the RS government. Some said that it duplicated the work of the ICTY unnecessarily, wasting precious resources. They also argued that if a commission was set up for Srebrenica, then there was an obvious need for commissions for Višegrad, Prijedor and Brčko, other places where numerous violations of international humanitarian law and genocide had taken place.

Čavić's comments, similarly, were rejected by others because they were too little, too late, and did not come with any real form of accountability. Politicians who had recently refused to admit that the crimes occurred at all were now seen as offering a "fictitious apology" under pressure. One Bosnian Serb MP, Nikola Špirić, reflected this sentiment in saying that it "is tragic that all the information in the Srebrenica Commission's report came from RS authorities," adding that if it were true, he did not "understand how RS officials are still in their positions."[103] The president of the Research and Documentation Center, Mirsad Tokača, argued that the Serb people had to take on more responsibility. He said that collective responsibility exists, "not [in] the legal sense but in a moral and political sense [on the part of] all of those who supported the criminal regime."[104] In the newspapers, representatives of the Mothers of the Enclaves of Srebrenica and Žepa argued that Čavić's comments meant nothing to them, particularly because they had to wait nine years to hear them.

The critiques were an understandable public position for Srebrenica's long-suffering survivors. But the Commission was a sign of at least modest progress; RS politicians had not previously discussed Srebrenica with any honesty. The

ali i odgovornost" (Dodik has absolute power but also responsibility), Interview, *Dani*, no. 582, August 8, 2008. "From the point of view of the political atmosphere which is dominant today throughout Bosnia-Herzegovina, that which I said then seems unreal. It is completely unthinkable that today anyone from the political elite in Bosnia-Herzegovina would try to say something at least somewhat conciliatory, and not to mention something similar to that which I said four years ago. As things stand today, it looks as if that happened in 2024, not 2004." Ibid.

[102] Discussion with Srebrenica family association representative, May 26, 2004. Author's notes.
[103] "Špirić on the Srebrenica Commission Report," *The Tuzla Night Owl*, June 13, 2004, <www.tfeagle.army.mil/tfeno/Feature_Story.asp?Article=85796> (accessed January 30, 2005).
[104] Almir Terzić, "Fiktivni čin za spas Republike Srpske" (Fictitious act to save Republika Srpska), *Oslobođenje*, June 24, 2004.

Commission's work brought the topic of Srebrenica to the public in a way in which the ICTY had been unable. Without the ICTY, though, the creation of a Commission would have been unlikely. The Commission also made some ideas more palatable in RS. The General Secretary of the Social Democratic Party, Svetozar Pudarić, argued that the report placed pressure on the RS public and the international community, and changed the atmosphere, making possible the arrest of Radovan Karadžić and Ratko Mladić.[105] A Srebrenica survivor said, "On the record, I will tell you that we need more, that we need names of the perpetrators, more trials and justice for the victims of these crimes, but off the record I will say that the Commission has done much more than I expected."[106] The High Representative said that Čavić's statement in relation to the events in Srebrenica was a "potentially historical moment ... when the Serbs in BiH [faced] the crimes committed in their name and [admitted] that those people who committed these crimes are not national heroes, but the worst sort of criminals who shamed the Serb people and for that they must face justice in The Hague."[107] Inside Bosnia, the international community had approached the topic of war crimes, and of dealing with the past more generally, very tentatively.[108]

Initial euphoria wore off quickly after two of the mass graves listed in the RS report produced no bodies. The head of the Federal Commission for Missing Persons, Amor Mašović, returned to the schedule of exhumations his commission had followed before the Srebrenica Commission's formation. He refused to continue to support the work of the Commission. The long-awaited final report was submitted to the RS government on October 15, 2004. After being endorsed by the government, it was forwarded to the Human Rights Commission of the Constitutional Court, set up to take over the cases of the Human Rights Chamber that closed in December 2003. The final report differed from the preliminary report: it admitted that over 7,000 individuals had been massacred. The Commission used over 30 sources to arrive at the figure, which, even so, was not final. The report contained an annex with the names of 8,731 residents of the enclave, of whom 7,793 had gone missing between the 10th and 19th of July, and the rest after that. The Mothers of

---

[105] Ibid.

[106] Discussion with Srebrenica survivor, July 16, 2004.

[107] "Reaction by Ashdown," OHR BiH Media Round-up, June 24, 2004, <http://www.ohr.int/ohr-dept/presso/bh-media-rep/round-ups/default.asp?content_id=32712> (accessed July 21, 2009).

[108] Historian Robert Donia recounts one example in Srebrenica, "Ambassador Robert Berry, the OSCE Head of Mission, chaired the opening session of the first postwar municipal council meeting in Srebrenica. Although thousands of the town's [Bosniak] residents were slaughtered by Serbian troops in July 1995 in one of the war's worst atrocities, Berry made no mention of the crimes that were initiated only a few hundred yards away and less than four years ago. The meeting's tone was set in the keynote statement of his opening remarks. 'In forming the Assembly, Srebrenica has established a new beginning,' he stated. His omission made it clear that the OSCE was hoping to achieve reconciliation in Srebrenica without confronting the hard realities of recent history." Robert J. Donia, "The Quest for Tolerance in Sarajevo's Textbooks," *Human Rights Review* 1, no. 2 (January–March 2000): 40.

the Enclaves of Srebrenica and Žepa had submitted considerable documentation to the Commission, including a list with 10,500 names.[109] They thought the report should lead to new ICTY indictments and make known the identities of those war criminals not previously named in public.[110] There were some calls for a new suit against the RS government.[111]

In November 2004, nine years after Srebrenica's victims had been moved to secondary and tertiary mass graves, the RS government apologized for the participation of VRS forces in the massacre. Not going so far as to call the massacre a genocide (even though the ICTY had by then established it as such), the government statement said, "The government of Republika Srpska sympathizes with the pain of relatives of the Srebrenica victims and expresses sincere regrets and apologies over the tragedy which has happened to them."[112] The government committed to take "decisive steps to bring to justice all those who committed war crimes." This concession was the result of the actions of the survivors, who had utilized all the legal instruments available to them to pursue their goals.

It also made inaction on the part of international officials more unacceptable. When Bosnia failed to be invited to join NATO's Partnership for Peace (PfP) for a second time in December 2004, largely because of non-cooperation with the ICTY, the High Representative responded. One of his new measures was "an instruction to RS Prime Minister Dragan Mikerević to set up a group under the supervision of the EU Police Mission to study documentation produced by the Srebrenica Commission and identify those officials whose names appear in connection to the events of July 1995."[113] In May the Commission had "identified 25,083 people involved in the massacre in Srebrenica, 19,473 of which are said to have given orders or actively taken part in the killings."[114] The others indirectly contributed to the slaughter. The list included members of the RS Defense Ministry, the Army of Republika Srpska (VRS), and the RS Ministry of Interior. It was slowly becoming clearer that the international community's goals of Euro-Atlantic integration meant that war crimes had to be addressed. This was more than an issue of retributive justice; high levels of participation in the crimes meant that the issue affected all of Bosnian society.

[109] "Na spisku imena 8731 Srebreničana" (On list of names, 8731 people from Srebrenica), *Oslobođenje*, October 16, 2004, 9.
[110] Ibid.
[111] A. Hadžić, "Mašović: Porodice žrtava genocida imaju pravo tužiti RS" (Mašović: Families of genocide victims have the right to initiate legal proceedings against RS), *Dnevni Avaz*, October 16, 2004, 9.
[112] Nicholas Wood, "Bosnian Serbs Apologize for Srebrenica Massacre," *New York Times*, November 11, 2004.
[113] "High Representative Maps Out Process to Tackle War Criminal Networks and to Reform BiH's Security Institutions," press release, Office of the High Representative, December 16, 2004, <www.ohr.int/ohr-dept/presso/pressr/default.asp?content_id=33742> (accessed February 9, 2009).
[114] Anes Alic, "25,000 participated in Srebrenica massacre," *ISN Security Watch*, May 10, 2005, <www.isn.ethz.ch/news/sw/details.cfm?id=13046> (accessed September 10, 2005).

ICTY Cases Relating to Srebrenica

The ICTY tried a handful of individuals for their involvement in the tragedy, setting important precedents and establishing facts that aided developments inside Bosnia. One of the first judgments for violations of international humanitarian law since the Nuremburg trials was issued in response to crimes committed after the fall of the enclave.[115] The accused, Dražen Erdemović, was a low-ranking Bosnian Croat soldier in the VRS who confessed to having taken part in the execution of an estimated 70 people on a farm near Srebrenica called Pilića – the site of one of the biggest massacres of the Bosnian war, where approximately 1,200 Bosniak men and boys perished.[116] The prosecution recommended a lenient sentence because of the defendant's remorse and cooperation with the Tribunal in identifying mass graves previously unknown to the prosecution, which aided other trials. On appeal, his sentence was reduced to five years, most of which had already been served. The sentence was not well received among the family associations. After the initial judgment, the headline of one Bosnian daily, *Oslobođenje*, decried: "Ten years for 70 Murders!"[117]

In August 2001, the highest-ranking VRS officer to be tried for war crimes was convicted of genocide. General Radislav Krstić was sentenced to 46 years in prison for the crime of genocide. This was the longest sentence given by the Tribunal, but was short of the eight consecutive life sentences sought by the prosecution, led by Mark Harmon.[118] The presiding judge, Almiro Rodrigues, stated: "In July 1995, General Krstić, individually, you agreed to evil."[119] This was the first time an individual was convicted of the crime of genocide in Europe by an international tribunal since the crime was outlined in the 1948 Convention on the Prevention and Punishment of the Crime of Genocide.[120] The Convention defined genocide as any of a list of specified acts "committed with intent to destroy, in whole or in part, a

---

[115] For background on the case see Mirko Klarin, "Defendant for the Prosecution: To the Prosecutors, Erdemović is Above All a Valued Witness," IWPR, *Tribunal Update*, November 1996.

[116] *Prosecutor v. Dražen Erdemović* (IT-96-22), Judgement, ICTY, March 5, 1998, <www.icty.org/x/cases/erdemovic/tjug/en/erd-tsj980305e.pdf> (accessed July 5, 2009).

[117] One survivor, whose father was killed by Erdemović, sought to file a civil suit against him but was unable to locate him. Having served his short sentence, Erdemović was rumored to be living somewhere in Western Europe.

[118] See "Za Genocid u Srebrenici Radislavu Krstiću 46 Godina Zatvora" (Radislav Krstić gets 46 years for genocide in Srebrenica), *Oslobođenje*, August 3, 2001; "Serb General Convicted of Genocide," *The Guardian*, August 2, 2002; and "Serb general to serve 46 years for war crimes," *Associated Press*, August 3, 2001.

[119] Trial transcript, August 2, 2001, p. 10191, <www.icty.org/x/cases/krstic/trans/en/010802it.htm> (accessed July 22, 2009).

[120] NB: In 1997, a German court convicted Bosnian Serb Nikola Jorgić of genocide for crimes committed in Bosnia. Jorgić had been a member of a paramilitary group during the war. The decision was significant because the crimes were committed in the Doboj area of Bosnia, not in Srebrenica.

national, ethnical, racial or religious group, as such."[121] Predictably, the sentence was perceived as too light by the family associations. Munira Subašić, head of the Mothers of the Enclaves of Srebrenica and Žepa, argued, "We, survivors of the Srebrenica massacre, don't think that justice has been served. ... He should have been sentenced to life." She added that although he could not possibly outlive his sentence, it was a symbolic matter.[122]

The Appeals Chamber reduced Krstić's sentence and charge; they found him guilty of "aiding and abetting genocide" and ordered him to serve 35 years in prison. Still, it was the first time a court of law determined that genocide had been committed on the territory of the Republic of Bosnia and Herzegovina; for many, any question about the character of the war was answered. The decision, however, did not spark major debates inside Bosnia, a fact that disappointed many local human rights activists. In addition, news of the decision rippled through Bosnia in different ways. One civil society leader recalled being on a trip to Banja Luka the day the final sentence was announced. The RS news outlet reported, "General Krstić received a lighter sentence today in The Hague for *so-called* crimes in Srebrenica."[123] Only when he got to the Federation and switched to another radio station did he learn that the court had issued a historic decision.[124] This was further evidence of other local obstacles the ICTY faced in Bosnia, such as the lack of a common public forum since new media were fragmented, largely along ethnic lines.

When Slobodan Milošević was found dead in his cell in March 2006, some in Bosnia felt that a chance to determine the character of the war had been lost. Milošević had been indicted for crimes in Bosnia resulting from both superior and individual criminal responsibility. His death meant that the court could not issue a final verdict. The prosecution team in his trial had presented evidence that he

[121] Convention on the Prevention and Punishment of the Crime of Genocide, December 9, 1948, Approved and proposed for signature and ratification or accession by General Assembly, Resolution 260 A (III), Office of the High Commissioner of Human Rights, <www.unhchr.ch/html/menu3/b/p_genoci.htm> (accessed February 5, 2009).
[122] "Survivors Condemn 'Lenient' Verdict," *BBC News*, August 2, 2001, <news.bbc.co.uk/1/hi/world/europe/1470706.stm> (accessed February 5, 2009).
[123] Interview with civil society organization representative, Sarajevo, April 23, 2004.
[124] A second genocide charge soon followed. Vidoje Blagojević, former commander of the VRS Bratunac Brigade, was sentenced to 18 years in prison for his complicity in the Srebrenica genocide. The trial chamber noted that the crimes were committed with a "level of brutality and depravity not previously seen" and were among the "darkest days in modern European history." Along with Blagojević, Dragan Jokić, former chief engineer of the Bratunac Brigade, received nine years for lesser charges. At the appellate level, Jokić's original verdict was upheld, but Blagojević was acquitted of the charge of complicity in genocide and his sentence was reduced to 15 years. That meant that the only ICTY judgment of genocide was in the trial of Radislav Krstić. See the Case Information Sheet Blagojević and Jokić (IT-02-60), <www.icty.org/x/cases/blagojevic_jokic/cis/en/cis_blagojevic_jokic_en.pdf> (accessed July 20, 2009); and "ICTY: Blagojević Acquitted of Complicity in Genocide," Balkan Investigative Reporting Network (BIRN), May 9, 2007, <www.birn.eu.com/en/82/15/2839/> (accessed July 20, 2009).

had advance knowledge of the genocide in Srebrenica.[125] The prosecution team had spent years building the case that tied him to the crimes, including identifying an order by the Interior Minister requesting Serbian police forces move to Eastern Bosnia to participate in the attack on the enclave. This fact came up in the testimony of former Assistant Interior Minister Obrad Stevanović and that of other related witnesses. One of the strongest pieces of evidence linking Serbia to the massacre came during the defense phase of the trial: a videotape was aired in the courtroom showing the Scorpions – a Serbian paramilitary force on the payroll of the Serbian Ministry of Interior – executing six Bosniak males after the fall of the enclave. It was quickly rebroadcast throughout the region. As the first strong visual evidence of Serbia's involvement in the crimes, the tape prompted a swift reaction in Serbia and numerous arrests in Belgrade followed.[126] It was a hint of the more extensive impact the court could have had if evidence had been disseminated more widely in the region and outreach had been given more resources.

ICTY witnesses sometimes presented evidence not favorable to the UN, which aided the efforts of the survivors. Ambassador Diego Arria, Venezuela's erstwhile United Nations representative and coordinator of the UNSC's mission to Bosnia in 1993, argued in his testimony, as he had in his report to the Security Council many years before, that the Srebrenica massacre was a process of what he called "slow-motion genocide" that could have been foreseen, not only by Milošević, but by the UN. He described the atmosphere of impunity created by UN actions, and the appalling conditions that existed in the enclave, information which, the Prosecution argued, must have reached Milošević himself through the course

---

[125] See this part of the indictment of Slobodan Milošević, *Prosecutor v. Slobodan Milošević* (IT-02-54), Amended Indictment "Bosnia and Herzegovina," ICTY, November 22, 2002, <www.icty.org/x/cases/slobodan_milosevic/ind/en/mil-ai040421-e.htm> (accessed July 20, 2009).

[126] Early reports about the impact showed that the public was still divided; a third of respondents in Serbia thought the tape was a fake. See Beth Kampschor, "Serbs Divided Over Grim Video," *Christian Science Monitor*, June 15, 2005, <www.csmonitor.com/2005/0615/p06s01-woeu. html> (accessed July 20, 2009). Another poll conducted by Banja Luka–based Alternative TV found that 95 percent believed that the ICTY caused Milošević's death. See Gordana Katana, "Bosnian Serbs Mourn Milošević," BIRN, *Balkan Insight*, March 14, 2006, <www.birn.eu.com/ en/25/10/1272> (accessed July 20, 2009). The ICTY President at the time, Theodore Meron, told PBS: "There is no question that this tape is having – has been having a real impact on public opinion in the region. I think it will act as a very strong antidote to the rampant denial that we have seen in countries like Serbia, for example. They did not want to realize how terrible were the events in Srebrenica, in its character, in its magnitude. Srebrenica is an atrocity reminiscent of the events that occurred during the Second World War." "Conversation: War Crimes," Online NewsHour, NewsHour with Jim Lehrer Transcript, June 14, 2005, <www.pbs.org/ newshour/bb/europe/jan-june05/meron_6-14.html> (accessed July 20, 2009). History arguably would side more with Meron. A survey taken in Serbia in June 2005 asked: "The film clips of the shootings in Bosnia provoked the following feelings in you" and allowed respondents to indicate more than one answer. The top responses were: pity (sažalenja) 51.7 %; sadness (tugu) 48.6%; anger towards the executioners (besa prema počiniocima) 43.2%. See Faktor Plus, *Aktuelna ekonomsko- politička scena Srbije* (Current Economic and Political Scene of Serbia), Belgrade, June 2005. Copy on file with the author.

of normal diplomatic channels.[127] Proof of advance knowledge of developments bolstered the charges laid out in the indictment. Principal Trial Attorney in the Office of the Prosecutor, Geoffrey Nice, asked Arria about the reporting requirements of the UN Security Council and how information flowed:

Nice: Returning to the issue of impunity that may or may not have been created, was the atmosphere and the attitude that was apparent to you in the United Nations something that should have been or would have been available to Yugoslavia?

Arria: Yes. So much so I remember that the Yugoslavian ambassador at the time, Jokić, used to send letters, Your Honours, to his colleague in Venezuela, informing exactly what we were doing in the private consultations of the Security Council. I remember one day telling to Jokić that I wasn't going to send more reports to my own government about my performance in the Security Council because his reports were more fully informed than even mine, and presented even faster.

Nice: So if it was coming to Venezuela from the Security Council, your inference is that it was going at the same speed and the same quality to Belgrade.

Arria: I have to imagine that, sir.[128]

This testimony emphasized that Milošević would have known about the situation in Srebrenica, at the very least through normal diplomatic channels.

Arria's testimony also focused on the role of the international community and gave activists in the region more material toward their effort to expand accountability for the massacre. During his cross-examination by Milošević, the accused noted that Arria's statement outlined how poorly informed the UNSC had been, and that Arria considered the poor flow of documentation a dereliction of institutional obligations. Arria had harsh words for the UN. Citing the Council's lack of accurate information about conditions in the enclave, Arria argued, "I consider this operation one of the most – the greatest cover-up operation of the United Nations officially because so much information was kept away from the – from the Security Council membership to act upon."[129] Still, the bulk of Arria's testimony reinforced the point that Milošević would have been informed about the humanitarian disaster in the enclave.

Srebrenica's survivors felt that tying Milošević to the massacre was an important aspect of the ICTY's work. Some argued that his death rendered the court a failure, never able to provide a judgment on its most important case.[130] In fact, success or

---

[127] Arria's testimony can be found in the trial transcripts for February 10, 2004, ICTY Trial Transcript, United Nations, February 10, 2004, <www.icty.org/x/cases/slobodan_milosevic/ trans/en/040210ED.htm> (accessed July 10, 2009). His testimony starts at p. 31711.

[128] Arria testimony, ICTY trial transcript, <www.icty.org/x/cases/slobodan_milosevic/trans/ en/040210ED.htm>, transcript. p. 31721 (accessed July 10, 2009).

[129] Arria testimony, ICTY trial transcript, <www.icty.org/x/cases/slobodan_milosevic/trans/ en/040210ED.htm>, transcript p. 31740 (accessed July 10, 2009).

[130] For another view, see Aryeh Neier, "Milošević Trial Not in Vain," Open Society Institute and Soros Foundations Network, March 24, 2006, <www.soros.org/resources/articles_publica- tions/articles/milosevic_20060324> (accessed July 10, 2009). See also "Weighing the Evidence,

failure could never have hinged on one case alone; events merely shifted emphasis to other ICTY trials and to the proceedings at the neighboring International Court of Justice (ICJ), in which Bosnia charged the Federal Republic of Yugoslavia (FRY) (later because of the dissolution of the country, just Serbia) with genocide, the first case of its kind. Scholars argued that the rich documentation from the trials provided for an understanding of the causes of the wars of succession.[131]

The court's decisions also provided evidence as to how the trial chamber felt the prosecution's case against Milošević was going. One decision in particular, overlooked in most popular discussion of the trial, gave survivors insight about the trial chamber's views of Milošević's role in the Bosnian war. This was the June 16, 2004, "Decision on Motion for Judgement of Acquittal."[132] After the prosecution's case, a motion for acquittal was filed by the Amici Curiae ("friends of the court"); in response, the court found sufficient evidence to support each count challenged in the indictments, which it described in a lengthy decision of June 16, 2004. This included the charge of genocide. By a vote of 2 to 1, with Judge Kwaan dissenting, the judges upheld the charge. All three judges supported the other charges. (Charges for certain municipalities were dropped, a change that often happens in this stage of a trial.)[133]

The court also started the largest collective trial since World War II, for crimes committed in the enclave. In July 2006, a trial began for seven Bosnian Serbs indicted for crimes that occurred during and after the fall of the enclave.[134] Many of the indictees participated in the effort to conceal the crimes that occurred in the fall of 1995.

From the survivors' perspective, the arrest of Naser Orić, commander of the joint armed forces of the sub-region of Srebrenica in the Bosnian Army, was one of the greatest sources of disappointment with the ICTY. Transferring a Bosnian Army officer before those most responsible for the fall of the enclave were arrested

Lessons from the Milosevic Trial," Human Rights Watch, December 13, 2006, <www.hrw.org/en/reports/2006/12/13/weighing-evidence> (accessed July 10, 2009).

[131] On the role of documentation, see also Nena Tromp Vrkić, "Understanding the Milošević Case: Legacy of an Unfinished Trial," paper presented at the annual meeting of the International Studies Association, New York, February 16, 2009.

[132] *Prosecutor v. Slobodan Milošević* (IT-02-54-T), Decision on Motion for Judgement of Acquittal, June 16, 2004, <www.icty.org/x/cases/slobodan_milosevic/tdec/en/040616.htm> (accessed July 10, 2009). It discussed the decision in Bosnia's case against Serbia at the International Court of Justice. See also Edina Bećirević, "ICJ Judgment Significant Despite Flaws," IWPR, *Tribunal Update*, No. 491, March 2, 2007, <www.iwpr.net/?p=tri&s=f&o=333778&apc_state=henptri> (accessed July 10, 2009).

[133] The decision was published as a book in Bosnian and English with forewords by American historian Robert J. Donia and Smail Čekić. See Robert J. Donia and Smail Čekić, *Milošević guilty of genocide: decision on motion of the Hague Tribunal of 16 June 2004* (Miloševiću dokazan genocid u Bosni) (Sarajevo: Institute for Research of Crimes Against Humanity and International Law of the University of Sarajevo, 2007).

[134] See Prosecutor v. Vujadin Popović, Ljubiša Beara, Drago Nikolić, Ljubomir Borovčanin, Radivoje Miletić, Milan Gvero, and Vinko Pandurević, Case Information Sheet, ICTY, <www.icty.org/x/cases/popovic/cis/en/cis_popovic_al_en.pdf> (accessed July 20, 2009).

gave the impression that the court lacked good judgment. Orić commanded forces in the enclave from 1992 and was charged with command and individual responsibility for the wanton destruction and plunder that took place during raids on Serb villages around Srebrenica in 1992 and 1993, including the Christmas day attack in Kravica.[135] The murder charges in the indictment were dropped when the prosecution failed to produce enough evidence. Orić eventually was found not guilty of any direct involvement in the crimes, but guilty of two counts of failing to "discharge his duty as a superior to take necessary and reasonable measures" to prevent the occurrence of murder and cruel treatment. He was sentenced to two years but had already been in prison for over three, and his immediate release was ordered.[136]

Even after his release, Orić had the reputation of a renegade commander, but many of the enclave's residents viewed him as one of the few who had made an effort to protect them. Of five NGOs working on issues relating to Srebrenica, all stopped short of proclaiming his innocence when asked about the indictment. Many felt that his arrest had had much to do with The Hague needing Bosniak defendants to "balance out" the numbers of Serbs indicted. They also thought that the manner in which he was arrested was inappropriate – a full SFOR operation with helicopters – given that Orić had not hidden after the war. It was seen as a travesty that the court would choose to arrest Orić before it had in its custody those they felt were most responsible for the massacre, Radovan Karadžić and Ratko Mladić. Orić's transfer was a dramatic event, as some survivors blocked the road, proclaiming their support for him. Orić was eventually acquitted of all charges at the appellate level.[137]

Ultimately, the court indicted 22 individuals for crimes in the Srebrenica region in different court cases, most for crimes that occurred in July 1995 (see Table 4.1). The highest military official in the enclave after it fell, VRS General Ratko Mladić, remained at large as of the end of 2009.

Outreach in the Municipality

The family associations had an uneasy and tendentious relationship with the court over the postwar period. Though hope in the institution was extremely high at the end of the war, it eroded over time, even though local outreach professionals in Bosnia made a particular effort to educate them about the limitations of international criminal law.

---

[135] See *Prosecutor v. Naser Orić* (IT-03-68), Initial Indictment, ICTY, March 28, 2003, <www.icty.org/x/cases/oric/ind/en/ori-ii030328e.pdf> (accessed July 10, 2009).

[136] The final judgment is at: <www.icty.org/x/cases/oric/tjug/en/ori-jud060630e.pdf> (accessed July 10, 2008).

[137] His freedom was short, however: Orić was arrested and charged with racketeering in October 2008. See "Naser Orić Arrested in Sarajevo," *B92*, October 3, 2008, <www.b92.net/eng/news/region-article.php?yyyy=2008&mm=10&dd=03&nav_id=53961> (accessed July 10, 2009).

TABLE 4.1. Srebrenica-related trials at the ICTY (in alphabetical order)

Indicted (ICTY Case Number)	Date of initial indictment	Rank/position at the time of (alleged) crimes	Trial and appeals completed	Sentence
Ljubiša Beara (IT-05-88) (joint trial)	March 26, 2002	Colonel, Chief of Security, Main Staff, Army of Republika Srpska,VRS	No; ongoing	
Vidoje Blagojević (IT-02-60)	October 30, 1998	Colonel, Bratunac Brigade, VRS	Yes	15 years (Serving)
Ljubomir Borovčanin (IT-05-88) (joint trial)	September 6, 2002	Deputy Commander, MUP Special Police Brigade (SPB)	No; ongoing	
Dražen Erdemović (IT-96-22)	May 29, 1996	Soldier, 10th Sabotage Detachment, VRS	Yes; Guilty Plea; Yes	5 years (Completed)
Milan Gvero (IT-05-88) (joint trial)	February 10, 2005	Assistant Commander for Morale, Legal and Religious Affairs of the Main Staff, VRS	No; ongoing	
Dragan Jokić (IT-02-60-T)	May 30, 2001	Major, Chief of Engineering, Zvornik Brigade, VRS	Yes	9 years (Serving)
Radovan Karadžić (IT-95-5/18)	July 25, 1995	President, Republika Srpska	No; Trial started Oct. 2009	
Radislav Krstić (IT-98-33)	November 2, 1998	General Major, Commander of the Drina Corps, VRS	Yes	35 years (Serving)
Radivoje Miletić (IT-05-88) (joint trial)	February 10, 2005	Chief of Operations and Training and Deputy Chief of Staff, VRS	No; ongoing	

(continued)

TABLE 4.1. *(continued)*

Indicted (ICTY Case Number)	Date of initial indictment	Rank/position at the time of (alleged) crimes	Trial and appeals completed	Sentence
Slobodan Milošević (IT-02-54)	November 22, 2001 (for Bosnia)	President of Serbia	No; Accused died in March 2006	
Ratko Mladić (IT-09-92)	July 25, 1995	Commander of the Main Staff, General, VRS	No; At large	
Drago Nikolić (IT-05-88) (joint trial)	September 6, 2002	Chief of Security, Zvornik Brigade, VRS	No; ongoing	
Momir Nikolić (IT-02-60/1)	March 26, 2002	Assistant Commander (Chief) for Security and Intelligence, Bratunac Brigade, VRS	Yes	20 years
Dragan Obrenović (IT-02-60/2)	April 9, 2001	Lt. Colonel, Zvornik Brigade, VRS	Yes; Guilty plea/ Plea agreement	17 years (Serving)
Naser Orić (IT-03-68)	March 28, 2003	Commander of the Joint Armed Forces of the Sub-Region Srebrenica, Army of the Republic of Bosnia and Herzegovina (ARBiH)	Yes	Acquitted of all charges
Vinko Pandurević (IT-05-88) (joint trial)	November 2, 1998	Lt. Colonel, Commander, Zvornik Brigade, VRS	No; ongoing	
Momčilo Perišić (IT-04-81)	February 24, 2005	Chief of General Staff of Yugoslav Army (VJ)	No; ongoing	
Vujadin Popović (IT-05-88) (joint trial)	March 26, 2002	Lieutenant Colonel, Drina Corps, VRS	No; ongoing	

Indicted (ICTY Case Number)	Date of initial indictment	Rank/position at the time of (alleged) crimes	Trial and appeals completed	Sentence
Franko Simatović (IT-03-69)	May 1, 2003	Commander, Special Operations Unit, of State Security Service, MUP, Republic of Serbia	No; ongoing	
Jovica Stanišić (IT-03-69)	May 1, 2003	Chief of State Security Service, MUP, Republic of Serbia	No; ongoing	
Zdravko Tolimir (IT-05-88-2)	February 10, 2005	Assistant Commander for Intelligence and Security of the Main Staff, VRS	No; Pre-trial stage	
Milorad Trbić (IT-05-88/1)	March 24, 2005 (amended indictment)	Captain, Zvornik Brigade, VRS	Case referred to Court of Bosnia and Herzegovina	

Source: ICTY. The ICTY's website introduced in 2009 has a geographically based representation of cases; see the Interactive Map at <www.icty.org>. Click on the Srebrenica map for a list of the cases in the chart above. Case information is from the Case Information Sheet (NB: The Trbić case is not listed there as it was transferred to the Court of Bosnia and Herzegovina).

To give but one example, the court's use of plea agreements was difficult for the family associations to understand. Plea agreements expedited the processing of cases and enabled the court to acquire information for future indictments. Family associations generally viewed such agreements negatively. However, the work of ICTY outreach coordinators had an effect: the leaders of family associations would eventually calmly articulate the benefits of the agreements when asked.[138]

Despite disappointment with the court, it remained the last hope of many survivors. On March 8, 2004, International Women's Day, approximately 50

---

[138] I observed a change in tone and a greater understanding of plea agreements between 2002 and 2008.

representatives of the Mothers of the Enclaves of Srebrenica and Žepa stood in front of the former UN headquarters, still home to the Tribunal's regional office, and demanded that it keep its door open. The Bosnian press had recently reported that the Security Council ordered the ICTY to wrap up all investigations in 2004 and all initial trials before 2008, but the survivors believed that the domestic courts were not yet ready to replace it. Munira Subašić said: "The Hague can't just give up on us now when we most need it. Because if that happens, justice will never see the light of day."[139] They had with them a petition bearing 10,000 signatures supporting their position that the ICTY should continue to operate. At the time, the War Crimes Chamber at Bosnia's State Court, which would localize the war crimes trials, was still a year from opening.

The people who occupied key roles at the ICTY influenced impressions of the court. Some of the family associations felt that some staffers traded on the Srebrenica cause for publicity rather than the work of the court. A scene from the 12th anniversary of the massacre was illustrative. Flanked by bodyguards and photojournalists, Carla Del Ponte, then Chief Prosecutor of the ICTY, had insisted on meeting with survivors of the Srebrenica massacre in Potočari. As she entered a building for the scheduled appointment, trailed by her staff, a widow screamed at her. Like hundreds of families, the widow was preparing to bury loved ones recently unearthed from mass graves and positively identified. Del Ponte's appearance in Potočari was against the wishes of many members of the family associations and was seen as an effort to grab attention. As Srebrenica's survivors prepared for a solemn day, Del Ponte's presence was viewed as another hollow gesture by the international community. These events demonstrated how perceptions of the court were often influenced by the people who led it, and not the decisions it produced.

The ICTY held an outreach event in Srebrenica in May 2005, following similar gatherings in Foča, Brčko, Konjic, and Prijedor. The goal of the event was to present the court's findings to the communities living near where the crimes occurred. The all-day event featured investigator Jean René Ruez, who discussed investigations, and prosecutor Mark Harmon, who addressed the intricacies of the Krstić trial.[140] It had taken almost exactly a decade for the ICTY to organize direct contact with the citizens in the municipality. Although outreach events were a welcome addition to the ICTY's activities in Bosnia, considering the enormity of the

---

[139] S. Rožajac, "Haški sud ne može dignuti ruke od nas" (Hague court can't abandon us), *Oslobođenje*, March 9, 2004.

[140] On Ruez, see Meg Bortin, "The Policeman Who Dug out the Horrors of Srebrenica," *International Herald Tribune*, July 11, 2008, <www.iht.com/articles/2008/07/11/europe/bosnia.php> (accessed February 9, 2009). Ruez's work for the court was addressed in Giacomo Battiato's film "Resolution 819," named after the UNSC resolution that set up the safe area. Writing about his impression of the film in a Sarajevo-based weekly was Hasan Nuhanović, "Drugi pišu našu historiju" (Others write our history), *Dani*, no. 596, November 14, 2008; Nuhanović's review recounts how he contacted the Mothers of the Enclaves of Srebrenica and Žepa to bring to their attention a scene in the film in which a Serb soldier holds a gun to the

problem, including the sheer numbers of citizens involved in the tragedy, a one-day conference addressed only the tip of the iceberg.

To be sure, the ICTY – especially local employees – understood this. Outreach coordinators spent a significant amount of time fielding questions from the family associations, explaining decisions and legal terminology. The groups were invited to other ICTY-sponsored seminars, including one about guilty pleas and plea agreements held in December 2003. It was during this seminar that ICTY officials had some of their first meetings with family associations and began to realize the importance of outreach. Prosecutor Mark Harmon also participated in a round-table organized by the Sarajevo group in July 2003, an event attended by activists, legal professionals, and members of the press. In 2007, former OTP Principal Trial Attorney Geoffrey Nice visited Srebrenica and showed a film about the Milošević trial to a meeting attended by 30 of Srebrenica's survivors.[141] There was, however, only one official outreach event in the municipality of Srebrenica itself.

The lack of more extensive outreach meant that residents in the area of the former enclave were largely unaware of the Tribunal's findings, with the exception of returnees and survivors who had made an effort to educate themselves. Local residents had only the Bosnian broadcast and print media as sources of information about the Tribunal; progressive publications often faced distribution problems in Eastern Bosnia where, for many years, hardline nationalists had controlled distribution channels.

Almost 15 years after the fall of the enclave, pictures of Ratko Mladić and Radovan Karadžić could be found openly displayed on wine bottles where they were celebrated as heroes in neighboring Bratunac, which was still controlled by the nationalist SDS (Serb Democratic Party). Returnees were faced with numerous daily (and traumatic) reminders about the tragedy they survived: one displaced person living in central Bosnia reported a 2 KM (1.02 euro) surcharge for the "Radovan Karadžić fund" on her electricity bill in Milići, a small town not far from Srebrenica.[142] On July 12, 2007, a group of young men wearing t-shirts displaying pictures of Ratko Mladić walked up and down a street in downtown Srebrenica populated by Bosniak returnees, in a clear effort to intimidate them. Later that day, a group in World War II uniforms of the Serbian-nationalist Chetniks lined up in front of the town's mosque while cars drove through town waving Chetnik flags.[143] In 2009, a similar gathering was even larger.

Around the time of the RS apology in the fall of 2004, the United Nations High Commissioner for Refugees (UNHCR) reported that only 2,931 Bosniaks,

---

head of a Dutch peacekeeper, an event that never happened. The family association agreed with Nuhanović that it was a "serious falsification of history."

[141] A.H., "Tužilac Najs u Srebrenici" (Prosecutor Nice in Srebrenica), *Dnevni Avaz*, June 21, 2007. Nice's visit was not an official ICTY event. The film, "Milošević on Trial," was made by Michael Christoffersen (Denmark, 2007).

[142] Interview with Srebrenica survivor, Zavidovići, July 24, 2004.

[143] Author field notes, Srebrenica, July 2007.

amounting to just 10 percent of the prewar population, had returned to the municipality fulltime.[144] The Srebrenica municipality was quietly contrasted with Prijedor in northwestern Bosnia, to which over 20,000 Bosniaks had returned to live full time. That municipality also had a high number of missing persons, as well as the sites of the Omarska and Trnopolje camps, but Prijedor also had the highest number of prosecutions per capita. Prosecutions were thought to help facilitate the process of return by lessening the fear faced by returnees.[145]

The development community started to take human rights issues into account when assessing developmental planning. A UNDP pilot project on "Rights-Based Municipal Assessment," which included a study on the Srebrenica municipality, argued that a lack of information about missing persons and the unwillingness of RS authorities to provide for the socioeconomic welfare of the families of the missing were hindering long-term development. RS officials denied assistance to Srebrenica's survivors, while the families of former VRS soldiers received benefits.[146]

Outside the municipality, survivors of the tragedy faced many difficulties and were publicly mocked without sanction. In 2002, at a soccer game in Sarajevo, fans of the Banja Luka–based team held up a sign which read "Nož, Žica, Srebrenica" (Knife, Wire, Srebrenica), a familiar insult and an unwelcome reminder of the events of July 1995. The fans of the Sarajevo team retorted with their own sign, displaying the characteristic dark humor of the region. It read: "Carla Del Ponte." The Tribunal was their answer to both the crimes and the public taunt.

Pockets of Denial in the International Arena

While the debate about the Srebrenica massacre continued inside Bosnia, those outside the country who accused the family associations and the international community of making up crimes to justify the NATO intervention were few in number, in part due to the documentation created by the court. Without the ICTY, it is likely that these voices of denial would have had a bigger impact in post-Yugoslav and international politics.

Some of the groups that refused to acknowledge the events surrounding the tragedy were easy to anticipate. Supporters of Slobodan Milošević continue to deny the

---

[144] Discussion with representative of the United Nations High Commissioner for Refugees (UNHCR), Zvornik office, November 1, 2004.

[145] Several Prijedor returnees attributed this level of return to several other factors as well, including a very organized community that was able to find all of its displaced persons. Some others point to the fact that many of the displaced had not traveled very far, just to nearby Sanski Most. One activist credited "unrelenting sheer will." Interviews with Prijedor returnees, June 2004. See also Chapter 5 of this volume.

[146] Rights-Based Municipal Assessment and Planning Project (RMAP), Municipality of Srebrenica, Republika Srpska, October 2003–February 2004, UNDP.

massacre. Commenting on the first RS report, they claimed: "In September of 2002 the Republika Srpska Bureau for Cooperation with the ICTY issued a report about the alleged massacre in Srebrenica. The report relied on UN documents, International Red Cross documents, BH Army documents, and photographic documentation. The report, which had been destined to be part of a larger final report, exposed the official Srebrenica story as a fraud."[147] A small Washington-based NGO, obscure to people in the United States but familiar to human rights activists in the region, echoed similar sentiments on the eve of the opening of the Srebrenica-Potočari memorial. Greg Copley of the International Strategic Studies Association (ISSA) called the number of casualties "vastly inflated and unsupported by evidence."[148] He accused Deputy High Representative Donald Hays of "[forcing] the Republica [sic] Srpska Government to issue a statement which accepted the radical Islamists' version of the Srebrenica affair, despite the fact that the Office of High Representative does not have any investigative capability of its own to make a valid assumption on the matter."[149] He argued that what he called the "memorialization of false numbers" would not serve reconciliation in the region.

Around the time of the 10-year anniversary of the massacre, discussion heated up yet again. In July 2005, the Serbian Unity Congress published its own "Srebrenica Report," an effort that included an unlikely group of former UN employees, representatives of the American far left, and members of the nationalist diaspora. Among those in the working group were academic Ed Herman; American journalist Diana Johnstone; and George Bogdanich, producer of a pro-Serb film called, "Yugoslavia: The Avoidable War." The report was a revisionist effort to forge a counternarrative to the facts determined by the ICTY and to divert attention from the ten-year anniversary. It claimed that "both the scale of the casualties at Srebrenica and the context of events have been misrepresented in official reports from governmental and non-governmental organizations as well as news organizations," and questioned the high numbers of missing persons cited in ICTY and ICRC documents.[150] The report argued that "the facts presented ... make a very cogent argument that the figure of 7,000 killed, which is often bandied about in the international community, is an unsupportable exaggeration. The true figure may be closer to 700."[151] After the release of the report, an opinion editorial in the *Globe and Mail* by Canadian Lewis MacKenzie, former UNPROFOR commander, also questioned the documented numbers of people killed. He based this on an

---

[147] The Forbidden Srebrenica Report, October 16, 2004, <www.slobodan-milosevic.org/news/smorg-sreb101604.htm> (accessed February 8, 2009).

[148] "Srebrenica Casualty Numbers Challenged by Experts as Politicized and Ethnically Divisive," press release, The International Strategic Studies Association (ISSA), September 20, 2003, <freerepublic.com/focus/f-news/986581/posts?page=226> (accessed February 8, 2009).

[149] Ibid.

[150] *Srebrenica and the Politics of War Crimes*, Srebrenica Research Group, July 2005, <www.srebrenica-report.com/> (accessed May 2, 2009).

[151] Philip Corwin, "Foreword," *Srebrenica and the Politics of War Crimes*, Srebrenica Research Group, July 2005, <www.srebrenica-report.com/foreword.htm> (accessed May 2, 2009).

argument that he himself called "distasteful," that, "if you're committing geno-cide, you don't let the women go since they are key to perpetuating the very group you are trying to eliminate."[152]

An interview with Noam Chomsky by *Guardian* journalist Emma Brockes received the most attention. Brockes asked Chomsky about journalist Diana Johnstone's article in a Swedish publication calling into question the number of deaths in the Srebrenica massacre. Chomsky had sent a letter endorsing her work. Brockes reported Chomsky's defense of his decision: "'No,' he says indignantly. 'It is outstanding [her work]. My only regret is that I didn't do it strongly enough. It may be wrong; but it is very careful and outstanding work.'"[153] Chomsky also claimed that Ed Vulliamy, who uncovered concentration camps in Bosnia, "got caught up in a story that probably wasn't true."[154] When the interview was published, Chomsky insisted that it misrepresented his views. The *Guardian* published a correction endorsing Chomsky's account of the interview. The correction, a capitulation to a prominent public intellectual, was criticized by a group of well-respected Balkan watchers including *New York Times* journalist David Rohde; UN mission coordi-nator Diego Arria; and Marko Attila Hoare, former ICTY employee and author of *How Bosnia Armed*.[155] The network of scholars, researchers, and activists around Srebrenica, which relied on the documentation created by the ICTY, continued to fight dissemination of false assertions.

Conclusion

Srebrenica became an international issue the moment the safe area was created. Consequently, to narrowly address the domestic effects of the ICTY's effort in Srebrenica would mean to capture only a part of the significance of the court's work in this area. This chapter has illustrated that the court influenced domestic developments in Bosnia (and the region), as well as local actors who mobilized around both domestic issues (locating war criminals, identifying missing persons, and memorializing the dead) and international ones (holding international actors responsible for the fall of the enclave).

The role of the court in the mobilization of Srebrenica's survivors was largely an unintended consequence of its work. Still, it is important to understand how

---

[152] Lewis MacKenzie, "The Real Story Behind Srebrenica," *The Globe and Mail,* July 14, 2005. MacKenzie, who usually publishes in Canada's more conservative *National Post,* has admit-ted to having received funds from the Serbian diaspora. His article followed an opinion edito-rial in the same paper written by the author and a colleague; see Lara J. Nettelfield and Sarah Wagner, "Bosnia's Muslims Still Cry Out for Justice," editorial, *The Globe and Mail,* July 11, 2005, <www.theglobeandmail.com/news/world/article890969.ece> (accessed July 10, 2009).
[153] Emma Brockes, "The Greatest Intellectual?" *The Guardian,* October 31, 2005.
[154] Ibid.
[155] "Srebrenica – defending the truth," January 3, 2006, *Bosnia Report,* The Bosnian Institute, March 10, 2006, <www.bosnia.org.uk/news/news_body.cfm?newsid=2137> (accessed February 12, 2009).

the court's decisions and indictments facilitated this domestic development, since this has implications for how we understand the impact of international courts more generally.

The ICTY created a space where accountability could be pursued; it was also a resource for family associations and survivors. In the climate of denial that was pervasive at the end of the war, the court helped legitimize their fight and prompted them to pursue other legal options. The ICTY's work also created a fact base that family associations, as well as international institutions, used in their work. The court's work was often adopted by other bodies in its entirety, a practice which had both positive and negative consequences.

The documentation produced by the ICTY helped illustrate the complicated role of the international community in the tragedy, aiding the survivors in their bid for international accountability. The court's decisions outlined the international community's role in the fall of the enclave, even though it was not the subject of specific indictments and the court ultimately refused to take up this issue. Elsewhere, survivors articulated their demands through courts in a strategy of legal mobilization. They channeled their demands through courts that often relied on ICTY documentation.

International courts can thus help facilitate democratic engagement. The activism of the family associations and survivors represented a form of political participation by those who would likely have had a more difficult time organizing themselves in the absence of the court. This case study suggests that scholars and analysts should look at the much broader implications of the work of international courts. The ICTY's work in Eastern Bosnia started a chain of events that led to concrete outcomes: investigative reports, decisions, and eventually, an apology by the RS government. They were small steps, but they represented progress in the quest for postwar transparency, accountability, the rule of law, and a state in which citizens could live free of fear of persecution based on their membership in an ethnic group.

Timeline of Significant Events Related to the Srebrenica Genocide

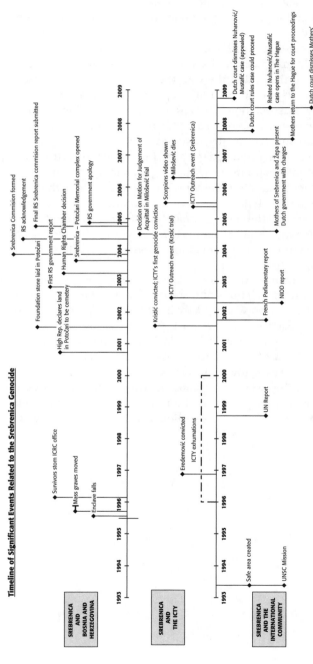

5 Making Progress with Few Resources

Civil Society and the ICTY

Ten years after the war, Bosnia and Herzegovina had a small and growing civil society. Most local nongovernmental organizations dealt in some ways with the social consequences of the war. The international community increasingly viewed civil society development as a priority in the postwar years, after it turned its focus from elections. It promoted the development of independent media outlets, legal aid societies, women's organizations, and human rights groups in an effort to create a layer of society that would lobby the state in the interests of its citizens. There was consistent support for human rights, but donor focus in this period rarely included international humanitarian law, war crimes, or the subject of "dealing with the past." What role did the ICTY have in the activities of these groups? What did civil society leaders think about the ICTY's work? If some of the ICTY's goals were "bringing justice to thousands of victims and giving them a voice," and "strengthening the rule of law" in the region, civil society leaders who work with victims on an everyday basis provide valuable insight into how an important segment of Bosnian society interprets the ICTY's work.[1] This chapter illustrates how, despite donor indifference to Bosnia's wartime past, the ICTY was relatively successful in getting its message out, changing attitudes toward the court for the better, and bringing its work closer to Bosnian citizens. This chapter illustrates the fluid nature of attitudes toward transitional justice institutions and is a reminder to critics that attitudes change over time even under unfavorable circumstances.[2]

Background on Bosnian Civil Society

A brief history of Bosnian civil society provides some context for this study. Civil society has been defined as "all of the organizations which exist outside of the

---

[1] Quotation from the list of the ICTY's achievements at <www.icty.org/sid/324> (accessed July 13, 2009).

[2] On the role of civil society and international courts, see Tullio Treves, Marco Frigessi di Rattalma, Attila Tanzi, Alessandro Fodella, Cesare Pitea and Chiara Ragni, *Civil Society, International Courts and Compliance Bodies* (The Hague: TMC Asser Press, 2005).

state and the market."[3] The exact number of civil society organizations in Bosnia is unknown, as an exact count has been complicated by the country's structure. Before the passage of the Law on Associations and Foundations in December 2001, civil society organizations could register only at the entity level (either Republika Srpska [RS] or the Federation of Bosnia and Herzegovina). Thus, government officials possess no statistics for the entire country.[4] Estimates range from 1,000 up to 8,000, but analysts guess that there are between 1,000 and 2,000 active groups.[5]

In the postwar years, foreign donors gave money to numerous civil society initiatives, especially those that fostered multiethnicity and inclusiveness in an effort to create a buffer to nationalist forces in the country. This initial availability of funding facilitated the establishment of many groups. When this transitional support subsided and donor fatigue set in, however, many organizations that relied solely on foreign grants or donations closed their doors. The attrition rate was particularly high in some sectors like media, where a large influx of funding had created more organizations than the market alone could support.

The sample in this study illustrates the high turnover rate in the sector. This chapter presents the results of a 2004 study that replicates a previous study of the perceptions and knowledge of Bosnian civil society about the ICTY.[6] The sampling frame for the previous study (the total universe of all possible NGOs), compiled in 1999, contained 550 organizations, of which only 147 still existed in 2004 when this study was carried out. Some groups, which focused on refugee return or strictly humanitarian assistance, had closed their doors after finishing their jobs. Many, though, closed because they lacked financial support. A common theme heard during the interviews for this chapter was that organizations temporarily had only a few or no program activities due to a deficiency of funds.

The situation is not entirely bleak, however. Despite financial and numerous other obstacles, today Bosnia has a small but thriving civil society sector, and the high attrition rate caused by the postwar donor environment is countered by the registration of new organizations every day. In any case, a high attrition rate

---

[3] Bill Sterling, "Serving the Community: An Assessment of Civil Society in Rural BiH," report, Dadalos Association for Peace Education Work Sarajevo, March 1, 2005, available online at: <www.dadalos.org/report/ngo_report_bih.htm> (accessed July 13, 2009).

[4] In October 2002, the Law on Associations and Foundations of the Federation of BiH was passed. This law replaced the 1995 Law on Citizens' Associations, the 1998 Law on Foundations and Funds, and the 1998 Law on Humanitarian Activities and Humanitarian Organizations. The Law on Associations and Foundations of Republika Srpska was passed in October 2001. Press releases about the legislation and English copies are available at the web site of the International Center for Not-for-Profit Law, *ICNL Knowledge Center*, <www.icnl.org/knowledge/index.htm> (accessed July 13, 2009).

[5] Discussions with civil society leaders, 2004 and 2005.

[6] Kristen Cibelli and Tamy Guberek, *Justice Unknown, Justice Unsatisfied?: Bosnian NGOs Speak about the International Criminal Tribunal for the Former Yugoslavia* (Boston, MA: Tufts University, 2000), <www.hrdag.org/resources/publications/justicereport.pdf>. They compiled their database and conducted their interviews in 1999.

should be expected in a sector in which society's changing needs require new organizations.

Human rights in general figured prominently in postwar donor mandates, but the war and the topic of international humanitarian law in general were not addressed as priorities. Some observers thought that donors felt it was too early to deal with the topic of the war, and by extension, the laws governing war. In contrast, many projects that emphasized "reconciliation" or "coexistence," bringing together members of different ethnic groups, received funding. International organizations emphasized democracy, democratization, and civil society; they organized seminars, trainings, and workshops around these themes. Foreign experts who arrived in Bosnia after 2000 would describe local activists as "overworkshopped." The Geneva Conventions, or on-going developments at the ICTY, however, were topics that donors rarely felt worthy of their attention until the ICTY Outreach Program helped bring about a slight change in attitudes.[7] As a report by Quaker Peace and Social Witness, based on numerous interviews with activists in the region, put it, "Whilst physical reconstruction and economic and social development is also continuing, there has been much less attention to the process of dealing honestly with the traumatic, horrific, difficult and contested events of the past decade, so important in building a lasting and sustainable peace in the region."[8] Nor was the nascent civil society in Bosnia necessarily ready to deal with the issue. Most postwar organizations were preoccupied entirely with humanitarian concerns. Although this somewhat changed in the period after this study was completed and funding increased to war related projects, there was a general reluctance on the part of donors to get too close to the subject of the war.

A lack of attention to these issues was not particularly surprising given that representatives of the international community inside Bosnia – from embassies, the Organization for Security and Cooperation in Europe (OSCE), the Office of the High Representative, and foreign foundations – had little or no knowledge of international humanitarian law or the ICTY. Its work was not a part of their organizations' efforts, and therefore they felt no obligation to understand what developments in The Hague might mean for politics inside Bosnia. Foreign experts had little incentive to look outside of their given mandates, the benchmarks used to measure success and determine future funding. Some even felt that the ICTY's work hindered their efforts on the ground to promote democratization. One OSCE press officer, in an interview with two journalists, went so far as to call the ICTY's work "counterproductive."[9] While this opinion was probably more extreme than that of the typical foreign worker, it was a telling declaration nonetheless.

---

[7] I am grateful to Mirsad Tokača for numerous helpful conversations about this point.

[8] "Dealing with the Past in Bosnia-Herzegovina, Croatia and Serbia and Montenegro," Quaker Peace and Social Witness, *Regional Synthesis Report*, September 4, 2003, 3. Copy on file with the author.

[9] Isabelle Wesselingh and Arnaud Vaulerin, *Raw Memory: Prijedor, Laboratory of Ethnic Cleansing* (London: Saqi Books, 2005), 150.

The problem was partly structural. There were no mechanisms in the Dayton Peace Agreement or in the ICTY's statute designed to use international organizations on the ground as a force to bring the court's work closer to Bosnian citizens. Local international community representatives could have helped facilitate the ICTY's goals of contributing to a lasting peace and strengthening democracy, yet it was rare that the ICTY had extensive contact with foreigners in the field. This meant that it lost potential allies. The court had few local representatives to which to assign the overwhelming task of conducting investigations and other court-room-related tasks.

Bosnian civil society did not agree with the de facto division of labor that kept the topic of the war primarily in The Hague. Of the organizations surveyed in this study, 79 percent felt there was not enough discussion about the causes of the war in Bosnia, and 70 percent felt that representatives of the international community within Bosnia had not paid enough attention to the issue of war crimes or "dealing with the past." The international community, which focused mostly on elections and other types of democratization projects, failed to adequately deal with the issues in postwar Bosnian society that local leaders thought were important.

Despite these structural obstacles, the court had some successes: it was able to get its message out to groups of local civil society organizations affected by its work, and over time these groups showed changing and improved attitudes. In late 1999, the ICTY's Outreach Program began the difficult task of bringing courtroom findings to local citizens. While perceptions were still divided along ethnic lines in some parts of the country, the court was starting to be accepted as part of Bosnia's political landscape. These changing attitudes illustrated that international standards of accountability were internalized by local elites, at least rhetorically.

Inspiration for Study

The impetus for this chapter was an earlier report by Kristen Cibelli and Tamy Guberek, *Justice Unknown, Justice Unsatisfied?: Bosnian NGOs Speak about the International Criminal Tribunal for the former Yugoslavia*, published in 2000.[10] The authors wrote their study while they were still undergraduates at Tufts University, under the supervision of an impressive board of advisors that included former ICTY Chief Prosecutor Richard Goldstone. Ms. Cibelli and Ms. Guberek shared with me their experience and methodology. In early 2004, I compiled a new database of NGOs from various sources, from which I could derive a sampling universe of Bosnian civil society organizations which was as comprehensive as possible. I consulted all of the same directories that Cibelli and Guberek had used that still

---

[10] Cibelli and Guberek, *Justice Unknown.*

existed, and added sources that had been created since their study. Seven sources, from domestic organizations and the international community, provided directories of NGOs in various fields. They included publications and lists from the OSCE, the International Commission on Missing Persons (ICMP) (both international organizations), the International Council of Voluntary Agencies (ICVA), the NGO Development Foundation, the Center for Civic Initiatives (centar civilnih inicijativa or CCI), and Medica Zenica (the latter four are Bosnian NGOs that have contact with a large network of organizations). Many NGOs appeared in more than one source. The new database was compared to a copy of the database from Cibelli and Guberek's study to see whether organizations listed had also been in the universe of the 2000 study.[11]

The resulting updated database listed over 1,500 NGOs and was probably the most comprehensive listing of NGOs in the country; even government officials did not have such a source. From this list of virtually all Bosnian NGOs, the universe for this study was created. The 2004 study utilized the same criterion as the 2000 study: a group was included in the population if it was a civil society organization dealing with some aspect of postwar reconstruction or humanitarian issues. As in the previous study, organizations such as hunting associations, choirs, and sports clubs were excluded. The database contained 775 NGOs once those groups were excluded; this was consistent with estimates by civil society leaders that there were approximately 1,000 active civil society organizations in all spheres of activity (some not represented in this sample) in the country at the time of the study. From this universe, a random sample was drawn for interviews. The sector's high attrition rate introduced possible bias in the sample, but this was unavoidable.

After the creation of the new database of local organizations concerned with social reconstruction, Ms. Cibelli, with guidance from Dr. Patrick Ball, drew a proportionally stratified random sample from both entities.[12] Similarly, in my sample 33 organizations are located in the Federation and 20 are in RS, which reflects the fact that there were a greater number of organizations registered in the Federation at the time of the study. This is consistent with the fact that the Federation is the more populous entity and has benefited from more foreign aid, which often was directed to local groups.

In addition, the 2004 sample was stratified between the Federation of Bosnia and Herzegovina and Republika Srpska, and between the main city in each

---

[11] As mentioned earlier, of the original universe of 550 organizations in 1999, only 147 organizations still existed five years later.

[12] Dr. Patrick Ball is the Chief Scientist and Director of the Human Rights Data Analysis Group (HRDAG) at the Benetech Initiative in Palo Alto, California. HRDAG was previously housed at the American Association for the Advancement of Science. See <www.hrdag.org> (accessed July 14, 2009). A proportional sample means that the number of organizations in the sample is relative to the numbers in the units from which they are drawn. As an example, take a universe of 1,000 NGOs in which 700 groups are located in the Federation and 300 in RS. If the sample size were 100, 70 organizations would be drawn from the Federation and 30 from RS.

entity – Sarajevo and Banja Luka, respectively – and the rest of the entity. Stratification is the subdivision of a population into smaller, more homogeneous units (often called strata); a stratified sample contains respondents from each of these subdivisions. In this study, each organization was coded from 1 to 4, 1 for organizations based in Banja Luka, 2 for organizations in Sarajevo, 3 for those in the Federation outside of Sarajevo, and 4 for organizations in RS outside of Banja Luka. This ensured that the sample would include organizations outside of the capital in each entity and, it was hoped, a range of views.

Primarily between April and August 2004, representatives of 53 local Bosnian NGOs in both entities were interviewed, asked about their attitudes toward the ICTY and its work. These interviews took place in person, usually at the headquarters of each organization. I asked interviewees a standard set of questions, some of which were additional to those of the 2000 study in order to reflect new developments in the country and the focus of this research project.[13] The director or president of each group (except two) gave the interview. The interviews were transcribed. From the complete transcripts of each interview, the qualitative, narrative information was transformed into structured, quantifiable data categories. The data was put into the statistical program SPSS with the help of a Bosnian student who also provided intercoder reliability (a measure of agreement among multiple coders for how they apply codes to text data). This enabled a statistical analysis to be performed.

Even though the database was compiled using the newest possible sources, some listed organizations did not exist when sought for participation in the study. This prompted the selection of a second sample in order to reach the desired total number of organizations.[14] The total sample size in this study was kept the same as in the previous study, due to financial and time constraints. Three organizations refused to participate in the study, claiming to have no competence in the subject area. The groups in the sample are from the sectors shown in Tables 5.1 and 5.2.

As indicated by Table 5.2, women's groups, youth groups, and organizations focusing on various forms of democratization formed the largest part of the 2004 sample. Increased numbers of NGOs focusing on youth, evident in the newer sample, are likely due to great donor interest in the topic in recent years. In addition, the smaller number of organizations involved with refugee return in the 2004 sample is to be anticipated, as many of these organizations finished their work when returns were completed.

This study provided a rich opportunity to measure how attitudes changed over time. It benefited from collaboration offered by the authors of the 2000 project, which had been well-received. Many things changed in that intervening period

---

[13] See Annex 1 for a complete list of interview questions.
[14] Although ideal, it would have been time consuming and costly to contact all of the organizations listed in each source before putting them in the database.

TABLE 5.1. Types of Organizations in 2000 Sample

Type of NGO	Number of organizations interviewed	Percentage of total
Civil Society	18	33.33
Women's	14	25.93
Return of Refugees and Displaced Persons	7	12.96
Information/Legal Aid	7	12.96
Youth	4	7.40
Victims/Refugee Aid	4	7.40
Total	54	100

TABLE 5.2. Types of Organizations in 2004 Sample

Type of NGO	Number of organizations interviewed	Percentage of total
Women's	13	24.53
Youth	11	20.75
Democratization	11	20.75
Development	4	7.55
Return	4	7.55
Psycho-social	4	7.55
Veterans	3	5.66
Humanitarian	2	3.77
Missing Persons/Victims	1	1.89
Total	53	100

and contributed to changing attitudes toward the ICTY, and though this study is not adequate to establish the relative influence of each variable, they are worthy of note.

In the earlier study, the results analyzed through cross tabulations on the entity level were a solid proxy for a type of elite view of the constituent nations (Bosniaks, Croats, and Serbs) in Bosnia. Individuals who chose to open and lead organizations were generally elites in their fields or in their communities. In the later study, however, changes in the country complicated the ability to use the views expressed in the entities as reliable proxies for Bosnia's ethnic groups. In the interim period, returns increased as authorities solved property claims, meaning that many of the organizations interviewed for the second study represented "minority" groups in their areas. This had several effects. As new civil society organizations with differing views and program activities interacted with other groups, issues such as the work of the ICTY and the question of the past entered the public debate in local communities all over the country. In addition, the somewhat improved political climate facilitated the growth of different types of organizations with different agendas.

ICTY Outreach

Another factor that contributed to changes in attitudes toward the court was the Tribunal's establishment of an Outreach Program to "explain the Tribunal's work and its relevance to the peoples of the former Yugoslavia."[15] Under the leadership of President Gabrielle Kirk McDonald, the ICTY established this program in response to a growing awareness that the court would not have its desired impact in the region if it did not make a concerted effort to inform citizens in the region about its work. The ICTY knew it was important that it "not be perceived as an alien institution."[16] It hoped to correct rampant misperceptions that resulted from the dissemination of erroneous notions about the court and its work, often spread via media outlets with connections to political forces opposed to the court. The ICTY opened field offices in four cities in the region: Zagreb, Sarajevo, Belgrade, and Priština. The Outreach Program focused on cooperation with the press, local groups, and family associations; organizing educational trips to the court; monitoring local press coverage; and sponsoring and participating in local events.[17]

The Outreach Program also created a version of the ICTY's web site in each of the languages of the region (Bosnian, Croatian, Serbian, and Albanian). Until then, the ICTY's materials were not available in local languages and the web site was only offered in French and English. Today, the web site contains translations of indictments, decisions, orders, judgments, and basic legal documents in local languages. Trial transcripts, however, are still only available in English, either on CD from the Outreach office or from the ICTY's website. Even witness testimony given in a language of the region is only available in the English transcript of the proceedings. This has prompted a transcription project in Serbia, for example, to produce trial transcripts in the local languages.[18] Despite the fact that web pages in the region's languages are less extensive than those in English, the ICTY site is an

---

[15] ICTY Outreach Program Summary. Copy on file with the author.

[16] Ibid.

[17] On ICTY Outreach see also Victoria Enaut, "The ICTY's Outreach Programme and the Challenges to its Success at Shaping Local Popular Perceptions of the Tribunal," unpublished M.A. Thesis, King's College London, 2006. For a more recent article that concurs with my findings about the need for significant resources for outreach, see Janine Natalya Clark, "International War Crimes Tribunals and the Challenge of Outreach," *International Criminal Law Review* 9 (2009): 99–116. On outreach at the ICTR, see Victor Peskin, "Courting Rwanda: The Promises and Pitfalls of the ICTR Outreach Programme," *Journal of International Criminal Justice* 3, no. 4 (2005): 950–61.

[18] The Humanitarian Law Center in Belgrade currently has one such project.

extremely important resource for Bosnian civil society: 43 percent of the organizations surveyed use the Internet to access information about the court.

From 2003 to 2005, the Outreach Program held several major events in Bosnia. The court's conferences on "Bridging the Gap Between the ICTY and Communities in Bosnia and Herzegovina" were organized in 2004 to inform local communities in Brčko, Foča, and Konjic about cases affecting their municipalities. In 2005, events were held in Srebrenica and Prijedor. The daylong events brought in members of the investigative and prosecution teams, legal advisers, and representatives of the Registrar's office from The Hague. ICTY representatives gave an overview of the entire judicial process from the phase of investigation, to indictment, arrest, and transfer of the accused, to the trial, plea agreement (if applicable), and judgment. Particularly powerful were presentations of video clips from an actual trial, during which an ICTY representative would often pause the tape and contrast the testimony of the defendant with the findings of the investigators. During the Foča seminar, for example, participants watched as one of the defendants, Dragoljub Kunarac, a member of a reconnaissance unit of the Army of Republika Srpska (VRS), testified under oath that a girl from the town, in his words, "forced herself on him." The court later found Kunarac guilty of rape.[19] He was sentenced to 28 years in prison in a joint trial at which Radomir Kovač and Zoran Vuković, both sub-commanders of the military police of the VRS and members of a local paramilitary group, were also found guilty. Seminar participants thus learned about the historic Foča case, the first trial at an international tribunal addressing sexual violence.[20]

A large cross-section of local citizens and members of the international community attended these Outreach events.[21] The local sponsor in Bosnia, the Helsinki Committee for Human Rights in Republika Srpska, working with the ICTY, invited members of the press, representatives of family associations, local prosecutors, judges, and government officials. For the Brčko conference, over 190 invitations went out, including 19 to members of the press.[22] Later, in 2006, the national broadcaster, Radio and Television of Bosnia and Herzegovina (Radio Televizija Bosne i Hercegovine or BHRT), aired a program about the ICTY outreach events,

---

[19] ICTY testimony of Dragoljub Kunarac, shown to Outreach event participants in Foča on October 9, 2004. Author's notes. For background see Kunarac, Kovač and Vuković (IT-96-23; IT-96-23/1) Case Information Sheet, ICTY, <www.icty.org/x/cases/kunarac/cis/en/cis_kunarac_al_en.pdf> (accessed July 14, 2009).

[20] For background see Michelle Jarvis, "Gender Perspectives on ICTY Practice and Procedure," in Gideon Boas and William Schabas, eds., *International Criminal Law Developments in the Case Law of the ICTY* (Leiden, The Netherlands: Martinus Nijhoff Publishers, 2003), 179.

[21] The local Outreach events took place on May 8, 2004, in Brčko; October 9, 2004, in Foča; and November 20, 2004, in Konjic. The Outreach conference "Plea Agreements and Guilty Pleas at the ICTY and Related Practice in National Systems," co-sponsored by the Human Rights Center at the University of Sarajevo, took place on December 5–6, 2003. In 2009, the ICTY published the proceedings of five events in English and Bosnian/Croatian.

[22] List of invitees, RS Helsinki Committee document. Copy on file with the author.

which was followed by one a few months later aired by the public broadcaster in Republika Srpska (Radio televizija Republike Srpske or RTRS).

"Localizing" the ICTY was not an easy task. On the day of the Brčko event on May 8, 2004, the local police and SFOR (the acronym for NATO's peacekeeping mission) closed practically the entire district to traffic as part of its security measures. The ICTY had to ensure the safety of its delegation, which included Geoffrey Nice, who was then leading the prosecution of Slobodan Milošević. Once the local police vetted guests, however, the presentations gave a glimpse of just how the ICTY's employees viewed their role in the developments of postwar Bosnia. Nice, also the prosecutor in the Jelisić case which addressed crimes in Brčko, told a full hall:

Are there advantages to the position in which we find ourselves? Including that we have no interest to serve, no ethnicity to favor or disfavor, and for us the only job satisfaction is helping the judges get, if and when they can, as near to the correct, right, truthful, and accurate answer if possible? Because of our position, I guess the last 12 years will seem different to us than they seem to you. Today we are in the same month, the same season of the year, with the same length of daylight as obtained during the time when these terrible offenses were committed.[23]

The details of the cases were interspersed with commentary about ICTY procedures. There were two cases relating to Brčko, those of Goran Jelisić and Ranko Češić. SFOR had arrested Jelisić on January 22, 1998, and he had been convicted and sentenced. In July 2001, the Appeals Chamber upheld a 40-year sentence for crimes against humanity and violations of the laws or customs of war, to which he pleaded guilty.[24] Jelisić was acquitted of the count of genocide. In the second case, FRY authorities had arrested Ranko Češić in Belgrade on May 25, 2002. He pleaded guilty to 12 charges, including six counts of the violations of laws or customs of war and crimes against humanity. The ICTY sentenced him to 18 years in prison.[25]

The final hour of these conferences – the question and answer period – was the most revealing part of the day for what was illustrated about expectations of the court. Lingering misperceptions about what the ICTY was and was not capable of doing were voiced. Conference participants wrote queries on bits of paper and forwarded them to the moderator who then grouped them by theme or interest. Many asked about specific victims or perpetrators, wondering when the ICTY would deal with "their" case. Some noted the suffering of victims of different ethnicities. Still others asked about civil cases, restitution, and things outside of the ICTY's jurisdiction. The questions made clear the truth in the observation that justice is local. Participants were understandably interested in forms of redress for their own problems and specific crimes that affected their social networks.

[23] Geoffrey Nice, Former Principal Trial Attorney in the Office of the Prosecutor of the ICTY, comments, ICTY Outreach Conference, Brčko, May 8, 2004. Author's notes. Nice was the Senior Trial Attorney for the OTP in the Jelisić trial.
[24] Jelisić (IT-95-10) Case Information Sheet. Document distributed at Outreach event.
[25] Češić (IT-95-10/1) Case Information Sheet. Document distributed at Outreach event.

These queries prompted ICTY representatives to explain the limitations of its intervention. Geoffrey Nice told the group: "When an international organization is to contribute to a local problem, it must make a decision as to when to withdraw its service. Doing that will never be at the right time."[26] Some of the participants, however, felt that the conference, in some ways, was more of the same kind of event that Bosnians had long grown tired of: members of the international community talk at them, and they listen. One argued that the time was ripe for more local ownership, making the process more interactive: "What has been going on today has been a one-way street. We have to stop looking to the ICTY. It has been five years since the district [of Brčko] was established and there has been no freedom to emphasize the rights of the victims. We should try, in the future, to give more attention to bringing the victim's communities closer to the experience of the ICTY and creating the proper climate in our communities."[27] That was precisely what was beginning to happen around the time of this event in Brčko: local groups that had formed around the issue of the wartime past were starting to receive support for their initiatives. The international community started to realize, especially after the creation of the Srebrenica Commission, that it had to support local institutions working on issues of documentation, trial monitoring, and victims' advocacy because these issues were the most important for many Bosnians. The ICTY's work brought this omission into the spotlight and the outreach events created a forum in which local needs became more visible.

The "Bridging the Gap between the ICTY and Communities in Bosnia and Herzegovina" conferences were some of the first efforts to bring the work of the ICTY directly to Bosnian communities affected by the court's work. They represented a new institutional attitude, recognizing that providing citizens in the region with an explanation of the ICTY's procedures and factual findings was an important responsibility. Family associations started showing a more sophisticated understanding of the court's work.[28] Outreach representatives tirelessly worked to explain the court in both public and private events.

But these conferences also showed that an international court could never address all of the problems associated with violations of international humanitarian law in Bosnia. The presence of war criminals continued to manifest itself in the lives of ordinary citizens, even at ICTY events. At one of the outreach events, which mixed local civil society organizations (including family associations), local prosecutors, and local officials, a court employee recognized a perpetrator seen in one of the archival videos relating to a case discussed that day. The man, apparently an invited conference guest, had become a local leader: another criminal who had evaded justice. The ICTY sent this wartime perpetrator home from the conference

---

[26] Geoffrey Nice, Former Principal Trial Attorney in the Office of the Prosecutor of the ICTY, comments, ICTY Outreach Conference, Brčko, May 8, 2004. Author's notes.

[27] Mirsad Tokača, President, Research and Documentation Center, comments, ICTY Outreach Conference, Brčko, May 8, 2004. Author's notes.

[28] Author field notes from 2003 to 2006.

with a complimentary packet of translated case summaries. Given that the court indicted only 161 persons out of an estimated several thousand perpetrators, events like this could have been anticipated.

The overall impact of the Outreach Program is difficult to measure, but there is reason to believe that it achieved some success in getting the court's message out. The task of assessing the program's impact is complicated by the fact that ICTY does not keep records on exactly how much money was dedicated to outreach by state, nor does it gauge opinions about the ICTY. Funding for the Outreach Program in The Hague from 2000 to 2004 was between 650,000–800,000 euros annually. Those funds paid for operating costs in the head office and four field offices. The European Commission was the major donor for this portion of the budget. Overall funding for Bosnia was higher in recent years than in other countries.[29] Many grants, however, went directly to local partners that organized ICTY-related events, such as the RS Helsinki Committee, further complicating state-by-state record keeping.

Outreach, interestingly, was never an activity the ICTY felt was necessary to finance from its own coffers, and it never dedicated its own budget line item to the cause. The entire program is supported by a United Nations Trust Fund and hence was funded entirely by voluntary contributions. This meant that representatives on the ground (and in The Hague) spent a good portion of their time searching for grants for future events, taking precious time away from their work with people in the region. Since the Outreach Program had a skeleton staff with only a handful of people in each office, this work involved a sacrifice on the part of employees who would routinely spend a workday traveling to the farthest corners of the country (and back) for Outreach events.

Nevertheless, despite limited staffing and resources, the program was able to make itself somewhat known in Bosnia. Of the organizations surveyed in 2004, 34 percent had heard of the ICTY Outreach Program, up from 17 percent in 1999. More organizations in RS (50 percent) had heard of the program than in the Federation (24 percent). An important 29 percent felt they had not received enough information from the program. Had the sample in this study been comprised only of family associations and other organizations related directly to wartime violence, it is likely that a larger percentage of respondents would have reported knowledge of the program, but the group sampled was broader because it used the selection criteria followed in the initial study.

While this study shows improved attitudes toward the ICTY, civil society still felt underutilized as a resource for the effort to educate Bosnians about the court's mission: 67 percent said that local civil society organizations had not been used to the extent possible to help with the ICTY's work. The director of one small NGO in Mrkonjić Grad observed that, "NGOs in the big city centers are used but those away

[29] Olga Kavran, e-mail to the author, February 15, 2005. Kavran was the Deputy Outreach Program Coordinator for the ICTY.

from the city center are not used for things, in general."[30] This finding addresses the limitations of the ICTY's impact on Bosnian civil society: while organizations generally reported mostly positive attitudes about the court, only a few local groups actually became involved with the work of the court.

The Outreach Program did succeed, however, in providing targeted groups with information about the ICTY's work. In 2004, one ICTY official told a group of regional activists, "The problem is not a lack of information, it is a problem of social awareness, including of public officials and journalists. And then that information is put through the filter of political identification."[31] The Outreach office started to channel and explain information to enhance greater social awareness. The seminar events continued this time-consuming and demanding process. Resource constraints at the local field offices meant they could not conduct all of the outreach necessary, but the program was a small step forward. Unfortunately, the program hit its stride just at the court was formulating an exit strategy. The ICTY's extended mandate would have benefited from hundreds of "Bridging the Gap" events all over the country.

Civil society representatives that were part of this study suggested it was important that the court speak for itself. Those in positions of power in Bosnia did not inspire trust among local groups that they would honestly relay information about the court: 70 percent felt that people in power manipulate information about the ICTY, a 7 percent increase over the previous study. Comments by participants at outreach events showed that it would take more than a one-day conference to bring up to speed even those key groups of Bosnian citizens affected by the ICTY's work. However, the creation of Outreach offices meant that at least there was always someone available to answer journalists' questions and to explain court procedures.

Media Coverage

Improved media coverage contributed additionally to changed attitudes about the ICTY. As the years following the war passed, media coverage improved in both depth and breadth. Media outlets received funds from foreign donors that made it possible for them to send representatives to The Hague for coverage of the trials. The Outreach Program also hosted study tours for journalists from the region. The start of the trial of Slobodan Milošević, in February 2002, prompted increased coverage and interest in developments at the ICTY. To ensure that domestic audiences did not miss the historic first trial of a head of state, donors subsidized journalists, paying for travel expenses and apartments in The Hague and providing them with per-diem allowances. For example, the International Research and Exchange Board (IREX), with a grant from the Charles Stuart Mott Foundation, funded the

---

[30] Interview with civil society organization representative, Mrkonjić Grad, May 13, 2004.
[31] Refik Hodžić, comments, Conference of the Humanitarian Law Center, Budapest, January 16, 2004. Hodžić was the ICTY Outreach Program representative in Bosnia. Author's notes.

Bosnian publications *Slobodna Bosna, Oslobođenje, Reporter,* and *Dani* so that they could send reporters to The Hague.[32] Even after donor funding ran out, many papers kept reporters there. When the Bosnia portion of the Milošević trial started, IREX provided support for coverage by a team of TV and radio journalists.[33] The effort was not without its problems, though. After the attacks of September 11, 2001, led to tightened security worldwide, the Dutch government did not want to issue visas to Bosnian journalists to cover the run-up to the start of the Milošević trial. An Amsterdam-based NGO, Press Now, came to their aid and visas were issued, but some affected reporters missed a few weeks of coverage.[34]

Media content in particular was a priority for the international community. The rules set up in the postwar period affected how broadcast outlets would cover sensitive issues, including war crimes. In the immediate postwar period, the OSCE, in addition to other organizations, conducted significant media monitoring efforts in an attempt to curb the hate speech and misinformation prevalent during the war.[35] By the time of the second general elections in 1998, international authorities realized that biased media coverage was hindering the citizens' ability to make informed decisions and was an obstacle to democratization. The international community designed an elaborate system of sanctions, especially in the months before elections. On several occasions, election authorities disqualified candidates from the ballot for violations of media rules. The primary problem with postwar media was hate speech, however, and was not directly related to the ICTY. In 2000, for example, Channel S, an RS-based station, was fined for a broadcast about the Markale marketplace massacre of February 5, 1994, attributing the attack to "the [Muslims]." The station's report claimed that an explosive device like those usually used by Hezbollah was found at the scene of the crime, a blatant lie.[36]

There were few such breaches relating specifically to coverage of the ICTY. Having witnessed the willingness with which the international community would reprimand uncooperative news outlets, most mass media responded to inquiries about violations of broadcast rules quickly. The temporary broadcast media

---

[32] Interview with Drew Sullivan, Sarajevo, February 26, 2005. Sullivan is an Advisor to the Center for Investigative Reporting in Sarajevo and a former employee of the International Research and Exchanges Board (IREX).

[33] "Bosnian Media Begin Live Coverage from the International Criminal Tribunal for the former Yugoslavia," *Supporting Independent Media in Bosnia and Herzegovina Program Highlights,* International Research and Exchanges Board (IREX), September 2002, <www.irex.org/media/bosnia/highlights/02.asp> (accessed February 27, 2005).

[34] Interview with Drew Sullivan, Sarajevo, February 26, 2005.

[35] For background on the use of media during the war, see Mark Thompson, *Forging War: The Media in Serbia, Croatia, Bosnia, and Hercegovina* (Luton, UK: University of Luton Press/Article 19, 1999).

[36] Interview with Dunja Mijatović, Sarajevo, March 2, 2005. Mijatović was Director of the Broadcast Division at the Communications Regulatory Agency, Government of Bosnia and Herzegovina (CRA). See <www.rak.ba> (accessed July 15, 2009). See the decision in the Channel S case: Case Analysis June 1998–December 2001, December 15, 2001, CRA Broadcast Division, <www.rak.ba/en/broadcast/cases-compl/?cid=185> (accessed July 15, 2009).

regulator, the Independent Media Commission (IMC), was transformed into Bosnia's national broadcast media regulator, the Communications and Regulatory Agency (CRA) in March 2001. The CRA issued and enforced regulations relating to broadcast media. As of late 2009, the CRA had received only one complaint dealing with content related to the ICTY.[37] A citizen, Senad Pećanin – editor of the local weekly publication *Dani* – complained that Television of the Federation of Bosnia and Herzegovina (Federalna televizija Bosne i Hercegovine or FTV), the Federation public broadcaster, had not aired the first day of the Milošević trial during which the ICTY had read the indictment against Milošević for crimes committed in Bosnia. The CRA's response declared that it was "without the intention to influence editorial decisions" but admonished FTV to "take into account the importance that the trial presents for the Bosnian public."[38] FTV did broadcast the trial on the second day. In RS, the public broadcaster, RTRS, dragged its feet for a while but eventually complied with its obligations. It was reluctant at first to air some of the programs offered by SENSE, an independent news agency created to cover events in The Hague, but by 2005 it was transmitting them regularly. Under the conditions for long-term licenses, broadcasters have a specific obligation to include the ICTY in their news programming:

Public broadcasters are reminded of their obligations under CRA Rule 01/1999 "Definition and Obligations of Public Radio and Television Broadcasting" according to which at least 40 per cent of program time in any week shall consist of news and other informative or educational programming. Such programming content includes broadcasts about the implementation by all authorities of Bosnia and Herzegovina of the General Peace Agreement for Peace in Bosnia and Herzegovina and coverage of the work of domestic judicial institutions and of the International Criminal Tribunal for the former Yugoslavia.[39]

Today, the ICTY and the topic of war crimes are given broad coverage in both entities. The nightly news programs feature ample coverage of daily developments in The Hague. ICTY authorities inside Bosnia spent a lot of time working with both regulatory agencies and journalists to improve reporting. Even though regulators report few serious problems, participants in this study nonetheless argued that coverage still needs improvement. Media discussion of the ICTY's work was often biased in ways that were difficult for the international community to sanction. Coverage in the two entities differed in both emphasis and tone, helping keep opinions divided about the work of the ICTY and the facts it has established. The lack of a common public space made the court's efforts in this area more difficult.

---

[37] Interview with Dunja Mijatović, Sarajevo, March 2, 2005. The CRA receives complaints relating to content in addition to technical issues. In 2004, for example, there were 112 complaints relating to content.

[38] Communications and Regulatory Agency, letter to Marija Topić-Crnoja, March 5, 2002. Topić-Crnoja is the Editor of FTV. Copy on file with the author.

[39] Definition and Obligations of Public Broadcasting, CRA rule 01/1999, BiH 33/03, November 13, 2003. Copy on file with the author.

All of the respondents in this study argued that media continued to be an "opinion shaper." When asked where they get information about the ICTY, most organizations mentioned both print and broadcast media. In addition, over 35 percent of respondents specifically mentioned "Tribunal", a 30-minute weekly news program focusing exclusively on developments at the ICTY, produced by the SENSE News Agency.[40] Today, the show airs all over the country.

Direct broadcasts of trials also brought news of day-to-day developments in The Hague directly to the living rooms of average Bosnian citizens. On most days during the time this study was conducted, Bosnian Federal TV was broadcasting the Milošević trial live, starting at 9 a.m. when proceedings began in The Hague. Some respondents claimed they had no choice but to watch the trials, as weak reception left them with few other options. Even though the percentage of respondents who said that the broadcasting of trials was useful for their organization equaled that of those who said it was not (48 percent), 83 percent of those surveyed said they did watch the broadcasts when their schedules permitted. When asked whether the broadcasting of trials is useful for Bosnia, 80 percent answered positively – 67 percent in RS and 88 percent in the Federation. There were, however, some caveats: several respondents in the Federation said that the way Slobodan Milošević conducted himself in his trial has had negative consequences in Bosnia in general, claiming that his "performance" only bolstered his support in RS.

Conditions for more balanced coverage in the print media improved as well over the interim period between the two studies. Progressive print media started to receive better distribution in places like Eastern RS, where views of the opposition had previously been impossible to find on newsstands because nationalists, who controlled means of distribution, kept them out of the entity's kiosks. These distribution monopolies were broken down over time, facilitating the circulation of new ideas.

One of the most striking findings of this study was that attitudes toward the ICTY drastically improved in RS, and slightly improved in the Federation, suggesting that civil society leaders likely internalize the views of other elites in their communities. Among other findings of the study were that many organizations believed that the trials affected other key aspects of democratization, such as refugee return and the rule of law. Also of note, however, was that the NGOs in 2004 reported roughly the same levels of understanding of the purpose, structure, and goals of the ICTY as they had in the first study five years earlier, despite reporting to be more comfortable with their levels of knowledge about the court.

---

[40] South East News Service Europe (SENSE) News Agency, <www.sense-agency.com> (accessed July 14, 2009).

In-depth Results of This Study

Most organizations reported having no direct connection with the work of the ICTY on a day-to-day basis.[41] Some groups with human rights and democratization in their mandates that might have been expected to incorporate ICTY-related activities, answered no to this question. Despite the lack of relevance of the court's activities to the direct mandates of the groups, almost half of them said that their work would be different if the court did not exist, a testament to the spillover effects of the court. This finding was roughly the same in both entities, and is especially interesting considering that the sample group had a wide range of interests, some rather removed from the work of the court. A number of those surveyed felt that the ICTY facilitated communication between the two entities. Many groups in the Federation echoed the sentiment of one representative of a Tuzla-based NGO who noted that, "it would be difficult to work in RS" without the ICTY, "so in that sense it's easier for us to work because there is this oversight of justice which is leading to some knots which will be untied."[42] Other organizations argued that the whole atmosphere in the country would be different. A member of a Sarajevo group observed, "If the court did not exist, the whole atmosphere in Bosnia-Herzegovina would be different as would the thinking of ordinary people. People would still have negative energy in themselves, thinking about the collective guilt of a people, group etc. However, just the existence of the Tribunal says that justice exists somewhere, that there are people with first and last names who are guilty of war crimes."[43] The numbers of those in civil society organizations who had direct experience with the court was relatively high: almost 20 percent of all groups had at least one employee who had served as a witness, given a statement, or been otherwise directly touched by the court's work.[44]

The number of respondents who felt comfortable with their knowledge of the ICTY increased over time. Almost half of all respondents said they were at least "more or less" comfortable with their knowledge about it. After over 10 years of work, Bosnian citizens had learned about the court, its judgments, arrests, and daily presence in the media. This was a marked change from the study five years earlier, when almost three quarters of all respondents said they were not comfortable with their knowledge levels.

---

[41] Percentages reported are valid percentages, which calculates the respective totals excluding the missing data. I have chosen to present valid percentages so that they are consistent with cross tabulations in SPSS. The program always calculates only valid percentages and thus their totals equal 100. I will make a note of questions where there are large amounts of missing data.

[42] Interview with civil society organization representative, Tuzla, July 20, 2004.

[43] Interview with civil society organization representative, Sarajevo, June 28, 2004.

[44] In contrast, only 2 percent of all 463 respondents in the armed forces had direct experience with the court. See Chapter 7 of this volume.

However, the concrete work of the ICTY remained a mystery to many study participants. Over 50 percent of all respondents said they did not know what criteria the ICTY uses for indictments, and only one respondent specifically mentioned crimes against humanity and international law. Four organizations (8 percent of all respondents) felt that indictments are at the whim of the court. One group in Travnik said the ICTY's position is: "Whoever I want, I will indict." The representatives of other groups felt ethnicity was a key criterion. Asked, "do you know what criteria are used for indictments?" a citizen in Zvornik said that, "I do not think the ICTY has ever answered that question ... . Mostly I see that Serbs and Croats are sent to The Hague, and Croats and a few Bosniaks were sent mostly because of the crimes between them and not because of the crimes against Serbs, so in that way, if criteria exist at all, they are unclear to me."[45] The lack of an understanding of the criteria used for indictments could be partly attributable to a failure on the part of the court to disseminate basic information to this important group.[46] On the other hand, it is possible many failed to inform themselves about the basic facts of the war, and the crime base the court was dealing with.

This lack of basic knowledge was in sharp contrast to reported levels of trust in the court. This significant increase in reported levels of credibility of the ICTY in both entities, particularly RS, was the most striking finding of this study. A considerable 69 percent of the organizations surveyed said that their organization believed the ICTY to be a credible institution. Another 10 percent said they could not speak on behalf of the whole institution, but that they personally believed the ICTY to be credible. When analyzed by entity, 88 percent of respondents in the Federation and 65 percent in RS believed the ICTY is a credible institution; this was a threefold increase in RS from the previous study.[47]

Several factors contributed to this change. First, even if cooperation with the ICTY was not forthcoming in the form of local arrests by RS authorities, elites had at least to feign the conviction that cooperation was a goal worth pursuing. This meant that politicians, obliged to speak of the legitimacy of the institution, introduced an idea that could spill over and influence the attitudes of civil society leaders in the entity.[48] Second, in the years between surveys, the ICTY had begun

---

[45] Interview with civil society organization representative, Zvornik, June 16, 2004.

[46] The 2000 study asked a slightly different question: "Have you received information about the criteria for an indictment?"; 34 percent of respondents said they had.

[47] Opinions within the public were somewhat different. A survey conducted by the Stockholm-based International Institute for Democracy and Electoral Assistance (IDEA) found that 51 percent of the residents in the Federation gave the ICTY a moderate to high trust rating, whereas only 4 percent in RS reported the same rating. IDEA conducted interviews in January and February 2002. For a summary of its findings, see IDEA, *South East Europe (SEE) Public Agenda Survey*, April 4, 2002, <www.idea.int/europe_cis/balkans/see_survey.cfm> (accessed July 14, 2009).

[48] Research in psychology shows that when issues are complicated, individuals look to the source of views and adjust their attitudes accordingly. See, for example, Geoffrey L. Cohen, "Party Over Policy: The Dominating Impact of Group Influence on Political Beliefs," *Journal of Personality and Social Psychology* 85, no. 5 (2003): 808–22.

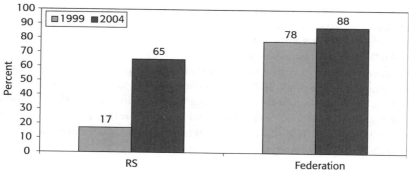

Figure 5.1. Is the ICTY a credible institution? (Percentage of respondents who answered yes.)

to process more criminals of non-Serb ethnicity – for example, from the Croat Defense Council (HVO) and the Army of the Republic of Bosnia and Herzegovina (ARBiH) – which helped change the perception of some that the ICTY had been created exclusively to prosecute Serb war criminals. Five years previously, this presumed bias had been one of the most significant factors damaging the credibility of the ICTY in RS. Third, in the 2004 study there were more organizations representing returnee groups in the entity. Lastly, better press coverage, discussed above, illustrated the day-to-day activities of the institution to the public and helped to create some degree of transparency, however slight (Figure 5.1).

Among these positive responses, however, other replies indicated a lack of basic knowledge of the court. Despite increased levels of credibility, it was not clear that civil society representatives really understood the court they labeled as credible. Three organizations, for example, expressed highly developed positions on things such as plea agreements and sentencing, and then made comments that indicated they were unaware that the ICTY is an ad hoc institution. One individual, who ran a group in the Federation, for example, mentioned that it was a shame Bosnia was forced "to exempt American soldiers," a clear reference to the Article 98 agreement Bosnia signed with the United States regarding the ICC, an entirely distinct institution. Another RS organization made remarks suggesting a belief that the ICTY was a direct continuation of the Nuremburg trials.

While these local organizations can be forgiven for not being able to navigate an international legal labyrinth that includes ad hoc institutions, a permanent world court, military courts, and the like, these comments were indicative of a larger problem. While the amount of available information about the ICTY improved, the ICTY, and international forces on the ground, failed to communicate some of the most basic information about its structure and purpose to the Bosnian public, even when possible venues existed. The SFOR billboards put out by the Psychological Operations Department of NATO could have been used to get the message out, for example. Some of these "psy-ops" campaigns were notorious blunders, unpopular all over the country. For example, in 2004, one poster campaign showed Ratko Mladić's "present," a one-way ticket to The Hague, with the message that SFOR "had not forgotten" his birthday. Most Bosnian citizens interviewed felt the poster was a waste of valuable resources. Some of the psy-ops campaigns could instead have been dedicated to educating the public about things as basic as the structure of the ICTY and the laws of war. This, however, would have required coordination among the international institutions on the ground and willingness on the part of NATO, which had a strained relationship with the court at best.[49] It is important to ask, also, what levels of knowledge are reasonable to expect of the public at large.

Division of Labor Among International Organizations in the Field

A lack of understanding of the complicated relationship between the various international institutions on the ground influenced perceptions of the ICTY. Respondents did not necessarily appreciate that the ICTY did not have control over the organizations with which it worked. For example, the fact that SFOR and the ICTY were separate institutions was not always clear to respondents. When asked whether SFOR's failure to arrest war criminals affected or jeopardized the credibility of the court, over 60 percent of organizations said it did at least somewhat. The representative of one organization in Tomislavgrad was honest about their confusion: "Now I'm not sure how SFOR and the Tribunal are connected. If SFOR is an arm of the ICTY, then it does affect the court. If SFOR is independent, then no."[50] The phrasing of the question in the 2000 study was slightly different. It had asked respondents whether they understood that the roles of SFOR and IPTF (the International Police Task Force) were separate from that of the ICTY. Close to half of all respondents did not understand that these were unconnected institutions with different mandates.

Further consequences of this confusion about the ICTY were illustrated when respondents were asked whether the way in which SFOR conducted arrests affected the credibility of the ICTY. Answers to this question illuminated some lingering divisions in attitudes between the two entities. A much higher percentage in RS (80 percent) than in the Federation (40 percent) believed SFOR's arrests hurt the court's credibility. Many respondents in RS cited the failed April 2004 operation in Pale to arrest Radovan Karadžić, when SFOR forces critically injured an Orthodox

---

49   For information about the campaign see "Mladić sjetili smo da danas ti je rođendan" (Mladić we remembered that today is your birthday), <www.24sata.ba>, March 12, 2004, <www.24sata.info/portal/pregled.php?ArtID=3141&act=refer> (accessed March 5, 2005).

50   Interview with civil society organization representative, Tomislavgrad, May 24, 2004.

priest, Jeremija Starovlah, and his son Alexander Starovlah.[51] For many groups, it remained unclear who had the responsibility to arrest war criminals. When asked whether they knew whose duty arrests are, almost three-quarters of respondents said SFOR, the Ministry of Internal Affairs (Ministarstvo unutarnjih poslova, or MUP), or local authorities. Sixteen percent of respondents were not sure. A handful guessed that the average citizen had this responsibility, or the Office of the High Representative (OHR).

The Work of the ICTY: Sealed Indictments, Plea Agreements, and ICTY Strategy

Opinions differed among respondents about the tools and strategy used by the ICTY. Sealed indictments were issued as part of the ICTY's practice of not making public the identities of some of the persons indicted for war crimes, to prevent individuals from escaping justice. Of the organizations surveyed in 2004, 46 percent had a positive opinion of the use of sealed indictments. A higher percentage of groups in the Federation than in RS thought they were important for the ICTY's work, but the contrast was not as stark as in the previous study. Five years earlier, almost all of the groups in RS had a negative opinion of sealed indictments, but attitudes and understandings had changed over time. The director of an organization in Srebrenica argued, "I think that just the fact that they are sealed creates for some people doubt and skepticism, but I personally believe that the fact that they are sealed is justified in the sense that sometimes a lot more time is needed to get to some kinds of information."[52]

In recent years, the ICTY has also used plea agreements to obtain further information about crime locations and perpetrators, to reduce the time needed to complete a case and the overall number of trials. A total of 85 percent of those surveyed were familiar with this process. Just over half of all respondents (53 percent) had a negative opinion of this practice, but of those, almost half (22 percent) of those acknowledged that the practice could have some positive effects. The director of an organization in Goražde said, "Plea agreements are a double-edged sword. The victim can't be happy with that, a victim is a victim and everyone should respect what they've been through."[53] Of the organizations that had a positive opinion of the practice, one civil society representative in Banja Luka emphasized the importance of time: "I'm completely for every type of procedure that speeds up the process because until The Hague process is finished our society definitely can't

---

[51] See "SFOR Operation in Pale – Additional Information," press statement, NATO Stabilization Force in Bosnia and Herzegovina, April 2, 2004, <www.nato.int/sfor/trans/2004/p040402a.htm> (accessed July 14, 2009).

[52] Interview with civil society organization representative, Srebrenica, June 17, 2004.

[53] Interview with civil society organization representative, Goražde, July 16, 2004.

begin finally confronting the past."[54] Others emphasized the gains from additional information: "I think that those agreements are part of the whole strategy of the Tribunal because if someone accepts the agreement, they put themselves in a situation in which the Tribunal can use it as a tool to get new information and because of that we've gotten closer to the idea of what it means to catch the big fish."[55]

Some organizations, however, felt that the practice did more harm than good. In Bratunac, one representative of a well-established organization argued:

I am very disappointed because it has all lasted so long. Dayton was signed in '95 and the madness stopped; now it is 2004, and everything is so slow. I live for the day, unfortunately, it still has not come, and personally, I call it D-day, when all those people who committed war crimes will be arrested and that those plea agreements do not exist on that day. It hurts a lot that these agreements exist .... It's a big injustice.[56]

In recent years, the ICTY turned its focus to those most responsible for violations of international humanitarian law, a strategy known colloquially as a search for the "big fish."[57] United Nations Security Council (UNSC) resolutions outlined target dates for the closure of the ICTY: to have completed all investigations in 2004 and to have begun all initial trials by 2008. This strategy seemed to be a logical approach for the respondents who supported it.[58] "We have a saying here in the Balkans that the fish stinks from the head and it's logical that the big fish should be caught first," said a representative of an organization in Čapljina.[59] A small number felt the ICTY should have focused on this set of perpetrators earlier. However, many respondents, when asked to evaluate this focus, simply lamented the fact that the two most wanted perpetrators from Bosnia, Radovan Karadžić (later transferred in 2008) and Ratko Mladić, were still at large. "The ICTY is under a big question mark until those big fish are in The Hague," one argued."[60] These sentiments provide further evidence that the reputation of the ICTY was tied to the work of institutions, like SFOR, over which it had no control.

A subset of organizations was asked whether they believed the arrest of Mladić and Karadžić was an important goal for the country.[61] Here, the results on the entity level were starkly dissimilar: 86 percent in the Federation said it was, whereas only 27 percent in RS concurred. One organization in Bijeljina argued,

---

[54] Interview with civil society organization representative, Banja Luka, January 20, 2005. (NB: This is one of two organizations interviewed in 2005; the rest were interviewed in 2004.)

[55] Interview with civil society organization representative, Kakanj, May 17, 2004.

[56] Interview with civil society organization representative, Bratunac, June 17, 2004.

[57] United Nations SC Resolution 1534 (2004) (S/RES/1534, 26 March 2004), <www.un.org/Docs/sc/unsc_resolutions04.html> (accessed July 14, 2009).

[58] A slightly smaller number of organizations answered this question: 24 in the Federation and 17 in RS.

[59] Interview with civil society organization representative, Čapljina, May 21, 2004.

[60] Interview with civil society organization representative, Banja Luka, January 20, 2005.

[61] This question was added later, resulting in a large number of missing data: only 21 organizations in the Federation and 15 in RS answered it.

"It could be important for media and politics but for any real change, really I don't think so. ... One man didn't cause all of this or give the orders for all of this. It was a complete machinery. His arrest won't change things."[62] Another in Čelinac said:

Most people in their position would surrender. I don't know what their surrender would actually solve, it's not like they could do anything on their own and now there is some kind of blackmail toward the people who live here [in RS]. [I previously said] that it's odd they haven't been able to catch them so far, but if they could and it would solve something in this region then that would be good. I don't see that it is a goal because a lot of things happened during the war and a lot of people suffered and no one knows how much that affected ordinary people.[63]

Many organizations in the Federation felt that The Hague's failure to find and try the "most wanted" was holding back progress in the country, while others argued that joining the European Union was the way forward, with or without their capture. One organization in Mostar emphasized the social setting in which the court worked: "The arrest of Karadžić and Mladić is not important as long as the structure of the country is not changed. They can arrest Karadžić and Mladić tomorrow and as long as we have Dayton BiH, the arrests will be false satisfaction. It's more important to change the structure of the country. We have had some small steps toward progress; Bosnia needs a big step now."[64] None of the respondents claimed that those most responsible for violations of international humanitarian law should not be sent to The Hague. The existence of the ICTY was generally accepted as an aspect of postwar Bosnia that would not, and should not, be altered. However, most respondents had not previously considered the long-term implications of the ICTY's strategy.

Respondents were rather divided on what they thought about the sentences issued by the ICTY. Many felt sentences were too short, or that politics influenced sentencing, or that sentencing was not equal for all ethnic groups. One organization in Sarajevo saw the issue of sentencing as part of a bigger problem: "I think sometimes they [the sentences] are really ridiculous, but it's a problem of developed democracies in general."[65] Grouping these categories suggested that the number of organizations unhappy with sentences was the same as in the first study. Even though many civil society representatives thought sentences were too short, when asked whether the length of a sentence or the fact that a person was held accountable for their crimes was more important, almost half of all respondents claimed accountability was more important to them; only 10 percent said the length of the sentence was more important; 37 percent said they were equally important.

Participants illustrated a willingness to help the work of the court even if they were unsure they would be safe doing it. Over three-quarters of respondents said

---

[62] Interview with civil society organization representative, Bijeljina, June 15, 2004.
[63] Interview with civil society organization representative, Čelinac, May 12, 2004.
[64] Interview with civil society organization representative, Mostar, August 2, 2004.
[65] Interview with civil society organization representative, Sarajevo, July 15, 2004.

they would be a witness for the ICTY if they were asked, even though they felt that some witnesses in its care were not adequately protected.

Respondents were asked to comment on the prosecution of one specific type of crime: rape. The overwhelming majority supported the court's decision to address this type of crime and 61 percent felt the court has not paid enough attention to it. Many respondents, predominantly in the Federation, argued that rape was part of the wartime strategy to humiliate Bosniak women and should be punished as a war crime. The court would, in fact, later become noted for convictions for rape as a war crime.

Broader Impact of the Court

The 2004 study gave respondents the opportunity to comment directly on the extra-legal aspirations of court. They were asked, for example, whether the ICTY serves as a deterrent to future war crimes, helps democratization, aids the return of refugees, and fosters the rule of law. Respondents answered positively in higher numbers to questions that addressed effects that were tangible, suggesting that they witnessed a relationship between the court's proceedings and other domestic developments in the country. They were less convinced that the court would help other goals such as deterrence and reconciliation, bigger conceptual issues that many felt were distant from their daily lives.

The most significant finding in regard to the effects of the court was an increase between 1999 and 2004 in the numbers of respondents who felt prosecutions facilitated the return of refugees. This was the only question about the expressivist effects of the court that appeared in the 1999 study. Almost three-quarters (74 percent) of all respondents in this study felt the ICTY at least somewhat contributes to the return of refugees, more than double the percentage in the previous study, in which 33 percent concurred. One group in Kakanj mentioned the trial of Bosnian Army officers: "Of course it has influence. Now, for example, take the example if there is a sentence for [Amir] Kubura and the others indicted. Of course those Croats who left for Stolac will return because the sentence was accepted. The war criminals will be held accountable and the Croats will return to Stup, Vareš, Vitez, and so on. When I speak, I'm talking about the long-term process."[66] Other respondents reasoned that trials help to decrease the fear returnees feel when moving back to areas where they may now be minorities or where major violations of international humanitarian law took place. One organization in Prijedor said the ICTY helped facilitate returns there because it started early in the region. "The ICTY had a role [in returns in Prijedor], because they started to arrest and take

[66] Interview with civil society organization representative, Kakanj, May 17, 2004. The reference is to the trial of Enver Hadžihasanović and Amir Kubura. See Hadžihasanović and Kubura (IT-01-47) Case Information Sheet, United Nations, <www.icty.org/case/hadzihasanovic_kubura/4> (accessed July 13, 2009).

people into custody earlier, before return and before everything, therefore the Tribunal had a role in the return and existence of these returnees."[67] Respondents had watched the process of returns and realized that the security situation on the ground was influenced by the continued presence of war criminals, many of whom had become involved in organized crime. Even though the numbers of criminals arrested by the ICTY were small, they sent a message that more arrests could follow. In upholding the norm of accountability, they signaled that the rule of law was being returned to these communities. Still, there were some differences of opinion on the issue: one person involved in the return process in Prijedor argued that prosecutions were more peripheral to their efforts to get people back to their prewar homes than the actions of elites who had kept meticulous records of citizens displaced from the municipality and later organized the return effort.[68] However, the fact that respondents claim that prosecutions have had a positive impact provides further evidence that perceptions are important and that trials were a positive sign to would-be returnees.

The ICTY received credit for other aspects of postwar relations in Bosnian society. When asked whether individual criminal responsibility – the idea that individuals and not ethnic groups are responsible for the commission of crimes – improves or worsens interethnic relations, a majority responded that it improves them. Many respondents argued that individual criminal responsibility takes away the temptation to attach collective guilt to an ethnic group for crimes. "We know that the criminals have first and last names," said one group in Tuzla. Still, for the 18 percent that thought it worsens interethnic relations, some felt there was no way to escape the problem of generalization: "It's logical that it worsens interethnic relations. If I'm an individual who committed a war crime and it is known which ethnic group I belong to, in the mind of the average person, they will generalize and simplify about the ethnic group. And then it's not me as a person but as a part of this ethnic group."[69] This view, however, was expressed by only a handful of organizations.

When asked whether the ICTY helps advance the rule of law, one of the goals the ICTY set out for itself, the majority answered that it did.[70] This result was almost identical in each entity: 70 percent in RS and 67 percent in the Federation. As Chapter 8 outlines, without the ICTY, it is unlikely that Bosnia would have made as much progress in developing local capacity to prosecute war crimes in the first decade after the war.

On the more elusive concepts of justice, democratization, and reconciliation, the majority thought that the work of the court positively influenced these areas, but their conviction was not as strong as it was for some of the more tangible effects of the court. Some respondents, unable to directly assess the court's impact on

[67] Interview with civil society organization representative, Prijedor, May 10, 2004.
[68] Discussion with human rights activist from Prijedor, Sarajevo, September 2005.
[69] Interview with civil society organization representative, Ribnik, May 13, 2004.
[70] See the list of the ICTY's achievements at: <www.icty.org/sid/324> (accessed July 13, 2009).

these less concrete concepts, simply stated that it *should* positively influence these processes. An organization in Bijeljina argued that, "Just removing war criminals from this area opens doors to democracy."[71] Some, though, felt that politicization of the work of the ICTY made this goal unobtainable. One group in Banja Luka said, "I expected that the Tribunal would help democratize; however, I'm afraid that with the politicization around the ICTY and all of the events, the opposite happened. All of the events that are connected to the Tribunal, internal and external, gave a base to extremist circles to politicize and destabilize, meaning permanently destabilize, the situation, constantly."[72]

On whether the court helped the process of reconciliation, the numbers of positive responses were lower: just over half said it at least somewhat helped the process. Most respondents felt that this was a generational issue and reconciliation could not be brought about so soon after the end of the war. One organization emphasized a different long-term value of the ICTY's efforts: its documentation. "The documentation that the ICTY has collected is capital. And probably in the future it will bring a historical interpretation of past events."[73]

Respondents were less sure about whether the ICTY could deter future crimes, or prevent individuals from taking revenge. History repeats itself, said one respondent in Goražde: "We had the Nuremburg trials for war crimes during World War II and we thought it would never happen again and some sentences were higher than those given by the ICTY. Later, on the territory of the former Yugoslavia, we had [another] war, so whether there is a deterrent effect is disputable."[74] Similarly, only a third of all respondents thought that the ICTY would prevent individuals from taking revenge. "The Tribunal can't stop revenge, revenge is like water," one respondent from an organization in Mrkonjić Grad commented.[75] The 2000 study had represented these issues in one question: "Do you believe the Tribunal has broader goals besides holding trials for those accused of war crimes?" Then, 76 percent of respondents answered positively.

A Biased Institution?

The questions asked of the respondents failed to formally capture one sentiment, expressed all over RS, or by almost all respondents of Serb ethnicity: why there are so many Serbs in The Hague, even though violations of international humanitarian law were committed by everyone. In Zvornik, one organization lamented that the ICTY had not addressed crimes against Serbs: "In every ear you can hear [about] Srebrenica. ... We can't say it didn't [happen], yes, it is, ok, but nobody wants to say

---

[71] Interview with civil society organization representative, Bijeljina, June 15, 2004.
[72] Interview with civil society organization representative, Banja Luka, May 12, 2004.
[73] Interview with civil society organization representative, Banja Luka, May 12, 2004.
[74] Interview with civil society organization representative, Goražde, July 16, 2004.
[75] Interview with civil society organization representative, Mrkonjić Grad, May 13, 2004.

how Bratunac and Kravica were completely destroyed and the man who did that is not answering for his crimes, but these people from Srebrenica are, [even though] he was the first one who committed crimes." In Modriča, another said: "maybe they didn't commit the same number of war crimes but there were war crimes everywhere, it doesn't have to be the same number but simply all three armies did a lot of things and there were war crimes toward civilians. It was inevitable, and now what's the number of the first, second, and third? I don't want to get into it." Similarly, in Prijedor came the assertion that: "we all have our Srebrenicas. Here you go: Sarajevo, graves around Sarajevo and Tuzla. Go to Lukavica and see." In general, Serb respondents in RS had come to believe that the existence of the ICTY was legitimate and even necessary, but the feeling was still prevalent that it was biased against members of their ethnic group.

Conclusion

This chapter addressed the question of what civil society groups thought about the ICTY's work and its broader mandate. As one of the sectors of society that deals with the social consequences of the war, local organizations were able informants about the court's work. Attitudes changed for the better, in some cases quite drastically, over the intervening five years. The court enjoyed increased legitimacy and, in greater numbers, NGOs reported that they felt it contributed to some crucial aspects of democratization, including the return of refugees.

This change in attitudes was accompanied by change at the court itself about taking steps to realize its extended mandate. In the immediate postwar period, the lack of awareness and knowledge of the court within Bosnia inhibited its stated goal to be a transformative force in the region. ICTY representatives realized that verdicts must be translated, journalists trained properly, and victims contacted if the court were to have any chance of helping the country's transition and of realizing its extended mandate, which included contributing to peace and stability. In addition to explaining its findings, the ICTY also needed to explain the limitations of international criminal justice in general, as well as those of the ICTY. To do so, it started translating its work into local languages and created an Outreach Program. This program facilitated contact with many different groups in the region despite having relatively few resources, relying on strong and motivated employees on the ground who had good relations with civil society representatives. Local outreach employees also anticipated the needs of the court's varied local constituents, including victims, legal professionals, and the press.

During the period under consideration, political conditions in Bosnia improved slightly: the nationalists' stranglehold on political power was somewhat diluted by electoral losses, politicians in RS understood that anti-court rhetoric would not be tolerated (they could be removed by the High Representative), and the media matured and developed. More journalists were trained on how to cover complex trials, which enabled better coverage of the court to reach the average citizen, including the leaders of civil society organizations, large and small, surveyed here. Civil society itself changed: new groups were started, many of which represented the interests of returnees. The cumulative result was that the court enjoyed increased legitimacy all over the country. There were still differences in attitudes between the country's two constituent entities; however, even respondents in RS reported higher levels of confidence in the credibility of the court, and more recognized the need to process violations of international humanitarian law and genocide, although many still regarded the court as a "political" institution.

Despite these positive changes, across the country there remained confusion about the purpose and structure of the ICTY, and its relationship to other international institutions on the ground. Although respondents felt more comfortable with their levels of knowledge, misunderstandings about the basic function of the court still hindered the achievement of some of its broader goals. Here, analogies to the domestic criminal justice system seem appropriate. How much do we expect informed citizens to know about courts? What is an acceptable level of knowledge in democratic societies, and what, precisely, would constitute a lack of knowledge? Who should know what, when, and how much? A future study may find it worthwhile to assess NGO knowledge about domestic courts as a source of comparison. Such a comparison might mitigate the fervor of one aspect of critiques of the ICTY.

Even if a reassessment of the role of civil society and courts were to temper expectations, it would not undercut a major conclusion of this study: civil society, a potential source of information and a conveyor of ideas, was largely an untapped resource, although, as respondents suggested, it would have been a willing partner in bringing the ICTY's work closer to local communities. The ICTY's outreach effort eventually did use local groups to facilitate its work, but it devoted only limited resources to the task and ultimately involved only a handful of organizations. The ICTY never made civil society a true partner in its work, which could have invigorated debates in the country and improved civil society's ability to lobby on issues related to the court's mandate.

To date, there have been few panel or quasi-panel studies conducted on ICTY attitudes in Bosnia. As one of the first studies to address this gap in the literature, this research has illustrated that civil society attitudes changed for the better. The levels of support and attitudes toward the court's extended mandate are consistent with those found in other sectors, notably in the military (see Chapter 7). It is impossible, however, for a study using a relatively small sample size to untangle which variables led to the greatest change in attitudes, nor to tease out the impact of outreach compared to other variables. In this sense, this type of study cannot uncover precise causal relationships and measurements, nor, consequently, reveal simple policy prescriptions. There simply is not enough good data here to make any bold claims with the confidence that a larger sample size might have allowed.

Nevertheless, some tentative conclusions seem reasonable. Insofar as the court's Outreach Program at least partly contributed to a change in attitudes toward the court – signaling more of an openness to discuss accountability, the rule of law, and the country's recent past with Bosnian civil society – it was part of a positive dynamic. Perhaps most importantly, this chapter illustrates that attitudes change over time. Individuals representing organizations that served as a layer between the state and its citizens felt that the court was making progress on its extended mandate. Even though the shortcomings and criticisms were numerous, for a court that had no road map about how to reach out to this critical sector, the change in attitudes was encouraging at the very least.

6 Narrative and Counter-Narrative
The Case of the Čelebići Trial

Two years after the war, the International Criminal Tribunal for the former Yugoslavia (ICTY) turned its attention to events that had taken place at the Čelebići prison camp an hour outside of Sarajevo. In 1997, three Bosniaks and one Croat were put on trial for crimes committed against Bosnian Serbs in a detention facility at Čelebići, a village in the municipality of Konjic. Seven hundred Bosnian Serb combatants and civilians were detained for over six months, from May to December 1992, at the hands of ruthless and sometimes murderous jailers. Thirteen of the detainees died there.

This was the ICTY's first trial of individuals not of Serb ethnicity. In some circles, hope existed that the trial would help foster a more positive reputation of the court, and strengthen the notion that it was, indeed, impartial. The impact of the proceeding was somewhat different, however. At first glance, ten years after the war, the Čelebići trial seemed to have affected postwar developments beyond Konjic's borders more than it had within the town. Among Serb nationalists in Bosnia, and in the diaspora, many saw the trial as evidence that all sides had committed comparable war crimes. Among Bosniak elites, it led to a new awareness that members of the Army of the Republic of Bosnia and Herzegovina (ARBiH) were also guilty of violations of international law. In the international arena, the trial set several precedents.

This chapter outlines the effects of the Čelebići trial, drawing from conversations with local residents in Konjic, the town near where the crimes took place. It shows that, even though differences in narratives of the war were among the ICTY's underestimated local obstacles, the trial added a judicial narrative that influenced the stories told by Bosnian citizens. In doing so, the trial prompted new discussions and raised questions that any country transitioning to democracy should contemplate.

Narratives and Social Science

Narratives provide valuable clues about how to understand social and political developments. Stories told by citizens about violence, war, and proposed efforts to redress human rights violations contain information about personal beliefs, reveal theories about causation, and give indicators of the effectiveness of a given political solution or proposed institution.[1]

Trials for mass atrocities often bring out competing narratives of events, motives, and purposes. To begin with, the different actors in a courtroom – the prosecution, the defense, the witnesses – utilize different narratives of what happened during the events in question. This process feeds into the narrative produced by the verdict, the narrative that tends to have the most lasting impact. As Mark Osiel has argued, trials are not particularly effective mechanisms to change those narratives.[2] But this chapter will illustrate how legal narratives can help to refute some of the more untenable claims espoused by nationalists. Trials also prompt debates within communities, as a result of evidence presented and issues raised in the courtroom, and the very fact that a trial was held with a particular set of defendants. Even if trials may not force committed nationalists to change their positions, they engender the type of discussions that should characterize developing democracies. The Čelebići trial showed that less than ideal legal proceedings could still stimulate these important conversations.

Some scholars, such as Hannah Arendt and, more recently, Martha Minow have argued that the use of narratives and storytelling may be even more important than other social science methods. They argue that more rationalist methods obscure what is new and extraordinary about periods of political violence because rationalists seek to explain these periods not as ruptures but by reference to prior events, which may lead to passivity by citizens who feel helpless to change outcomes.[3] Drawing on Arendt, Minow argues that narratives "are crucial in constructing a sense of self in the face of traditions that have crumbled and human hopes that risk being forgotten."[4] Narratives enable the expression of multiple viewpoints and "only through the variety of relationships constructed by many people seen from different perspectives can truth be known and community be created."[5]

In support of this insight, this chapter draws on the stories told by citizens of a small town about nearby wartime events. It also explores their attitudes toward a trial that examined a few of the violations of international humanitarian law

---

[1] For a discussion of what narrative analysis has to offer to social scientists, see Roberto Franzosi, "Narrative Analysis – Or Why (And How) Sociologists Should be Interested in Narrative," *Annual Review of Sociology* 24 (1998): 517–554.

[2] Mark Osiel, *Mass Atrocity, Collective Memory and the Law* (New Brunswick, NJ: Transaction Publishers, 2000), especially pp. 6–10 and 51–55.

[3] See Martha Minow, "Stories in Law," in Peter Brooks and Paul Gewirtz, eds., *Law's Stories: Narrative and Rhetoric in the Law* (New Haven, CT: Yale University Press, 1996), 32–33.

[4] Ibid., 33.

[5] Ibid., 34. Minow also emphasizes Arendt's description of the role of storyteller, that "the storyteller selects and necessarily judges while excavating the past, just as a deep-sea diver finds pearls. The storyteller uses bits of the past to unsettle the present and deprive it of peace of mind." Ibid., 33.

that took place there. It addresses the understandings and effects of the trial, and shows how the ICTY's work was received both in that community and in Bosnia in general. This chapter first lays out the details of the trial, then describes how the constantly changing political climate in Bosnia meant that attitudes toward the court slowly changed, mostly, but not always, for the better. Citizens' narratives revealed strongly held positions, but also some new admissions and ruminations about what the trial meant for Konjic and beyond.

The Municipality of Konjic

Konjic is located an hour's drive southwest of Sarajevo, in Canton 7, the Herzegovina-Neretva Canton, on the road from Sarajevo to Mostar. Like Sarajevo, Konjic is nestled in a valley, an unfavorable place during war, as the only retreat is over the hills. From a military point of view, the town was strategically important for several reasons. First, the municipality was home to an ammunition factory that would later supply the ARBiH with bullets. Second, its placement between two of the country's major cities meant that it was a place of interest to all of the parties involved in the war. Some saw Konjic as problematic because it occupied an undecided space between the planned "Greater Serbia" and "Greater Croatia," but was not a part of the plan for either. The municipality's demography complicated such a division. The prewar population of Konjic was mixed: 55 percent Bosniak, 26 percent Croat, 15 percent Serb, and 4 percent other. It was one of 37 municipalities (of 109) in Bosnia where Bosniaks made up more than 50 percent of the population.

As of October 2008, there were records of 801 persons killed in the municipality of Konjic during the war. Of those, 360 were Bosniaks, 221 were Serbs, and 220 were Croats. The first two years of the war accounted for the largest number of casualties, with 252 deaths in 1992 and 394 in 1993. In 1994, 104 people were killed. Even after the signing of the Washington Agreement, 43 people perished in 1995.[6] Wartime events in Konjic reflected the various stages of the larger Bosnian war. Čelebići, a village within the municipality of Konjic but outside the city itself, housed a military storage facility for the JNA (Jugoslovenska narodna armija or Yugoslav People's Army); images of its sizeable grounds were among the prosecution exhibits shown to the judges and trial participants. Most of the facility was used for military storage but a small part of it housed detainees. Bosnian Serb citizens would later say that memories of the existence of the camp still kept many from returning to their prewar residences 10 years after the war ended.

---

[6]   Research and Documentation Center, "Human Losses 1991–1995" project, October 2008. Data provided to the author on June 29, 2009. The Research and Documentation Center listed eight additional individuals for whom the year of death is unknown. Commemorating (and documenting) the dead was a difficult process requiring decisions on whom to memorialize and how to do it. For example, a memorial in the center of the town for the ARBiH's victims listed almost 400 deaths, which included those born in Konjic but killed in other municipalities.

The Trial

ICTY Chief Prosecutor Richard Goldstone issued the original Čelebići indictment on March 21, 1996, just months after the signing of the Dayton Peace Agreement (DPA). In addition to having non-Serb defendants, the trial was the first ICTY case that sought to convict based on command responsibility for crimes, and it was the first collective trial for violations of international law since World War II. There were four accused: Zejnil Delalić was a commander of the First Tactical Group of the Bosnian Army and was alleged to have had command responsibility over the Čelebići prison camp. Zdravko Mucić commanded the camp from May to November 1992, the period during which the crimes in question took place. Hazim Delić was deputy commander of the camp. Esad Landžo was a camp guard. Delić and Landžo and were charged primarily with direct participation in the crimes that occurred in the camp, whereas Delalić and Mucić were charged with superior command responsibility.[7] The four defendants were tried at the same time, in the same courtroom, for crimes they were alleged to have committed in the same facility. The case was assigned one number, IT-96-21.

The trial established that some of the most horrific violations of international humanitarian law to occur in Bosnia took place in Čelebići. The "evidence demonstrated that an atmosphere of fear and intimidation prevailed at the prison-camp, caused by the beatings meted out indiscriminately upon the prisoners. Each of the former detainees who testified before the Trial Chamber described acts of violence and cruelty which they themselves suffered or witnessed and many continue today to sustain the physical and psychological consequences of these experiences."[8] The trial lasted 19 months, included over 1,500 exhibits, and created over 16,000 pages of documentation. Video footage of detainees being taunted visually confirmed the atmosphere.[9] However, not all went well for the prosecution.

Zejnil Delalić, who ICTY documents stated was "coordinator of the Bosnian Muslim and Bosnian Croat forces in Konjic from April to September 1992," was accused of superior criminal responsibility, grave breaches of the Geneva Conventions, and violations of the laws or customs of war, but was acquitted of all charges and released from detention in 1998, finding that he did not have command and control over the camp and its guards.[10]

---

[7] *Prosecutor v. Zejnil Delalić, Zdravko Mucić a.k.a. "Pavo," Hazim Delić, Esad Landžo a.k.a. "Zenga"* (IT-96-21), Judgement (In the Appeals Chamber), ICTY, February 20, 2001, <www.icty.org/x/cases/mucic/acjug/en/cel-aj010220.pdf> (accessed April 15, 2009).

[8] *Prosecutor v. Zdravko Mucić, Hazim Delić, Esad Landžo and Zejnil Delalić* (IT-96-21) Case Information Sheet, ICTY, <www.icty.org/x/cases/mucic/cis/en/cis_mucic_al_en.pdf> (accessed May 15, 2009). See also Jennifer M. Rockoff, "Prosecutor v. Zejnil Delalić (The Čelebići Case)," *Military Law Review* 166 (2000): 172–98.

[9] See the documentary film "Justice Unseen," directed by Aldin Arnautović and Refik Hodžić (Sarajevo: XY Films, 2004).

[10] *Prosecutor v. Zdravko Mucić, Hazim Delić, Esad Landžo and Zejnil Delalić* (IT-96-21) Case Information Sheet, ICTY, <www.icty.org/x/cases/mucic/cis/en/cis_mucic_al_en.pdf> (accessed May 15, 2009).

Zdravko Mucić, commander of the camp from May to November 1992, was found guilty and convicted, based on superior criminal responsibility, of eight counts of violations of the Geneva Conventions and seven counts of violations of the laws or customs of war. He was sentenced to seven years, increased on appeal to nine. He was granted early release in 2003, having served two-thirds of his sentence, a common practice at the ICTY.[11]

Hazim Delić, deputy commander of the Čelebići camp from May to November 1992, was found guilty of eight counts of violations of the Geneva Conventions and seven counts of violations of the laws or customs of war, including the rapes of two detainees. He was sentenced to 20 years imprisonment, which on appeal was decreased to 18 when one murder charge was dropped. His further appeal was dismissed. He was granted early release in 2008 after receiving credit for time served since 1996.[12]

Esad Landžo, the camp guard, was found guilty of nine counts of grave breaches of the Geneva Conventions and nine counts of violations of the laws or customs of war. He was sentenced to 15 years, a sentence upheld on appeal, and he was granted early release in 2006, also receiving credit for time served since 1996.[13]

This was a trial in which "everything that could go wrong did go wrong."[14] The stories that emerged out of the courtroom sometimes seemed scripted as a parody of an international trial. One day, a judge fell asleep in court, an infamous incident that seemed to symbolize the international community's indifference to the suffering of the people in the region. Procedural delays caused the proceedings to drag on; a judge fell ill; a prosecution witness was hit by a car a day before his testimony.[15] Such missteps, combined with instances of bad luck, catalogued by analysts and journalists, were offered as evidence that the court was biased toward this or that party. These were the early days of the court's life, though, and no international institution functions optimally in its early years.

Even this relatively flawed legal intervention, however, prompted a series of discussions about the nature of the new Bosnian state, what the political community would look like, and how people would relate to one another. These discussions were good for the democratization process. The effects of the trial are best

---

[11] Ibid., 3.

[12] Ibid., 3.

[13] Ibid., 3. See also the initial indictment for *Prosecutor v. Delalić et al.*, <www.icty.org/x/cases/mucic/ind/en/cel-ii960321e.pdf> (accessed April 15, 2009).

[14] Journalist Mirko Klarin of the SENSE News Agency quoted in Elizabeth Neuffer, *The Key to My Neighbor's House: Seeking Justice in Bosnia and Rwanda* (New York: Picador, 2001), 299. Klarin had been one of the first people in the region to lobby for the creation of an international tribunal. See Mirko Klarin, "Nuremberg Now!," *Borba*, May 16, 1991, reproduced in *The Path to the Hague: Selected Documents on the Origins of the ICTY* (The Hague: International Tribunal for Prosecution of Persons Responsible for Serious Violations of International Humanitarian Law in the Territory of the former Yugoslavia since 1991, United Nations Publications, 1995), 43.

[15] Neuffer, *Key to My Neighbor's House*, 299.

understood within the context of larger narratives about the war in Bosnia in general and how those narratives and counter-narratives impeded the court's ability to positively influence developments in Bosnia.

The Lack of an Official Narrative

Fifteen years after the signing of the DPA, there are still many contrasting narratives of the war. Bosnia's citizens continue to offer different accounts of the causes, events, and purpose of the three and a half years of bloodshed. Even basic questions, such as whether it was a civil war or an aggression, remain contested. In the short term, the ICTY's work seemed to fuel these differing accounts. There were no agents who could impose a narrative about the character of the war and any attempt to do so would have been regarded as illegitimate by the parties who understood the war in another way. The fragmented public space in the country contributed to this state of affairs.

A likely candidate to craft such a narrative might have been the international community, but the DPA represented a fragile resolution by way of an impractical agreement, in which international actors had been forced to balance the competing interests of the nationalist parties still in power after the war. Consequently, they did not come out strongly in favor of any one party to the conflict. The DPA punished noncompliance, for example, withholding aid in Republika Srpska, but refrained from judgment and offered no official interpretation of events that took place before it was signed in November 1995. The only exception was that it provided that wartime violations of international humanitarian law could be addressed by the ICTY, and eventually by local courts. As a result, international actors present in the country approached the topic of the war very tentatively. The U.S. Embassy, for example, did not even use the term "war" (*rat*) to describe what occurred in Bosnia; internally, embassy employees referred to it as a "conflict" (*sukob*). The latter term was a source of contention for many Bosniaks who felt it trivialized the level of violence they had experienced and did not accurately represent what happened in the country, which they considered an aggression. Many Serb nationalists, by contrast, welcomed the U.S. terminology, and referred to the war as either a conflict (*sukob*) or a civil war (*građanski rat*).

The ICTY's jurisprudence slowly pieced together a picture of the conflict, built by the court's documentation. The court's focus on individual indictees, however, coupled with the fact that outreach efforts were relatively limited, meant that overall interpretations of the general findings of the court's work would largely have to wait for later analysts. In addition, embassies on the ground were not obliged to promote, or even support, the court's findings. Furthermore, the court's analyses of the overall structure or demographics of war crimes, including those of the Demography Unit in the Office of the Prosecutor (OTP), were used for specific trials, although they were accessible to enterprising journalists and researchers who might care to interpret them.[16] Thus, although it produced micro-narratives through its trials, the court's job was not to provide an overarching picture of the war, or a comprehensive narrative. The potential of the court to produce "history" was often exaggerated.

The ICTY's internal structure also tacitly endorsed the argument that a civil war of equal parties had occurred: the caseloads of investigative teams at the Office of the Prosecutor were grouped by the ethnicity of the perpetrators and not by the crimes committed.[17] This created institutional pressure to indict individuals of each ethnic group in equal proportion. Historian and former ICTY employee Marko Attila Hoare observed:

The Tribunal also suffers from structural problems that have hindered its effective operation. Established in 1993, at the height of Western appeasement of Milošević's Serbia, the organization of the Tribunal reflects the dominant Western precepts of the day: that atrocities were being "committed by all sides"; that Serbia was quantitatively but not qualitatively more guilty than the other parties; and that the war in Bosnia-Herzegovina was a "civil war" in which Bosnian Serb crimes were carried out autonomously from Belgrade. Instead of beginning with the "joint criminal purpose" of Serbian, Montenegrin and JNA leaders that brought about the war, and working downwards and outwards, the Tribunal's Office of the Prosecution began by fragmenting the war crimes according to ethnicity and territory: different investigative teams dealt with Serb crimes in Croatia, Serb crimes in Bosnia, Serb crimes in Kosovo, Croat crimes in Croatia, Croat crimes in Bosnia, Muslim crimes, Albanian crimes and – most recently – Macedonian crimes.[18]

The court's focus on individual criminal responsibility left the issue of state (and entity) responsibility to the case that Bosnia filed against the Federal Republic of Yugoslavia (FRY) at the International Court of Justice (ICJ), charging it with genocide. The ICTY's staff was aware of the limits of its concentration on individual criminal responsibility. OTP Principal Trial Attorney Geoffrey Nice, on a break from the Milošević trial in 2005, told a group of human rights activists: "A question for us here is whether trials of individuals can deal adequately with the accountability of states."[19] He noted that some of history's observers of justice were divided

[16] In 2009, a book of many of the collected reports of the ICTY Demography Unit was published by the Helsinki Committee for Human Rights in Serbia. See Ewa Tabeau, *Rat u brojkama: demografski gubici u ratovima na teritoriji bivše Jugoslavije 1991–1999* (War in figures: Demographic losses in the wars on the territory of the former Yugoslavia 1991–1999) (Belgrade: Helsinki Committee for Human Rights in Serbia, 2009).
[17] John R.W.D. Jones, "ICTY and Command Responsibility," manuscript; a more developed version of this argument can be found in John R.W.D. Jones and Steven Powles, *International Criminal Practice,* 3rd ed. (Ardsley, NY and Oxford: Transnational Publishers/Oxford University Press, 2003).
[18] Quotation from Marko Attila Hoare, "The Capitulation of the Hague Tribunal," Open Letter, June 2005, <www.glypx.com/BalkanWitness/hoare2.htm> (accessed April 15, 2009).
[19] Geoffrey Nice, Former Principal Trial Attorney in the Office of the Prosecutor of the ICTY, presentation, Meeting of the International Center for Transitional Justice, Cape Town, South Africa, March 2005.

on the topic of where and how to enforce accountability. He quoted Sir Hartley Shawcross, Britain's chief prosecutor at Nuremberg: "There can be no reconciliation unless individual guilt for the appalling crimes of the last few years replaces the pernicious theory of collective guilt on which so much racial hatred hangs." In contrast, he noted, Hannah Arendt had argued in *Eichmann in Jerusalem* that: "Crimes of this kind were, and could only be, committed under a criminal law and by a criminal state."[20] Discussing his work in Brčko, Nice noted that the trial "achieved nothing of state, municipality or even town accountability." The absence of overall claims about state responsibility allowed competing narratives of the war to flourish. The ICTY's role was never meant to be an arbiter of their accuracy, but its documentation and evidence, with pages numbering in the millions, pointed fingers at Serbia, Croatia, and a war effort that began long before the "official" start of the war in April 1992.

Bosnia's case against the FRY (later because of the dissolution of the country, just Serbia) at the ICJ, filed in 1993, was completed in February 2007. Its decision was upsetting for the Bosnian government and citizens who believed that the FRY had committed aggression and genocide on Bosnian territory. The court found that the VRS was guilty of genocide on Bosnian soil, but in Srebrenica only, and it found Serbia not guilty of direct participation in the crime. The court had relied solely on ICTY documentation and did not conduct any investigations of its own. It consequently inherited the flaws of the ICTY's work, notably the court's decision to accept the redacted documents of FRY's Supreme Defense Council (SDC).[21] Still, the decision was not a total victory for the Serbian defense; it acknowledged Serbia's failure to cooperate with the ICTY and its obligations under the Genocide Convention. As the only court that could have affirmed state responsibility, international judges appeared to be extremely timid.

Antecedents

The international community had been aware of suspected crimes in Konjic for a long time. When the ICTY was still only a concept, its proponents cited the names of suspects from Konjic in their advocacy for creation of an institution that would prosecute violations of international law. On October 5, 1992, when the Čelebići prison camp had been open for some months, the UN Security Council passed Resolution 780, which created the United Nations Commission of Experts to Investigate Violations of International Humanitarian Law in the

---

[20] Ibid.

[21] The documents contain minutes of the meetings of the FRY's wartime political and military leaders. See Marlise Simons, "Genocide Court Ruled for Serbia without Seeing Full War Archive," *New York Times*, April 9, 2007. Simons reports: "Serbia, heir to Yugoslavia, obtained the tribunal's permission to keep parts of the archives out of the public eye. Citing national security, its lawyers blacked out many sensitive – those who have seen them say incriminating – pages."

former Yugoslavia.[22] The Commission, headed by M. Cherif Bassiouni, a well-known law professor and specialist in international law, gathered documentation to justify the creation of the ICTY. A few months later, in December 1992, when the Commission was still collecting evidence in support of creation of a tribunal, U.S. Secretary of State Lawrence Eagleburger, at a conference on the Balkans attended by 29 nations, publicly noted that some high-ranking Serb leaders might be in violation of international humanitarian law.[23] His list contained several names that have become notorious: Ratko Mladić, Radovan Karadžić, Slobodan Milošević, and Željko Ražnatović, the paramilitary leader also known as Arkan. Also listed was Hazim Delić, a Bosniak who would be one of the four defendants in the Čelebići trial.[24] The existence of detention facilities in the Konjic municipality appeared in the report of the Commission, probably corroborated by members of the UN peacekeeping mission or by the EU monitoring mission.[25] This information later traveled up to the highest offices of the American government.

The Narrative that "All Sides Committed Comparable Numbers of War Crimes"

When the Čelebići trial opened in 1997, a *New York Times* headline read, "A War Crimes Trial, but Not of Serbs."[26] This was a nod to the perception prevalent at the time that the ICTY targeted only Serb war criminals. As it turned out, this trial, as well as others of non-Serbs, only slightly changed that perception, at least in the first decade after the war. Serb nationalists often pointed to the trial not as evidence that the ICTY was fair, but as confirmation that Serbs had suffered equally in the war. The Čelebići trial fueled this view by exposing atrocities committed by the "other side." It was an argument that dovetailed with the Bosnian Serb nationalist elite's position that a civil war of three equal parties – and not an international war – had occurred in the country. Along this line of thinking, some argued, all three ethnic groups, equal in their resolve not to live together, fought for control of territory. Even though the statements of Bosnian Serbs detained in the camp would show otherwise, some citizens internalized this narrative.

---

[22] See UNSC Resolution 780 (1992) (S/RES/780, 6 October 1992), October 6, 1992, <www.un.org/documents/sc/res/1992/scres92.htm> (accessed May 1, 2009).

[23] Don Oberdorfer, "Eagleburger Urges Trial of Serb Leaders: Milošević, Karadžić Would be Judged on Balkan War Crimes," *Washington Post*, December 17, 1992.

[24] Ibid.

[25] United Nations Security Council, Final Report of the United Nations Commission of Experts established pursuant to Security Council resolution 780 (1992), no. S/1994/674/Add.2 (Vol. 1), December 28, 1994, <www.ess.uwe.ac.uk/comexpert/Summary.htm> (accessed May 2, 2009).

[26] Marlise Simons, "A War-Crimes Trial But Not of Serbs," *New York Times*, April 3, 1997.

The Čelebići trial started in April 1997 at a time when denial, which had begun years before, prevailed in Republika Srpska. The first article about the commission of war crimes by the Army of Republika Srpska (VRS) was published by an RS newspaper in August 1999. Several months later, the editor of the paper, Željko Kopanja, lost both of his legs when a bomb exploded under his car.[27] No one was charged in the attack, but the perpetrators of the crimes highlighted in that article, and the network behind them, were seen as prime suspects.

By 2004, when the ICTY held an Outreach event in Konjic, some progress had been made. The RS government had acknowledged the Srebrenica massacre of July 1995, though it stopped short of using the term genocide and later backpedaled.[28] RS officials granted these concessions on an "ad hoc" basis, usually as a result of a court order or international pressure. RS politicians never made any general admissions or conceded that the Army of Republika Srpska, funded and aided by counterparts in Belgrade, had committed the vast majority of war crimes during the war (over 90 percent, by an early CIA estimate).[29]

In this environment, nationalist Bosnian Serb politicians made outlandish claims with relative impunity. In March 2005, Pero Bukeljović, Prime Minister of Republika Srpska, charged at a conference of the Serb Democratic Party (SDS) in Pale that "perhaps a greater genocide was committed against the Serbs in Sarajevo than against Bosniaks in Srebrenica" and declared that the RS government was "committed to prove that Serbs were the victim of genocide."[30] The nationalist elite continued to try to make Bosnian Serbs feel like a threatened minority who had suffered equal injustices that continued to go unaddressed. These claims resonated in some places. The Bosnian Serb public did not object strongly to such statements, although they lacked any empirical basis. Some observers argued that this was a conscious strategy of victimization used to slow down the wheels of reform, which threatened the existence of the VRS (which no longer exists), entity-level

---

[27] The editor's car was bombed on October 22, 1999. See also: "Position of the Media Within Context of Human Rights, reporting period: 01.01-31.12.1999," Report, Helsinki Committee for Human Rights in Bosnia and Herzegovina, 1999, <www.bh-hchr.org/Reports/reportmedia1999.htm> (accessed May 1, 2009).

[28] Pero Bukeljović would later assert that the RS government never conceded that 8,000 Bosniaks had been killed after the fall of the enclave; "Bosnian Serb Cabinet Never Said 8,000 Bosniaks Died in Srebrenica – Premier," *BBC Monitoring Media Reports*, August 2, 2005. The Office of the High Representative disputed this assertion; "OHR: RS Government Did Accept the Number of Srebrenica Victims," *Federation News Agency*, August 2, 2005, <www.fena.ba/uk/vijest.html?fena_id=FSA287799&rubrika=ES> (accessed April 30, 2005).

[29] Roger Cohen, "C.I.A. Report on Bosnia Blames Serbs for 90% of the War Crimes," *New York Times*, March 9, 1995.

[30] See Aldijana Omeragić, "Nad Srbima u Sarajevu počinjen genocid veći nego u Srebrenici" (A bigger genocide was committed against the Serbs in Sarajevo than in Srebrenica), *Oslobođenje*, March 26, 2005; "Bosnian Serb PM says Sarajevo Serbs Suffered More than Srebrenica Muslims," *Agence France Presse*, March 25, 2005; and Anes Alic, "Bosnian Serbs allege Sarajevo massacre," *ISN Security Watch*, January 5, 2005.

police forces, and even Republika Srpska itself.[31] This perspective included a corollary opinion that the further devolution of power to the entities was necessary. The argument that all sides suffered equally in the war made Bosnia's further integration – first toward a more centralized state, and then into the European Union – seem premature and politically naïve.

Nationalists, however, eventually did have to confront the facts uncovered by the work of the ICTY and issues raised in the courtroom. Nationalist politicians in Republika Srpska seemed to have a "one step forward, two steps back" approach to talking about the recent past, i.e. acknowledging the Srebrenica massacre and then making outlandish claims comparing Sarajevo to Srebrenica. The work of the ICTY, however, revealed some extremist claims for what they were: lies. Except among the most strident nationalists, the comparison of crimes committed in Srebrenica and Sarajevo enjoyed only a brief moment of apparent acceptance. This was in part also because human rights groups emboldened by the court's work had collected and publicized information to illustrate that this claim was false. The claim also had a more positive unintended effect by prompting more introspection within the circles of the Sarajevo elite about what to do about crimes that were committed by Bosnian government forces.[32]

Fueling the Domestic Fires: Diaspora Nationalism

The myth that all parties to the conflict were equally guilty was not limited to the Serb nationalist political circles of the successor states. It took on an even more fervent tone among the Serb diaspora, whose role in providing misinformation about the character of war was significant, although impossible to measure. Diaspora groups provided an external source of support for the assertions of nationalists inside the country. In small towns all over Bosnia, local citizens were connected with members of the diaspora by web sites, chat rooms, newsletters, and blogs. They shaped the meta-narratives about the war, and their allegations were dispersed through electronic media or visits by diaspora organization representatives. Diaspora groups sought support for nationalist political goals in foreign states and also tried to influence the foreign policies of their own countries.

---

[31] I am grateful to Mirsad Tokača, President, Research and Documentation Center, Sarajevo, for sharing this insight.

[32] A commission was formed to examine the number of Serbs killed in Sarajevo during the war. While some human rights activists opposed such an ad hoc institution, Serb politicians and Serb civil society organizations argued it was sorely needed. Some felt it would set the record straight. See Cécile Jouhanneau, "'Si vous avez un problème que vous ne voulez pas régler, créez une Commission.' Les commissions d'enquête locales dans la Bosnie-Herzégovine d'après-guerre" (If you have a problem you do not wish to solve, create a commission: Local Inquiry Commissions in postwar Bosnia and Herzegovina), *Mouvements* 53 (March–May 2008): 166–174.

Abroad, the Čelebići trial was woven into a story of equal suffering in gatherings of nationalist diaspora groups all over North America and Europe. Far away from the day-to-day developments in their home countries, including the facts being unearthed through prosecutions and exhumations, some promoted misinformation even more egregious than their nationalist counterparts back home.

Some diaspora groups followed the Čelebići trial with particular interest. A web site called "Serbianna.com," designed primarily by and for the Serb diaspora, began its account of the trial with a scenario mirrored in many Bosniaks' stories of being forcibly expelled from Eastern Bosnia. It reads:

In May, 1992, Bosnian Muslim and Croat forces attacked and occupied Bosnian Serb villages around the Konjic municipality in central Bosnia-Herzegovina. The Muslim and Croat forces began rounding up and expelling the Bosnian Serb residents, a policy that came to be known as ethnic cleansing. Serbian villages and towns were burned down and destroyed and Bosnian Serb civilians were massacred. The Bosnian Serb civilians who survived, men, women, and children, were herded into collection or detention centers. Many of the Serbian women and children were confined in a local school. Approximately 400 men and some women were taken to the former JNA (Jugoslovenska [n]arodna [a]rmija, Yugoslav [People's] Army) military base in the town of Čelebići, where the Muslim and Croat forces set up the Čelebići camp.[33]

This narrative omits some pertinent information, most notably why Bosnian government forces attacked. As explained below, the Territorial Defense Forces (TOs) and Croat Defense Council (HVO) attacked the village in an effort to end two road blockades on the north and south that threatened the population of the municipality with starvation. Former TO members explained that the operation took place only after successive negotiations could not end the blockade. They also stated that Serb residents in the local villages had received arms up to eight months before the war formally started in April 1992.[34]

The Serbianna article endorsed the "civil war" thesis of the war, asserting that the JNA had withdrawn from the Konjic region in May 1992 and therefore was not a party to the conflict.

The Čelebići case is meant, moreover, to maintain the characterization of Yugoslavia as the "aggressor" in the Bosnian civil war and the Bosnian Muslims as the victims of aggression by an outside country. The sequence of events during the war, however, disproves this contention. The Čelebići camp opened on May 21, 1992. The JNA had withdrawn from the Konjic region on May 5, 1992.[35]

---

[33] Carl Savich, "Čelebići," *Serbianna.com*, November 11, 2003, <www.serbianna.com/columns/savich/047.shtml> (accessed May 2, 2009).
[34] Statements of Čelebići detainees, Research and Documentation Center archive, Sarajevo. Archival research conducted by the author in February–March 2005, and follow-up research conducted in December 2008.
[35] Savich, "Čelebići."

It is true that in May 1992, the rump Yugoslavia ordered all of its military personnel to return to Serbia, but this was a withdrawal in name only: the JNA transferred its resources and personnel to the Army of Republika Srpska (VRS), a creation of the Milošević regime.[36] These forces merely changed hats: the Bosnian Serb Assembly voted on May 12, 1992, to form the VRS under the command of Ratko Mladić, and it was constituted just a week later.[37] Belgrade continued to provide resources and financing, and sent paramilitary formations throughout the war.[38]

The Serbianna article also argued that the Čelebići case was a political trial:

The ICTY needed a token show trial to demonstrate that it was not biased against the Serbs. The Čelebići case was the obvious choice. It was the most documented case. Richard Boucher of the U.S. State Department had even acknowledged that it had existed and war crimes were committed there. The camp was notorious and the information and knowledge of war crimes committed there could not be suppressed. So the Čelebići case served a useful function. The ICTY acknowledged that the Bosnian Muslim and Croat factions had committed war crimes against Bosnian Serbs, but at the same time limited the scope of criminal liability of the Bosnian Muslim political and military leadership.[39]

This was a common assertion: that it was a case chosen precisely to show that the ICTY was unbiased, yet the court was said to be predetermined not to establish criminal liability too far up the chain of command. In fact, however, the Čelebići trial was the first case dealing with command responsibility since World War II. It tackled the notion in international law that those who occupy superior positions may be deemed to be responsible for crimes of their subordinates, or for failing to prevent and punish their crimes, and thus may be held accountable. The court established superior responsibility in convicting Zdravko Mucić (although not against Zejnil Delalić).

In reality, the ICTY did not shy away from senior figures in the ARBiH; it continued to indict high-ranking officials, including those of its Croat equivalent, the HVO, until it announced its final indictments in early 2005. Even the indictments of Sefer Halilović, Chief of the Supreme Command Staff of the ARBiH, and Rasim Delić, Commander of the ARBiH, elicited few acknowledgements from Serb nationalists that the ICTY was, in fact, interested in addressing violations of international humanitarian law and not in trying a nation.

---

[36] Marko Attila Hoare, *How Bosnia Armed* (London: Saqi Books, 2004) 31.
[37] See, for example Robert J. Donia, "The Origins of Republika Srpska, 1990–1992: A Background Report," ICTY, *Prosecutor v. Momčilo Krajišnik* (IT-00-39 and IT-00-40), Exhibit P934, July 22, 2005.
[38] As late as 1999, the VRS reported over $13 million dollars in military aid from the Federal Republic of Yugoslavia; some experts claimed even this was a gross underestimate. "Serbia After Milošević: A Progress Report Briefing by ICG analyst James Lyon to the U.S. Congress Commission on Security and Cooperation in Europe," International Crisis Group (ICG), March 6, 2001, <www.crisisgroup.org/home/index.cfm?id=2178&l=1> (accessed April 15, 2009).
[39] Savich, "Čelebići."

Some observers felt that the timing of indictments against senior military leaders of the Bosnian Army, which were made at the end of the court's tenure, sent the wrong message and contributed to the dominant Serb nationalist narrative.[40] By finishing its indictments with senior (Bosniak) leaders, the ICTY "balanced out" the charges, gave the impression of equal guilt, and supported the "civil war" thesis. Marko Attila Hoare argued that those most responsible for bloodshed in the region continued to elude justice, while resources were devoted to the trial of Slobodan Milošević.

The Yugoslav political and military leaders who organized and implemented this genocide, involving at least one hundred thousand dead, have mostly not been indicted ... . The scandal is that the principle of "command responsibility" therefore applies to the Croatian and Bosnian victims of aggression, but not to the Serbo-Montenegrin aggressor. As the sole member of the top Serbo-Montenegrin political leadership to be indicted for war crimes in Bosnia and Croatia, Milošević is effectively being made the villain of crimes that were the collective responsibility of this leadership. It is as if Hitler were punished while Himmler, Goering, Goebbels, Keitel, and Jodl were let off.[41]

The ICTY itself was thus an inadvertent ally in the construction of myths promoted by both the diaspora and nationalists at home.

The prosecution team in *Prosecutor vs. Zejnil Delalić et al.* argued that the crimes committed in Čelebići were as egregious as any exposed by its work or that of its sister institution, the International Criminal Tribunal for Rwanda (ICTR) in Arusha. They implied that the Čelebići trial could be compared with the Kambanda case in Rwanda, in which the ad hoc tribunal convicted Jean Kambanda, former Prime Minister of Rwanda, of genocide and sentenced him to life in prison, a sentence upheld on appeal. ICTY prosecutors argued:

Your Honours have heard about the gravity of the offenses, and you have heard for how, over seven months, persons were imprisoned in Čelebići, many of whom, most of whom, should never have been imprisoned at all, much less for months on end, and how they were treated. I won't repeat the evidence. I can't even repeat all of it. I would just ask, when finally deciding on a sentence, that you think about and remember the hundreds of victims of the Čelebići camp, that you think about what their lives were like, how a large number of them did not survive, and how even those who did survive will be scarred, physically or emotionally or both, for the rest of their lives. As found by the Chamber in the Kambanda case in the Rwanda Tribunal, sentences should reflect the predominant standard of proportionality between the gravity of the offence and the degree of responsibility of the offender. As also noted in that decision, fair sentences contribute to the respect for the law and the maintenance of a just and peaceful society.[42]

---

[40] I am grateful to Dino Abazović, Lecturer, University of Sarajevo, for sharing this insight.
[41] Hoare, "The Capitulation of the Hague Tribunal."
[42] *Prosecutor v. Zdravko Mucić, Hazim Delić, Esad Landžo and Zejnil Delalić* (IT-96-21) Trial transcript, October 15, 1998, ICTY, <www.icty.org/x/cases/mucic/trans/en/981015IT.htm>, pp. 16275–16276 (accessed June 15, 2009).

The prosecution team argued that, given these appropriate criminal parallels, the sentences meted out should be similarly analogous: a life sentence for Esad Landžo and Hazim Delić, 20 years for Mucić, and 10 years for Zejnil Delalić. The defense team reacted strongly, saying that the comparison was deplorable. The indictment listed only 13 dead. A Sarajevo newspaper also protested, arguing that the deaths of 800, 10,000, or 800,000 in the cases of Keraterm, Srebrenica, or Rwanda should not be compared to events in Čelebići.[43]

All Bosnian citizens suffered greatly in the war. The JNA and VRS's strategy to forcibly displace non-Serbs largely succeeded, creating ethnically homogeneous areas all over the country by the end of the war. This meant that members of all ethnic groups had to move in order to meet this goal. Prewar and postwar maps of Bosnia show stark changes in the ethnic distribution of the population. Although the ICTY found that war crimes were committed by all sides, a demographic representation of loss of life in the war reveals the differences in military strategies of the hostile parties; 83 percent of civilian casualties were Bosniaks. In addition, by arming local Serb civilian populations in advance, the JNA, and later the VRS, forced the ARBiH to see local populations as potential combatants, even if they were often unwilling participants in a war that started outside their communities (a point discussed further below).

The Čelebići trial, in documenting crimes committed by the ARBiH, established an empirical basis for claims made by Bosnian Serb nationalists. One former ARBiH officer called the camp "a stain on the reputation of the army." In Sarajevo, however, many argued that the horror could not, and should not, be compared to other war crimes. This was an important topic for the nascent state to address in the early days of its existence.

Views of the War from the Capital

In Sarajevo, the war was viewed as an aggression on sovereign territory, as the Republic of Bosnia and Herzegovina had been admitted to the United Nations on May 22, 1992. Rulings of the ICTY were consistent with this assertion, but stopped short of using the term aggression. In the Tadić and Čelebići judgments, for example, the trial chamber said that the war had an international character. There were two prevailing positions on the issue of war crimes committed by Bosnian government forces. As in Republika Srpska, the Bosnian government never addressed the issue comprehensively, but individual disclosures revealed what amounted to a *de facto* policy. Among Sarajevo elites, the Čelebići trial prompted a largely internal conversation, primarily in Bosniak circles. Any lack of effort to explore the

---

[43] "Slučaj Čelebići pred međunarodnim sudom u Hagu. Tužilac traži 90 godina zatvora za optužene" (Čelebići case in front of an international court in The Hague: Prosecutor seeks 90 years in prison for the indicted), *Dnevni Avaz*, October 19, 1998.

wartime record of the ARBiH was excused because its crimes were silently measured against those perpetrated by the aggressor's army. They were less numerous and mostly less egregious than those perpetrated by Bosnian Serb and Serbian forces, the VRS (Army of Republika Srpska), the JNA (Yugoslav People's Army), the MUP (Ministry of Internal Affairs), and related paramilitaries and therefore viewed as less urgent. It was common to hear the rhetorical question: were the ARBiH's camps the same as Omarska, Trnopolje, and Keraterm in political intent and design?[44] The numbers of people who perished in ARBiH camps were far fewer than the deaths in Bosnian Serb camps. The essential difference was (so the narrative went) that many of those sent to camps run by the Bosnian Serbs never made it out, whereas the Bosnian government released or exchanged their prisoners. Many had survived intolerable cruelties and violations of international humanitarian law, but their lives were spared, unlike those in the camps of Serb forces.[45] Individuals partial to this narrative often endorsed the position that international justice should be directed at the most heinous crimes and the party who committed the greatest number of them.

The Čelebići trial did serve as a wakeup call, however, and prompted discussion in Bosnia. It created awareness that all parties to the conflict were guilty of violations of international law, even if not equivalent in extent. As the head of the Federal Commission for Missing Persons, and leading SDA politician, Amor Mašović, put it:

The trial of Delalić, Landžo, and Delić showed the other side of the truth, that members of the Bosnian Army are not immune from committing crimes. The trial clearly showed this. We until then maybe believed, and a large part of the Bosnian public believed, that members of our army did not commit war crimes and that they never would.[46]

Even Mašović, in conversation, pointed out the difference between the crimes of the ARBiH and the systematic pattern of destruction conducted by the VRS and RS police forces. The court's work, however, complicated the narrative that the Bosnian government was only an innocent victim of Serb aggression. Most international tribunals dealt only with one side of a conflict, but the ICTY was addressing all.

Lingering questions would crop up occasionally in the newspapers, such as: to what extent did Bosnia's former president, Alija Izetbegović, know about crimes

---

[44] Bosniak civilians had been detained in the camps at Omarska, Trnopolje, and Keraterm, which were the subjects of other ICTY cases.

[45] Reflecting the de facto position of the Bosniak elite, Bakir Izetbegović (son of Bosnia's former president Alija Izetbegović) told a journalist, "at the end of [the] day the Serbs from [the ARBiH camp] Silos came out alive," while "there was never a trace found" of the Bosniaks from Hadžići, near Konjic. See "Bakir Izetbegović u intervjuu *Nezavisnim Novinama*: Moj otac je za neke zločine znao" (Bakir Izetbegović in *Nezavisne Novine* interview: My father knew about some crimes), *Oslobođenje*, March 14, 2005.

[46] Interview with Amor Mašović, Director, Federal Commission for Missing Persons, Sarajevo, March 25, 2005.

committed in the government's name? Did he know that gangs sometimes terrorized Serb civilians in Sarajevo? Who was responsible for letting the foreign fighters (mujahedin) into the country? Izetbegović's son, Bakir, told a Banja Luka–based newspaper: "My father knew about some of the crimes committed by individuals in the Bosnian Army."[47] He recalled being with his father while waiting to return from peace negotiations in Geneva when the former President received news of a massacre of Bosnian Croats. Stunned by the report, Izetbegović apparently said that he would not return to the country next time if the "Bosnian Army continues mistreating people like the aggressor's army."[48] Some argued that, because Federation media, more than their RS counterparts, often raised the issue of war crimes committed by Bosnian government forces, a false impression about the war developed.[49] Until August 1999, when Željko Kopanja, editor of the Banja Luka-based *Nezavisne Novine*, first published on the subject, the issue was not addressed in the RS press.

Many elites viewed the Federation government's relationship with the ICTY as evidence that it had a starkly different stance toward the issue of war crimes than did its RS equivalent. From the signing of Dayton, Federation officials supported full cooperation with the Tribunal and never offered protection to any of those indicted. In support of the Čelebići case, Federation police forces cooperated with IFOR (NATO's postwar forces) in the arrests of two of the indicted, Delić and Landžo.[50] (The other two indictees were arrested abroad, beyond the reach of NATO or the Federation police.)

A decade after the war, RS police had not arrested a single person indicted by the ICTY. In 2005, RS authorities arrested 16 Bosnian Serbs wanted in local courts suspected of committing war crimes against Bosniaks and Croats. In addition, that year, they transferred Savo Todović, the former deputy commander of a camp in Foča, to the ICTY. The OHR reported it was the first transfer made by the RS government in nine years.[51]

A group made up largely of human rights activists from all over the country pushed for a comprehensive approach to the research and prosecution of war crimes, regardless of the ethnicity of the perpetrators. They were a minority in postwar Bosnia where only a few organizations were committed to researching and documenting war crimes as a whole, and not just crimes committed against members of their ethnicity.[52]

47   Izetbegović interview, *Oslobođenje*, March 14, 2005.
48   Ibid.
49   Interview with Edina Bećirević, Lecturer, University of Sarajevo, Sarajevo, August 17, 2005.
50   "Delić i Landžo izručeni Hagu" (Delić and Landžo handed over to The Hague), *Oslobođenje*, June 14, 1996, 1.
51   See "Key Events Since Dayton," Office of the High Representative, February 12, 2005, <www.ohr.int/ohr-info/key-events/default.asp?content_id=35971> (accessed June 15, 2009).
52   These human rights groups included the Research and Documentation Center Sarajevo, the Center for Human Rights at the University of Sarajevo, and the Helsinki Committee of the Republika Srpska and the Federation of Bosnia and Herzegovina. The Helsinki Committee split into two organizations when the leading Serb member, Branko Todorović, withdrew to form his own group.

In Konjic, for example, each of the books about crimes committed in the municipality was written by a Bosnian Croat, Serb, or Bosniak, all of them documenting injustices done to their own ethnic group. The handful of local human rights groups advocating a holistic approach to the problem struggled to make their voices heard as politics were filtered through an ethnic lens endorsed by the DPA, while at the same time they observed how the ICTY's pattern of indictments seemed to promote the "civil war" thesis.

The dominant "unofficial narrative" in Sarajevo was based in fact. The numbers of crimes were not comparable. Rather than part of a wartime strategy to achieve military goals, as was true of the VRS, war crimes committed by the ARBiH generally occurred because it "lacked the discipline of a professional army, ... [and was] prone to abuse by self-willed elements at the local level."[53] Marko Attila Hoare argued that this was in part because of the institutional structure of the ARBiH, which developed slowly and not always cohesively.

The ARBiH made much greater efforts to discipline unruly soldiers during the war than did their counterparts in the VRS.[54] In Sarajevo, when two local commanders, Ramiz Delić Čelo and Musan Topalović Caco, showed a pattern of terrorizing local (largely Serb) populations, the ARBiH organized an offensive, authorized by President Izetbegović, known as Operations Trebević 1 and 2, to rein them in.[55] As a result, 180 state officials and police officers were arrested.[56] The task of reining in noncompliant soldiers and civil servants was part of a more unwelcome development for those who wanted a multi-ethnic Bosnia, as Hoare observed in his history of Bosnia's army:

The Bosnian government was asserting control in its backyard. While this meant a restoration of the rule of law and a stronger and more stable state, it also ensured the unhindered imposition of the SDA's political ideology on the ARBiH and eventually the complete abandonment of the latter's multinational character. [57]

This meant, in practice, that the army became largely mono-ethnic, even if this new reality did not match the wishes of many of the citizens who had voted for the independence of the Republic of Bosnia and Herzegovina.

This empirical reality, however, was not comforting to the numerous Serb victims of the war who had harrowing stories of their own. The war touched every Bosnia citizen: the logic and ideology of ethnically "clean" territory meant that very few Bosnian citizens had not been displaced. In addition, the dominant narrative about the crimes of the ARBiH in Sarajevo, even if true, did little to inspire trust in a Bosnian Serb population told consistently by nationalist elites to question the

[53] Hoare, *How Bosnia Armed*, 75.
[54] Hoare, *How Bosnia Armed*, 100.
[55] Musan Topalović Caco was killed in the offensive.
[56] Hoare, *How Bosnia Armed*, 100.
[57] Hoare, *How Bosnia Armed*, 100.

motives of Sarajevo's (primarily Bosniak) politicians. It was not as if Bosnia's Serb population was unhindered by obstacles after the war either; while it was much easier for a Serb to return to Sarajevo than a Bosniak to return to say, Bratunac, local conditions did not always allow a smooth transition. In Konjic, would-be Serb returnees cited a lack of representation in the police force and municipal offices as a factor that inhibited returns. Some argued the court's judgment fueled further mistrust by providing evidence of harm done, but others said it provided at least some measure of justice for a community that felt it had been denied a chance to present its side of the story.

Wartime Narratives

Stories about the war told by Konjic's citizens revealed interpretations that differed from the judicial narrative of the court, but offered clues about why that legal story was accepted in varying ways. This section distills the author's conversations with citizens in 2005, highlighting the differences in their narratives. The court's findings influenced these narratives. Most citizens conceded that the ICTY's work was important for the municipality.

Konjic's residents, when asked about the first signs that there would be a war in their municipality, begin their narrative with the 1991 elections that put nationalist parties in power all over the country. The elections split power among the SDS (Serb Democratic Party), the HDZ (Croat Democratic Union), and the SDA (Party of Democratic Action). Shortly thereafter were the first signs of uneasiness. One municipal official reported: "And then started some excesses which were committed by members of the Serb ethnicity. I don't know, from setting fire to certain buildings, to scare attacks and thefts ... . I don't think anyone realized that was a beginning of something, of course."[58]

As in other parts of the country, Serb residents largely boycotted the referendum on independence in which 99.43 percent of voters supported an independent Bosnia. (However, 63 percent of the country's residents turned out, larger than the total number of Bosniaks, Croats, and Yugoslavs registered in Bosnia, so the Serb boycott was not absolute.) One Konjic resident remembered troubles during the referendum itself:

They [the Serbs] boycotted the referendum, following the instructions of the Serb Democratic Party. There was even one incident as far as I remember with the distance of time, I believe on the polling place in Bijela ... . A hand grenade was thrown on the polling place. Their representatives, political representatives, meaning of the Serb people – I always say "so-called" because no one has the exclusive right in [a] political sense to represent a whole nation, one national group; it's only nationalist parties with

---

[58]   Interview with J.D., Konjic, March 21, 2005. (Even though permission was given for full identification, I have chosen to use only the initials of several interviewees.)

that type of platform – they left all the political bodies of the municipality of Konjic, left all governing bodies, even my colleagues from the Territorial Defense Forces with whom I had worked for years together. At the beginning of April, all of them left their places [of] work.[59]

When asked about Serb turnout during the referendum, a Serb resident did not mention particular instructions, but emphasized the lack of potential impact: "They [the Serbs] didn't go [to vote in the referendum] simply because they were a minority; because of that they wouldn't have been able to influence the outcome in any important way."[60]

The war in Croatia was the backdrop to all of the events in the municipality. The JNA mobilized soldiers to fight against Croatia's secession, and this increased tensions everywhere in Bosnia, Konjic included. The war in Croatia began in July 1991, following its June declaration of independence. At the same time, in these months before the war in Bosnia – according to some, even the summer before the war – citizens reported that ethnic Serbs began leaving Konjic en masse.

Before, on the eve of the war, in those two, three months, it was not clear to us where they were going. They took their things from their apartments and left in the middle of the night and headed up toward Borci [a village in the Konjic municipality]. During the whole war, it was under Serb control.[61]

Serbs who had been detained in the Čelebići camp confirmed that plans to leave the city center were long in the making. Others Konjic residents mentioned efforts to form a Serb Municipality of Konjic after the Serb boycott of the referendum. The former head of Konjic's wartime Crisis Committee, Rusmir Hadžihusejnović, remembered:

I could not allow it to happen … . The Serbs are forming their own Serb municipality, you understand, they won't go [even though] a mobilization was proclaimed. The state had proclaimed a mobilization for the defense of the country that was in effect for everyone. However, the Serbs will not go, will not join the mobilization effort … . They form their own special [municipalities]. They listened to the orders given to them by Serb leaders Karadžić and others and they founded, made a decision to form, their own Serb municipality of Konjic. We, back in 1991, caught Serbs distributing weapons, distributing weapons to Serb residents when the war still had not started at the end of 1991.[62]

According to Hadžihusejnović, those weapons belonged to the JNA and were distributed in villages to civilians and combatants alike. To avoid alarming the public, he said, information about arms distribution was kept out of the papers, even

---

[59] Interview with a former member of the Territorial Defense forces, Konjic, March 22, 2005.
[60] Interview with N.S., Konjic, March 25, 2005.
[61] J.D. interview. Borci is a small village in the hills above Konjic.
[62] Interview with Rusmir Hadžihusejnović, Konjic, March 22, 2005. Hadžihusejnović is the former president of the Crisis Committee in Konjic.

though political elites realized that an armed conflict was in the making. A former member of the Territorial Defense Forces remembered that even the Serbs who lived in the city center were quietly being armed in 1991.

The narrative of a Serb resident in Konjic, however, was quite different from that of his Bosniak counterparts. For him, in the early days of the war, there was an equal effort to grab territory and influence:

Before the war, more or less, Serbs, Croats, and Bosniaks surrounded the territory where they were the majority. Understand? And then the Serbs tried, and at the same time tried to proclaim Serb territory in the part of these villages where they were a majority, so that it becomes Serbian territory. They called that the Serb Autonomous District, then Croat Autonomous District, the Bosniak Autonomous District, etc. Those were some kind of attempts to form those zones where they were a majority. And that is that.[63]

The Serb resident's narrative emphasized the "civil war" thesis. There are no records of a Bosniak or Croat autonomous district in the municipality of Konjic, but a defense witness for the ICTY, Professor Iljas Hedžibegović, testified that the Assembly of the Serb People of Bosnia and Herzegovina created a "Serb Konjic Municipality" on March 22, 1992, after the passing of the "Decision on proclamation of the Serb territories in the Konjic municipality."[64] His report stated that this decision came from the SDS in Konjic itself, as outlined in the "Instructions for the Organization and Activities of the Organs of the Serbian People in Bosnia and Herzegovina in Emergency Conditions," which was adopted in November 1991.[65]

Residents complained that, in April 1992, JNA reservists from Montenegro started causing trouble in the municipality: "They were the worst," one resident commented.[66] Then there were reports of the first mortar shells falling in the municipality, and the first bloodshed occurred then, residents said.

All residents of Konjic, in different ways, agree that the most important event of the war was the fall of Bradina, a village 25 miles southwest of Sarajevo inhabited by Serbs, on May 26, 1992. The attack by the forces of the TO (Territorial Defense Forces) and HVO (Croat Defense Council) on Bradina was precipitated by a series of blockades put up by Serb forces on the only road link with Sarajevo. One Bosniak remembered:

---

[63] Interview with N.S.
[64] Professor Iljas Hedžibegović Ph.D., Expert Report, ICTY, no date (English version). Copy on file with the author.
[65] See "Instructions for the Organization and Activities of the Organs of the Serbian People in Bosnia and Herzegovina in Emergency Conditions," Serb Democratic Party, Bosnia and Herzegovina, December 19, 1991, ICTY document number 0025-2738–0025-2747-ET/ Translation. *Prosecutor v. Momčilo Krajišnik* (IT-00-39).
[66] Interview with J.D.

We couldn't go anywhere. We couldn't go toward Tarčin, Hadžići; it was all cut off. Then it had to be done because of the strategic meaning of that road. We had to free it. They [the Serbs] were called several times for discussions, through Radio Konjic, the local radio station ... . We tried, we went up to talk with them; however, they had their own conditions, because they considered that that part of the Neretva bank completely belonged to them, to that Serb state, which they planned in their sick heads. And I know that on May 26, Bradina fell. I mean the members of the joint army, that is the TO and the HVO entered Bradina.[67]

In Bradina, residents reported, there were Serbs from all over, armed with weapons from neighboring Hadžići. One mentioned that the village was full of "Serb extremists." Another said of Bradina:

At the end of May they organized, created barricades, blocked the road. And you couldn't pass without [permission]. Those who they wished to let pass did, and those they didn't, didn't pass, but I don't know of one person who was killed while that blockade remained in place. That is the main road, as you yourself know, it is the only link with Sarajevo.[68]

Before the attack on Bradina, residents reported, there was another offensive in a small village south of Konjic, Donje Selo, where Serb soldiers had also put up a blockade. Access to the town was cut off and residents reported that the blockade even prevented some patients from getting to Sarajevo for medical treatment.

According to one former soldier in the Territorial Defense Forces (TO), the attack on Bradina was a necessary intervention from a military point of view.

We came to a situation where we had to look for a solution for a large number of our patients who went for dialysis treatment in Sarajevo. At the same time, they were forming blockades in certain other territories, that is, the Konjic-Lisičići line of communication, meaning the right bank of the Jablanica river, in the village of Donje Selo. Also Serb paramilitary formations or militants of the SDS whatever you would like to call them, blockaded that road as well. The political and military leadership of the municipality of Konjic tried to have discussions with the representatives of those armed parastate formations in Donje Selo and in Borci and in the village of Bradina to find the best solution. Solution in the sense of avoiding that conflict. Solution in the sense of unblocking communication, so that we could conduct a normal life, a life fit for a human being. However, it was obvious that they, the armed formations, were proceeding according to certain plans that were made beforehand.

Another citizen who was not a part of the armed forces related that:

In May 1992 they freed Bradina and then they arrested some [people], some ran into the hills, some were killed ... because there were bunkers set up according to military

---

[67] Interview with J.D.
[68] Interview with S.N., Konjic, March 23, 2005.

laws and norms. All of that was very professional, because the person who did it had previously worked in the municipal TO headquarters and he set them up in a true military fashion. As the JNA did before. And then it was, already easier, there we found many people, not just from Konjic and Bradina and nearby villages, but even from Tarčin, Serbs from Hadžići who came there, because those from Hadžići brought munitions, up there is a technical maintenance center in Hadžići, that was a military installation. And those Serbs who worked there brought the munitions from Hadžići here and our men went to get those munitions. But then it [the town] fell. That was some sort of beginning.[69]

The Bosniaks and Croats maintained that TO forces entered Bradina only after many failed attempts at negotiations to open up the blockade.

Representatives of the Serb residents of Konjic viewed the Bradina attack quite differently. From their perspective, the attack on Bradina was an act of gratuitous violence. When asked the reason for the attack, one representative argued that it took place "because the Serbs were there and they thought they wouldn't put up resistance. In fact the war started there. And then all those people were taken to prison."[70] The blockade did not figure into this resident's narrative. Another Serb resident mentioned the blockade, but emphasized the loss of life on the Serb side:

Bradina was charged, charged with blocking the connection between Sarajevo and Konjic, that they were stopping vehicles and simply blocking communication between armed forces. That was more or less the reason [for the attack]. On the territory of Bradina a lot of old people, women and children were gathered, because a lot of people thought that nothing was going to happen up there. However, then came the attack. Some say [it was] a fight, however if someone defending his house doesn't kill anyone, then it isn't a fight. Namely, on the Muslim-Croat side only one man was killed, one fighter. And on the Serb side, the data differs, but I think the numbers are somewhere between 50 and 60 people.[71]

Another Serb resident of Bradina, who was later in the Čelebići camp, argued: "That was the worst, I couldn't imagine that they could do that. For 20–30 years, there wasn't anything that we didn't do together. And then they came for me."[72]

The foreign press reported the Brandina attack as evidence that all sides were committing violations of international humanitarian law. For example, a *New York Times* report said:

In accounts that appeared to confirm that atrocities against civilians are being committed by all sides in the ethnic war here, Serbs from a mountainous area outside Sarajevo said today that Muslim Slav and Croatian gunmen swept through at least six

[69] Interview with J.D.
[70] Interview with N.S.
[71] Interview with L.I., Konjic, March 29, 2005.
[72] Nikola Mrkajić, interview, in the film "Justice Unseen."

villages in the region last week, executing Serbian men after they had been forced to kneel and recite the Muslim incantation "God is Great."[73]

The report added that those taken prisoner in the offensive were kept in a railway tunnel for several days without food or water. Some estimates at the time claimed that the tunnel held several thousand people.[74]

The attack on Bradina prompted the use of the Čelebići facility as a camp for prisoners of war. Serbs arrested in the village, over 700 people in total, were taken in June to the Čelebići facility, the only place large enough to house so many people. They were held until the end of the year, when many prisoners were exchanged and the remaining detainees (estimated between 110 and 170 people) were moved to the Musala detention facility, a school grounds in the center of Konjic. By that point in the war, Serb forces had control of two-thirds of Bosnian territory.

Statements taken from detainees in the Čelebići camp confirmed some of the Bosnian government's suspicions that preparations for the war had begun among Serb citizens in Bosnia well before it formally started in April 1992.[75] In Bradina, as in other villages all over the country, members of the SDS quietly armed local residents while the war raged in neighboring Croatia. One detainee mentioned a meeting in June 1991 that was held to discuss what actions the Serb population would take in the event of war. It was decided that all Serbs would move en masse to the villages of Borci and Bijela, Serb villages in the municipality.[76] Many indeed moved to those villages, and to Bradina, as the situation deteriorated in Bosnia.

After the June 1991 meeting, shipments of arms made their way to local Serb villages all over the municipality of Konjic. Detainees reported receiving arms in Bradina as early as October 1991 from SDS leaders. They also described seeing several military convoys of weapons intended for other Serb villages in the municipality, such as Donje Selo and Brđani. A typical individual was given an automatic weapon and over 100 bullets. One stated, "the arms which we were given were intended for the defense from eventual enemies."[77] Having admitting to receiving

---

[73] John F. Burns, "Serbs Say Muslim Slav and Croatian Gunmen Killed Civilians in 6 Villages," *New York Times*, June 4, 1992.

[74] Storer H. Rowley, "The Brutal Killing Fields of Bosnia," *Toronto Star*, June 24, 1992.

[75] The JNA had already destroyed the Bosnian Croat village of Ravno in October 1991; the month before, two Bosniaks had been shot in Bratunac. Hoare, *How Bosnia Armed*, 30.

[76] Republika Bosna i Hercegovina, Opština Konjic, Štab TO i HVO Opštinski Stožer. Document number 11.288/97. Statement taken June 3, 1992. These citations refer to statements of the Čelebići prison camp inmates archived at the Research and Documentation Center, Sarajevo, taken by the Bosnian Army and by the State Commission for Gathering Facts on War Crimes formed by the Presidency of the Republic of Bosnia and Herzegovina in 1992, which in 2004 became the Research and Documentation Center. See <www.idc.org.ba> (accessed June 15, 2009).

[77] Predsjedništvo Bosna i Hercegovina, Državna komisija za prikupljanje činjenica o ratnim zločinima na području R BiH, number 11.269/97 (State Commission for Gathering Facts on War Crimes on the Territory of the Republic of Bosnia and Herzegovina). Statement taken August 11, 1993.

the arms, however, he added that he "wished to live in a Republic of Bosnia and Herzegovina created without nationalism, in a country with equality for all."[78] Another noted that guns were distributed house to house; residents were told they would be necessary for "self defense" (*za samoodbranu*).[79]

Some who moved to Bradina after the war's start in April 1992 reported that local residents were already armed.[80] Hundreds of statements reveal that it was primarily two individuals who armed the village; their names came up repeatedly in statements. Once the village had been armed and those arms had been paid for, the person most responsible for distributing arms was not seen again, according to archival documents. One prisoner reported driving to pick up a yellow packet in Bileća (a town in Bosnia) labeled "SDS Konjic," intended for the party's municipal president, indicating coordination between different branches of the party.[81]

Furthermore, even those Serbs who admitted to taking guns were not necessarily the willing participants in an ethnic war fueled by ancient hatreds, as some of the foreign media portrayed them to be. One man, who confessed to receiving an M48 rifle and 90 bullets at the end of 1991, told the TO's investigatory commission:

Regarding the politics of Radovan Karadžić, I don't know what his politics are, people are being killed and that will never be to the good of all people [in Bosnia]. I'm 65 years old and would like to stay with my neighbors until my death and continue to live together and I would like to emphasize if I didn't live here then I wouldn't have a life.[82]

Despite this assertion, this pensioner reported that he was a member of the SDS from its founding. Another SDS member who was given a rifle and 105 bullets in 1991 declared: "I won't go to the prisoner exchange because I wish to live in the municipality of Konjic with my neighbors and help in the defense of the Republic of Bosnia and Herzegovina."[83] Far from expressing extreme ethnic affiliations or sentiments, some prisoners offered to join the ARBiH. Of his membership in the SDS, one said, "Why I was a member of the SDS, I myself do not know."[84] Suggesting that many average citizens did not even contemplate the larger consequences of the call of their nationalist colleagues to take up arms, he added: "I never even thought about the fall of Konjic and in case of the fall of Konjic I would stay here; I wouldn't run off anywhere because I'm a sick man and I'm not capable

---

[78] Ibid.
[79] Republika Bosna i Hercegovina, Opština Konjic, Vojna istražna komisija (Military Research Commission), Državna komisija za ratne zločine (State Commission for War Crimes), Document number 11.367/97. Statement taken January 15, 1993.
[80] Ibid., Document number 11.366/97. Statement taken January 21, 1993.
[81] Ibid., Document number 11.334/97. Statement taken January 21, 1993.
[82] Republika Bosna i Hercegovina. Opština Konjic, Štab TO i HVO Opštinski Stožer 12.08.1993, Document number 11.270/97. Statement taken August 12, 1993.
[83] Republika Bosna i Hercegovina, Opština Konjic, Vojna istražna komisija (Military Research Commission), Državna komisija za ratne zločine (State Commission for War Crimes), Document number 11.271/97. Statement taken August 22, 1993.
[84] Ibid., Document number 11.273/97. Statement taken August 12, 1993.

of anything."[85] Another Serb resident of Bradina, and former student in Sarajevo, represented himself as a victim of circumstances in the unfolding war:

At the beginning of April 1992 I stopped studying in Sarajevo because of the deteriorating situation and I returned to my birthplace, Bradina. I intended to stay until the situation in Sarajevo normalized, however, the situation got worse in Sarajevo, and in the whole republic, and I decided to stay in Bradina and get involved in the military organization of Serbs. I decided this because I didn't have another choice and I couldn't leave Bradina.[86]

The camp itself started to change the thinking of some of the Serb residents about their future in the municipality. One detainee argued: "I think this [war] is unnecessary for all people and I thought, and that's what my Muslim neighbors said to me, 'don't go, stay, we'll live together,' but now I hesitate because I see that I'm extremely threatened without any reason." Most detainees in the Čelebići camp were arrested after the fall of Bradina, just a few days after Bosnia was admitted to the United Nations. The Military Research Department of the Territorial Defense Forces, working with the State Commission for Gathering Facts on War Crimes, took individual statements over the course of their internment. It should be noted these statements were collected from prisoners by Bosnian government representatives; even so, they are revealing for their lack of strong positions.

Given the differing views about the events that led to the war, it is not surprising that the views of the trial were similarly divided. Still, the legal narrative forced many to confront their assumptions about what went on in the camp in 1992 and how the community should best confront the facts presented by the court. Far from resolving these issues, the court prompted further communication, dialogue, and disagreement.

Konjic's residents expressed varying perceptions of the intent of the Čelebići camp by how they referred to it. To a former member of the TO (and later the Bosnian Army), Čelebići was a collection center. "[It was] a collection center for prisoners of war. That means that there were only people found with military weapons, meaning, persons who in searches were found carrying a certain amount of weapons used in the military."[87] He explained that the government of the SFRY had strictly regulated "military weapons"; citizens could carry arms for protection or for hunting, but military weapons were limited to certain places and facilities.

The Serb residents of the community saw Čelebići in a different light. One citizen said it was a "classic prison," inaccessible by family members. In addition, they viewed the decision to open the Čelebići site as facilitating criminal activity on the part of those who wanted access to the property of the Serb population in the municipality.

---

[85] Ibid.
[86] Ibid., Document number 11.345/97. Statement taken June 9, 1992.
[87] Interview, former member, Territorial Defense Forces.

They opened [Čelebići] so that they would have somewhere to place the civilians, so they could rob them and their homes, so that they could mistreat them, lock them up, simply so that they could expel them from the territory of the municipality of Konjic. That was the basic reason.[88]

Many felt that this was a decision that had come from the highest offices in the municipality, "from the Crisis Committee and the war presidency in that time, as an organ of the government of the municipality of Konjic."[89] As they saw it, the trial had left those most responsible for the facility untouched, including the members of the wartime Crisis Committee and its president.

By the end of 1992, many of Čelebići's detainees had already been exchanged, and a smaller number were transferred to the Musala detention facility, a school grounds in the center of town. The Čelebići camp shortly thereafter ceased to exist. In the Musala facility, another 14 inmates were killed by a mortar shell. The party responsible for those deaths is still in dispute. One Serb resident said:

And in Musala ... now, there are estimates. There were also 14 [deaths], but that raises the question of who launched the shell on the sports center where the detainees were. They were killed by a mortar shell. You have two versions: One is that the Serbs shelled the prison, which is pretty much impossible, because there were only Serbs in the prison. It looks like the latter version, which is official, that the Bosnian Army launched the attack on the prison.[90]

After a time, the conflict between the ARBiH and VRS subsided and gave way to a war between the ARBiH and the HVO. From time to time, HVO forces would cooperate with the VRS, but the early months of 1993 saw the end of the major chapter of the war in the municipality, which led to the trial at the ICTY.

Views of the Čelebići Trial and the ICTY

Bosnians' attitudes toward the ICTY transformed over the postwar years. Immediately following the war, Serbs felt it was a strictly anti-Serb organization, while Bosniaks argued that it provided them with a small amount of long-awaited justice. Thereafter, those positions grew somewhat less polarized as Serbs (and for that matter Croats) moderated their stance, and Bosniaks grew more disillusioned. As the wheels of justice moved slowly and some of the ICTY's most wanted indictees continued to elude justice, Bosniaks more frequently expressed discontent with the institution. However, as the ICTY proved itself through the consistency of its work and its indictment of members of all ethnicities, it changed elite views and some Bosnian Serbs moderated their rhetoric about the court.

---

[88] Interview with N.S.
[89] Ibid.
[90] Ibid.

The position of those in Konjic was no exception. The municipality's Serbs generally felt the country was nominally better off with the institution than without it, but doubted whether it was truly independent. One commented in 2005:

I think the ICTY is a good thing because it probably would have been difficult to get any country of the former Yugoslavia to officially try its criminals. That is evidence they are willing to try them, would not hide them, would not help them hide, etc. So in that sense it's a positive thing … . But if, and I use the word *if,* if the [ICTY] is really neutral, well it raises the question if that is clean neutrality or it is part politics. That is now the problem.[91]

The ICTY's work had only made slight progress in changing the dominant narrative that all sides were equally guilty for crimes, and many in Konjic recognized this. One resident said:

The problem is that every side thinks that it isn't guilty to the extent attributed to it, that the other side is much more to blame. And, as an example, now when the commander of the Bosnian Army, Delić, was summoned to The Hague, all of the Bosniak people said "he's not in the least bit guilty, he's not guilty for anything, where does the court get the right to call him up?" And then when they summon someone on the Serb side then [they would say] "that's it, there should be hundreds more of them!"[92]

This "trading in victimization" flourished, especially in the absence of agreed facts about the war. Still, the ICTY's documentation did make a tremendous contribution. Case by case, the mounting archives provided a more complete picture of the war. With every witness statement and testimony, the court's work added a piece to the puzzle of the war crimes committed in the country. The ICTY's work made it impossible for reasonable individuals to deny the extent of these crimes, especially in places like Prijedor, Višegrad, and Srebrenica where thousands of persons were missing. In Konjic, in contrast, the court chipped away at the narrative in which the Bosnian government was seen as purely the victim of aggression by a neighboring state.

The ICTY was distant from the people of the region and consequently less effective than a tribunal located inside the country might have been. A former (Serb) resident of Konjic, later living in Bijeljina said:

The Hague Tribunal is something that is unknown to us, which is far away. We can't follow it, we can't participate in it. I think that those people, and I say in quotes, "deserve" to be tried here, to be tried by our people, that in the public are our own people who were affected. I think it would be a lot more effective.[93]

For one Bosniak resident still living in Konjic, the court's presence was more of an absolute good. "The Hague is necessary. Nuremberg was necessary for Europe,

---

[91] Ibid.
[92] Ibid.
[93] Dr. Petko Grubac, interview in the film "Justice Unseen."

and The Hague is necessary," he argued.[94] Not all residents felt the court's work was relevant to them, however. The ICTY's work failed to capture the interest of the municipality's youth. According to the head of one local youth group, they viewed cooperation with the court only as a necessity on the path to European integration:

For me it sometimes seems more like a farce, or a comedy, rather. I have the feeling that ... I don't know ... after so many recordings of some people ... they always stick to the same line and that it is, in effect, classic demagoguery. However, the existence of a court like that is certainly important for Bosnia and Herzegovina ... . However I also think it isn't always necessary to insist on criminals, criminals ... . [The youth] don't look at it [the ICTY] that seriously. They don't see it as something that could change their future. Maybe only in the sense that there is always talk of how we can't get into the European Union if we don't respect all of the requests.[95]

The fact that many of the people of the region were never consulted about the work of the ICTY fed skepticism of it. Local residents were not real stakeholders but, still, most citizens of all ethnicities agreed that its formation was important for the country.

Serb residents felt the court's work validated their narrative at least somewhat. This judicial validation that others had suffered in the war was important to maintain momentum in the democratization process, even if many felt that it was an imperfect court. One Serb resident commented, "Part of the Serbs [in Konjic] are satisfied that justice has been served by The Hague; however, the Croats are not happy."[96] Moreover, others emphasized that while there may have been "justice," the court was influenced by "politics" as well. As one Serb resident commented, "There is some justice in my opinion [resulting from The Hague's work], but there is more politics; in the system of who ordered the court and the prosecutors, there is politics."[97]

In general, when asked about the Čelebići trial, many observed that the focus on measuring the impact of the court so soon after the crimes took place was somewhat misplaced and that time was a crucial factor. Amor Mašović argued:

The court played its role [in the process of democratization of Bosnia]. It is very important and it will be much more important in 10, 20, 30 years. We are not in a position now to look at the Hague's contributions ... . The decisions the court will make, once the emotions on the territory of the former Yugoslavia calm down, will be more important; when someone gets those decisions in their hands, when they read about the horrible things that members of their ethnicity, or any ethnicity, did against entire groups of other ethnicities that weren't their own, I believe that many people will much more objectively

---

[94] Interview with former member of the Territorial Defense forces.
[95] Interview with the director of a non-governmental organization representing youth in Konjic, March 21, 2005.
[96] Interview with N.S.
[97] Ibid.

look at things that happened in the Balkan territories from 1992 to 1995. The point is, now we are still too emotional, too vengeful. Mostly, there are a lot of emotions.[98]

Those emotions, however, have already moderated over the course of the postwar period.

Establishing the Truth

In Konjic, there were no local actors in the municipality working strictly on the issue of war crimes. In Sarajevo and Banja Luka, there were a few organizations addressing the topic, but establishing credibility and trust across the country was a formidable task. Faced with alternatives to choose from, citizens were more likely to support institutions and initiatives close to their already held beliefs. A representative of the Serbs in Konjic illustrated this in comments in March 2005 about two institutions in Sarajevo:

The Bosniaks already in 1990 founded an Institute for War Crimes. Meaning, there wasn't an inkling [then] about the war. The Bosniaks founded an [Institute for Research of Crimes Against Humanity and International Law], and they made Dr. Čekić the head of it. And then already back then they were preparing enough documentation, without names and last names, with invented insinuations. And then after that they used anyone's name and said the perpetrator was so and so. However, the Serbs simply until 1994 had little documentation dealing with those crimes, so that it wasn't until very late that they completed the documentation given to The Hague, [when] they had already started to talk about closing the court down, etc. And that documentation, which subsequently was delivered, raised the question until when will [cases] be processed or will they be processed at all or simply returned to Bosnia-Herzegovina for proceedings. And that is the main difference. For example, I know that in Konjic there was a Commission for War Crimes formed. And they were personally questioning some women from, say, Foča, because there were enough resettled refugees from Foča that came to the municipality of Konjic. I personally know that that Commission ... listened to those women, taped them, video taped them, took pictures, this and that, and they had already arrived in the municipality of Konjic when the war was just preparing. Then they gave statements how they were raped and this and that. Clearly, fake documentation. The Bosniaks' advantage in demonstrating everything, I tell you, started two years before the war with that Institute and then they created documentation, and they completed video tapes and photos and now its very difficult to prove whether [it's real] or not.[99]

The narrator thus argues that the Bosniaks knew about the war in advance and had prepared fake documentation in anticipation of future events, but

[98] Interview with Amor Mašović.
[99] Interview with N.S. Čekić was not, in fact, the first director, as this conversation implied, nor was the organization founded in 1990 but rather in fall 1992.

his statement conflates two separate institutions. The Institute for Research of Crimes Against Humanity and International Law, which is part of the University of Sarajevo and is headed by Professor Smail Čekić, was founded in the fall of 1992. The State Commission for Gathering Facts on War Crimes was founded by the Presidency of the Republic of Bosnia and Herzegovina in April 1992, and was later transformed into a non-governmental organization called the Research and Documentation Center. In other words, neither organization predated the start of the war, as the speaker asserted in support of his argument that Bosniak claims were faked.

Moreover, when the subject turns to the number of deaths in the war, the same speaker invokes a recent initiative by one of these same organizations in support of his interpretations:

And now you have an interesting thing. It is always mentioned in the various means of informing [the public], in a lot of media and written material, that you had 200,000 victims during the war. However, now you have one institute on the level of Bosnia-Herzegovina, which started an initiative [the "Human Losses 1991–1995" project of the Research and Documentation Center] to really confirm the number of missing, killed, etc. And the director of that institute now says that the number is closer to 100,000 instead of 200,000. However, the Bosniaks drummed up the theme that it is 200,000, 200,000, and constantly defend it, and that is supposed to raise a fuss. It's the same in Srebrenica. It raises the question.[100]

The "Human Losses 1991–1995" project to which the speaker refers (which is discussed in Chapter 3), was about half way through completion at the time of this interview in March 2005. Based on the data collected to that time, the project estimated that the deaths in Bosnia likely did not exceed 100,000. The director of this initiative, Mirsad Tokača, had been the director of the State Commission for Gathering Facts on War Crimes during the war. Thus, this speaker gave credence only to the report that matched his preconceptions, while remaining suspicious of the same institution when its report seemed contrary to his views.

Postwar Developments

Konjic was the first "Open City" in postwar Bosnia. The United Nations High Commissioner for Refugees (UNHCR) encouraged Bosnian cities to proclaim themselves as "open," that is, where "local authorities officially [commit the city] … to return in general, minority return specifically, reconciliation between different ethnic groups, reintegration of refugees and displaced persons, and respect for human rights."[101]

---

[100] Interview with N.S.
[101] Refugee and Displaced Persons Return Information Contacts, November 23, 1997, Bosnian NGO Development Unit, UNDP, <www.ddh.nl/fy/refuorgs.html> (accessed August 30, 2005).

Returns to Konjic, however, were slow in coming. Some residents who were interviewed believed that the municipality had the fewest minority returns in the Federation. By April 30, 2005, only 1,216 Serbs, out of a prewar population of 6,647, had returned, as had just 2,583 Croats, out of a prewar population of 11,530.[102] Counting returnees was a difficult task. In many municipalities, the registered number of returns did not match "real" returns. Some people claimed their prewar municipality as home but continued to live elsewhere, where housing or jobs were more plentiful. Local Serb representatives in the municipality, for example, reported that only 583 Serbs had returned, a figure that differed from UNHCR data.

The reasons for scant returns were multifold: many had left the country as refugees and they remained in the countries where they had relocated to, eventually being granted legal residency. Others sought out larger cities that offered more employment opportunities. Municipal officials in Konjic also cited organizations in RS – such as Udruženje za opstanak, or "Organization to Remain" – that offered financial incentives for ethnic Serbs to remain in Republika Srpska. Many people detained in the Čelebići camp moved to Višegrad, a town in Eastern RS, and would be eligible for such incentives. Those who did return were often elderly persons hoping to spend their retirement years in the municipality of their birth. Serb residents also identified a lack of influence in the municipality as hindering returns. By 2005, they said, there were only four Serbs employed by the municipality, none of them in positions of authority; in addition, there were only two Serb police officers and one Serb judge.

The reconstruction of churches was also important to the Serb community. The local NGO representing Serb residents lobbied to repair houses of worship in the hopes that this would encourage returns. Before the war there had been four Orthodox churches in the municipality – in Bradina, Čelebići, Konjic, and Borci; all suffered damage during the war. Residents repaired the Konjic church, but the two buildings (parohijske kuće) attached to the church that would normally house a visiting priest had been torched during the war; requests by the organization "Active Serb Residents" to have them rebuilt had been unsuccessful. In a letter to the Ministry of Displaced Persons and Refugees, they noted:

The repair of this house would secure a place for the visit of a priest and the fulfillment of religious needs of those of the Orthodox faith and surely would have a big effect on the return of citizens and on the morale of those who now live here, as I can often hear commentary that "if no one will repair the house and enable the priest's visit then they don't want us to be here."

Interest in the church signaled an interest in the life of its Serb residents. While the organization's board was disappointed by the lack of resources in Konjic to rebuild

---

[102] Discussion with UNHCR Representative, Sarajevo, June 15, 2005. According to the 1991 Census in Bosnia and Herzegovina there had been 24,164 Bosniaks, 11,530 Croats, 6,647 Serbs, and 1,932 others. The numbers of returns peaked in 2002 (781 Croats and 632 Serbs) after property legislation was passed.

the priest's quarters, it was grateful to a local radio station for airing a religious program for the Orthodox community on a regular basis.

Croat returns were more numerous, but still low. Croat residents in the town reported that the nationalist parties discouraged returns as a matter of policy. Most displaced Croats remained in Herzegovina, the site of the wartime parastate of Herceg-Bosna. A school for Croat children opened in Konjic in 1997, hoping to foster returns with the promise of an education tailored toward its Catholic residents, but it closed at the end of the 2005 school year and its students were absorbed into another school.[103]

Demographic changes, which started before the war and continued even after it ended, were an obstacle to rebuilding relations among different communities. Bosnia's citizens no longer interacted as much with individuals of different ethnicities; many lived in ethnic ghettos. There was little chance for an average citizen to put aside his or her ethnicity, because politics were ethnicized to a degree unprecedented in the SFRY. For many, these changes in the country represented the victory of Milošević's plan for ethnically pure territories. The former president of the wartime Crisis Committee in Konjic reasoned:

In essence, I personally think that the destruction and dissolution of Bosnia-Herzegovina simply did not succeed, which is the most important. But there is another thing that is important, regardless of the fact that BiH remained one state. That which happened, that is surely a consequence, a very important consequence, is that the ethnic cleansing was accomplished, you understand. That means that the results of Milošević's project live *de facto* because the population has moved. There will never be the ethnic composition of the population as it was before the war. In part, people will return, that is true, but it [ethnic composition] will never be the same, and, regardless, the country survived, but in some sense, we can say in quotes that Milošević "succeeded," succeeded in the sense of the result of ethnic cleansing.[104]

In Konjic, 26 villages had primarily Serb populations before the war; after the war, at the time of these interviews in 2005, Serbs lived in only nine of those villages. Many Serb residents in Konjic blamed the former mayor for the existence of the Čelebići camp. They contended that returns would have been much greater had the Čelebići camp never existed.

The postwar years presented concrete obstacles to minority returns as well. Local residents recalled one incident in particular. On Christmas Eve 2002, three members of the Andrei family, Croat returnees, were murdered in the village of Kostajnica in the municipality. A local Bosniak resident named Muamer Topalović later confessed to the murders but refused to admit that they were motivated by religious hatred. He did, however, acknowledge that he was frustrated with the attacks on Bosniaks in Bosnia, the situation in Afghanistan, and the crisis in

[103] Interview with Fra. Ante Ledić, Konjic, April 1, 2005.
[104] Interview with Rusmir Hadžihusejnović.

Iraq.[105] Even though this was an isolated incident, it fueled rumors that the municipality was filled with Muslim extremists.

ICTY Outreach Seminar

On November 20, 2004, the ICTY held a conference in Konjic, entitled "Bridging the Gap between the ICTY and Communities in Bosnia and Herzegovina – ICTY cases in relation to war crimes committed in Konjic." There were over 100 invited guests, ranging from former inmates in the Čelebići camp to local municipal officials, members of the press and civil society organizations, and international observers. The municipality's cultural center was packed with Bosnian citizens invited to hear the details of the trial and about ICTY procedures in general.

In Konjic, as in many other postconflict municipalities, there was some disagreement about whether the local residents had been aware of the prison camp and of the wartime atrocities committed in Čelebići. The question of "do you know what happened during the war?" is one that looms large after every conflict. It is a question that hints at the moral obligation ordinary citizens have to prevent commission of heinous crimes in their name. The issue divided the city's residents and local human rights activists. One seminar participant declared, "I can confidently say for Konjic that [the citizens of the town] did not know what was happening in Čelebići."[106] Others disagreed:

Many were aware of what was happening in Čelebići at the time and many were opposed to it. But those were moments when you couldn't do anything to change the situation here. Those were circumstances when people fell into the hands of criminals, I don't know what else to say ... criminals. Criminals from the line of the Bosniak people. Those were just criminals and nothing else. For me it's good that they've been tried and that for our government it wasn't a dilemma whether to extradite or to protect them.[107]

In Sarajevo, the head of the Federal Commission for Missing Persons said that the trial was the first time he had heard of the crimes at Čelebići. The trial and the outreach seminar forced citizens to discuss their role in the war, their knowledge of the events that transpired in the town, and whether or not they were obligated to do something with that knowledge.

That is not to say that all positions expressed were most desired, only that the discussion itself was a positive development. The ICTY had facilitated a discussion about the crimes committed in the municipality and participation by civil society

[105] Tina Jelin, "Počelo Sudjenje Topaloviću" (Trial of Topalović started), *Radio Slobodna Europa*, March 10, 2003, <www.danas.org/programi/aktuelno/2003/03/20030310173544.asp> (accessed September 5, 2005).
[106] Interview with J.D.
[107] Interview with S.N.

in a conversation about the country's wartime past. Some seminar participants, however, felt that the Čelebići camp inmates should not have been given the right to speak about the conditions in which they were kept, because their stories did not include the suffering of other residents of the municipality. One commented:

For me the seminar was acceptable (*prihvatljiv*). I am happy that it was held ... . I don't think they needed to bring in the witnesses, however. They brought in witnesses from Bratunac, Višegrad, surviving camp internees ... . It was too much, needless (*suvišno*). Because we were all internees in Konjic. We were all in one camp; Konjic was a big camp, completely, you know? They were on the CD, in the photos, their statements were seen and heard. They didn't need to interview them here again. The journalists interviewed them and they spoke about how they spent their days in the camp. On the other hand we don't know how the citizens of Konjic lived. That has not been shown anywhere, you know. It must be known that we were surrounded.[108]

For this resident, the trial did not capture the most important dynamic of the war. The outreach event, by extension, created a somewhat false impression. But questions about who gets to participate in these discussions, and when, where, and why violence harmed their community, had been started on one cold day in an unheated cultural center. The dialogue was itself constructive because, despite the grumblings of some, everyone was given the chance to speak.

Spillover Effects

Many argued that the Čelebići case was the likely impetus for another war crimes trial for the murder of the Golubović family in July 1992, events which also took place in Konjic. Mr. Đura Golubović, a Serb, lived in the municipality and worked as a professor. He was remembered by residents as a frail and quiet man. He, his wife, Vlasta, and their two children, Petar and Pavle, were taken from their house and murdered. The perpetrators stole the family's car and later robbed their house. The trial, which started in October 1998, was the first war crimes case for the newly established Herzegovina-Neretva Cantonal Court, and represented an important test for it.[109] Three Bosniak policemen from Konjic, Miralem Macić, Adem Landža, and Jusuf Potura, were charged with the murders in January 1999. Authorities had detained two of the policemen after an investigation in 1994, but later released them.[110] The bodies of the Golubović family were exhumed from a mass grave in May 2000. In July 2000, the Mostar Cantonal court found the three men guilty of

108 Interview with J.D.
109 Human Rights Monthly Report, October 1999, Human Rights Coordination Center, Justice Watch Listserv, <listserv.acsu.buffalo.edu/cgi-bin/wa?A2=ind9911& L=justwatch-l&P=R79874&I=-3> (accessed September 1, 2005).
110 Daria Sito-Sucic, "Serb Victims Exhumed in Bosnian War Crimes Trial," *Reuters*, May 6, 2000.

the murders and sentenced them to a total of 33 years in prison.[111] The lawyer for the family, Duško Tomić, told the courtroom that non-Bosniaks in the municipality had "understood the murders as a message that all of them must leave Konjic if they wanted to stay alive."[112] Trials did continue in the municipality, but the Golubović trial was not immediately followed by other indictments, as many had hoped. That would have to wait until 2009, when Bosnia's State Court announced an indictment against Safet Bukvić, for allegedly shooting a Croat civilian in a school in Čelebići in 1993, the first case at the court to deal with crimes committed there.[113]

Conclusion

Narratives provide information about how citizens view the world. This chapter has shown the differing views of the war with which the court's legal narrative had to contend. The court's findings in Konjic, while sometimes feeding into existing attitudes and, indeed, prejudices of citizens, also prompted new discussions and forced individuals to revise their knowledge, opinions, and assumptions about the town's recent past. It also challenged the (largely) Bosniak elite's de facto position about the war. As the court's findings reverberated through a highly charged political and emotional environment, they slowly reshaped that environment in a manner that was, on the whole, positive for the transition process.

---

[111] "Muslim Police Sentenced in Bosnia-Herzegovina," *FreeB92 News*, July 26, 2000, B92.net, Justice Watch Listserv, <listserv.acsu.buffalo.edu/cgi-bin/wa?A2=ind0007& L=justwatch-l&P=R102777&I=-3> (accessed September 1, 2005).

[112] Ibid.

[113] See "Indictment confirmed in the Safet Bukvić case," Court of Bosnia and Herzegovina, May 15, 2009, <www.sudbih.gov.ba/?id=1253&jezik=e> (accessed May 17, 2009); and "Indictment for Čelebići Crimes Confirmed," Balkan Investigative Reporting Network (BIRN), *Justice Report*, May 15, 2009, <www.bim.ba/en/166/10/18936/> (accessed May 17, 2009).

7 From the Battlefield to the Barracks

The ICTY and the Armed Forces

"When you are cold, tired, and wet, you must make split-second choices on the battlefield. Later, the judges will make decisions about your actions from the comfort of their warm offices." These were the comments of an Organization for Security and Cooperation in Europe (OSCE) advisor on military reform to a group of battalion commanders of the Armed Forces of Bosnia and Herzegovina (AFBiH) at a seminar on international humanitarian law.[1] For more than 15 years, officials at the International Criminal Tribunal for the former Yugoslavia (ICTY) assessed the actions of the region's political and military leaders. Have the decisions of warm, dry judges in The Hague affected the attitudes of the armed forces in Bosnia and Herzegovina? What are soldiers' views toward the court's extended mandate, which includes the aspirations to contribute to peace and stability in the region and to influence various aspects of the development of the postwar state that are important for democratization?

This chapter explores these questions based on a qualitative survey of the AFBiH taken between September and December 2005. It probed for levels of knowledge about the ICTY and international humanitarian law; changes in knowledge of wartime events as a result of the court's work; and attitudes toward the court's extended mandate and contribution to such goals as the rule of law, justice, and reconciliation. This survey represents a "hard case" for the court, as the respondents represented a population whose wartime colleagues were often targeted by ICTY prosecutions, and who could therefore be expected to be critical of its work. However, anonymous survey data reveals that the court has positively influenced the attitudes of most soldiers of all ethnicities. These attitudes signal that the court has played a positive role in Bosnia's ongoing transition to democracy and has even contributed to its nascent democratic political culture, a culture that recognizes

[1] Major General (retd.) K. J. Drewienkiewicz, presentation, Seminar on International Humanitarian Law and Conflict Control, OSCE Mission to BiH, the Office of the Personal Representative of the OSCE Chairman in Office for Articles II and IV and the German Foundation for International Legal Cooperation, Munich, October 23, 2004, author's notes. Drewienkiewicz was a senior advisor for the OSCE Mission to Bosnia and Herzegovina.

that those who committed violations of international humanitarian law should be held accountable for wartime transgressions.[2]

The ICTY, through its decisions, sought to have impact in the countries of the former Yugoslavia. Its architects hoped that the enforcement of universal norms of international law would contribute to the establishment of peace and security in Bosnia, as well as in all the other countries affected by its mandate.[3] More specifically, the ICTY has described its legal and extra-legal achievements as "holding leaders accountable, bringing justice to victims, giving victims a voice, establishing the facts, developing international law and strengthening the rule of law."[4] The court's architects also hoped that trials would be a catalyst for future transitional justice initiatives in the region. In short, the court aspired to be a tool of peace and democracy building. Respondents indicated that it has at least partially realized this extended mandate.

Scholarship on Armed Forces

The military is a segment of society often overlooked in scholarly analyses of transitional justice. States, however, are often born from political violence and repression, a process that usually involves established militaries, or groups that evolve into militaries. Bosnia, as shaped by the Dayton Peace Agreement (DPA), was no different in this regard. The agreement formally acknowledged territorial gains made by the Army of Republika Srpska (VRS) by dividing the country into two autonomous entities: the Federation of Bosnia and Herzegovina and Republika Srpska (RS). The RS comprises 49 percent of Bosnia's territory, and its creation was a result of systematic violations of international humanitarian law, namely the forcible expulsion of the Bosniak and Croat populations and a military strategy that included genocide.[5] Throughout the war, the VRS often held more than 60 percent of the territory of a sovereign Republic of Bosnia and Herzegovina, admitted to the United Nations in May 1992. Politics were ultimately shaped by the military reality on the ground. A change in the balance of power at the end of the war did not change the structure of the country: when the Bosnian Army (ARBiH) (with assistance from Croatia) was close to a victory on military grounds, international forces

---

[2] International humanitarian law is defined as the law of conflict or the law of war and includes the Geneva and Hague Conventions. See the International Committee of the Red Cross fact sheet, <www.icrc.org/web/eng/siteeng0.nsf/html/humanitarian-law-factsheet> (accessed June 15, 2009).

[3] A norm is a "shared (social) understanding of standards for behavior." See Audie Klotz, *Norms in International Relations: The Struggle Against Apartheid* (Ithaca, NY: Cornell University Press, 1999), 14.

[4] See, for example, Achievements, ICTY, <www.icty.org/sid/324> (accessed May 28, 2009).

[5] On war crimes as a military strategy, see James Gow, *The Serbian Project and Its Adversaries: A Strategy of War Crimes* (London: Hurst and Company, 2003).

threatened the Bosnian government with military action if they upset the entity structure that had already been quietly negotiated.[6] The Federation of Bosnia and Herzegovina, the second of Bosnia's two entities, was created with the signing of the Washington Agreement in March 1994, which ended the war between the Bosnian Army and Croat Defense Council (HVO).

The international community thus rewarded the wartime behavior of the VRS and Serb nationalist politicians with such a political configuration, but it also agreed that crimes committed during this process of statecraft exceeded acceptable international norms and constituted an assault to human dignity everywhere. This prompted the creation of the ICTY under the auspices of Chapter VII of the UN Charter. In light of such inconsistent indications about appropriate behavior, it is important to determine whether former parties to the conflict were influenced by enforcement of those norms at the ICTY.

An understanding of the attitudes of the AFBiH toward the ICTY is a crucial case study for several other reasons as well. Civil-military relations are an important element in postwar processes of democratization. The reconstruction of armed forces is one of the most complicated undertakings of an international intervention.[7] The development of the AFBiH from what were in essence three armies at the war's end is a good indicator of progress in the country at large. If norms enforced by the ICTY have a positive effect on the attitudes of the members of a recomposed military, this should have positive effects on civil-military relations. In addition, because many of the ICTY's indictees had been military personnel, these soldiers often had first-hand knowledge of the events addressed in the court and thus were important informants about its work.

Scholars of transitional justice have solicited the opinions of many segments of postwar populations after previous conflicts. Civil society leaders, political elites, academics, journalists, and victims have all been considered valuable informants about both the nature of a conflict and postwar developments, but the military is often overlooked.[8] Many analysts possess a general bias against members of armed forces, as they are assumed to be merely thugs or perpetrators of violence.[9] In fact, armed forces are an influential part of the state, separate from the bureaucrats that staff central administrations. Militaries often include individuals possessing high levels of education who play important roles in young states.

The number of studies based on field research conducted with members of armed forces in transitional states is growing, however. This chapter is inspired by

---

[6]   Marko Attila Hoare, *How Bosnia Armed* (London: Saqi Books, 2004), 121–127.

[7]   Some scholars are examining the recomposition of armed forces in divided societies; see Roy Licklider, "Merging Militaries after Civil War: South Africa, Bosnia and a Preliminary Search for Theory," paper presented at the Annual Meeting of the American Political Science Association, Boston, August 28–31, 2008.

[8]   Jennifer Schirmer, "Whose Testimony? Whose Truth? Where Are the Armed Actors in the Stoll-Menchú Controversy?" *Human Rights Quarterly* 25, no. 1 (2003), 60–73.

[9]   Ibid.

one such study: Jennifer Schirmer's *The Guatemalan Military Project: A Violence Called Democracy*.[10] Schirmer, an anthropologist, conducted interviews with 50 military officers who played a role in the recomposition of the state in Guatemala.[11] While the dynamics of transition in Guatemala were different from those in Bosnia, her study provided a starting point for analysis. Schirmer's research in Guatemala demonstrates the importance of such inquiry by illustrating how a military in peacetime can adapt to civilian rule without fundamentally changing. In addition, other more recent studies in Burundi, Sierra Leone, and elsewhere have probed for attitudes about justice and postconflict reintegration.[12]

This research area is critical because, as political scientists Juan Linz and Alfred Stepan argue, a functioning state bureaucracy is necessary for the consolidation of democracy.[13] As the part of a bureaucracy that commands the state's monopoly on use of force, militaries play a vital role in the construction of a state. If democracy is to be the "only game in town" – to borrow Linz and Stepan's term – then soldiers, like other citizens, must be confident that political conflict will be solved within the confines of democratic institutions.[14] But the beliefs of those in the military are shaped, like their civilian counterparts, by past human rights violations and responses to them, and their views of acceptable uses of state violence influence their opinions about the nature of the developing polity and whether "exit" from the democratic arena is an option.[15]

Building a State-level System of Defense

After the war, the defense of the territory of Bosnia and Herzegovina was not initially the responsibility of the state, but fell to the country's two constituent entities.

---

[10] Jennifer Schirmer, *The Guatemalan Military Project: A Violence Called Democracy* (Philadelphia, PA: University of Pennsylvania Press, 2004).

[11] There is increasing research conducted on whether participation in foreign peacekeeping missions affects civil-military relations. See, for example, Arturo Sotomayor, "The Peace Soldier from the South: From Praetorianism to Peacekeeping?" (Ph.D. diss., Columbia University, 2004).

[12] Former combatants are a focus of several recent research efforts. See, for example, Macartan Humphreys and Jeremy Weinstein, "Disentangling the Determinants of Successful Demobilization and Reintegration," paper presented at the Annual Meeting of the American Political Science Association, Washington, D.C., September 2005), <www.columbia.edu/~mh2245/papers1/DDR.pdf> (accessed May 29, 2009). See also Cyrus Samii, Eric Mvukiyehe, and Gwendolyn Taylor, "Wartime and Postconflict Experiences in Burundi: A Micro-level Study of Combatant and Civilian Conflict Experiences," project homepage, <www.columbia.edu/~cds81/burundisurvey/> (accessed May 29, 2009).

[13] Juan J. Linz and Alfred Stepan, *Problems of Democratic Transition and Consolidation: Southern Europe, South America and Post-Communist Europe* (Baltimore, MD: Johns Hopkins University Press, 1996), 5–6.

[14] Ibid.

[15] On exit as an option, see Albert O. Hirschman, *Exit, Voice and Loyalty: Responses to Decline in Firms, Organizations and States* (Cambridge, MA: Harvard University Press, 1970).

The Dayton Peace Agreement established two armed forces in the country (de facto there were three), each governed by entity-level defense ministries.[16] Even the peace agreement's architect, Richard C. Holbrooke, would later lament that the existence of more than one army in Bosnia was Dayton's biggest flaw.[17] A Joint Military Commission (JMC), staffed with representatives of the international community and entity-level ministries, was created to monitor allegations of ceasefire violations, but it was not a consensual body. The JMC allowed the international community's military forces to police violations of the Dayton Agreement. The JMC would summon the Entity Armed Forces (EAF) when violations were reported.

Military reform was slow in the immediate postwar years but picked up momentum when the Office of the High Representative formed the first Defence Reform Commission in 2003, which oversaw reforms and helped integrate the disparate armed forces into one institution. The Defence Reform Commission was inspired by Bosnia's desire to join NATO's Partnership for Peace (PfP), but its formation was triggered by the High Representative's exasperation with the behavior of the RS Army, including non-cooperation with ICTY.[18] The backdrop for reforms was a scandal involving the sale of arms to Iraq by firms based in RS.[19] The forerunner to the Commission was the Standing Committee on Military Matters (SCMM), a consensual body set up in the Dayton Agreement to serve as a coordinating mechanism for Bosnia's armed forces. In 2003, the country's Law on Defense was passed, the first significant piece of legislation on military reform in the postwar period.

The first Defence Reform Commission led only to the creation of a state-level defense ministry, which was superimposed on top of the existing entity-level ministries. In other words, a third defense ministry was created in a country that already had two. This structure stalled long-term plans in the military. Eventually, one of the international community's biggest tasks was to unite the two separate military forces under one ministry and chain of command. In mid-2004, military personnel were disappointed when Bosnia was not extended an invitation to join the PfP because it lacked parliamentary control and a functioning state-level Ministry of Defense. International pressure prompted another commission to be set up at the end of December 2004. The second Defence Reform Commission facilitated the handing over of all functions of the entity-level defense ministries to the state level. Entity-level defense ministries closed their doors at the end of 2005.

---

[16]   De facto there were three armed forces because the Croat and Bosniak parts of the Federation Army were highly autonomous in the immediate postwar years.

[17]   "Bosnia peacemaker sees Dayton flaws," *BBC News*, November 18, 2000, <news.bbc.co.uk/2/hi/europe/1029867.stm> (accessed May 28, 2009).

[18]   For background on the process see: Defence Reform Commission, *AFBIH: A Single Military Force for the 21st Century* (Sarajevo: DRC, September 2005), 11–13, <www.afsouth.nato.int/nhqsa/.../Report2005-eng.pdf> (accessed June 30, 2009).

[19]   See Nick Hawton, "Bosnian Firm Aiding Iraq, U.S. Suggests," *BBC News*, September 10, 2002, <news.bbc.co.uk/2/low/europe/2250117.stm> (accessed July 15, 2009); Alix Kroeger, "Bosnia Mired in Arms Scandal," *BBC News*, October 31, 2002, <news.bbc.co.uk/2/low/europe/2381095.stm> (accessed July 15, 2009).

In addition, this second Commission emphasized the arrest of war criminals and their transfer to the ICTY, a subject that had been neglected entirely by the first.[20] As a result of the second Commission's work, a single command structure was imposed, a single budget established, and conscription abolished.[21] These were significant accomplishments considering that the constitutions in the Federation and RS gave responsibility for organizing the armed forces at the end of the war to each respective entity.

The work of the second Commission proceeded slowly and incrementally. In April 2005, however, progress in defense reform faced what some felt was a setback. Professionals involved in the process called it "a gasp of the old regime."[22] At a public (and televised) swearing-in ceremony for new military recruits in the RS towns of Bileća and Manjača, the young men attending refused to swear allegiance to defend Bosnia and Herzegovina. In Manjača, all 550 swore allegiance to RS. In Bileća, they initially swore allegiance only to RS, but repeated the oath a second time, then swearing allegiance to Bosnia and Herzegovina.[23] This was the first time RS recruits were asked to swear allegiance to the country, not the entity, and these events were watched closely.

Western and domestic press reported the event as evidence of the continued fractured nature of the country. Although it signaled the fragility of reforms that had been undertaken to date, and even of the state itself, those knowledgeable about such military events noted that the mishap was the result of political miscalculation by RS politicians who had committed to the new oath. They had failed to anticipate how these new political commitments would translate into a large ceremony – traditionally a public display of nationalism in Yugoslav times – involving priests and, more significantly, veterans. In the socialist era, inclusion of disparate groups had often indicated obligatory participation and public displays of patriotism.[24] The presence of these disparate groups in the postwar ceremony meant that there was pressure from members of the public audience to forego the new, and still not universally accepted, commitments.

The event combined two formal procedures normally kept separate in, for example, the U.S. and U.K. military traditions: the oath and the graduation ceremonies that mark the completion of initial training duties.[25] In most Western European

---

[20] See Office of the High Representative, *Decision Extending the Mandate of the Defence Reform Commission: Article 2*, December 31, 2004, <www.ohr.int/decisions/statemattersdec/default. asp?content_id=33873> (accessed May 29, 2009).

[21] Defence Reform Commission, *AFBIH: A Single Military Force*.

[22] Interview with Raffi Gregorian, Deputy High Representative, Office of the High Representative, Sarajevo, August 11, 2008. Gregorian was NATO Co-chair of the Defence Reform Commission (DRC) of Bosnia and Herzegovina from January 2005 to December 2005.

[23] Antonio Prlenda, "RS Army Chief of Staff Sacked Over Oath-Taking Incidents," *Southeast European Times*, June 6, 2005, available online at: <www.balkan-info.com/cocoon/setimes/xhtml/en_GB/features/setimes/features/2005/06/06/feature-02> (accessed July 15, 2009).

[24] Interview with Major General (retd.) K.J. Drewienkiewicz, December 9, 2004.

[25] Major General (retd.) K.J. Drewienkiewicz, e-mail to the author, March 6, 2006.

armies, oaths are taken in the presence of a limited number of people.[26] While these two events are often combined in military ceremonies in the region, the presence of war-era fighters and nationalists who supported the cause of separate armed forces made it tempting for the master of ceremonies to forego new political commitments to the entire territory of BiH. The international community had to show resolve on the matter, and the RS Army Chief of Staff was eventually fired over the affair.[27] Internally, there was a lot of debate about this decision, with some arguing that he should be required to find a solution to the problem instead of being let go.

By the end of that same year, however, institutional reforms had advanced so far that the events of April were already in the distant past: On January 1, 2006, the entity-level ministries of defense ceased to exist and a joint command structure took over the armed forces, covering all of the territory of Bosnia. The modernization of the AFBiH also included preparing for Operations Other than War (OOTW), a reference to deployment in postconflict peacekeeping missions. Bosnian soldiers have participated in peacekeeping operations in Eritrea and, more recently, have been sent by the government to Iraq to aid in the de-mining effort.[28] In order to train the officer corps, the international community set up the Peace Support Operations Training Center, a project supported by 12 countries. The Center offers courses for young officers (lieutenants, captains, and majors) from both entities, in addition to officers from partner and neighboring countries. Located on the EUFOR base in the Sarajevo suburbs, the Center will eventually become the Staff College of the AFBiH. For the next several years, international military officers will maintain stewardship of the center as the new command structure of the Bosnian Army completes its transition. Since 2005, the Center has held officer training courses that run for 14 weeks. Officers who were on opposite lines just over 10 years ago now freely discuss issues of war and peace and the proper ways to conduct postconflict peace operations.[29] The course covers such topics as urban conflict, NATO military doctrine, and international humanitarian law (IHL).[30] Experts in the field report that the course on IHL is remarkable by any standards, even compared to similar efforts in more developed European countries.[31] However, the findings of the ICTY regarding relevant issues such as command responsibility have not yet been integrated into the program.

---

[26] Interview with Major General (retd.) K.J. Drewienkiewicz, December 9, 2004.

[27] Prlenda, "RS Army Chief of Staff Sacked."

[28] Bosnian participation in the Iraqi mission was rumored to be a quid pro quo for continued U.S. engagement in Bosnia, although Bosnian authorities would not admit this when pressed. On Bosnian participation in peacekeeping missions, see Aida Cerkez-Robinson, "Postwar Bosnia's Surprising Export: Peacekeepers," *Associated Press*, November 12, 2008.

[29] Interview with Brigadier General H. Brøchmann Larsen, Sarajevo, November 25, 2005. Larsen was head of the Peace Support Operations Training Center BiH.

[30] See the web site for the Peace Support Operations Training Center Bosnia and Herzegovina, <www.psotc.org/> (accessed June 30, 2009).

[31] Interview with Major General Drewienkiewicz.

The Bosnian Armed Forces Today

Social scientists have not much studied the postwar state of the armed forces in this region. At the end of the war, there were 264,500 soldiers in the Federation Army and 154,500 in that of RS.[32] Recent research shows that more deaths in the war were suffered by the military than by the civilian population.[33] "The Human Losses 1991–1995" project, carried out by the Research and Documentation Center in Sarajevo, records 30,966 Bosniak, 5,625 Croat, 20,830 Serb, and 102 "other" soldiers killed (or missing) during the war, totaling 57,523 – 59 percent of the total lives lost.[34] Civilian deaths, the remaining 41 percent of losses, numbered 39,685.[35] This preponderance of military deaths suggests that members of the armed forces deserve considerations usually offered to civilian victims of war by researchers' scholarly attention, both as important actors in the postwar transition and as the population that suffered the conflict's largest losses. The drastic transformation of the armed forces in the country is striking: three armed forces of 400,000 were systematically reduced to one army of 10,000. The first and biggest step occurred within three months of the end of the war, when everyone who wanted to return to civilian life did so, leaving fewer than 100,000 forces. By 2002 this figure was down to 34,000, and by early 2004 there were just 19,800 troops.[36] At the time of this survey, there were approximately 12,000 soldiers, roughly 80 percent of whom had served in the war.

Background on Survey Methodology

The field research for this chapter consists of a questionnaire, followed up by a larger self-administered survey and a number of in-depth, oral history interviews with officers. (See Annex 2.) The first questionnaire was administered in 2004 to Bosnian battalion commanders (or their equivalent) at the conclusion of a three-day seminar on international humanitarian law in Munich. Out of 40 seminar participants, 35 returned the anonymous questionnaire. This seminar was significant in that it was the first time most of the battalion commanders of the two entities had met; it was also one of the first formal trainings on international humanitarian law since the war ended and followed a series of "Code of Conduct" seminars run by the OSCE.

---

[32] Defence Reform Commission, *The Path to Partnership for Peace* (Sarajevo: DRC, September 2003) 68.

[33] As many people register as military casualties because of the higher state benefits associated with such status, these statistics will change. However, these changes will not be likely to significantly alter the number of civilian and military casualties.

[34] Details about the project can be found at the Research and Documentation Center web site, <www.idc.org.ba>. See also Aida Cerkez-Robinson, "Research Shows Bosnian War Death Toll Guesses Severely Inflated," *Associated Press*, June 21, 2007.

[35] Research and Documentation Center, Sarajevo (CD from presentation of initial results, June 21, 2007). On file with author.

[36] Major General (retd.) K.J. Drewienkiewicz, correspondence with the author, January 15, 2009.

The Munich questionnaire was followed by a more comprehensive survey of 463 Bosnian soldiers of all ranks, administered by the author and a colleague, Selma Korenjić, in five Bosnian cities in September and December 2005.[37] Working with the entity Ministries of Defense (now defunct) as well as the state-level Ministry of Defense, cities were chosen so that the sample population would reflect different regional attitudes and the ethnic diversity of the armed forces. They were also cities in which there were enough soldiers to reach the desired number of a total of 450 or more respondents, or almost 5 percent of the entire military population. The Defense Ministry required that at least one person in each entity review the survey before it was distributed. In order to prevent officials in the ministries from instructing colleagues about how to answer, only one officer in each Defense Ministry saw the instrument before the survey was administered. To gain access to the barracks, written permission was obtained from the respective ministries. An officer was required to accompany the interviewers to each location, but spent little time in the rooms in which soldiers completed the survey during its administration. Upon arrival at each barracks, a meeting was held with the senior officer at the location, who was presented with a directive from the Defense Ministry authorizing the research. The officers were not informed in advance of our arrival and did not have prior knowledge of the survey contents. The surveys were self-administered, meaning that each respondent completed an anonymous questionnaire. The precise administration of the survey differed in each location: In some cases, soldiers filled the instrument out by themselves in their offices. In others, surveys were distributed at once to a group in a large room. In these cases, where possible, soldiers were instructed to leave at least one empty seat between themselves and the next respondent. After survey administration, the senior officer was given a copy of the instrument and informed that they would receive a copy of the codebook results when the data was processed.

Although the sample population was not strictly random, procedures were followed to ensure that as unbiased a sample as possible was chosen. Nevertheless, it should be acknowledged that the results may not be representative of the population. Out of the 12,000 members of the armed forces at the time, 8,000 were located in the Federation and 4,000 in RS. In order to reflect this distribution, the survey was administered at four different locations in three Federation cities – Sarajevo, Tuzla, and Mostar – for a total of 309 respondents, and in two cities in RS – Banja Luka and Bijeljina – for a total of 154 respondents. In Mostar, two barracks were visited in order to sample the views of both Croat and (largely) Bosniak soldiers, still divided in different parts of the city.[38] In Banja Luka, two different barracks

---

[37] The results of the Munich questionnaire were consistent with the findings of the larger five-city survey. Note that both the questionnaire and the survey dealt primarily with international humanitarian law and addressed genocide only tangentially in specific questions.

[38] The survey was administered in both the eastern and western parts of Mostar. The barracks in the western part of the city, at the time of the survey, were home to Croat members of the

representing different branches of the armed forces were visited. In total, 463 individuals were surveyed. Three others declined to participate, citing their right to withdraw as outlined by human subjects provisions on the survey instrument. In some instances, soldiers declined to answer most or all of the questions and turned in a folded but blank survey; in these cases, missing data was coded where appropriate.

At each location the sample population was determined by who was at work that day. The armed forces were in a state of transition during the survey period and in certain places there were high absentee rates due to activities occurring off the base. In Sarajevo there are three main buildings in the barracks, each housing a different branch of the army. A roughly equal number of instruments were divided among the buildings. In each building, offices were randomly selected on each floor and surveys were distributed to each person in the office. In general, each respondent spent up to 25 minutes filling out the instrument.

In Mostar, the two barracks visited were on the eastern and western sides of the city. In the western side, in the first of two groups surveyed, many soldiers were in the field conducting exercises and were later brought together into one room where the survey was administered. For the next group, surveys were distributed to offices chosen randomly in one building. In the eastern side of the city, a smaller number of surveys were administered. Similarly, in Tuzla, surveys were distributed to offices in one location, while in another part of the barracks they were administered to a group collected in one room. In Banja Luka, four different buildings and two different barracks were visited. In Bijeljina, two different buildings on the base were visited.

The first section of the survey instrument contained questions about age, rank, and education levels of both the respondent and his or her parents. Questions about trust in government and military reform, and general questions about attitudes toward the ICTY, were included in the next section. Questions were drawn from the U.S. National Election Survey instruments, studies of former combatants, and previous survey research on the ICTY and ICTR.[39] The survey instrument contained 89 questions, which were later translated into 119 variables using the statistical program SPSS.

After the survey was completed, each instrument was coded by at least two people in order to insure accuracy. When coding was finished, a consultant from

armed forces; those in the east housed primarily Bosniaks. The city was formally united in 2004.

[39] See American National Election Studies, Stanford University and the University of Michigan, <www.electionstudies.org/> (accessed May 29, 2009). For a recent survey instrument on former combatants, see Macartan Humphreys and Jeremy Weinstein, "What the Fighters Say: A Survey of Ex-Combatants in Sierra Leone June–August 2003," survey instrument, 2005, <www.columbia.edu/~mh2245/SL.htm> (accessed May 29, 2009). I also consulted Eric Stover and Harvey M. Weinstein, eds., *My Neighbor, My Enemy: Justice and Community in the Aftermath of Mass Atrocity* (Cambridge: Cambridge University Press, 2004).

the Human Rights Center at the University of Sarajevo randomly selected surveys to check the work of the two initial coders. Consequently, the survey has a high degree of what is known as intercoder reliability, which is a measure of agreement among multiple coders for how they apply codes to text data.[40] A high degree of intercoder reliability means that multiple coders assign the same values to the same text data. Given that the majority of questions were not open-ended, this was to be expected.

Several possible sources of bias should be noted. First, some respondents were not monitored while they completed the survey instrument in their offices, which provided an opportunity for them to consult with colleagues about how to answer, even though they were instructed not to. Second, as with any survey, there is always the problem of "truth telling" – the risk that respondents will answer according to what they think the researcher expects, sometimes offering answers that differ from their true opinions. In addition, some of the questions were rather provocative and it is possible that respondents were uncomfortable answering them honestly. The summary that follows notes some questions that may have been especially sensitive for respondents, as well as some where respondents might not have presented their honest views.

Lastly, some information about the survey universe was not provided despite numerous requests. An exact breakdown of the number of soldiers at each military base in the country was not made available, nor was the numbers of soldiers of each rank in each location. This would have facilitated a more sophisticated analysis. Because the armed forces were in a state of transition, it is possible that such a breakdown did not exist, or perhaps it was not accessible due to a culture of secrecy left over from the Tito era.[41]

Summary of Major Findings

Some of the questions addressed in this chapter are: Did the ICTY shape perceptions about the causes and purposes of the war among soldiers, many of whom had fought in it? Did the court change beliefs about acceptable behavior during wartime? Did it influence the emerging security doctrine in the AFBiH? Did the work of the ICTY influence postwar mentalities, understandings of recent history, or views on the use of violence for political goals? In the first scholarly look at the AFBiH since the end of the war, the data presented here provides the first summary of participants' attitudes about these issues. The survey was designed to gather information about attitudes toward the ICTY and international humanitarian law, preferred ways to deal with Bosnia's wartime past, and more general issues such

---

[40] The few errors on individual questions were corrected before the data was entered into the statistical program SPSS.
[41] Major General (retd.) K.J. Drewienkiewicz, correspondence with the author, January 15, 2009.

as defense reform and perceptions of various branches of the government. This survey also contained general questions, some of which are not described here, so that it would also be of relevance to those interested in defense reform in the country.

Some of the major findings include:

- A high number of members of the armed forces suffered loss of family during the war; they thus are important informants about the ICTY, which deals directly with the crimes that led to those losses.
- Among members of the military, there is a noticeable lack of knowledge about the work of the ICTY, considering that the institution addresses their actions. The majority of soldiers feel they are not adequately educated in international humanitarian law. Some stated it is of little importance to their day-to-day work.
- Despite a lack of personal knowledge, most believe that the ICTY has contributed to a proper understanding of the appropriate conduct of military personnel, as well as to other important aspects of democratization in Bosnia.
- Most respondents agree that the ICTY's work has led them to think differently about various aspects of recent history in the country.
- Soldiers of all ethnicities believe that a failure to cooperate with the ICTY should not have kept Bosnia out of NATO's PfP.
- Overwhelmingly, soldiers believe that trials are the best way to deal with their country's legacy of violations of international humanitarian law. Most feel there have not been enough trials dealing with wartime atrocities.

General Findings

The survey was carried out in five Bosnian cities, three of which are in the Federation of Bosnia and Herzegovina (66 percent of respondents) and two in Republika Srpska (33 percent of respondents). Bosniaks represented 44.9 percent of respondents, Croats were 22.4 percent, Serbs constituted 32 percent, and other ethnicities made up 0.7 percent. The survey sample is representative of the overall ethnic composition of the armed forces. In the Federation, there are 2.3 Bosniaks for every Croat soldier. In RS, with few exceptions, the army is comprised entirely of ethnic Serbs. Almost 100 percent of the sample there declared themselves to be Serb. In Mostar and Bijeljina there were a slightly smaller number of respondents, reflecting that these are smaller barracks and fewer people are at work at any given time.[42]

---

[42] Percentages reported are valid percentages, which calculates the respective totals excluding the missing data. I have chosen to present valid percentages so that they are consistent with cross-tabulations in SPSS. The program always calculates only valid percentages and thus their totals equal 100. I note those questions where there are large amounts of missing data.

During the period in which the survey was conducted, there was a moratorium on conscription as the army transitioned to a fully professional force. While the respective defense ministries have not provided a precise breakdown of the numbers of soldiers of each rank, higher ranks are clearly represented disproportionately in the sample population, as slightly over 50 percent were officers and high officers.[43] Of all respondents, 85 percent served in the war, which is slightly higher than the approximate percentage in the armed forces overall. However, it is worth noting that only 57 percent of respondents in RS claimed to have served in the armed forces during the war, as compared with 97 percent of Bosniaks and 100 percent of Croat respondents. Thus, a large percentage of soldiers in RS reported that they did not share the experience of the war with their colleagues in the Federation.[44]

Questions relating to the demographic profiles of the respondents were included on the survey instrument in order to understand some attributes of the individuals surveyed. Many respondents suffered considerable trauma during the war, and 17 percent reported losing a member of their family to the conflict. Comparable statistics for the Bosnian population as a whole do not exist, although the best data on the total number of deaths in the war (approximately 97,000 individuals) suggests that approximately 2 percent of the overall population was killed.[45] Bosniak soldiers reported the highest numbers of loss (21 percent of respondents), whereas Serbs and Croats indicated lower percentages (15 and 11 percent, respectively), which is consistent with the demographic structure of overall population losses in Bosnia. In addition, members of the armed forces have been displaced considerably, resulting either from the conflict directly or the need to live near the base where they are stationed. Over 40 percent of respondents live in a municipality other than that of their prewar residence. These demographic realities make this population an important source of information about attitudes toward the court. It is also worth noting that the armed forces are highly educated, especially when compared to their parents. Almost 50 percent of respondents had achieved education beyond high school, a great deal more schooling than their parents attained;

---

[43] The RS and Federation utilized different systems of rank, as outlined in the survey instrument. In the survey, however, those ranks were collapsed into four categories, based on the advice of current officers: Soldiers, Sergeants, Officers, and High Officers.

[44] This is a somewhat surprising finding and may point to a lack of truth-telling. However, other data suggests that this statistic is plausible even considering that overall participation rates are much higher in RS-based forces altogether. Fifty-three respondents were between the age of 18 and 29, and thus were, at most, 15 years of age when the war started. It is likely this population did not fight in the war. In addition, over 75 Serb respondents are "soldiers" or "sergeants," the lowest of the four rank categories; these ranks contain some individuals who did not serve in the war. Generally, however, the armed forces downsized after the end of the war. It is fair to estimate that up to 10 percent of Serb respondents did not answer this question truthfully.

[45] Research and Documentation Center "Human Losses 1991–1995," Project results, June 21, 2007. Copy of project results on file with the author.

less than 20 percent of respondents' fathers and only 7 percent of their mothers had any education beyond high school.

Findings on International Humanitarian Law and the ICTY

Soldiers' self-assessments of their knowledge of the principles of international humanitarian law indicated that they felt it was lacking: just over half responded that they were adequately educated in these principles. In the postwar period, this may not have been so important, as many felt humanitarian law did not affect their day-to-day work in peacetime. In fact, almost 70 percent replied that their work would be no different if such laws did not exist at all. This response is perhaps not surprising given the absence of war and the fact that the armed forces are currently more focused on training for peacekeeping duties abroad.

A considerable portion of those who served in the war reported seeing what they considered to be violations. When those who served in the war were asked whether "soldiers in their unit undertook actions against civilians that they felt qualified as criminal violations of the laws of war," 10 percent replied "yes." It is possible that some respondents were afraid to answer this question truthfully, for fear of further inquiry. Interestingly, only 3 Serb respondents (2 percent of all Serbs surveyed) answered positively to this question, as compared with 15 Bosniak and 25 Croat respondents (8 percent and 26 percent of respondents, respectively). CIA estimates in March 1995 suggested that approximately 90 percent of all war crimes were committed by Bosnian Serb and Serbian forces; the fact that a high percentage of Bosnian Serbs in this sample reported that they served in the military (85 of 154 respondents in RS) but very few reported observing violations suggests a possible lack of truth telling among them.[46] Such a high percentage of Croat respondents reporting having witnessed violations is a remarkable finding and deserves further study. Of all those respondents who reported witnessing criminal violations, 7 percent said commanding officers punished those soldiers responsible for violations.

Many respondents (over a quarter) were unsure, however, that they could even accurately identify a violation of international humanitarian law. When asked, "Do you think you could identify a violation of the Geneva Convention in a conflict situation?" 19 percent answered that they did not know, and another 7 percent answered no. In the prewar period, training in international humanitarian law was a part of the soldiers' peacetime preparation. Of those who served in the war, 74 percent reported that they were instructed in how to treat civilians and combatants. Again, the percentage of Croats who said they did not receive instructions was the highest (16 percent of all Croat respondents versus 7 percent for Bosniaks

---

[46] See, for example, Roger Cohen, "C.I.A. Report on Bosnia Blames Serbs for 90% of the War Crimes," *New York Times*, March 9, 1995.

and 12 percent for Serbs). Overall, it is striking that so many Croat respondents reported having seen violations but also that they were not instructed in the rules of war.

Misperceptions exist in the AFBiH about the numbers of war crimes committed by each party to the conflict, a fact that inevitably influences attitudes toward the ICTY. One-third of respondents answered that all parties in the war were equally guilty of violations of international humanitarian law. Within that group, respondents were overwhelmingly Serb: 65 percent of all Serbs, compared with 25 percent of Croats and 8 percent of Bosniaks, believed that all parties were equally guilty. When asked to rank parties' guilt on a scale of one to six, each group ranked the armies of their own ethnicity as least guilty. Most respondents did not question the need for the creation of the ICTY, although support for it was higher among Bosniaks and Croats than among Serbs. Seventy-three percent of those surveyed felt it was necessary for the ICTY to be formed; however, those who answered "no" or "don't know" included 50 percent of all Serb respondents and 39 percent of all Croat respondents. Nonetheless, these percentages show support for the creation of the court among all members of the armed forces.

Lack of knowledge about the court was evident: just over one-third of respondents felt comfortable with their understanding of the ICTY, a result that was roughly the same across all ethnic groups. This was not for lack of effort by the soldiers themselves: 84 percent reported that they at least sometimes followed the court's trials. Even though a considerable number of Croat and Serb respondents were unsure as to whether the ICTY should have been created, they found it to be a credible institution, with over three-quarters of all respondents answering that the ICTY was at least somewhat credible. An overwhelming 95 percent of all Bosniaks found it to be at least somewhat credible, versus 75 percent of Croat and 58 percent of Serb respondents (see Figure 7.1). A study of Bosnian nongovernmental organizations (NGOs) found that 65 percent of respondents from RS also reported that the ICTY was a credible institution, indicating that there are comparable levels of support in both segments of society.[47] However, when the armed forces were asked, "In your opinion, does the ICTY work in the best interests of Bosnia-Herzegovina?" only 22 percent answered "always" or "most of the time," with 39 percent responding "sometimes" and 32 percent answering "rarely."[48]

Although there were ICTY outreach efforts such as "Bridging the Gap Between the ICTY and Communities in Bosnia and Herzegovina" that targeted all sectors of society, the ICTY made no attempt targeted specifically at educating members of the armed forces about its findings.[49] Consequently, like most Bosnians, soldiers rely heavily on broadcast media for information about the court: 88 percent

---

[47] See Chapter 5 of this volume.
[48] Significance levels for this survey were not calculated, as the survey was not a probability sample.
[49] See "Outreach Activities," ICTY, <www.icty.org/sid/241> (accessed May 30, 2009).

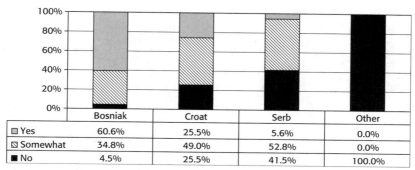

	Bosniak	Croat	Serb	Other
☐ Yes	60.6%	25.5%	5.6%	0.0%
☒ Somewhat	34.8%	49.0%	52.8%	0.0%
■ No	4.5%	25.5%	41.5%	100.0%

Figure 7.1. Is the ICTY a credible institution?

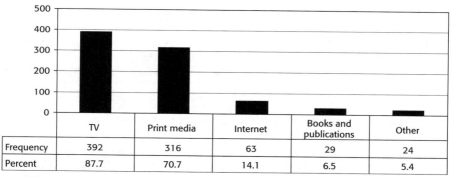

	TV	Print media	Internet	Books and publications	Other
Frequency	392	316	63	29	24
Percent	87.7	70.7	14.1	6.5	5.4

Figure 7.2. How do you get information about the work of the ICTY? (Percentages do not add up to 100, as respondents could check more than one option.)

reported getting ICTY-related news from the TV, while print media followed at just over 70 percent. The Internet was also an important source, although not as much for soldiers as for members of NGOs. Books and publications were consulted by only a small percentage of respondents in either sector (see Figure 7.2). These statistics make clear that the accuracy of media sources is crucial, as only a tiny percentage of the Bosnian population has had any direct experience with the ICTY – in this sample, only 2 percent of respondents. Nevertheless, discussion of the court's work is a daily part of the life of a soldier: 65 percent reported that the ICTY comes up at least sometimes in conversations with other military personnel during the workday.

The armed forces of a democratic country are expected to uphold the laws and norms of appropriate behavior for military personnel in both war and peacetime. Most participants in this study felt that the ICTY had contributed to a better understanding of the rules of conduct during wartime; 71 percent claimed that it at least somewhat did so. Again, support for this assertion was strongest among Bosniak respondents. When asked a follow-up question about whether the ICTY positively

TABLE 7.1. Does the ICTY affect the rule of law in Bosnia and Herzegovina?

	Ethnicity				
	Bosniak	Croat	Serb	Other	Total
Positive effects	47	15	7	0	69
% within Ethnicity	23.5%	16.0%	5.3%	0.0%	16.0%
Somewhat positive effects	139	57	61	3	260
% within Ethnicity	69.5%	60.6%	45.9%	100.0%	60.5%
Negative effects	8	9	35	0	52
% within Ethnicity	4.0%	9.6%	26.3%	0.0%	12.1%
Somewhat negative effects	6	13	30	0	49
% within Ethnicity	3.0%	13.8%	22.6%	0.0%	11.4%
Total	**200**	**94**	**133**	**3**	**430**
% within Ethnicity	**100.0%**	**100.0%**	**100.0%**	**100.0%**	**100.0%**
% of Total	**46.5%**	**21.9%**	**30.9%**	**0.7%**	**100.0%**

affected soldiers' relationships to international humanitarian law, 69 percent said that it did at least somewhat.

To other questions regarding the court's contributions to its extended mandate, answers varied. Just over half of all respondents (52 percent) felt the ICTY would deter people from committing crimes in the future, and 63 percent felt it at least somewhat contributes to justice in Bosnia and Herzegovina. As for the elusive idea of reconciliation, popular in the international community, 58 percent said the ICTY would at least somewhat contribute to its realization. Roughly the same findings were found in the NGO sector, again suggesting that soldiers hold views very similar to the rest of the population. As shown in Table 7.1, support for the ICTY's effects on the rule of law in Bosnia was stronger among Bosniaks than Croats and Serbs, although opinions were all mostly positive. Among Bosniaks, 93 percent said that the ICTY has positive or somewhat positive effects, compared with 77 percent of Croats and 51 percent of Serb respondents. Almost a quarter of all respondents felt the ICTY has had somewhat or entirely negative effects on the rule of law in Bosnia, largely accounted for by the views of Serb respondents.

When asked whether the ICTY aided the democratization of Bosnian society, 89 percent of Bosniaks concurred; this was 30 percent more than their Croat colleagues (58.6 percent of whom answered positively) and more than twice as many as their Serb colleagues (42 percent). Many Serb and Croat respondents failed to weigh in on the issue at all, with an average of 20 percent in each group answering, "don't know," compared to only 3 percent of Bosniaks.

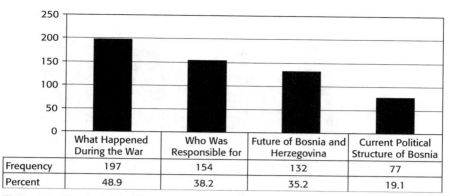

	What Happened During the War	Who Was Responsible for	Future of Bosnia and Herzegovina	Current Political Structure of Bosnia
Frequency	197	154	132	77
Percent	48.9	38.2	35.2	19.1

Figure 7.3. Has the ICTY affected your views about the following?

After the opening of the War Crimes Chamber of the Court of Bosnia and Herzegovina in March 2005, and the steady increase in prosecutions in lower courts, focus shifted from the ICTY to local courtrooms across the country. Bosniak respondents, who so whole-heartedly support the ICTY, were less enthusiastic about domestic trials than their Croat and Serb colleagues. Asked whether domestic trials would positively affect democratization, justice, reconciliation, and the rule of law in Bosnia, 44 percent of Bosniaks answered they would do so less than the ICTY, compared with 24 percent of Croat and 17 percent of Serb respondents. On the same question, a more similar percentage across all groups felt domestic trials would have more impact than the ICTY (average 18 percent). Almost a third of all respondents answered "don't know."

The ICTY also appears to have influenced attitudes toward certain aspects of current developments in Bosnia. To the question, "Has the ICTY affected your views of the following?" (what happened in the war, who was responsible, the future of the country, its current political structure) many felt that the court's work influenced their understandings about the country. Almost half of all respondents, for example, said that the court influenced their views about events of the war, suggesting that the court's findings are making soldiers more aware about the country's recent past. Respondents could check more than one answer to this question (see Figure 7.3).

Previous studies have shown that respondents are likely to answer positively to questions that include a norm in the question itself.[50] Thus, if respondents are asked, "Is the ICTY good for democracy?" they will likely respond positively because the norm of democracy was posited in the question. However, this phrasing may obscure true views. In order to overcome this bias, the survey instrument

---

[50] See, for example, Paul Sniderman and Edward Carmines, *Reaching Beyond Race* (Cambridge, MA: Harvard University Press, 1997).

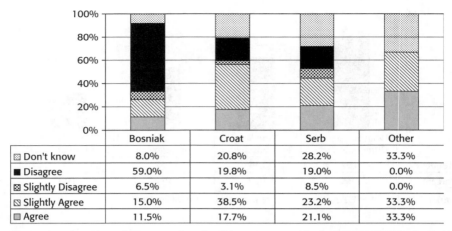

	Bosniak	Croat	Serb	Other
▨ Don't know	8.0%	20.8%	28.2%	33.3%
■ Disagree	59.0%	19.8%	19.0%	0.0%
▨ Slightly Disagree	6.5%	3.1%	8.5%	0.0%
◩ Slightly Agree	15.0%	38.5%	23.2%	33.3%
▢ Agree	11.5%	17.7%	21.1%	33.3%

Figure 7.4. Bosnia and Herzegovina should cooperate with the ICTY ONLY because if it does not it will be punished by the international community.

offered similar questions rephrased in different ways, in an effort to get at underlying attitudes.

This approach was used to address an important question throughout the region: why people believe compliance with the ICTY is necessary.[51] Do they believe that states should comply with the ICTY because they believe in the norms of justice it represents or simply because they are concerned about the consequences if cooperation is lacking? Some respondents see cooperation only instrumentally, as a way to gain membership in regional organizations and as a "ticket" to increased foreign aid. While Serb respondents favor this view more than their Croat counterparts, the numbers show more indifference to the ICTY than vehement opposition. For example, when asked to evaluate the statement, "Bosnia and Herzegovina should cooperate with the ICTY ONLY because if it doesn't it will be punished by the international community," 56 percent of Croats, 44 percent of Serbs and 27 percent of Bosniaks agreed or slightly agreed with this statement. More than a quarter of all Serb respondents answered "don't know." When asked to evaluate the statement, "Bosnia and Herzegovina should cooperate with the ICTY because perpetrators of war crimes should be brought to justice," support was highest among Bosniaks, among whom 96 percent agreed or slightly agreed; Croats and Serbs, however, trailed not far behind, at 82 percent and 72 percent, respectively. This data suggests that the norm of justice is slightly stronger than that of strategic cooperation for material gain, even among Serb respondents. (See Figures7.4 and 7.5.)

---

[51] On cooperation with the court, see Victor Peskin, *International Justice in Rwanda and the Balkans: Virtual Trials and the Struggle for State Cooperation* (Cambridge: Cambridge University Press, 2008).

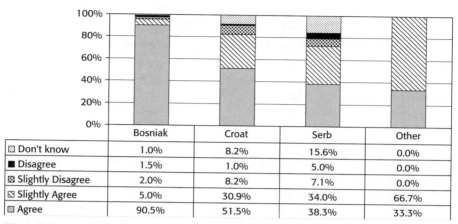

	Bosniak	Croat	Serb	Other
⊠ Don't know	1.0%	8.2%	15.6%	0.0%
■ Disagree	1.5%	1.0%	5.0%	0.0%
⊠ Slightly Disagree	2.0%	8.2%	7.1%	0.0%
⧅ Slightly Agree	5.0%	30.9%	34.0%	66.7%
▢ Agree	90.5%	51.5%	38.3%	33.3%

Figure 7.5. Bosnia and Herzegovina should cooperate with the ICTY because perpetrators of war crimes should be brought to justice.

The feeling that politics had an influence on the way trials were initiated and conducted at the court is prevalent among all respondents and is strongest among Croats: 73 percent of Croats, 67 percent of Bosniaks, and 66 percent of Serbs agreed or slightly agreed that politics have influenced developments at the ICTY in a way that inhibited its ability to dispense justice fairly. But, when asked to assess bias at the ICTY, Serbs reported in the highest numbers that the court was biased against them. The statement, "The ICTY is biased against members of my ethnic group" was positively received by 72 percent of Serbs, 63 percent of Croats, and only 28 percent of Bosniaks. Some respondents agreed that the ICTY has been a misuse of limited resources: 19 percent of those surveyed agreed with the statement "the ICTY is a waste of money" and 26 percent slightly agreed – 45 percent in total, a figure that included 67 percent of Croats, 60 percent of Serbs, and 21 percent of Bosniak respondents.[52]

Implicit in the argumentation of many human rights advocates is that documentation of atrocities create a rational basis for discussion of wartime events. The ICTY has generated hundreds of thousands of pages of documentation containing facts about the wars in the region. That documentation establishes microhistories of the war in the areas that pertain to each case tried. Respondents were asked to assess whether they thought international prosecutions would help their country discover facts about wartime events; 74 percent at least slightly agreed that they would. A follow-up question asked respondents to assess the effects of

---

[52] A similar question also appeared on the survey about the ICTR discussed in Timothy Longman, Phuong Pham, and Harvey M. Weinstein, "Connecting Justice to Human Experience: Attitudes Toward Accountability and Reconciliation in Rwanda," in Stover and Weinstein, *My Neighbor, My Enemy*, 214.

TABLE 7.2. What is the best way to address war crimes? (Percentages do
not add up to 100, as respondents could check more than one option.)

	Frequency	Percent
Trials	385	83.5
Reparations	145	33.3
Other	26	6
Amnesty	19	4.4

facts revealed over the postwar period. The statement, "Factual knowledge about
wartime events has improved interethnic relations in Bosnia Herzegovina" elicited some interesting responses, worthy of further research. While 28 percent
answered that factual knowledge has worsened relations, only 11 percent said it
had improved them. The question did not elicit, however, whether the respondent believed this to be a short-term or long-term effect. Despite their sense that
the knowledge bank created by the court has not helped interethnic relations,
soldiers still overwhelmingly believe that trials are the best way to deal with war
crimes. Over 83 percent of respondents indicated a preference for trials, whereas
just 33 percent supported reparations and only a scant 4 percent felt amnesty was
the best course.[53] The breakdown in Table 7.2 shows that even though respondents
could check more than one answer, they overwhelmingly indicated a preference
for trials.

The respondents were also canvassed for their views on the two most wanted
ICTY indictees at the time of the survey's administration. When asked to assess
the statement, "The arrest of Radovan Karadžić and Ratko Mladić is an important
goal for the future of Bosnia and Herzegovina," answers were divided: 98 percent
of Bosniaks and 75 percent of Croats agreed or slightly agreed, compared with only
22 percent of Serbs.[54]

Even if Bosnian soldiers supported the creation of the ICTY, many felt it exerted
a structural influence on the armed forces that was unwarranted. Bosnia's membership in NATO's Partnership for Peace was conditioned upon cooperation by
Bosnia (in reality by RS's) with the Tribunal. The country was refused membership at the June 2004 NATO summit in Istanbul and again in December of that
same year. Many soldiers felt the country was being unfairly held hostage by political elites. Membership in PfP is the first step toward full NATO membership and
an important indicator of progress in all of the countries of Eastern Europe. Of
those surveyed, 89 percent thought that Bosnia should have been admitted to PfP

[53] One question asked whether or not the respondent supported the creation of a truth and
reconciliation commission; 63 percent of respondents said they did, although 24 percent of
respondents indicated they were not informed about it and another 8 percent answered "don't
know."
[54] Radovan Karadžić was arrested and transferred to the ICTY in July 2008.

TABLE 7.3. Do you believe the issue of non-cooperation with the ICTY should continue to be a bar to PfP entry?

| | Ethnicity | | | | |
	Bosniak	Croat	Serb	Other	Total
Yes	74	18	4	0	96
% within Ethnicity	37.0%	18.6%	2.9%	0.0%	21.9%
No	102	51	94	2	249
% within Ethnicity	51.0%	52.6%	67.6%	66.7%	56.7%
Don't know	24	28	41	1	94
% within Ethnicity	12.0%	28.9%	29.5%	33.3%	21.4%
Total	**200**	**97**	**139**	**3**	**439**
% within Ethnicity	**100.0%**	**100.0%**	**100.0%**	**100.0%**	**100.0%**
% of Total	**45.6%**	**22.1%**	**31.7%**	**0.7%**	**100.0%**

already. However, when this question was phrased differently and respondents were asked whether the issue of non-cooperation with the ICTY should continue to be a bar to membership, 22 percent answered that it should, suggesting that some respondents changed their mind when reminded about the issue of ICTY cooperation, shown in Table 7.3. Bosniak respondents answered positively in the largest numbers: 37 percent of all Bosniak respondents agreed that non-cooperation was a reasonable obstacle versus only 18.6 percent of Croats and 2.9 percent of Serbs. Bosnia was admitted to PfP in December 2006.

Conclusion

This analysis of the first qualitative survey conducted with the AFBiH since the end of the war finds that, although attitudes toward the ICTY are divided along ethnic lines, members of all ethnic groups support the ICTY and believe that the court has made contributions toward its extended mandate. These results are significant, especially considering that an earlier survey conducted in the general population in Bosnia and Croatia, in 2000 and 2001, found that the ICTY was viewed through a nationalist lens.[55] Although this survey of the AFBiH does not represent repetition of this early research, its results suggest that nationalistic absolutes may have lessened over the intervening period.

[55] Miklos Biro, Dean Ajdukovic, Dinka Corkalo, Dino Djipa, Petar Milin, and Harvey M. Weinstein, "Attitudes toward Justice and Social Reconstruction in Bosnia and Herzegovina and Croatia," in Stover and Weinstein, *My Neighbor, My Enemy*, 200.

The survey instrument contained questions phrased both positively and negatively in an effort to discern underlying attitudes. It found that support for the norm of justice was higher among respondents than the need for strategic cooperation with the court. On most questions dealing with the court's extra-legal impact – such as its contributions to values such as justice, reconciliation, democratization, and the rule of law – more than half of all respondents felt that the ICTY had constructively impacted the attainment of those goals. In addition, it is noteworthy that levels of support for the ICTY and various aspects of its extended mandate among members of the military are consistent with the findings for NGOs presented in Chapter 5 of this volume.

Further, there is considerable support for judicial forms of transitional justice. Soldiers overwhelmingly believed that trials are the best way to deal with violations of international humanitarian law committed in Bosnia. Similarly, a considerable majority believes that there have not been enough trials yet. The selectivity of both international and domestic trials means that many alleged perpetrators will likely never be brought before a court, but there is a high level of support for this mechanism in the military.

During their workdays, soldiers speak frequently about the ICTY and its work, yet they claim that their knowledge about the court is insufficient. The mass media are the primary source of information about the court and thus play an important role in shaping attitudes. These findings show that television, slightly ahead of newspapers, is relied upon the most for information about the court. The continued training of news reporters on issues related to international justice is crucial, not only to properly inform this segment of the population, but also to offer trustworthy reporting and analysis to the public as a whole.

Several other general findings are significant and introduce a note of caution to overly optimistic interpretations. Overall, there is a group of respondents in RS who do not support the work of the court, even though this sentiment is far from universal there. Croat respondents are also quite critical of some aspects of the court's work. In addition, many respondents in RS felt that all parties were equally guilty of violations of international humanitarian law, a feeling which has led to persistent and widespread views that the institution is biased against Serbs, despite the fact that most estimates show that the police and military forces of RS committed a striking majority of war crimes.

Other limitations of this research should be acknowledged. This survey, being the first of its kind in the postwar period, was meant to ascertain a broad overview of attitudes. It did not deal with important subjects such as the topic of genocide (apart from several questions about Srebrenica). Further surveys of this type would be necessary to understand how attitudes evolve over time in response to changing circumstances. It is hoped that future researchers will replicate this effort. The initial data presented here, however, illustrates how the court's work has influenced attitudes in the most unlikely places, in a segment of the population often scrutinized by ICTY prosecutors. The respondents believed the court made contributions to peace and security in Bosnia. Measuring their attitudes represents an important step in analyzing the court's influence on Bosnia's transition to democracy. One survey is not enough and should be seen as a small step in an ongoing research trajectory that seeks to understand the role of international tribunals in the region and beyond. This chapter has addressed only a small population, many of whom had recently undergone a significant transition themselves, from the battlefield to the barracks.

8 Localizing War Crimes Prosecutions

The Hague to Sarajevo and Beyond

In March 2005, with the opening of Bosnia's long-awaited War Crimes Chamber, High Representative Paddy Ashdown confidently declared that: "By showing itself willing and ready to handle these cases, Bosnia has underlined that crimes committed in this territory can be tried here, should be tried here, and should not be sent to a foreign country."[1] Several years in the making, the War Crimes Chamber would try those responsible for violations of international humanitarian law and genocide and begin taking over cases from the ICTY. The opening of the Chamber represented a big step for Bosnia and its still developing legal system: it meant that the prosecution of war criminals would be shared among The Hague, the State Court, and local courts, and that in a short time trials would only be held in Bosnia.[2] Although fraught with some of the inevitable difficulties of institution building in a transitional environment, the progress made in Bosnia demonstrates that foreign trials can lead to local ones. The development of local judicial capacity in coordination with the ICTY may be the clearest example of the court's contribution to the rule of law and to democratic development in Bosnia.

This chapter outlines the development of local prosecutorial capacity, including efforts to review and reappoint judges and prosecutors, the process of referring cases to Bosnia, and the country's initial experience with war crimes trials. The rule of law emerged as an international priority relatively late, but when it finally found a place on the agenda, local institutions were built rather quickly. There were considerable difficulties transferring knowledge and shaping local institutional capabilities, but within a few years Bosnian courts had reached verdicts in cases that included even the gravest offense in international law: genocide. The ICTY and the parties implementing reform efforts on the ground, though an imperfect alliance, achieved considerable progress in the advancement of Bosnia's justice system in the first 15 years after the war. The architects of the ICTY hoped that

---

[1] Daria Sito-Sucic, "Bosnia to Open Own War Crimes Court," *Reuters*, March 6, 2005.
[2] The full name of the court is the Court of Bosnia and Herzegovina, but I will use the more common name "State Court" throughout.

their work at the international level would bolster the rule of law in the region, and it did. The creation of local capacity was a domestic initiative funded separately by donors and, later, by the Bosnian government, but it was the ICTY that created the pressure and expectation for local trials, referred cases, and shared experience from the international level. Many of the professionals who spearheaded the localization effort had worked in The Hague and improved upon its institutional shortcomings.

The Rule of Law after Dayton

The average Bosnian's experience with the justice system in the immediate postwar period did little to breed confidence that it would ever be able to try complicated cases fairly, such as those for violations of international humanitarian law. By all accounts, the rule of law was in a state of ruins in the postwar years, and included a patchwork of public institutions that Bosnians had no choice but to interact with regularly. Petty, nonresponsive, and power-hungry bureaucrats often violated the human rights of the country's citizens through the exercise of significant influence and discrimination in a labyrinth of prewar, postwar, and wartime institutions.[3] This inefficient public administration affected the daily lives of most.[4] Many people, unable to avoid the labyrinth, were forced to resort to legal proceedings to do things such as reclaim prewar property. Bosnians often found judgments influenced by ethnic politics. While this was blatantly obvious in most cases, other less overt strategies were also employed. As one analysis commented: "Rather than openly use ethnicity as grounds, the courts and governmental agencies often [masked] their prejudices in dubious rulings, or in unexplained delay[s] in procedure."[5] This was compounded by the postwar transition of the judiciary, which was completely restructured by the international community. Many members of the judiciary did not fully understand their new roles as part of an independent force.

The Dayton Peace Agreement gave the entities responsibility for the administration of justice; each had its own justice department, and associations in both the Federation and RS monitored legal professionals. One of the greatest postwar challenges for the international community was to build legal infrastructure at the state level, and this challenge was tackled relatively late. Many argued that the rule of law and the criminal justice system should have emerged as a priority earlier in

---

[3] International Crisis Group (ICG), "Rule of Law in Public Administration: Confusion and Discrimination in a Post-Communist Bureaucracy," *Bosnia Legal Project Report N° 2* (Sarajevo: ICG, 1999),<www.crisisweb.org> (accessed June 10, 2009).

[4] Ibid. For an excellent account of how the socialist state monopolized the hours of its citizens, see Katherine Verdery, *What Was Socialism and What Comes Next?* (Princeton, NJ: Princeton University Press, 1996), Chapter 2, which uses an example from Romania.

[5] International Crisis Group, "Denied Justice: Individuals Lost in Legal Maze," *Bosnia Legal Project Report No. 3* (Sarajevo: ICG, 2000): 19, <www.crisisweb.org> (accessed June 10, 2009).

the international intervention.[6] Bosnia had five years of peace before major pieces of legislation that started the process were implemented. Consequently, as many foreign workers in Bosnia were packing their bags for home or for other international hot spots such as Kosovo, Afghanistan and, later, Iraq, many lawyers arrived in the country to fill available positions demanding their expertise and assistance in transforming the country's judiciary, raising standards and undertaking new roles.

Key laws that set the framework for the eventual trial of war crimes in the country were drawn up with the assistance of the High Representative's Bonn Powers.[7] The Court of Bosnia and Herzegovina was created by legislation drafted in 2000 and imposed by High Representative Wolfgang Petritsch (who preceded Ashdown) when the targeted date was reached.[8] The War Crimes Chamber was Section 1 of the State Court's three criminal divisions.[9] (Figure 8.1 outlines the court's structure.) This new institution was entrusted with the authority to process criminal cases covering all of Bosnia and Herzegovina. In 2003, the Bosnian parliament passed a new criminal code, which set the legal foundation for prosecution of war crimes at the state level. Once the legislation was passed, the State Court would share the burden of war crimes prosecutions with cantonal courts in the Federation and district courts in RS.[10]

The Prosecutor's Office of Bosnia and Herzegovina (PO BiH) had responsibility for State Court prosecutions.[11] The Prosecutor's Office was, however, an institution separate from the State Court, with a separate budget; the two institutions shared only office space. The Law on the Prosecutor's Office of BiH was adopted in October 2003. The Special Department for War Crimes (Department I), set up a little over

---

[6] See, for example, Michael H. Doyle "Too Little, Too Late? Justice and Security Reform in Bosnia and Herzegovina," in Charles T. Call, ed., *Constructing Justice and Security After War* (Washington D.C.: United States Institute for Peace, 2007), 231, 248; "Courting Disaster: The Misrule of Law in Bosnia and Herzegovina," International Crisis Group, *Europe Report No. 127* (Brussels, ICG, 2002).

[7] As described in Chapter 3, the December 1997 Peace Implementation Council (PIC) meeting in Bonn gave the High Representative the ability to remove officials from office and to implement legislation; these were known locally as the "Bonn powers."

[8] See the "Law on Court of Bosnia and Herzegovina," Laws of Bosnia and Herzegovina, OHR Legal Department, Office of the High Representative and EU Special Representative, <www.ohr.int/ohr-dept/legal/laws-of-bih/default.asp?content_id=31549> (accessed June 10, 2009); also see Office of the High Representative and EU Special Representative, "Decision Imposing the Law on the State Court of BiH," November 12, 2000, HR's Decisions: Judicial Reform, <www.ohr.int/decisions/judicialrdec/default.asp?content_id=5228> (accessed June 10, 2009).

[9] The Criminal Division has three sections: Section I for War Crimes; Section II for Organized Crime, Economic Crime and Corruption; Section III for General Crime.

[10] There is also the Constitutional Court of Bosnia and Herzegovina, outlined in Annex 4 of the Dayton Peace Agreement. The court has its prewar origins in the Constitutional Court which was established in 1964, in accordance with the 1963 constitution. See <www.ccbh.ba/eng/p_stream.php?kat=503> (accessed June 10, 2009).

[11] See "Jurisdiction," Office of the Prosecutor of Bosnia and Herzegovina, <www.tuzilastvobih.gov.ba/index.php?opcija=sadrzaj&kat=1&id=3&jezik=e> (accessed June 30, 2009).

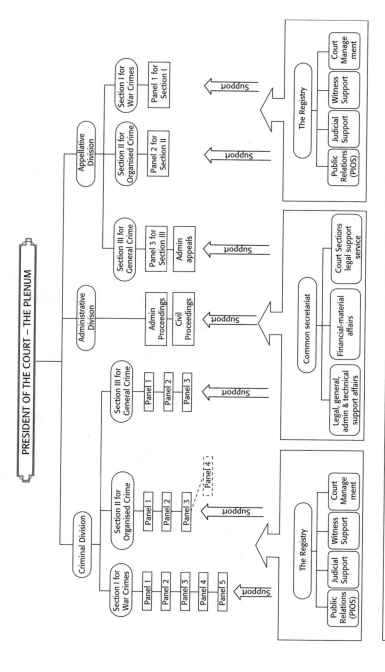

Figure 8.1. Court of Bosnia and Herzegovina Organization and Structure.

The Registry provides support also to the Appellative Division Criminal Pannel 1 for Section I for War Crimes and Appellative Division Criminal Pannel 2 for Section II for Organised Crime. Common Secretariat provides support to the Appellative Division Criminal Pannel 3 for Section III General Crime.

Source: Court of Bosnia and Herzegovina, <www.sudbih.gov.ba/?opcija=sadrzaj&kat=3&id=3&jezik=e> (accessed June 20, 2009).

a year later, was to become the lead institution for development of a plan to work through war crimes cases in the country. In the meantime, the international community undertook an extensive process of reappointing those judges and prosecutors found acceptable after review of their qualifications and employment histories, including wartime activities.

Major Pillars of Judicial Reform

One of the goals of Bosnia's push for integration with the European Union (EU) was a modern and efficient legal system that met Western European standards. In 2001, the Office of the High Representative set up the Independent Judicial Commission (IJC) and made it the lead international agency for judicial reform in Bosnia. The IJC outlined its proposals in a detailed paper. After receiving support from the Peace Implementation Council (PIC), the IJC was tasked with key aspects of the reform process, including:

(1) the establishment of High Judicial and Prosecutorial Councils (HJPC) (at the Entity and State levels) with appointment and disciplinary authority over judges and prosecutors;
(2) reappointment of all judges and prosecutors by the three councils with international support;
(3) the restructuring of courts and prosecutorial offices.[12]

Reappointment and resizing was necessitated by the fact that there were too many judges and prosecutors for the size of the country, and a patchwork of over 20 different councils and commissions that oversaw the appointment and disciplinary processes.[13] In order to be considered for reappointment, existing judges and prosecutors were obligated to submit their resumes, in addition to detailed information about where they had spent their time during the war. Many legal professionals had been residing outside of the country, and the promise of a job in the newly formed judiciary could facilitate their return. Judges' and prosecutors' salaries were some of the highest in the country, at approximately 3,000 KM (approximately 1,500 euros) per month – a rate decided upon to prevent corruption. In 2001, this figure was approximately six times the national average monthly salary in Bosnia of 500KM (approximately 250 euros) per month. At the end of the reappointment process, 629 judicial positions remained of the previous 868. The number of prosecutors (275) remained unchanged in order to help facilitate their new, more active

---

[12] Tim Hughes, former Head of Investigation and Verification Department, Independent Judicial Commission (IJC), e-mail to the author, April 6, 2006.
[13] However, the reappointment process did not cover every court; the Constitutional Court of Bosnia and Herzegovina, Entity Constitutional Courts, and Brčko Courts were excluded, as was the State Court. The High Representative later appointed seven judges to the State Court that enabled it to become operational.

role in the courtroom. The reappointment process lasted until the IJC's mandate expired in March 2004.

The changes to the structure of the justice system, and to the way trials were carried out, represented a major shift for the country's legal professionals. Under the legal system of the SFRY, investigatory judges (rather than prosecutors) had coordinated the investigation of a case. Prosecutors served primarily as bureaucrats who filed paperwork and attended hearings. In the new system, prosecutors were tasked with the burden of fact-finding for trials in an adversarial system, creating a "party-driven" process.[14] This change in roles was part of the overall reform of the country's criminal procedure.[15] The subject of war crimes, however, was not new: Chapter 16 (Articles 141–145) of the Criminal Code of the SFRY had already provided a basis for trying violations of international humanitarian law and genocide in domestic courts.

There were multiple demands to be addressed in the reappointment process: the international community had to keep ethnic parity, in addition to reappointing minority judges and prosecutors for work in regions of the country where, before the war, they may have been the majority. Thus, for example, Bosniaks were needed for Eastern Bosnia and Serbs for some parts of Herzegovina. Applicants were asked to check their geographical preferences when they filed for reappointment. There was not always a willing pool of individuals of specific ethnicities for the regions in question, and this led to charges of foul play by nationalist politicians. For example, in late 2003, the SDA put ads all over Sarajevo claiming the OHR had stacked the deck in favor of Serb appointees, discriminating against Bosniaks. The Steering Board of the Peace Implementation Council (PIC) reacted strongly to the provocation, stating in a press release, "The Ambassadors were confident that when this process was complete, BiH's judiciary would again reflect the country's multiethnic nature, and reaffirmed their full support for the ongoing work of the HJPC. However, they underlined in the most serious terms that the media campaign against the HJPC was discouraging [Bosniaks] from applying to positions in RS, and therefore making it harder to restore the multi-ethnic balance."[16] The SDA's accusations were later debunked. Table 8.1 shows the ethnic composition of the judges and prosecutors at the local level before and after reappointment.

The politicization of the process by nationalists was short-lived, however. Admittedly, it was poorly managed. Consisting mostly of a group of foreign lawyers, those overseeing the reappointments were more skilled at assessing the legal qualifications of the applicants than at managing the public relations aspect of the transformation. The reappointment process coincided with a growing awareness of the need for outreach and public information campaigns by programs dealing

[14] Hughes, e-mail to the author, April 6, 2006.
[15] Hughes, e-mail to the author, September 22, 2005.
[16] Office of the High Representative and EU Special Representative, "Steering Board Ambassadors Warn against Attempts to Politicise HJPC Process," January 7, 2004, Peace Implementation Council, <www.ohr.int/pic/default.asp?content_id=31499> (accessed June 10, 2009).

TABLE 8.1. Ethnicity Chart of the Composition of the Judiciary and Prosecutors at the Entity Level[a]

	Bosniaks	Croats	Serbs	Others
	Pre-R/Post-R	Pre-R/Post-R	Pre-R/Post-R	Pre-R/Post-R
RS Judiciary	1.9%/21.9%	3.8%/7.3%	91.5%/65.1%	2.6%/2.8%
RS Prosecutors	3.2%/23.8%	1.6%/7.9%	95.1%/66.6%	0.0%/1.5%
FBiH Judiciary	65.7%/57.2%	23.1%/21.8%	8.8%/19.4%	2.2%/1.5%
FBiH Prosecutors	65.4%/54.1%	21.2%/22.6%	10.9%/19.8%	2.4%/3.4%

Source: Organization for Security and Cooperation in Europe, Human Rights Department, *War Crimes Trials before the Domestic Courts of Bosnia-Herzegovina: Progress and Obstacles* (OSCE Mission to Bosnia-Herzegovina: 2005).
[a] Percentages listed are for pre-reappointment (pre-R) and post-reappointment (post-R).

with legal issues in the country. They faced internal challenges as well. There was little indication that High Representative Paddy Ashdown considered this operation, and the way it was carried out and presented, a priority for his office. There was anecdotal support for this: Ashdown was said to meet rarely with the head of the IJC, and never on a daily basis, as he did with department heads. When his term expired in January 2006, however, judicial reform was one of the major achievements of his mandate.

The reappointment process was not without controversy. The lack of transparency of the decisions of the IJC, coupled with the inability to appeal decisions, fueled criticism. As was true of many other vetting programs in Central and Eastern Europe, there were charges that the reappointment process in Bosnia lacked specific criteria. Some protested. Ahmed Žilić, a well-known Sarajevo-based lawyer and former candidate for a judgeship at the European Court of Human Rights (ECHR) in Strasbourg, presented a case on behalf of his wife, Aida, a former judge in a Sarajevo municipal court, who was not reappointed. Žilić charged that the lack of clear criteria for reappointment of judges and prosecutors violated the European Convention on Human Rights.[17] His efforts to secure a full review of her file were unsuccessful.[18] In other instances, individuals filed complaints with the Constitutional Court of Bosnia and Herzegovina, which, on several occasions, said it did not have the authority to review the decisions, given that an international legal body outside of its jurisdiction made them.[19]

---

[17] Materials submitted to IJC on file with the author.
[18] There were similar problems with the police. The International Police Task Force (IPTF), part of the United Nations Mission in Bosnia, conducted a review of all of the country's 40,000 policemen after the war, reducing the force to 15,000; 64 were found unsuitable because of their war backgrounds. A small group of those dismissed challenged the UN-sponsored reappointment process. See Aldin Arnautović, "Bosnia: Police Blamed for War Crimes," Institute of War and Peace Reporting (IWPR), *Balkan Crisis Report*, No. 394, January 2, 2003, <www.iwpr.net/index.php?apc_state=hen&s=o&o=p=bcr&l=EN&s=f&o=158563> (accessed June 10, 2009).
[19] See, for example, Decision of the Constitutional Court of Bosnia and Herzegovina, Case no. AP-545/04. Copy on file with the author.

In addition, despite the Commission's efforts, the reappointment of some existing members of the judiciary left Bosnians feeling that people with questionable
wartime backgrounds maintained a hold on positions of influence and power.
This initially fed ordinary citizens' distrust in Bosnian courts. In Modriča, a small
town in RS, the head of the court was a high-ranking member of the SDS, a fact
that disturbed some local nongovernmental organizations.[20] In addition, the State
Prosecutor, Marinko Jurčević, who would become the "face" of the Prosecutor's
Office of Bosnia and Herzegovina in its early years, had been a wartime prosecutor
in the parastate Herceg-Bosna (Croatian Community of Herceg-Bosna or HZHB) at
the time of the 1993 Ahmići massacre, during which over a hundred Bosniak civilians were brutally murdered. Some Bosnian citizens were understandably uncomfortable with the fact that the office was led by a man who had failed to prosecute
crimes committed in the territory under his court's jurisdiction.[21] The harsh reality
was that there were not always ideal candidates for some positions in the judiciary.

The IJC also set up three High Judicial and Prosecutorial Councils (HJPCs).
Funded by the state, they had been created to take over the selection and appointment of judges and prosecutors after the mandate of the IJC expired, in addition
to dealing with training, disciplinary, and ethics issues. The new councils merged
and became one in June 2005, when the entities agreed to confer authority to a
single council pursuant to the BiH constitution.[22] It was another example of the
localization of an initiative spearheaded by internationals, and represented the
unification of the judiciary in Bosnia. As it was not a particularly titillating issue
for the local press, the process of setting up the HJPC was quiet and without fan-
fare, even though it was one of the more successful results of the reform process.

The ICTY and National Courts

There were three main groups of cases referred from the ICTY to Bosnia:

1) cases reviewed under the auspices of the "Rules of the Road" agreement and unit
   (described below);
2) so-called 11bis cases (a reference to ICTY Rules and Procedure, "Referral of the
   Indictment to Another Court"), in which individuals indicted in The Hague
   could be sent to be tried in other courts, including courts in the region, where
   the accused was arrested, or in states willing to prosecute;[23]

---

[20] Interview with civil society organization representative, Modriča, July 21, 2004.
[21] The ICTY, however, addressed the crimes committed in Ahmići in several trials. See, for example: *Prosecutor v. Zoran Kupreškić et al.* (IT-95-16); *Prosecutor v. Dario Kordić and Mario Čerkez*
(IT-95-14/2); *Prosecutor v. Tihomir Blaškić* (IT-95-14). The State Court addressed crimes committed in Ahmići in the trial of Paško Ljubičić (KT-RZ-140/06).
[22] Hughes, e-mail to the author, April 6, 2006.
[23] The latest ICTY Rules and Procedure were published in December 2009, see <www.icty.org/
x/file/Legal%20Library/Rules_procedure_evidence/IT032_rev44_en.pdf> (accessed January
26, 2010). On the Bosnian side, see also the "Law on the Transfer of Cases from the ICTY to the
Prosecutor's Office of BiH and the Use of Evidence Collected by ICTY in Proceedings Before

3) cases in which investigations were initiated in The Hague but the suspects did not meet the ICTY's completion strategy criteria, which stipulated that it focus on those most responsible, and where the ICTY therefore did not file an indictment.[24]

The system that developed resulted from both the postwar experiences in the region and, later, the UN Security Council's push for the execution of a completion strategy. After the war, local prosecution of war crimes was a pressing issue, if not a priority. In some cases, politicians were using accusations of war crimes to discredit their political rivals. Some discriminatory arrests necessitated coordination between the ICTY and local authorities to prevent such abuse. In addition, the need for more oversight was illustrated by postwar publicity surrounding a wartime case in which two Serbs, Sretko Damjanović and Borislav Herak, were condemned to death for killing two Bosniaks who were later found alive.[25]

The Rome Agreement of 1996 set up the "Rules of the Road" that would govern the relationship between the ICTY and local courts. Under the Rules of the Road, a case first had to be approved by the ICTY before an arrest warrant could be issued for the prosecution of a suspect in local courts. In total, "OTP staff reviewed 1,419 files, involving 4,985 suspects, and advised local prosecutors whether they had enough evidence to proceed. Approval was granted for the prosecution of 848 persons."[26] Files were given a "Standard Marking" from A to H, depending on whether the evidence provided was sufficient or additional investigation was required. An A ranking meant there was evidence sufficient to provide "reasonable grounds" for concluding that the persons named committed violations of international law.[27] A B ranking meant "insufficient evidence," and a C ranking meant "unable to determine sufficiency of evidence." Other rankings of D, E, F, or G were given for reasons not always related to the evidence.[28]

Even though the coordinating mechanisms were created soon after the war, the referral of cases faced numerous obstacles. In earlier years, while the Rules of the Road department existed, the ICTY's priorities were in the courtroom and not on

the Courts in BiH," <www.sudbih.gov.ba/files/docs/zakoni/en/BH_LAW_ON_TRANSFER_OF_CASES_-_Consolidated_text.pdf> (accessed June 10, 2009).

24 See Department I (Special Department for War Crimes), The Prosecutor's Office of Bosnia and Herzegovina, <www.tuzilastvobih.gov.ba/?opcija=sadrzaj&kat=2&id=4&jezik=e> (accessed July 20, 2009).

25 See Chris Hedges, "Jailed Serbs' 'Victims' Found Alive, Embarrassing Bosnia," *New York Times*, July 1, 1997.

26 ICTY, Working with the Region, Rules of the Road, <www.icty.org/sid/96#rules> (accessed July 10, 2009).

27 Briefing book, "Background and Introduction," Office of the Prosecutor of Bosnia and Herzegovina, document dated July 7, 2009. Copy on file with the author.

28 Ibid. See also OSCE, Human Rights Department, *War Crimes Trials before the Domestic Courts of Bosnia and Herzegovina: Progress and Obstacles*, OSCE Mission to Bosnia and Herzegovina, March 2005, 5, <www.oscebih.org/documents/1407-eng.pdf> (accessed June 10, 2009).

the localization of the process. Cases languished in file cabinets at The Hague as the court took three years to establish a formal review procedure.[29] Some prosecutors in Bosnia reported a response time of up to two years.[30] A number of people argued that the importance the ICTY placed on these cases was symbolized by their location in The Hague: in an annex outside of the Tribunal's main building.

ICTY interest in the referral of cases would, however, increase. In addition to fulfilling its obligation to review locally-initiated cases under the auspices of the Rome Agreement, the ICTY would eventually refer its own cases to Bosnia, as part of the court's completion strategy. These included both the so-called 11bis cases and instances where investigations had not yet led to an indictment. With the passage of UN Security Council resolutions making the closure of the ICTY imminent, the efficient referral of cases became a priority. UN Security Council Resolution 1503 of August 2003 endorsed the completion strategy of the ICTY and called upon the international community to "assist national jurisdictions, as part of the completion strategy, in improving their capacity to prosecute cases transferred from the ICTY."[31] Follow-up Resolution 1534, in March 2004, called on ICTY prosecutors to review which cases should be transferred to national jurisdictions, and to outline the measures taken and needed to fulfill the completion strategy.[32] The resolutions outlined the timeline for this strategy: the completion of investigations in 2004, first instance trials in 2008, and all work by 2010, dates which were eventually extended.

Around the time the ICTY started to focus institutional energy on referring its own cases, the process of reviewing locally initiated ones was handed over to Bosnian authorities. This responsibility was handed to local Bosnian authorities in 2004, finally "localizing" the process. The Prosecutor's Office of Bosnia and Herzegovina (PO BiH) was entrusted with the task of reviewing cases to determine which would go to the State Court and which to the lower courts. The State Court was to focus on the "highly sensitive" cases, with the entity courts handling the "sensitive" cases; these criteria, however, seemed imprecise to many prosecutors in the field.[33] The ICTY's process of certifying cases based on the Rules of the Road in support of these domestic goals, PO BiH representatives argued, did not mean these cases were ready to be prosecuted at the local level once certification was

[29] Laurel E. Fletcher and Harvey M. Weinstein, "A world unto itself? The application of international justice in the former Yugoslavia," in Eric Stover and Harvey M. Weinstein, eds., *My Neighbor, My Enemy: Justice and Community in the Aftermath of Mass Atrocity* (Cambridge: Cambridge University Press, 2004), 42.

[30] OSCE, *War Crimes Trials*, p. 5.

[31] UNSC Resolution 1503 (2003) (S/RES/1504, 28 August 2003), <www.un.org/Docs/sc/unsc_resolutions03.html> (accessed June 10, 2009).

[32] UNSC Resolution 1534 (2004) (S/RES/1534, 26 March 2004), <www.un.org/Docs/sc/unsc_resolutions04.html> (accessed June 10, 2009)

[33] Human Rights Watch (HRW), "Still Waiting: Bring Justice for War Crimes, Crimes against Humanity, and Genocide in Bosnia and Herzegovina's Cantonal and District Courts," July 2008, 10–15 <www.hrw.org/en/node/62137/section/1> (accessed June 25, 2009).

completed. This was not only because the cases were old, but also because most were incomplete.

Bosnia's War Crimes Chamber opened in March 2005. By the end of that year, the ICTY had referred two individuals to Bosnia for trial. Most of the cases waiting for referral at the ICTY had to do with crimes committed in Bosnia. The progress became so swift that, after less than a year of operation, the jail of the State Court had for a time 33 persons in cells awaiting trial for charges related to corruption and war crimes, thereby exceeding its capacity.[34] At the cantonal and district level, this problem became so severe that all new trials were temporarily halted.[35] The process had picked up much needed speed. By 2009, a total of six so-called rule 11bis cases had been referred to the State Court involving 10 defendants. The OSCE was tasked with monitoring these cases and produced a series of reports.[36]

The limits of judicial reform in the absence of comprehensive reform of the police (the last major institution to be targeted for integration at the state level) was illustrated in 2007, when convict Radovan Stanković escaped from a Foča prison cell, with what appeared to be the assistance of Republika Srpska police (although this was vehemently denied by RS authorities). Stanković initially had been a success story of the localization process. Indicted in The Hague for rape and enslavement, his was the first case referred to Sarajevo as part of the ICTY's completion strategy outlined under Rule 11bis.[37] He was convicted in the State Court and sentenced to 20 years in prison. Stanković was serving time in his hometown when he escaped on the way to a dentist's appointment.[38] The escape received a lot of news coverage, and while it represented a setback for the localization process, it also put the spotlight on the pressing issue of police reform and gave local reformers tangible evidence of how dire the situation could be in the absence of real change. In the context of events like this one, which affected public attitudes toward the court, State Court officials intensified their efforts to counter inaccurate reporting about it.

Unwanted Influences on the Diplomatic Front

Despite the fact that the effort to build the rule of law in Bosnia picked up speed five years after the war, around the same time, foreign donor nations sometimes worked at cross-purposes with their local efforts in Bosnia. Some interventions,

---

[34] "Bosnian War Crimes Trials Halt as Local Courts Swamped with Backlog Cases," *BBC Worldwide Monitoring*, January 30, 2006.

[35] Ibid.

[36] For background, see "Monitoring and Reporting on Rule 11bis cases," OSCE Mission to Bosnia and Herzegovina, <www.oscebih.org/human_rights/monitoring.asp?d=1> (accessed June 14, 2009).

[37] See "Court of Bosnia-Herzegovina renders first judgment in a case transferred by the Tribunal," Press Release, ICTY, November 14, 2006, <www.icty.org/sid/8681> (accessed June 14, 2009).

[38] For background, see "Stanković Still at Large," Balkan Investigative Reporting Network (BIRN), *Justice Report*, June 1, 2007, <www.bim.ba/en/65/10/3139/> (accessed June 15, 2009).

motivated by national interest, shaped Bosnians' attitudes toward the development of local capacity, even though the work of foreign prosecutors and diplomatic initiatives were entirely separate endeavors. Global developments also had
a concrete impact inside Bosnia, in ways that soured local attitudes. Most notably, U.S. priorities in Bosnia were affected by the policies formed in the aftermath
of the 9/11 attacks and the subsequent "war on terror." One episode stands out.
In January 2002, the United States transferred six Algerians, many of whom held
Bosnian passports, from Bosnia to Guantánamo Bay; they were accused of plot-
ting to bomb the U.S. and U.K. Embassies in Sarajevo, and of being affiliated with
the Al Qaeda network. Their transfer violated a ruling of Bosnia's Human Rights
Chamber that four of them could not be extradited; the move was vehemently
protested by both local and foreign human rights organizations.[39] The "Algerian
Six" case, as it came to be known, raised questions in the minds of many Bosnians
about the true desires of the United States to strengthen the rule of law in Bosnia,
as it was flagrantly willing to violate the decisions of the courts it was helping to
develop.[40] The opposition was vocal and forceful. During the transfer of the six
detainees, approximately 500 people, including their families, protested, fearing
the treatment they would receive in the American military prison.

The prisoners languished in Guantánamo for years. After a U.S. Supreme
Court decision affirming the principle of *habeas corpus* recognized the detainees' right to challenge their detention in federal court, the Algerian Six finally
had legal recourse. Five were ordered released, and three of those, Boudella al
Hajj, Mohammed Nechle, and Mustafa Ait Idr, returned to Sarajevo in December
2008.[41] The other two (Lakdar Boudmediene and Sabir Mahfouz Lahmar) did not
have Bosnian citizenship and could not be transferred to Bosnia. Sabir Mahfouz
Lahmar was transferred to France in November 2009. The sixth, Belkacem
Bensayah, remained in custody as of the end of 2009 because of evidence of his
ties to Al Qaeda. Lakhdar Boumediene was held in Guantánamo from January
2002 to May 2009, when he was released and transferred to France. The decision in
the case that carried his name, *Boumediene et al. v. Bush, President of the United
States, et al.*, set the stage for hundreds of similar filings.[42] Even if there had been
little public support for these and other foreign mujahedin who had entered the

[39] "Bosnia-Herzegovina: Unlawful Detention of Six Men from Bosnia-Herzegovina in
    Guantánamo Bay," press release, EUR 63/013/2003, May 30, 2003, Amnesty International,
    <web.amnesty.org/library/Index/ENGEUR630132003?open&of=ENG-2MD14>   (accessed
    June 10, 2009).
[40] Lara J. Nettelfield and Sarah Wagner, "For the Bosniaks, the U.S. Ideal is in Ruins," op-ed, *Los
    Angeles Times*, September 19, 2004.
[41] "Guantánamo Algerians back in Bosnia," ISN (International Relations and Security
    Network),   December   19,   2008,   <www.isn.ethz.ch/isn/Current-Affairs/Security-Watch/
    Detail/?ots591=4888CAA0-B3DB-1461-98B9-E20E7B9C13D4&lng=en&id=94887>   (accessed
    June 10, 2009). This article speculates that U.S. pressure may have had something to do with their
    return as well, despite the fact that local authorities still believed they constituted a threat.
[42] The Supreme Court's decision can be found here: <supremecourtus.gov/opinions/07pdf/06-
    1195.pdf> (accessed June 10, 2009).

country during the war, the U.S. flouting of local court decisions was a source of disappointment in Bosnia.[43]

In addition, the United States exerted influence in 2003 when it forced Bosnia to sign an Article 98 agreement exempting American soldiers in Bosnia from prosecution in the International Criminal Court.[44] Bosnia was more crucial than other Eastern European nations that had been strong-armed into signing the agreement, partly because it had more U.S. soldiers on its territory. Nevertheless, some political elites in Sarajevo felt that the Article 98 agreement was a small price to pay for continued U.S. involvement, especially in the face of the often-uneven engagement of the EU.[45] Given that the United States was one of the main funders of the efforts to reform the rule of law in Bosnia, this blatant interference with its developing judiciary did not serve the norms of universal accountability espoused by the ICTY and the donors themselves. Furthermore, foreigners in the country often got away with blatant violations of local laws. In Bosnia (and Kosovo), peacekeepers of all nationalities accused of visiting brothels staffed with trafficked women, and of other unlawful activity, were generally simply sent home without further punishment.[46]

Prosecutors sent by foreign governments, however, were aware of the global context but labored in Bosnia isolated from their counterparts in the embassies. They faced, and overcame, resistance at every step. The foreign policies of donor nations were far removed from the process of building a new institution – the State Court. There even was great protest at the choice of the building that would house the new court.

Opening the Doors of the State Court

The site chosen to house the State Court, the former Viktor Bubanj barracks, suffered legitimacy problems from the outset. The Bosnian Army had occupied the location during the war and Bosnian Serbs alleged that it was home to a camp in

[43] On the role of Al Qaeda in Bosnia, see Vlado Azinović, *Al Kai'da u Bosni i Hercegovini: Mit ili stvarna opasnost* (Al Qaeda in Bosnia and Herzegovina: Myth or present danger?) (Prague: Radio Slobodna Europa, 2007).

[44] For the government explanation, see "Open Letter from U.S. Ambassador to Bosnia and Herzegovina Clifford Bond on Article 98," *News Release*, U.S. Embassy Sarajevo, Office of Public Affairs, May 19, 2003, <sarajevo.usembassy.gov/press/2003/en/030519e0.htm> (accessed February 14, 2006).

[45] Discussion with Bosnian government employee, Sarajevo, September 10, 2004.

[46] There were many cases, but the firing of Kathy Bolkovac, an American police officer working for the IPTF in Bosnia, illustrated that the international community was not keen to investigate the problem. Bolkovac outlined the involvement of UN workers in the sex trade in Bosnia in a document for her superiors and was later fired for it. A British labor review board later found that she was dismissed unfairly. See Magin McKenna, "Sins of the Peacekeepers," *Sunday Herald*, June 30, 2002, <www.sundayherald.com/print25914%20> (accessed February 15, 2006).

which many Bosnian Serbs perished between 1992 and 1995.[47] This led to protests over the appropriateness of placing the court in this location. Former detainees and representatives of Serb victims were opposed to the site, seeing it as further evidence that the international community was not interested in the losses they had suffered.

An organization called the Union of Camp Detainees of Republika Srpska (Savez logoraša Republike Srpske) had petitioned unsuccessfully to place a commemorative plaque at the site. It then organized a ceremony at the barracks to commemorate Serbs killed there. In September 2003, several buses transported Bosnian Serbs to Sarajevo for the ceremony, the same day that former President Bill Clinton delivered the opening speech at the Srebrenica-Potočari Memorial in Eastern Bosnia for the victims of the Srebrenica genocide. Sarajevo-based *Dani* magazine sent a reporter to the Sarajevo ceremony and found that, in fact, many on the bus headed to Sarajevo had no connection whatsoever to the Viktor Bubanj barracks.[48] The plaque they hoped to place at the site claimed that close to 2,000 people had been "tortured, mistreated or killed" in the barracks. Human rights organizations offered to facilitate investigations of crimes committed there, and requested that the organization sponsoring the commemoration ceremony provide a list of names of those who perished, or other supporting documentation. Such a list was not forthcoming. State Court representatives later met with the heads of the association to hear their grievances.[49] While the Serb detainees' association had initially threatened to boycott the proceedings at the court, after their meetings with the court's President Meddžida Kreso, in February 2005, public protest waned. Court representatives tried to impart to the group that the court would be a place where the suffering of all parties would be addressed, and justice served.[50] As with other similar events, the protest was short-lived; this one had been timed to steal attention from the opening of the Srebrenica-Potočari Memorial. The issue disappeared from the Bosnian newspapers after the opening of the court, in part because representatives were able to convince the association, at least temporarily, that its work would address their grievances too.

Organized Crime, Economic Crime, and Corruption

The international push for local war crimes prosecutions was predated by efforts to fight corruption in the country; the development of capacity to fight corruption and organized crime affected those later efforts. For numerous reasons, the

---

[47] Snježana Mulić, "Predsjedničko izdavanje spomen-ploče" (Presidential issuance of memorial plaque), *Dani*, September 26, 2003.
[48] Ibid.
[49] The commemoration service followed a decision by the organization to erect a memorial at the site, <www.logorasi.rs.sr/> (accessed June 15, 2009).
[50] Refik Hodžić, e-mail message to author, March 1, 2006. Hodžić was a Spokesman for the State Court.

problem of corruption was given priority over war crimes by the international community. The first major initiative to tackle the issue was an Antifraud Unit within the Office of the High Representative, opened in 1998 at the recommendation of the Peace Implementation Council (PIC); it was tasked with investigating cases of economic crime, corruption, and money laundering. A front page *New York Times* article in 1999 reported that the Unit's investigations had uncovered theft of over 1 billion dollars of foreign aid money by public officials.[51] Even though this revelation turned out to be an exaggeration, it shocked both domestic political elites and internationals, and briefly called into question the efficacy of whole postwar intervention.

When the State Court opened in 2003 with eight judges, the Prosecutor's Office of Bosnia and Herzegovina had four prosecutors and one functioning department: the Department for Organized Crime, Economic Crime, and Corruption.[52] The Antifraud Unit, which predated the court, assisted with its cases. Some local observers argued that this extrajudicial investigatory body, set within the Office of the High Representative, inhibited the development of domestic institutions.

Distinct employment structures in the two main divisions of the Prosecutor's Office (the War Crimes Department and the Corruption Department), and the selection of cases chosen for trial, showed that different philosophies were at work in each division in the early years. The most apparent contrast was the reliance solely on foreign prosecutors in the Corruption Department, while the War Crimes Department had a mixed staff of foreign and local prosecutors, which presented a decidedly more "Bosnian face" to the community observing it.

The Corruption Department turned out a series of indictments involving some of the country's highest political elites. Prosecutors admitted that the volume of illicit activity in the country overwhelmed them, and that their small staff could not possibly keep up with it.[53] Until 2006, Canadian John McNair led the prosecution team in the Corruption Department, where he managed a group of mostly North American and Western European lawyers. His job was eventually turned over to Drew Engel, an American. Some of the court's personalities became local celebrities. During his tenure at the court, McNair, for example, appeared in Bosnia's papers almost daily.

The Department set out to tackle some of the country's biggest cases, many involving representatives of the nationalist parties. The indictments that flowed

51 Chris Hedges, "Leaders in Bosnia are Said to Steal Up to $1 Billion," *New York Times*, August 17, 1999. While Hedges grossly overstated the degree of corruption and was later temporarily suspended from reporting for the *New York Times* because of the article, it created momentum for change inside Bosnia, at least in the short term.

52 "U BiH zvanično otvoreni državni sud i kancelarija tužilastva" (State Court and Prosecutor's Office formally opened in Bosnia and Herzegovina), *Southeast European Times*, January 28, 2003, <www.setimes.com/cocoon/setimes/xhtml/sr_Latn/document/setimes/newsbriefs/2003/01/030128-WMI-00510> (accessed February 15, 2006).

53 Interview with foreign prosecutor working in Bosnia, Sarajevo, December 10, 2005.

out of their department targeted many highly-placed Bosnian elites, including one former member of the Presidency, Ante Jelavić. Jelavić, former president of the HDZ, the party of Croat nationalists, was indicted for "the purchase of shares in Hercegovačka Banka using the funds of the Ministry of Defense of the Federation BiH; the misappropriation of Ministry of Defense funds to purchase share capital in Hercegovina osiguranje (insurance); misuse of funds during the period December 1997–November 1998; releasing a mandate loan program without risk assessment and the assessment of the credibility of the requestor; the failure to pay pension and disability insurance or to file with the relevant agencies the required forms concerning the amounts that were due to be paid."[54] He was found guilty of abuse of office and sentenced to 10 years in prison. Jelavić's verdict was read while the accused was in absentia; 500,000 KM (approximately 256,000 euros) was placed in an account as bail. Jelavić, thought to have stolen much more than his bail amount, fled to Croatia upon hearing the verdict.[55] This was not Jelavić's first run-in with authorities. He had appeared in a Sarajevo court in 2001, shortly after being removed from the presidency, over his attempt to create an autonomous mini-state in the region of Herzegovina. More than 300 people had loudly demonstrated in his support, carrying banners that read, "The trial of Ante Jelavić is the trial of the Croat people."[56] In 2005, however, there were no supporters protesting in his favor. Bosnians were starting to become aware that many nationalist representatives, of all parties, worked for their own interests and not for the interest of their members, lining their pockets with tax and foreign aid dollars. The persistence of this disenchantment was evident in local survey data. When asked, "Which party's political views are closest to your own?" almost 60 percent of respondents in one survey answered, "none."[57]

Dynamics in the State Court reflected the difficulties of combining local and international forces. There were differing opinions about whether the problem was due to stressful relations between locals and foreigners or to the challenges of understanding and implementing the new laws. One prosecutor argued that local judges and prosecutors, while arguing publicly that foreigners were needed to kick-start sensitive local prosecutions in the country, created obstacles for them in the courtroom. "I've never seen so much due process in my whole career [in my home country]," one commented. "At a time when 'hanging judges' are needed in Bosnia, many things get turned over on the slightest technicalities."[58] This prosecutor attributed this enthusiasm for overturning the work of foreign prosecutors at the appellate level partly to the desire of local judges not to be shown how to do

54 "Sarajevo: Ante Jelavić Found Guilty in 'Hercegovačka Banka' Case and Sentenced to Ten Years of Imprisonment," *Federation News Agency*, October 6, 2005.
55 "Croat Leader Flees from Herzegovina to Croatia," *RFE/RL Newsline*, October 12, 2005.
56 Alix Kroeger, "Former Bosnian Croat Leader in Court," *BBC News*, August 29, 2001.
57 United Nations Development Programme, *Early Warning System Quarterly Report: April–June 2005* (UNDP, 2005), 79.
58 Interview with foreign prosecutor, December 10, 2005.

their job in their own country. That was by no means a universally held opinion. Other prosecutors pointed out that things moved quickly at the State Court when compared to similar trials in the domestic courts of developed democracies. Still, there were difficulties in interpreting the new Bosnian codes, which combined elements of common law, civil law, U.S. law, Western European law, and Yugoslav law. International and local lawyers combined their different legal experiences to interpret this new hybrid code together.[59]

In addition, some observers felt that criminals in the country were being treated lightly, in part due to the lack of police reform and the manner in which international observers treated the existing forces. The EU advised on police reform inside Bosnia and had an observer mission, the EU Police Mission (EUPM). Many argued that European policing styles, emphasizing the rights of the accused and a lack of the use of force, were enabling criminals to slip through the cracks. Admittedly, it was difficult for foreign nationals working in the country to strike an effective balance and still maintain the appearance of conducting a benevolent intervention.

Pursuing those entrenched in illicit activity carried real risks that further slowed the development of local capacity: it was clear that security conditions were questionable for local prosecutors if they wished to take on certain individuals. Some of the foreign prosecutors in Bosnia were given 24-hour security details after credible threats to their well-being were received. Some were even forced to move onto NATO's base in the Sarajevo suburbs due to the severity of threats uncovered by local and foreign intelligence. Even if most criminals were slipping through the cracks, some of the country's most powerful individuals stood to lose a lot if they were targeted, and responded in kind.

Apart from investigating the private fortunes amassed at the public's expense, the work of the Corruption Department revealed the complexities of prosecutions in post-Dayton Bosnia. Because the peace agreement left wartime powers in place, individuals targeted for prosecution were often close associates of those running the country or others who gained wealth or power in the wartime years. This had the effect of weakening domestic support in some powerful circles for the whole endeavor. The clearest example was seen when rumors emerged in the Bosnian press that the Prosecutor's Office and State Investigation and Protection Agency (SIPA) was conducting preliminary investigations for corruption against RS Prime Minister Milorad Dodik and other RS officials. Dodik responded with an all-out campaign against the court, in which he challenged its legitimacy – a strategy also used by many indictees at the ICTY.[60]

---

[59] Jonathan Schmidt, prosecutor with the Prosecutor's Office of Bosnia and Herzegovina in the trial of Abduladhim Maktouf, e-mail to the author, July 15, 2009.

[60] See Srećko Latal, "Bosnian Serb Leader Criticises State Judiciary," BIRN, *Balkan Insight*, May 13, 2009, <balkaninsight.com/en/main/news/18832/> (accessed June 12, 2009).

The First War Crimes Trial

The first war crimes case prosecuted in the State Court broached an issue that the ICTY was only beginning to address: the role of foreign mujahedin in the country who had fought for the Bosnian government, and the war crimes many had committed. The court's first indictment was of an individual born outside of Bosnia, a fact that enabled it to start war crimes prosecutions in the country while not invoking the ire of any one of the country's constituent groups. The prosecution was organized under the auspices of the Department of Organized Crime, Economic Crime, and Corruption instead of taking place in the War Crimes Department, as might have been expected. Abduladhim Maktouf, an Iraqi national also holding a Bosnian passport, was the first individual to be charged with war crimes at the new state-level court.[61] He was a member of Army of the Republic of Bosnia and Herzegovina (ARBiH) and its Al Mujahid Unit, the army's home for the foreign mujahedin fighters who entered the country. Maktouf was originally arrested on charges of tax evasion and forgery, but later, based on new information, the prosecution broadened its investigation to include war crimes.

Ultimately, Maktouf was convicted of the kidnapping of one Serb and four Croat civilians, whom he took to the Al Mujahid camp in Orašac; there, one of the abducted was beheaded. Proven to have transported the victims, Maktouf was sentenced to five years in a Bosnian prison; the conviction was upheld on appeal.[62] The court may use confirmed facts adjudicated at the ICTY in domestic cases. The Maktouf decision cited the Kordić and Blaškić cases at the ICTY to establish that an international conflict occurred in Central Bosnia during the time in question.[63]

Even if Maktouf was a relatively low-level perpetrator, his case enabled the Prosecutor's Office to address numerous issues awaiting it in Bosnia: how to work with the ICTY, deal with evidence, frame charges, and generally interpret the new legal system.[64] It is worth noting that both the State Court and the ICTY started with prosecutions of relatively low-level perpetrators. In both cases, it was not part of an overall strategy; prosecutors first tried the cases for which defendants were most accessible, sometimes referred to as the "low hanging fruit." At the ICTY, the first defendant, Duško Tadić, a former café owner from Kozarac, a small town near

---

[61] See the amended indictment Ref. no. KT/H/1/04, *Prosecutor vs. Abduladhim Maktouf*, <www.sudbih.gov.ba/files/docs/optuznice//maktouf_amended_eng.pdf> (accessed June 12, 2009). NB: As noted in Chapter 3, ICTY documents transliterate *Al Mujahid* as *El Mujahed*.

[62] See "Maktouf story," *Izvor*, Center za istraživačko novinarstvo (CIN) (Center for Investigative Reporting), July 1, 2005, <www.cin.ba/Stories/P3_Reconciliation/?cid=218,1,1> (accessed June 25, 2009).

[63] Court of Bosnia and Herzegovina, First Instance Decision, Case No. K-127/04, July 1, 2005, <www.sudbih.gov.ba/files/docs/presude/2005/Maktouf_ENG_K_127_04.pdf> (accessed June 25, 2009).

[64] Jonathan Schmidt, prosecutor with Prosecutor's Office of Bosnia and Herzegovina in the trial of Abduladhim Maktouf, e-mail to the author, July 15, 2009. Peter Kidd, however, was the prosecutor at the appellate level.

Prijedor, had played only a small role in the crimes committed there. After both initial cases, however, there was optimism that arrests of more significant offenders would follow. "The prosecution is going after a little fish because it knows that a big fish will come out," commented Slobodan Kovač, Bosnian Minister of Justice, and a former prosecutor.[65] Unlike in The Hague, Bosnia's War Crimes Chamber wasted little time testing that assumption, quickly filling its cells to capacity.

Furthermore, the Maktouf case brought important legal issues to the fore in Bosnia. His five-year sentence was upheld at the appellate level. He later filed a case in Bosnia's Constitutional Court, arguing that the application of the Bosnia's new Criminal Code, instead of the criminal code of the Socialist Federal Republic of Yugoslavia (SFRY), violated his rights outlined in the Constitution of Bosnia and Herzegovina and in the European Convention for the Protection of Human Rights and Fundamental Freedoms. He also argued that the presence of international judges breached "the impartiality of the court."[66] The Constitutional Court ruled that the appeal could be heard, but then dismissed all counts as unfounded.[67] However, the court found that the application of different criminal codes undermined the rule of law in the country. There are five criminal codes currently being applied in Bosnia: the old Criminal Code of the SFRY, the Criminal Code of the two entities, the Brčko Criminal Code (covering the district of Brčko), and the Bosnian Criminal Code adopted at the state level and currently used at the State Court.[68] The issue was not entirely resolved with the decision, as the old codes continued to be applied.[69] This was significant because the Supreme Courts at the entity level had ruled differently on whether the nature of an armed conflict must be established before violations of international humanitarian law could be addressed.[70]

In January and September 2007, the State Court faced hunger strikes by 22 and 25 detainees, respectively, who demanded to be tried under the old criminal code, which had lesser maximum sentences.[71] The second hunger strike ended when

---

[65] "Maktouf story."

[66] Decision of Constitutional Court of Bosnia and Herzegovina, Case No. 1785/06, March 30, 2007, <www.ccbh.ba> (accessed June 25, 2009). One judge drafted a dissenting opinion.

[67] Ibid.

[68] Iva Vukušić, Analyst, Special War Crimes Department, Prosecutor's Office of Bosnia and Herzegovina, unpublished conference paper for the International Graduate Legal Research Conference, King's College London, School of Law, July 2–3, 2009. Copy on file with the author.

[69] The OSCE argued for a court at the national level that would harmonize case law. See "Moving Toward a Harmonization of the Law Applicable in War Crimes Cases before Courts in Bosnia and Herzegovina," OSCE Mission to Bosnia and Herzegovina, August 2008. Copy on file with the author.

[70] Ibid., 10–11.

[71] Registry Annual Report, Special Departments for War Crimes and For Organised Crime, Economic Crime and Corruption of the Prosecutor's Office of Bosnia and Herzegovina, 2007, 18; "Hunger strike halts Bosnian war crimes court," *Reuters*, January 10, 2007, <www.alertnet.org/thenews/newsdesk/L10358717.htm> (accessed June 15, 2009).

detainees were transferred to other detention facilities and eventually agreed to participate in court proceedings.[72]

Material from the Maktouf case was almost used at the ICTY, as well. The prosecution team in the case against Enver Hadžihasanović and Amir Kubura filed a motion to reopen the case because of new materials discovered, a request which included two documents about Maktouf. The trial chamber noted, "The Prosecution submits that the full relevance of Abduladhim Maktouf to these proceedings became clear only after the close of its case when he was indicted by the State Court of Bosnia and Herzegovina."[73] Ultimately, however, the trial chamber found that the prosecution had not exercised due diligence and rejected the motion.

Building the War Crimes Chamber

High Representative Wolfgang Petritsch had initiated the project for a War Crimes Chamber in 2001; the effort was bolstered along the way by cooperation between the OHR and ICTY, but Bosnian authorities were late to join in.[74] The OHR initially entrusted the creation of the War Crimes Chamber to a French diplomat with no legal experience. The idea languished under his leadership and when he was sent back to Paris, many in the legal community in Bosnia were relieved. The arrival in June 2004 of Michael Johnson, former head of Prosecutions at the ICTY, marked a real beginning for the Chamber. He spearheaded the mapping out of the institutional structure of a soon-to-be-created registry for the State Court. There were nine working groups on the War Crimes Chamber, with concentrations ranging from the actual building itself to procedural issues. Members of the Court Management System met with ICTY staff early in the process to discuss all aspects of management and to assure cooperation between the two bodies.[75] By the fall of 2004, the Bosnian parliament, after some foot-dragging, passed the package of laws necessary to create the War Crimes Chamber. The courtrooms had advanced design, complete with video conferencing links to enable testimony from remote locations. The stage had been set.

The War Crimes Chamber was an expensive undertaking by Bosnian standards, but amounted to just a fraction of the cost of justice in The Hague.[76] Between 2004 and 2009, donors had pledged just over 45 million euros to set up the Court, of

---

[72] Ibid., 19.
[73] See *Prosecutor v. Enver Hadžihasanović and Amir Kubura* (IT 01-47-T), Decision Regarding the Prosecution's Application to Re-Open its Case, Trial Chamber II, ICTY, June 1, 2005.
[74] Refik Hodžić, comments at "Pathways to Reconciliation and Global Human Rights, " Sarajevo, August 17, 2005, author's notes. Hodžić was a Spokesman for the State Court.
[75] War Crimes Chamber Project, Project Implementation Plan Registry Progress Report, Office of the High Representative, October 20, 2004, 16. Copy on file with the author.
[76] Court of Bosnia and Herzegovina, Registry Annual Report 2007, 93. Copy on file with the author.

which almost 38 million had been received.[77] International judges and prosecutors meant that initial operating costs would be higher than in future years, but these costs were often exaggerated by opponents of the court. The court's Registry reported that an average first-instance judgment in the War Crimes section cost 650,000 euros, but was forecast to decline more than 200,000 euros in 2008, in part due to declining labor costs.[78] However, some close to the process argued that these figures were unreliable and meaningless.

Observers in and outside the country watched developments in the local judiciary carefully. The foreign presence brought with it foreign journalists, analysts, and academics. Many of their analyses of developments inside Bosnia, amid the slow pace of overall reform, failed to see real progress in the courts when it in fact existed. As had happened with the ICTY, outsiders who underestimated the challenges of institution building in a transitional environment implicitly compared the situation to an ideal in which the hand-off from international to local prosecutions was seamless. This often created an extra obstacle for the architects of judicial reform; they had to defend themselves from those making somewhat unreasonable criticism, or who simply failed to appreciate real accomplishments.

The problem of how to measure progress and impact, and what yardstick to use, was illustrated in a series of articles about justice in Bosnia by the Center for Investigative Reporting.[79] Published just at the point when the War Crimes Chamber was finally getting off the ground, the series was highly critical of the State Court and the limited progress made in the transitions to local trials. However, while the planned opening was about six months behind schedule, viewed in another light, the project coordinators had accomplished a lot in an unfavorable environment in a very short amount of time – once the political will existed and the right combination of personnel was found. Similarly, advocacy groups, notably HRW, wrote a series of reports documenting the shortcomings of local prosecutions. Titles such as "Still Waiting" and "Narrowing the Impunity Gap" revealed their positions.[80]

Research by advocacy organizations outlined the failings of the court, all of which were already well known to individuals inside the court. They gave the stamp of independent authority and boosted the credibility of Court and Prosecutor's Office

---

[77] Ibid., 92.
[78] Ibid., 122.
[79] The series is available online at the Center for Investigative Reporting, <www.cin.ba/Reports/1/?cid=235,1,1> (accessed June 13, 2009).
[80] "A Chance for Justice: War Crimes Prosecutions in Bosnia's Serb Republic," Human Rights Watch, 2006; "Narrowing the Impunity Gap: Trials Before Bosnia's War Crimes Chamber," Human Rights Watch, February 2007; "Still Waiting: Bringing Justice for War Crimes, Crimes against Humanity and Genocide in Bosnia and Herzegovina's Cantonal and District Courts," Human Rights Watch, July 2008. UNDP printed a short report titled, "Solving War Crimes Cases in Bosnia and Herzegovina: Report on the Capacities of Courts and Prosecutor Offices' within Bosnia and Herzegovina to Investigate, Prosecute and Try War Crimes Cases," but with a print run of 500 it reached only a small audience.

employees' requests for specific resources. To the public, however, they sometimes created the perception that progress was nonexistent, especially in an environment with no real benchmarks. Advocacy groups and investigative reporters, like family associations (although in different ways), made comparisons to ideal worlds and pointed out the differences between ideals and what was happening on a given day. Both family association and advocacy groups often failed to realize that there would often be protracted discussions about what to admit in court, for example.[81] A general lack of understanding about how the judicial system works contributed to associations' sense of disappointment with the pace of prosecutions.

That is not to say this research was unimportant. All of these reports made valid points about local developments, but the context of these implicit comparisons to the ideal affected views of real developments within Bosnia. As with the ICTY, there were no scholarly or practical road maps to which to compare developments. The rules were being made up as they went along. Criticism fueled conventional wisdom about the futility of criminal trials.

The localization of war crimes prosecutions in Bosnia was slow in the early years, but the problem was political, not legal. As soon as the political will to tackle the issue of the rule of law existed in the international community, legal professionals worked rapidly, building institutions, forming working groups, and conducting investigations. By 2009, there was a plan in place that would facilitate the processing of these cases. The institutional building blocks had been set. The localization of war crimes prosecutions was a domestic initiative, but the body of knowledge created at the ICTY aided the process. The local architects of the process adapted mechanisms so they could best utilize the evidence and jurisprudence developed in The Hague. Soon the ICTY would begin to cite local decisions, showing that the flow of information went both ways between Sarajevo and The Hague.

Learning from ICTY: Outreach

The State Court integrated several important lessons from the shortcomings of the ICTY, notably the importance of outreach. In contrast to The Hague, outreach was part of the court's operating budget from day one. Court officials made an early effort to detail its purpose and mission to civil society groups, explaining what they could and could not expect from it. Also, soon after the court opened its doors, a round table for these groups was organized to describe the court's role in the overall process. Public Affairs coordinators set out a plan to train local NGOs to do some outreach for the court in smaller communities where these organizations could serve as intermediaries.[82] However, the Court Support Network, as

---

[81] Interview with Iva Vukušić, Analyst, Special War Crimes Department, Prosecutor's Office of Bosnia and Herzegovina, Sarajevo, July 14, 2008.

[82] The High Judicial and Prosecutorial Council (HJPC) also realized the importance of outreach; it created a staff position for a public relations officer.

the project was called, lost its financial support from the court's registry at one point, illustrating that outreach efforts would still need to wage internal battles for limited resources.[83] A series of public service announcements created awareness about the War Crimes Chamber. It was sorely needed. One survey showed that 72 percent of Bosnians were still not familiar with the institution several months after it had opened.[84] Over time, however, attitudes changed drastically. Another survey, conducted in 2008, found that 40.2 percent of respondents said they were somewhat informed about the work of the court, followed by 39.3 percent who said they had a little information, while 6.3 percent said they knew a lot about it.[85]

Media capacity to cover local trials increased as well. The Institute for War and Peace Reporting (IWPR), founded in 1991, which began its activity in the countries of the former Yugoslavia, gave way to the development of BIRN, the Balkan Investigative Reporting Network. IWPR placed its reports on the web and distributed them to email lists free of charge, and BIRN kept this distribution model. Local publications in the region were welcome to run these stories for free, with attribution. BIRN is an entirely regional publication with over 10 staff members in Bosnia.[86]

BIRN's engagement with the State Court started early. It trained both media and civil society, mindful that each group had separate needs. From March to September 2005, BIRN held intensive trainings for the journalists and editors of 13 media outlets in both entities in an effort to develop beat reporters focused on legal issues.[87] Having attended the many one-off seminars in postwar Bosnia, organizers realized that effective training would require a sustained interest and follow-up. The financial reality of Bosnia's press corps, however, meant that many reporters did not have the luxury of covering one event in depth. Journalists had to file multiple stories every working day, which precluded following a trial in its entirety. In response to this problem, in January 2006, BIRN launched its *Justice Report* initiative, staffed with five reporters and one editor. Reporters were dedicated to one trial and their reports were sent directly to family associations; articles were archived on the web. BIRN also supported the creation of a court reporters' association.[88]

The State Court had 150 reporters accredited by late 2005, after the War Crimes Chamber had been operational for little more than half a year. The difference between international and domestic trials had already been made visible in earlier

[83] Refik Hodžić, e-mail to the author, March 1, 2006.
[84] "CIN survey," *Izvor*, Center za istraživačko novinarstvo (CIN) (Center for Investigative Reporting), June 23, 2005, <www.cin.ba/Stories/P3_Reconciliation/?cid=201,1,1> (accessed June 25, 2009).
[85] "Public Perceptions of the Work of the Court and the Prosecutor's Office of BiH," Final Report, Prism Research, July 23, 2008, pp. 43–44. Copy on file with the author.
[86] IWPR continued to exist in the region, but with a reduced staff and presence.
[87] Interview with Nerma Jelačić, former Country Director, Balkan Investigative Reporting Network (BIRN), December 12, 2005.
[88] Ibid.

reporting on the Maktouf case. Journalists often stopped by the court every day and news articles appeared in the papers the day after a trial session. The reporting reflected knowledge of the indictment, the content of testimony, and its significance to the overall proceedings. While the coverage was still not as analytic as some would have hoped, it was an improvement over many reports filed from The Hague. Local trials were also much easier for the Bosnian public to follow and enabled more communication with the various parties to the proceedings. BIRN journalists in Sarajevo reported receiving letters in their office which were addressed to the indictees of State Court trials. The authors outlined their feelings, opinions, and recollections of the events in question at the court.[89] At the BIRN web site, citizens posted commentary about ongoing developments. The State Court's web site also featured daily updates of the court schedule, information much more up to date than the web sites of the courts of many Western nations. The staff of the State Court's Public Information and Outreach office could respond to requests quickly; for example, some courtroom audio recordings from a trial taking place were produced within a week after a request.[90] Other journalists, however, reported having less positive experiences with the office.[91]

Still, there was not a massive public presence in the courtrooms of the State Court. On most days, BIRN journalists were the only constant visitors, along with OSCE monitors who were tasked with following the trials.[92] Day in and day out, BIRN reporters sat in the courtroom taking notes in generally empty galleries and producing summaries of the day's events. Often there were more foreign researchers than local citizens. BIRN reporters even filed a story arguing that Bosnians were bored by war crimes trials.[93] The exception was when a big verdict was expected. In one way, this could be seen as some evidence of success: war crimes and their prosecution had become normalized in a country in which trials had previously ignited passions along nationalist lines. Experts, however, warned of the dangers of society's lack of familiarity with the facts discussed in the trials. Harvard University's András Riedlmayer, a frequent ICTY witness, argued, "The public is not much oriented towards accepting the facts. It is often not very well informed in the beginning. Many are not even interested in learning about the facts, which may interfere with their prejudices and what they think they know

[89] Interview with Nidžara Ahmetašević, Country Director, BIRN, Sarajevo, July 21, 2008.
[90] The request was filed with the Court of Bosnia and Herzegovina by Nidžara Ahmetašević of BIRN and the author on July 22, 2008; the court made the materials requested available on July 28, 2008.
[91] "Public Perceptions of the Work of the Court," 20.
[92] Author's field notes from court sessions, Sarajevo, June–August 2008.
[93] Aida Alić, "War-Crime Trials 'Bore' Public in Bosnia," BIRN, *Justice Report*, February 26, 2009, <www.bim.ba/en/155/10/17022/> (accessed June 25, 2009). Still, State Court President Meddžida Kreso reported that during the first eight months of 2009, 1000 people and representatives of over 30 organizations had visited the court. Meddžida Kreso, comments, BIRN Regional Conference on the Transparency of Courts and Responsibility of Media, Sarajevo, September 1, 2009. Author's notes.

about the war."[94] Yet lack of presence did not necessarily mean lack of interest, as many citizens followed developments in the press.

The Entity Courts

With the State Court to try only "very sensitive" cases, most of the war crimes trials were left to cantonal courts in the Federation, district courts in Republika Srpska, and the Basic Court in Brčko.[95] In the spring of 2005, the OSCE, having followed developments in the judiciary since 1996, outlined progress in a detailed report: between 1996 and January 2005, when the War Crimes Chamber came into existence, 54 category A cases, involving 94 defendants, had reached the trial phase.[96] In 2004, there was a drastic increase in activity in the Federation courts relating to war crimes, and fifteen trials had reached first instance verdicts.[97] Between 1996 and 2004, the Rules of the Road Unit had received files pertaining to 5,789 persons suspected of war crimes and assigned categories to 3,489 of these before referring them back to local courts.[98] These numbers were misleading, though, as they included many duplicates and therefore overestimated the numbers of potential suspects in the country. In fact, in later years, prosecutors would make it clear that most of the reported numbers of potential cases and suspects were wildly inaccurate.

Numerous research reports based on interviews with prosecutors, judges, and court employees all over the country, revealed very different capacities to carry out court work.[99] Staff shortages, including a lack of trained investigators, in addition to basic material conditions, inhibited progress. Some offices were closed in the winter due to a lack of heat. Others lacked basic offices supplies. Many were ill equipped to conduct the investigations required in complex war crimes trials. The reform to the system meant that prosecutors had to manage many different aspects of cases, often without staff to assist them. Furthermore, prosecutors themselves were being asked to perform multiple roles, working in many different areas of the law, from misdemeanors to violations of international humanitarian law.[100]

It was reasonable to be cautiously optimistic about the progress made in the Federation, but in Republika Srpska, the situation was dire in the early years. By January 2005, only two local trials had been started in RS. The international

---

[94] Alić, "War-Crime Trials ..."
[95] Brčko is a district in Bosnia that belongs to both entities. It was established after an arbitration process conducted by the High Representative.
[96] OSCE, *War Crimes Trials*, 6.
[97] Ibid., 6.
[98] Ibid.
[99] Ibid.
[100] Interview with David Schwendiman, Deputy Chief Prosecutor and Head of the Special Department for War Crimes, Prosecutor's Office of Bosnia and Herzegovina, Sarajevo, July 28, 2008.

community had high hopes that the first trial in Bosnia's smaller entity would produce the first war crimes convictions. Ranko Jakovljević and ten other RS police officers had been arrested in 2002 and charged with detaining Catholic priest Tomislav Matanović and his family for over a month in 1995. Returnees in the Prijedor municipality found the bodies of Matanović and his parents in a well in September 2001. The case had a long history in local institutions. In 1997, the Ombudsman for Bosnia-Herzegovina had filed a submission to Bosnia's Human Rights Chamber on behalf of the family, charging violations of their rights under Article 5 of the European Convention on Human Rights and Freedoms.[101] The Chamber ruled in favor of the family, ordering RS authorities to investigate their disappearances. RS authorities claimed that the family had left the country of their own accord; from 1997 to 2000, they took no action.[102] At the urging of the OHR, the investigative team was changed and put under the supervision of the International Police Task Force (IPTF).[103] Suspects in the disappearance were found among the police officers that the IPTF had refused to recertify, and a Banja Luka court charged them under the SFRY criminal code. In February 2005, after a ten month trial, all eleven were acquitted. This raised fears that the RS judiciary would never be capable of trying ethnic Serbs for crimes committed against non-Serbs.[104] Impetus for a new trial had been assisted by attention from Amnesty International, but in this case even their prodding could not overcome the reality in RS and its judiciary.

However, the same year saw the first conviction in an RS court for war crimes committed against Bosniaks; it was announced in November 2005, almost 10 years after the end of the war. Three Bosnian Serbs were found guilty of crimes committed against Bosniaks in a Banja Luka court. The initial indictment had not charged the men with war crimes, but with murder (there is no obligation to try violations of international humanitarian law as war crimes per se; prosecutors are free to try defendants on charges of murder, rape, theft, etc., as set out in the code).[105] Civil society activists closely watched the proceedings and protested the initial charges.

[101] "Bosnia-Herzegovina: The 'Disappeared' Father Tomislav Matanović and His Parents, Josip and Božena Matanović," press release, Amnesty International, EUR 63/006/2002, February 1, 2002, <www.amnesty.org/en/library/asset/EUR63/006/2002/en/dom-EUR630062002en.html> (accessed June 24, 2009).
[102] Ibid.
[103] Ibid.
[104] "Banja Luka: 11 Prijedor Police Officers Acquitted," *Federation News Agency*, February 11, 2005. The RDC, Humanitarian Law Center, and other partner organizations later complained about the judgment stating that the Matanović family had not received justice. See "Prvo suđenje za ratni zločin u Republici Srpskoj" (First judgment for war crimes in Republika Srpska), Humanitarian Law Center, no date, <www.hlc-rdc.org/PravdaIReforma/Sudjenje-za-ratne-zlocine/SudjenjaZaRatne-Nacionalna-sudjenja-za-ratne-zlocine/Sudjenje-za-ratne-nacionalna-BiH/152.sr.html> (accessed June 25, 2009).
[105] A similar event occurred in Canada. A Canadian of Serb descent who had fought with the Bosnian Serbs during the war had taken UN peacekeepers hostage in May 1995; he was charged only with kidnapping and not with violations of the Geneva Conventions, disappointing

The Sarajevo-based Research and Documentation Center (RDC), typically not an advocacy organization, held a press conference in which they argued to have the indictment changed to include war crimes.[106] RS prosecutors refused at first, but later made the change.

This first war crimes conviction was a small step for the judiciary in RS. The next convictions to come out of Banja Luka and other local courts would illustrate that the public could accept war crimes prosecutions, if not welcome them: there were no public outcries or demonstrations against the court, as some had expected. The public in RS was growing used to the subject of war crimes and accountability, even if many felt the justice meted out to Serb victims was insignificant. Bosniak victims, unsurprisingly, were unmoved by this first decision; they had been waiting on RS courts for a decade. But the slow wheels of justice had started turning inside the entity, with hundreds of cases waiting, and likely more to come. Still there was the looming problem of the will to try cases and ICTY officials reported that they received few calls from RS prosecutors for assistance.[107]

The Missing Links: Regional Cooperation, Harmonization, and Resources

Successful local war crimes prosecutions in Bosnia required extensive regional cooperation. Evidence, witnesses, and suspects were often found in neighboring territories of Southeastern Europe. Many had gone to the United States or to locations throughout Europe, making them difficult to find. Some new cases even addressed crimes committed on foreign soil. Victims began to travel to attend these trials, increasingly accessible by bus, train, or car. When the Belgrade District Court's War Crimes Chamber began the trial for five members of the Scorpions Unit of the Serbian Ministry of Interior, Srebrenica victims, sponsored by the Belgrade-based Humanitarian Law Center (HLC), traveled to observe the proceedings. The HLC also provided the families with legal representation.[108] This flow of victims and information swelled throughout the years that followed.

Legal professionals knew that cross-border networks were integral to their efforts. In a poll conducted by the University of Sarajevo's Human Rights Center

the victims. See Derek Puddicombe, "Hostage-Taker Jailed 3 Years; Canuck Detained UN Observers in War," *The Ottawa Sun*, September 16, 2005.

[106] "Prve presude za ratne zločine u Republici Srpskoj" (First war crimes verdict in Republika Srpska), press release, Research and Documentation Center, November 17, 2005, <www.idc.org.ba/onama/presude.html> (accessed June 25, 2009).

[107] "Still Waiting: Bringing Justice for War Crimes, Crimes against Humanity and Genocide in Bosnia and Herzegovina's Cantonal and District Courts," Human Rights Watch, July 9, 2008.

[108] "The Humanitarian Law Center Attorneys will represent the families of killed people from Srebrenica," press release, Humanitarian Law Center, October 12, 2005, <www.hlc.org.yu/english/Facing_The_Past/Press_Releases/index.php?file=1269.html> (accessed February 15, 2006).

and UNDP in 2004, 72 percent of the region's judges and prosecutors in Dubrovnik for a seminar on war crimes responded positively to the statement that local war crimes trials necessitate regional judicial cooperation.[109] There were, however, considerable obstacles to communication, as the judiciaries in the region were developing at different paces. Prosecutors all over the region, depending on where they were located, as in Bosnia, had vastly different resources available to them. In some places, they lacked basic things like computers and office supplies, let alone effective measures to protect sensitive information. Urged on by their superiors and the international community, members of the court made do, and attended numerous training events to become more familiar with their new roles as independent forces in the emerging justice system.

Beyond these functional obstacles, those in the judiciary were also keenly aware that the effective administration of justice was contingent upon political developments in the region. Of the process, a judge in one of Bosnia's cantonal courts told his colleagues:

At the end, when those rules are established, we will enter into court proceedings, because on the one [hand] we are forced to, and on the other [hand] because we want to. What is of extreme importance to emphasize is that it cannot be without politics. Thus, we professionals keep talking about the segments related to the craftsmanship part and the necessary preparation of such administration of justice. And I wanted to make an appeal, having the subjects we are talking about in my mind, that regardless of what is agreed, international cooperation may only continue with political agreements, interstate agreements. The experts must [provide] the minimum that is indispensable, so that a witness from Belgrade could be brought to a court in Sarajevo ... and then [to a] trial in Zagreb.[110]

Successful cooperation requires a network of professionals who trust each other, willing to exchange information and experience. There was substantial progress yet to be made on this front. Only just over 30 percent of the group polled in Dubrovnik said that they had both contacts and significant cooperation with their colleagues in neighboring states.[111] But the trials had just begun. As time passed, cooperation slowly increased. Video links enabled testimony from neighboring cities and countries to be aired in court. Politics, though, proved to be a constant problem. The lack of extradition agreements among the countries in the region inhibited the pace of trials and remained an obstacle to regional cooperation. For

[109] "In the Shadow of a Common Legacy: Conditions and possibilities for regional cooperation on prosecution of war crimes in Bosnia and Herzegovina, Croatia, and Serbia and Montenegro," survey report presented at the seminar "Crimes of War and Legal Legacy," Human Rights Center, University of Sarajevo and UNDP, 2005. The survey was administered in Dubrovnik, Croatia, September 2–5, 2004; copy on file with the author. Thirty-five respondents completed the survey.
[110] Ibid.
[111] Ibid.

example, when Croatian member of Parliament Branimir Glavaš was convicted of war crimes in 2009 at the first instance, he fled to Bosnia and the State Court refused to send him back to Croatia, citing a domestic law that prohibits the extradition of a Bosnian national.[112] (He held both Croatian and Bosnian citizenship.)

Searching for a Strategy

The fact that war crimes prosecutions were split between the State Court and local courts raised the issue of the priorities for prosecution at all levels and the need for the harmonization of the various criminal codes.[113] The question loomed about how to process the remaining caseload effectively. Previously, case selection criteria had been ad hoc and overarching principles nonexistent. The State Court was tasked with trying the "highly sensitive" cases, with the entity-levels court responsible for the "sensitive" ones. Even those involved in the process thought this criterion was vague.[114]

A complete and comprehensive strategy was a long time in the making. In July 2007, following a decision by the Council of Ministers, a Working Group was set up with the task to draft a plan for processing the backlog of cases.[115] The group proceeded in fits and starts, and in the summer of 2008, journalists reported having received multiple drafts of the "strategy" paper.[116] The various documents were eventually merged into one.

Among the reasons given for the necessity of a strategy were: 1) the existence of a large number of unresolved war crimes cases; 2) the lack of an exact number of existing and open cases; 3) the lack of a unified practice in the court with respect to those cases; and 4) the existence of missing data about the management of cases after the adoption of the new criminal code.[117] In short, there were numbers everywhere but no one was quite sure how many cases there were, exactly where they were, or how difficult the task of investigating them all would be. The strategy prompted an overall accounting of the state of affairs. It also proposed a timetable for the completion of all war crimes cases: finish the most difficult and

---

[112] "Branimir Glavaš Will Not be Extradited to Croatia," BIRN, *Justice Report*, June 23, 2009, <www.bim.ba/en/172/10/20462/> (accessed June 24, 2009). He had obtained Bosnian citizenship in 2008.

[113] The Council of Europe Parliamentary Assembly also argued for the harmonization of the country's criminal codes. See Resolution 1626 (2008), "Honouring of obligations and commitments by Bosnia and Herzegovina," Council of Europe Parliamentary Assembly, <assembly. coe.int/Main.asp?link=/Documents/AdoptedText/ta08/ERES1626.htm> (accessed July 14, 2009).

[114] "Still Waiting: Bringing Justice for War Crimes," HRW.

[115] Erna Mačkić, "Long-awaited War Crimes Strategy Close to Completion," BIRN, *Justice Report*, December 24, 2008, <www.bim.ba/en/147/10/15768/> (accessed July 14, 2009).

[116] Ibid.

[117] "Državna strategija za rad na predmetima ratnih zločina" (State strategy for work on war crimes cases), December 2008. Unpublished manuscript; copy on file with the author.

high priority cases in the next seven years, and the rest within fifteen. Prosecutors insisted these target dates were overly optimistic, but nevertheless resolved, in internal court documents, to try to adhere to them.

The strategy paper outlined some empirical details that were long the subject of speculation in Bosnia, one of which was the number of individuals suspected of war crimes in the country: 5,895 individuals were suspected of war crimes and another 1,285 cases were in the investigative phase. The numbers themselves are misleading, however, as they combine both extremely complex and time consuming trials – for which there may or may not be good evidence – with more straightforward ones. Many cases were also redundant, dealing with the same crimes. The Prosecutor's Office said that more reliable numbers would only be available once it completed its database outlining its "strategic inventory" of cases, a project which was slated to be completed by November 2009.[118]

A background document titled "A Crime Centered Approach to War Crimes Case Selection" utilized various sources, including those at the ICTY and local documentation efforts, to outline the overall crime base in the country. This project was initiated by Marko Prelec, an analyst in the Prosecutor's Office (PO BiH) (and former ICTY staffer), in conjunction with other experts. The paper, finalized in the summer of 2008, provided the empirical basis for the Prosecutor's Office's priorities for the processing of war crimes cases. The PO BiH had already divided up the country into six regions, including a special investigative group for Srebrenica. In addition, PO BiH documents outlined criteria for the division of cases between the State Court and entity courts. Cases that had been started at the entity level before the Criminal Code was passed were to stay at that level, except in certain circumstances where the State Court decided that a case initiated there satisfied its mandate to focus on the most sensitive cases.[119]

Three local family associations expressed their disappointment with their lack of inclusion in the process of developing a local strategy, posting a note at the bottom of a BIRN report, complaining: "Two months ago we presented the suggestion to the Working Group that there should be a representative of the nongovernmental sector, however, we never received a response. We ask that they leave us the new strategy in order to study it and eventually propose amendments. Do victims have the right to the truth, do we have the right to whatever deals with war crimes?"[120] The relationship with family associations and local courts has been complicated: while they have demanded formal participation, they have largely neglected their rights as citizens to be a presence in the courtroom, except when

---

[118] David Schwendiman, Deputy Chief Prosecutor and Head of the Special Department for War Crimes, Prosecutor's Office of Bosnia and Herzegovina, e-mail to the author, July 15, 2009.
[119] Ibid.
[120] Erna Mačkić, "Long-awaited War Crimes Strategy." The organizations that signed the comments were the Association of War Detainees (Savez logoraša BiH), the Association of Women Victims of War (Udruženje "Žena-žrtva rata"), and the Mothers of the Enclaves of Srebrenica and Žepa (Udruženje "Pokret majki enklava Srebrenica i Žepa").

important judgments have been announced. This was often for good reasons, though, such as the need to travel, to the proceedings, a lack of resources, or the difficulty of the listening yet again to the painful details of the war.

The strategy paper was drafted in part to satisfy the Peace Implementation Council's so-called "5 + 2" (5 objectives and 2 conditions) for Bosnia. These were required to be fulfilled before the Office of the High Representative could transition to the Office of the European Union Special Representative (EUSR). This transition is significant because the OHR's Bonn powers – the ability to impose laws and remove politicians – will not be available to the new EUSR. The strategy paper supported the fifth objective: entrenchment of the rule of law.[121] The document represented a compromise among the various parties involved in the process. The ambitious target dates outlined in the paper were not matched by resources to meet them, however.

The multiple demands on prosecutors in Bosnia prompted other perhaps even more significant changes in strategy that enabled them to do more with fewer resources. The way prosecutions were conceived and executed was changed. The PO BiH's office started working on an "event" basis. That meant that crimes committed in one place would be considered a situation, with many events surrounding one situation. This complemented the fact that prosecutors were assigned to different geographic regions. There were many benefits to such a strategy. It decreased the need to use the same witnesses in multiple cases, and the competition for witnesses that sometimes resulted. In addition, it also necessitated more cooperation among prosecutors working in courts at all levels.[122] Event-based prosecutions helped make up for the fact that the Prosecutor's Office had to work faster with fewer resources than the Office of the Prosecutor (OTP) at the ICTY.

There were other important developments at the local level. In October 2009, Milorad Trbić (X-KR-07/386) was found guilty of genocide and sentenced to 30 years imprisonment.[123] Those proceedings were coordinated with civil cases, and prosecutors handled several thousand property claims statements in conjunction with courtroom developments.

[121] See "Declaration of the Steering Board of the Peace Implementation Council," February 27, 2008, Office of the High Representative, <www.ohr.int/pic/default.asp?content_id=41352> (accessed July 20, 2009). See an assessment of these goals by the Democratization Policy Council (DPC), "DPC assessment of the PIC," March 9, 2008, <democratizationpolicy.org/2008/03/09/new-dpc-assessment-of-peace-implementation-council-decisions/> (accessed July 20, 2009).

[122] Interview with David Schwendiman, Deputy Chief Prosecutor and Head of the Special Department for War Crimes, Prosecutor's Office of Bosnia and Herzegovina, Sarajevo, September 28, 2009.

[123] This was a first instance judgment. See "Milorad Trbić found guilty," News, Court of Bosnia and Herzegovina, October 16, 2009, <http://www.sudbih.gov.ba/?id=1403&jezik=e> (accessed October 31, 2009).

First Genocide Judgment

The so-called Kravica trial decision was arguably the most significant first instance judgment at the State Court to date. In August 2008, a judgment was reached in the trial of 11 individuals suspected of participating in the murders at the Kravica warehouse, where over 1000 Bosniaks were executed after the fall of the Srebrenica enclave in July 1995. The trial lasted from May 2006 to July 2008. The indictment listed 11 indictees, most of them members of the Šekovići Second Police Brigade.[124] The War Crimes Chamber acquitted four individuals and found seven guilty of genocide.[125] The decision was significant because the court had concluded that genocide had occurred in the country, a judgment that followed the decision in the Krstić trial at the ICTY.[126] It was a test of the State Court's capacity and ability to handle complex cases with multiple defendants.

The Kravica trial was not widely attended until the reading of the verdict, which necessitated an overflow room for journalists and family members of the accused. Representatives of family associations also attended, which made for a tense exit from the courtroom as their representatives encountered the family members of the accused.[127] The verdict in such a complex case was significant, and something the court had been working up to, in a sense. It had been steadily increasing the numbers of successfully completed trials every year, as shown in Table 8.2.

Despite the successful completion of this trial, more structural changes threatened the development of the fledgling judiciary and its ability to continue working through a backlog of war crimes cases. In May 2009, the Council of Ministers voted not to extend the mandate of foreign judges and prosecutors working in the country. Although a 2009 phase-out date had been envisioned, when the time came it was still too early to make a full transition to Bosnian staff. The State Court president and representatives called for the mandates to be extended; however, only two ministers voted for their renewal.[128] The mandate was set to expire at the end of 2009. RS Prime Minister Milorad Dodik campaigned hard to get the foreign

---

[124] The cases of two individuals, both of whom testified in court, were severed from the originally indictment; Petar Mitrović and Miladin Stevanović were tried separately. See the first instance verdict, *Prosecutor's Office of Bosnia and Herzegovina vs. Petar Mitrović* (Case No. X-KR-05/24-1), <www.sudbih.gov.ba/files/docs/presude/2008/Petar_Mitrovic_-_1st_instance_verdict.pdf> (accessed July 14, 2009); the verdict again Stevanović, <www.sudbih.gov.ba/files/docs/presude/2009/Miladin_Stevanovic_(Kravice)_-_1st_instance_verdict.pdf> (accessed July 14, 2009); and the verdict against the rest, Miloš Stupar and others (X-KR-05/24), <www.sudbih.gov.ba/files/docs/presude/2008/Milos_Stupar_i_dr_-_1st_instance_verdict.pdf.> (accessed June 25, 2009.)

[125] "Bosnian Court in Landmark Genocide Verdict," BIRN, *Justice Report*, July 29, 2008, <balkaninsight.com/en/main/news/12146/?tpl=299&ST1=Text&ST_T1=Article&ST_AS1=1&ST_max=1> (accessed June 14, 2009).

[126] Ibid.

[127] Author field notes, June–July, 2008.

[128] "Bosnia: No Mandate for Foreign Prosecution," BIRN, *Balkan Insight*, June 5, 2009, <balkaninsight.com/en/main/news/19951/> (accessed June 11, 2009).

TABLE 8.2. Court of Bosnia and Herzegovina Judicial Activity

	2005	2006	2007	Total
	Cases/ Accused	Cases/ Accused	Cases/ Accused	Cases/ Accused
War Crimes				
Commenced Trials	2/2	13/27	17/27	32/56
First Instance Judgments	1/1	8/8	10/11	19/20
Organized Crime, et al.				
Commenced Trials	11/28	21/76	13/23	45/127
First Instance Judgments	8/18	7/18	14/40	29/76

Source: Registry Annual Report, 2007.

judicial staff to leave the country, part of his overall strategy to discredit all international forces in Bosnia so as to hasten their departure. It also stemmed in part from the international community's declaration of victory on the issue. The decision came at an inopportune time for the court, just as prosecutions were starting to pick up and plans that would serve as the motor for future prosecutions were being executed.

Other Challenges

ICTY employees would later state that most of the problems encountered during the referral process stemmed from the fact that the hand off of cases had not been planned at the outset of the Tribunal's work. That meant that State Court, Prosecutor's Office, and ICTY staffers would have to create procedures as they went along.[129] Other challenges were on the demand side: ICTY officials were ready to help prosecutors in the entities, but received almost no requests from RS. Most problems, however, were resource-based: local offices did not have the staff or technology to handle their workload effectively.

Other obstacles that inhibited the ability to process cases stemmed from issues of institutional design at the local level and had little to do with the ICTY's work in the region. To cite but one example, the productivity of prosecutors was assessed based on the numbers of cases completed and not on their content. This created an institutional incentive to work on small and easily-prosecuted cases, and not the complex cases involving multiple defendants and multiple crime scenes.[130] This institutional challenge required large policy changes at the High Judicial and Prosecutorial Councils, which took time. The most formidable challenges to local

---

[129] Author discussions with ICTY employees, The Hague, December 2008.
[130] Interview with foreign prosecutor working in Bosnia, July 15, 2008.

prosecutions, however, stemmed from a lack of political will to support prosecutions and to finance them. Members of the judiciary were forced to wait for sorely needed funds in order to do their jobs. That task increasingly fell to the Bosnian government. For war crimes prosecutions to continue at an even pace, the Bosnian government would eventually need to support the effort, especially with all foreign involvement slated to stop at the end of 2009. It was unclear whether it would maintain the momentum. In September 2009, the Bosnian Parliament voted not to extend the mandate of the foreign judges and prosecutors working in Bosnia, a decision that meant that the momentum of the process could be threatened. It also left the High Representative with the task of deciding whether or not to impose an extension and use the "Bonn powers" to do so, which ultimately was done, at the last possible moment.[131]

On December 14, 2009, the day their mandate expired, High Representative Valentin Inzko imposed an extension for the judges and prosecutors working in the War Crimes Department of the State Court. An extension was not imposed for the Corruption Department, but the OHR stated they could serve advisory roles if asked by the Bosnian government to do so.[132] The decision was a blatant attempt to appease Milorad Dodik and reflected the fears of the Peace Implementation Council member states that a decision to impose an extension for all foreign personnel would trigger severe backlash in RS. This strategy failed as Dodik immediately called a special session of the RS government during which 27 conclusions were adopted, including a rejection of the High Representative's decisions, a resolve not to implement them, and a declaration that war crimes prosecutions should occur at the entity courts.[133] For the time being, however, the institutional momentum for local war crimes prosecutions was maintained.

Conclusion

The work of the ICTY led to the development of local capacity to prosecute war crimes in Bosnia. First, a series of procedures and coordinating mechanisms in The Hague certified cases for prosecution. At the same time, reforms restructured Bosnia's judicial system. Later, a War Crimes Chamber was created, and the number of prosecutions at the entity level increased. Although the effort of

---

[131] The Democratization Policy Council (DPC) sent a letter to High Representative Valentin Inzko, signed by 75 individuals and organizations including two former High Representatives, urging him to impose an extension. See "Letter to High Representative Valentin Inzko," Democratization Policy Council, December 10, 2009, <democratizationpolicy.org/> (accessed December 14, 2009).

[132] "Statement by the Ambassadors of the Steering Board of the Peace Implementation Council," Office of the High Representative and EU Special Representative, December 14, 2009, <www.ohr.int/pic/default.asp?content_id=44274> (accessed December 15, 2009). Turkey was the only country to publicly express its desire that both departments receive an extension.

[133] Summary of Press Conference of Milorad Dodik, e-mail to the author, December 14, 2009.

the international community to craft local institutions was not always popular, the modern courtrooms of the State Court erected with its help will continue to hold trials long after the international intervention has ended. The ICTY was part of a democratizing dynamic that improved the rule of law in Bosnia, confirming that the court's architects were correct to insist that their work would have positive effects in this arena. It is likely that Bosnia will eventually work through at least some of its backlog of cases, fulfilling a key part of the ICTY's extended mandate.

9 Conclusion

In October 2009, the trial of former Republika Srpska President Radovan Karadžić started in The Hague. ICTY prosecutor Alan Tieger opened the prosecution's case with some of the accused's more distressing comments. The three-member panel of judges heard – in Karadžić's own words – a description of his ultimate intentions when he armed Bosnian Serbs in Bosnia, long before the formal onset of war in April of 1992. Karadžić had told a colleague, "They have to know that there are 20,000 armed Serbs around Sarajevo. ... They will – they will disappear. Sarajevo will be a black caldron ['karakazan'], where 300,000 Muslims will die."[1] Karadžić's indictment included 11 counts of genocide, crimes against humanity, and violations of the laws and customs of war.[2] The ICTY maintained that his words had the force of his position of authority at the time as "the highest civilian and military authority in [Republika Srpska]" during the Bosnian war.[3]

The trial had been long awaited. In July 2008, Karadžić had been arrested on a Belgrade bus and transferred to The Hague. The news of his arrest served as a reminder that below the surface, the structures and ideologies that produced the horrific crimes of Bosnia's war remained largely intact. This was evident in Serbia's role in protecting Karadžić. He had been living in the Serbian capital for many years. His capture illustrated the extent of the state's effort to give a new identity to a fugitive from the law. Karadžić had eluded The Hague's arrest warrant for almost 13 years.[4]

Analysts had warned that the transfer of suspects accused of major crimes could lead to bloodshed and violence, but arrests for war crimes had become somewhat normal by the time of Karadžić's arrest. Even in Pale, the wartime

---

[1] Prosecutor v. Radovan Karadžić, Trial transcript, ICTY, October 27, 2009.

[2] See the Prosecutor v. Radovan Karadžić (IT-95-5/18-PT), Marked Up Indictment, ICTY, October 19, 2009, 2, <www.icty.org/x/cases/karadzic/ind/en/markedup_indictment_091019. pdf> (accessed October 25, 2009).

[3] Ibid.

[4] Unfortunately, a lot of the press coverage of the arrest, both in the region and abroad, focused on the accused's "new" identity as an alternative healer and not on the crimes for which he was charged. See, for example, Jack Hitt, "Radovan Karadžić's New Age Adventure," *New York Times Magazine*, July 22, 2009.

capital of Republika Srpska, some reported a noticeable absence of passion about the transfer of their erstwhile leader.[5] In Belgrade, demonstrations in support of Karadžić were short and sparsely attended. There was a brief flurry of excitement in Sarajevo at the news of his arrest, announced late on a Monday: cars horns blared through the downtown streets until a sudden rainstorm swept the celebrations indoors.[6] In the following days there were plans for additional events. An event to mark the arrest was to be held on Alija Izetbegović Square in the downtown center; however, when the scheduled time arrived, there were more journalists than participants gathered there.[7] People in Bosnia, and in the region, had become used to the work of the ICTY. The arrest restored a bit of its waning credibility both in Bosnia and abroad.

The relationship between the court and Bosnian citizens had continued to evolve. The normalization of arrests in the general population, however, did not mean that those close to its work would be indifferent to its decisions or trial proceedings. In September 2009, before the start of the trial, survivors demonstrated against the ICTY, burning pictures of the court's judges to protest the proposed shortening of the indictment against Karadžić.[8] Though the indictment was shortened, it still contained charges relating to genocide in 1992 and 1995, which were crucial from the perspective of the protestors. Many of the people who attended the Sarajevo protest traveled by bus to The Hague to hear the prosecutor's opening statement. Munira Subašić, of the Mothers of the Enclaves of Srebrenica and Žepa, told reporters, "We are going there [The Hague] to show to Europe and the world that we are still here, still searching for the truth and still waiting for justice."[9] Representatives of 16 non-governmental organizations, 160 people in total, from all over Bosnia, attended the opening of the trial. This showed that the court was still important to Bosnia's citizens: while its missteps and shortcomings evoked ire, frustration, and even disdain, its existence and work still mattered.

If the start of the Karadžić trial held out the promise of international justice, a concurrent event illustrated the limits of the ICTY's transformative potential. Biljana Plavšić, erstwhile member of the RS Presidency, having served just two-thirds of the prison term to which she had been sentenced by the ICTY, was freed from her Swedish prison cell. She returned to Belgrade where she received a hero's welcome; RS Prime Minister Milorad Dodik sent a government plane to Sweden and personally welcomed her return to Belgrade. Plavšić and Dodik were photographed walking through the streets of Belgrade, Plavšić draped in a fur coat and smiling for the cameras. Declining to give journalists an interview, she

5   Interview with Alida Vračić, Executive Director, Populari, Sarajevo, July 23, 2008.
6   Author field notes, Sarajevo, July 2008.
7   See Lara J. Nettelfield and Sarah Wagner, "Justice Has Become a Normal Thing," *Vancouver Sun*, July 26, 2008.
8   "Protesters Burn Photos of UN Judges in Sarajevo," *Associated Press*, September 16, 2009.
9   "Bosnian War Survivors to Attend Karadžić Trial," *Agence France Press*, October 24, 2009.

nonetheless told them she felt "free."[10] Nusreta Sivac, who had been one of thousands of internees in the Omarska camp near Prijedor, argued: "That is just evidence that in RS a climate still pervades in which there is no readiness to confront war crimes even when a judgment has been made by The Hague Tribunal. Regardless, it is unacceptable that Dodik waited [for Plavšić]. That means nothing other than the fact that he too believes that crime pays."[11]

Dodik grew increasingly more brazen in his disregard of court findings over time. In 2009, he argued that a massacre of 71 civilians in Tuzla in May 1995 was the work of the Bosnian government, even though the State Court had recently found VRS Commander Novak Đukić guilty of the crime and sentenced him to 25 years in prison.[12] Dodik expected that international officials in Bosnia would not respond to his provocation as sharply as they had in years past.

By 2009, the court had largely accomplished most of its primary goals. Only two of the 161 individuals indicted by the ICTY remained at large. One of them was Ratko Mladić, the VRS general wanted for genocide in addition to a long list of violations of international humanitarian law relating primarily to the fall of the Srebrenica UN enclave. Local trials were continuing at a rapid pace, although there were reasons for concern. The ICTY, near the end of its mandate, had enabled Bosnia to address some of the ghosts of its wartime era.

In so doing, it had broached the painful question all postwar countries must address: What to do about the past? The international community sent a decidedly mixed answer to Bosnia. It rewarded behavior that violated international norms of human dignity, but it also punished that same behavior, in fits and starts, in dribs and drabs, with various instruments: criminal trials, vetting procedures, and the removal of intransigent politicians. Its tools were honed over the postwar period, but only some High Representatives were willing to use them to effect change. The Dayton Peace Agreement, an expensive Faustian bargain, which left wartime politicians in place, sent the signal that war crimes could be rewarded with territory, hardly a departure from the processes of state building of centuries past. In fact, Dayton effectively enshrined the nationalism that led to the commission of mass atrocities that cost the lives of 100,000 of the country's citizens.[13]

[10] Bojana Barlovac, "Biljana Plavšić Arrives in Belgrade," Balkan Investigative Reporting Network (BIRN), *Balkan Insight*, October 27, 2009, <www.balkaninsight.com/en/main/news/23201/> (accessed October 28, 2009).

[11] Gordana Katana, "Biljana Plavšić na slobodi: U slobodu doletjela Dodikovim avionom" (Biljana Plavšić freed: Flown to freedom on Dodik's airplane), *Oslobođenje*, October 27, 2009.

[12] Srećko Latal, "Bosnian Serb Leader Shocks Victims' Families," BIRN, *Balkan Insight*, September 15, 2009, <www.balkaninsight.com/en/main/news/22220/> (accessed October 28, 2009). See the first instance judgment against Novak Đukić (X-KR-07/394), <www.sudbih.gov.ba/?opcija=predmeti&id=68&jezik=e> (accessed October 28, 2009).

[13] See Aida Cerkez-Robinson, "Research Shows Bosnian War Death Toll Guesses Severely Inflated," *Associated Press*, June 21, 2007; and Ewa Tabeau and Jakub Bijak, "War-Related

The ICTY was tasked with a different message and mission: even though its prosecutions were selective, it sought to uphold universal norms. It sent a different message, too, about statecraft. The court's prosecutions implied that, in the post–Cold War world, statecraft should conform to a new model. Dealing with the consequences of nationalism and aggression, the ICTY denounced them through the indictment of a handful of individuals blamed for crimes in Bosnia. The court was a weak institution created by an international community willing to do only so much for the people of Bosnia. The same institution that created the court, the United Nations, had given the Republic of Bosnia and Herzegovina membership in 1992, including the rights and duties associated with a spot in the General Assembly, yet maintained an arms embargo that prevented the country from defending itself effectively. Other international forces, many part of the UN, airdropped rice and blankets, doctors and peacekeepers, but were unwilling to use force until the crimes were so brazen and ruthless that even the most cynical observer could no longer be complacent. After the war, attempts to deal with complex issues such as war crimes would always be compromised by the need to negotiate with a political elite that had wartime origins. Many of those actors were implicated in the international crimes of the recent past. The political project of a unified territory comprising only ethnic Serbs continues to have considerable support today.

Consequently, whatever was done in The Hague lacked the conditions to obtain maximum impact in Bosnia, nor did the international institutions on the ground necessarily aid the court in its work. The transformative power of the ICTY was limited by the social setting in which the court worked, as this book has shown. It is no wonder that, even in October 2009 as Karadžić's trial started, the subject of war crimes was still a dominant issue in newspapers, on television, and as part of daily discussions in the lives of many Bosnians. Bosnian citizens' thirst for justice has only just begun to be slaked, 15 years after the founding of an institution that promised to transform the country through laws, procedures, and judgments.

This study found that, nevertheless, the ICTY aided the transition in post-Dayton Bosnia. The case studies here have implicitly compared the evidence to an unknowable counterfactual: one in which the court was never created, in other words, a postwar Bosnia without the ICTY. Although the subject of this book has been limited to one country, many of the findings are applicable to the role of international criminal tribunals in transitional states more generally.

The secondary findings deal with the field of transitional justice and the accumulation and dissemination of knowledge about mass atrocity. Conventional wisdom about various instruments is often affected by the fact that different constituencies compare to different ideals, leading to inflated expectations all

Deaths in the 1992–1995 Armed Conflicts in Bosnia and Herzegovina: A Critique of Previous Estimates and Recent Results," *European Journal of Population/Revue Européenne de Demographie* 21, nos. 2–3 (June 2005): 187–215.

around about the role and promise of international criminal law. The first wave of scholarship in this field overemphasized the potential of international courts in postconflict environments, and thus set unrealistically high bars for measuring success. Unsurprisingly, early studies tended to see only the failings. Furthermore, the various scholarly constituents in the discussion of mass atrocity have yet to have a conversation about what is reasonable to expect of international criminal trials. In this chapter, I discuss each point in turn.

Major Findings of This Study

The overarching question of this book has been whether transitional justice measures aid processes of democratization in postconflict states. Human rights advocates argue that such measures are integral to the transition process: that an evolving polity will be stronger if a violent past is explored, and that the international community has an obligation on behalf of victims everywhere to punish perpetrators for violations of international humanitarian law and genocide. Critics contend that these mechanisms are better used when nascent institutions have become stronger, because the pursuit of justice can jeopardize a fragile peace and feed the narratives of nationalists. Conventional wisdom, a moving target, has tended to be either overly optimistic or overly critical about the transformative potential of international criminal law. In recent years, most scholarly writings about the effects of the ICTY have been critical, arguing that the court's work has been a divisive force in the countries of Southeastern Europe, or at best ineffective.

The case studies here do not support that view. This book shows that the court's work has indeed aided processes of democratization in numerous ways. The ICTY has contributed by facilitating social mobilization, political participation, and the internalization of human rights norms. It has also challenged extreme versions of dominant nationalist narratives and assisted with the development of democratic institutions that bolster the rule of law.

The concept of democratization is complicated, as is the idea that democratic states can consolidate and not face a return to their violent pasts. Previous scholars have pointed to the need for development of political, economic, and civil societies.[14] By creating an opening in Bosnian society in which the past is discussed, the work of the court encouraged political participation by representatives of family associations and civil society groups who might otherwise have lacked legitimacy; it provided them and elites with a language about accountability and,

[14] Juan L. Linz and Alfred Stepan, *Problems of Democratic Transition and Consolidation: Southern Europe, South America and Post-Communist Europe* (Baltimore, MD: Johns Hopkins University Press, 1996).

in some cases, a set of tools – namely, law – with which they could lobby for further forms of redress.[15]

Furthermore, in the period under consideration, political forces opposed to the court had to support, at least rhetorically, the work of the court and the promotion of human rights. In many cases, this rhetorical support was not matched by effective measures to arrest indicted persons and was strategically employed only in order to receive specific benefits. Other scholars, nevertheless, have shown how such adaptation can be the first step in the process of internalization of norms.[16] And, while support of the court by those elites may have been somewhat compulsory, attitudes evolved in other segments of the population, suggesting a positive spillover effect from a change in elite rhetoric. Progress in establishing postwar institutions and creating a democratic political culture was slow and unsatisfactory from many survivors' perspectives, but norms modeled by the court were at least somewhat internalized, despite its distance from the region it served.

The court, additionally, enabled the expansion of the notion of who and what should be held responsible for the crimes committed in Bosnia. Bosnian citizens asserted that the international community, which they felt had been committed to the protection of their country and their lives, should apply its own ideals of accountability to itself and should examine the responsibility and even liability of the international institutions that had failed to prevent the bloodshed.[17] The ICTY was crucial in establishing the facts about the role of the international community in the region, which facilitated the expansion of this discussion.

Different communities inside Bosnia continue to understand the causes and events of the war in differing ways, and those differences are often exaggerated for political gain. The ICTY's work, however, has weakened the impact of some of the more untenable assertions by providing an empirical basis on which to judge them. In the case of the Srebrenica massacre, for example, evidence brought forth at the ICTY made it more difficult for politicians in Republika Srpska to deny that the crime took place. Similarly, as a result of the court's work, Bosniak elites were confronted with the fact that the Bosnian Army was also guilty of having committed war crimes, even if not on the same scale as their counterparts in the wartime RS. Interactions in the courtroom allowed the beginning of communication between parties that otherwise would have lacked incentives to do so. In many trials, to be sure, the interactions and courtroom proceedings were far from what one would hope for a model of transitional justice. Thus, while this study articulates a positive legacy, it occupies a middle ground that, to date, has been absent in the scholarship on international criminal tribunals.

---

[15] For a compilation of recent scholarship on law and social movements, see Michael McCann, ed., *Law and Social Movements* (Aldershot: Ashgate, 2006).

[16] Thomas Risse, Stephen C. Ropp, and Kathryn Sikkink, *The Power of Human Rights: International Norms and Domestic Change* (Cambridge: Cambridge University Press, 1999).

[17] See also Adam LeBor, *Complicity with Evil: The United Nations in the Age of Modern Genocide* (New Haven, CT: Yale University Press, 2007).

Conventional Wisdom and the Production of Knowledge

In addition to measuring the effects of an important transitional justice mechanism, this book has attempted to draw attention to the state of knowledge about trials for mass atrocity. The field has exploded in the post–Cold War era, but in many ways the academic debate is still in its infancy. There are many voices weighing in on the subject. The multiple constituencies in the aftermath of political violence – lawyers, survivors, academics, policy makers, international community representatives, to name only a few – all have different ideals about what justice should look like, and how courts should function. Each has different priorities. For example, the counterfactual underpinning of this book has been: "What might Bosnia look like if the ICTY had never existed?" That is largely an academic question, drawing from a methodology commonly found in the social sciences.[18]

For most Bosnian citizens, however, this is the wrong question. Most want to know how the court can be better, process more cases, and secure more convictions. In short, many citizens want international trials to work toward the ideal visions of retributive justice each holds in their mind's eye. Some of their ideas are incompatible with how courts work. The relationship between the scholarly and advocacy communities has often been contentious. It is worth noting that one of the great scholars of the Holocaust, Raul Hilberg, had a complicated relationship with survivors, not to mention other scholars, until his death. Some complained that he dealt with the "how" of the Holocaust instead of the "why," which they felt was a more important focus.[19] This is a difficult chasm to navigate, as today there are more researchers in every postwar country studying some aspect of reconstruction efforts. Advocacy organizations and human rights groups also have different agendas with respect to international trials. Policymakers, too, want to know how they can improve the courts in which they have made considerable investments, but they are influenced by foreign policy objectives that also alter their counterfactual ideals. As a result of these multiple constituencies, conventional wisdom has tended to be rather negative: no institution could possibly fulfill all of these expectations.

In scholarly circles, most academic research has tended to look at the aspirations expressed by the court itself, and has then applied social science methodologies – generally positivist ones – to "measure" the outcome, and as a result has found international law falling short. But are these the right measures of success? Where do these criteria come from? There are no common criteria for assessing international courts. A conversation about precisely this issue is needed at this

---

[18] See Philip Tetlock and Aaron Belkin, eds., *Counterfactual Thought Experiments in World Politics: Logical, Methodological, and Psychological Perspectives* (Princeton, NJ: Princeton University Press, 1996).

[19] Yehuda Bauer, "A Human Being Without Fault," *Haaretz.com*, September 26, 2007, <www.haaretz.com/hasen/spages/907398.html> (accessed July 4, 2009).

point in the research trajectory. The current approach underestimates the positive legacy of international law, in part because the methods used to study "impact" and "effects" – methods with an explicitly policy-oriented agenda – have neglected to take into consideration some of the findings of the literature on law and society and anthropology of law (which have not necessarily cast their research agendas in terms which are consumable by the policy community).

The ICTY was tasked with being more than just an average court. Policy makers hoped it would be a tool of postwar social change. They argued that the ICTY would contribute to peace and stability, and more specifically, to values such as reconciliation and the rule of law, in addition to deterring further crimes and providing a sense of justice to the victims. The inclusion of these secondary goals in the court's promotional material helped to foster often unrealistically high expectations. However, these criteria must be understood within their proper context.

First, social science research should dig deeper than the policy rhetoric used to justify the creation of an institution. This rhetoric is not necessarily a reliable guide by which social scientists should measure impact. Furthermore, rarely do institutions honestly advertise what they will in fact deliver. In this case, the ICTY's promotional materials could never have stated: "This selective and imperfect court will only touch the surface of the needs of the people in the region. Survivors will consider it to be slow and inefficient, and world powers will sometimes try to interfere with its work."[20] Transitional justice is by definition limited and selective. It points to a more liberal order in the future.[21] It does not deliver that liberal order; it is only the beginning. This point has been lost in the race to measure impact by scholars studying mass atrocity. Many studies measured international trials as if they were expected to be magic bullets, but no proponent of an international tribunal has claimed it would solve the region's postwar challenges. Much research to date has focused on a promise of international law that was not, in fact, offered.

This book has drawn upon Mark Drumbl's framing of the rationale for the application of international criminal law to mass atrocity. Outlining the retributive, deterrent, and expressivist goals of international courts, Drumbl notes that the first two goals are often derived from the misapplication of analogies from the domestic criminal law.[22] Indeed, there is reason to be skeptical about the capacity of a mechanism that is, by definition, so selective to deter crimes. Furthermore, some scholars have argued that retribution is a form of expressivism, in that the act of punishing the criminal sends a message both to the criminal and to society at large.[23]

---

[20] This is a paraphrase of a point that was made by Mark Drumbl at the panel, "Law and Society: Understanding the International Criminal Tribunal for the former Yugoslavia ICTY," annual meeting of the International Studies Association, New York, February 16, 2009.

[21] Ruti Teitel, *Transitional Justice* (Oxford: Oxford University Press, 2002).

[22] Mark A. Drumbl, *Atrocity, Punishment, and International Law* (Cambridge: Cambridge University Press, 2007), especially Chapter 2.

[23] Jean Hampton, "Moral Education Theory of Punishment," *Philosophy and Public Affairs* 13, no. 3 (Summer 1984): 212.

If we are left with just expressivism as a rationale for international criminal trials, is expressivism enough? A model of international criminal law that furthers retributive and expressive functions is still powerful. However, it is worth addressing the expressivist criteria offered by the court itself.

Reconciliation

There is much discussion about the relationship between trials and reconciliation. To reconcile generally implies a normalization of common life between parties. Almost all of the survivors interviewed for this project reported good postwar relations with those who may have spent the war on the other side of the front line. Most felt, however, that the vision of reconciliation that they were forced to accept by international officials and foreign NGOs also demanded that they reconcile with the unrepentant perpetrators of the crimes against their families. Such a version of reconciliation is a lot to ask. Furthermore, most survivors argue that true reconciliation, however defined, is a process that will take place over generations, but not before they have received their property back, or can send their children to schools tolerant of people from different walks of life. In Bosnia, there are still over 10,000 persons missing from the war, and there is much denial about the crimes committed. There is reason to be skeptical of this focus; there is still a great deal we do not yet know about reconciliation processes in still-divided postwar societies.

Rule of Law

The court's aspiration to contribute to the rule of law in Southeastern Europe was more realistic, if only for the simple reason that the establishment of local capacity was part of its completion strategy. Many of the problems that occurred during the handoff to the region had to do with the fact that rules and procedures were developed over the life of the Tribunal, and were not spelled out from the beginning. Thus, the ICTY, in coordination with regional courts, had to play catch-up. But if international courts are increasingly courts of last resort, to be applied only in situations where local conditions make local judicial solutions impossible, the development of local capacity will be difficult to sustain as a primary extra-legal aspiration in other contexts, because the starting point means that it is a much more difficult task to complete.

In addition, the "justice cascade" – to borrow Sikkink and Lutz's term[24] – will occur differently in different places. Sometimes local initiatives will make up for the symbolism and selectivity of international trials. In Rwanda, for example, the "gacaca" system emerged to address, implicitly, many of the failings of the

---

[24] Ellen Lutz and Kathryn Sikkink, "The Justice Cascade: The Evolution and Impact of Foreign Human Rights Trials in Latin America," *Chicago Journal of International Law* 2, no. 1 (2001).

international criminal tribunal, the ICTR, including the fact that no international court could possibly handle the great number of perpetrators of the genocide there.[25] The gacaca model was adapted from a traditional grassroots justice system; all parties to a crime appear at local gacaca courts, where judges mediate resolutions which often involve reparations, some act of contrition or, in many cases, a lengthy prison sentence. Gacaca is conducted in coordination with the ICTR.

Respond to Needs of the Victims

The survey data in this study has shown that survivors in Bosnia want atrocity trials. Survivors in different places will want different things, however. Trials are institutions focused on perpetrators, and this fact needs to be explained to court constituents, including survivors, clearly and early. International courts should continue to support witnesses long after they have left the courtroom, but trials, by definition, are and will remain focused on indictees. International criminal law has clearly delineated parameters and should remain focused on what it does best: investigations, presenting of evidence, and rendering of judgments. That does not mean that courts must give up extra-legal aspirations. There are worrying signs, however, that court constituents may unduly influence the application of international law. For example, at the International Criminal Court, victims may participate in the early stages of investigations.[26] However, there are many unknowns about how intensive participation by victims might affect the integrity of the whole process.

We need to question some of the basic rationales used to gauge the effectiveness of international courts. Drumbl's definition of expressivism suggests other potential effects of international courts, including that they: "extol the messaging value of punishment to affirm respect for law, reinforce a moral consensus, narrate history and educate the public."[27] Different aspects of expressivism may be more or less important depending on the social context. The partial contribution of international law to any of these goals must be recognized. Narrating history does not mean writing a definitive history, nor does educating the public mean that courts need to take on the functions of schools. Scholars of transitional justice need to

---

[25] On gacaca see: Alice Urusaro Karekezi, Alphonse Nshimiyimana, and Beth Mutamba, "Localizing Justice: Gacaca Courts in Post-Genocide Rwanda," in Eric Stover and Harvey Weinstein, *My Neighbor, My Enemy: Justice and Community in the Aftermath of Mass Atrocity* (Cambridge: Cambridge University Press, 2004); Peter E. Harrell, *Rwanda's Gamble: Gacaca and a New Model of Transitional Justice* (New York: Writers Club Press, 2003); and Jina Moore, "No Small Mercy," *The Walrus,* April 15, 2009, <www.walrusmagazine.com/articles/2009.05-no-small-mercy-jina-moore-rwanda-genocide> (accessed July 4, 2009).

[26] See, for example, Fiona McKay, "Victim Participation in Proceedings before the International Criminal Court," *Human Rights Brief* 15, no. 3 (Spring/Summer 2008), <https://www.wcl.american.edu/hrbrief/15/3mckay.pdf?rd=1> (accessed July 11, 2009).

[27] Drumbl, *Atrocity*, 12.

have a conversation that outlines the reasonable aspirations of international law, and then measure against those standards.

The post-Cold War academic field of transitional justice is relatively young, even if the issues and debates it addresses are not.[28] Even so, it has spawned journals, at least one international organization (the International Center for Transitional Justice), and specialized courses and seminars. There is a lot of "transitional justice" going on in Bosnia that falls outside of the field's accepted definition and thus is not considered part of the landscape – because it is neither a trial, nor a truth commission, nor part of a lustration proceeding. There are, for example, many documentation projects, former soldiers giving talks in local communities, and community video projects. These instruments are missing because researchers may lack the time or the ability to put it all together. But citizens are addressing mass atrocity in various ways. Even scholarship that urges researchers to take a holistic approach to crime often overlooks some of these important developments.

In addition, though few would admit it, scholarship may be affected by the implied incentives to gain attention by overturning conventional wisdom or being overly critical. Alan Bennett's play, *The History Boys*, portrays this: the old headmaster is displaced by a newly minted "Oxbridge" graduate, who urges his students cramming for their exams to produce something original – "something new!" – perhaps to show that "Stalin was a sweetie," in order to gain a seat at Cambridge or Oxford.[29] Bennett's satire contains kernels of truth about the production of academic knowledge in the current climate, and suggests lessons of caution for the study of transitional justice.

The current emphasis on mixed-method research presents new problems, even as it enriches our understandings of big questions. Making headway in one discipline is challenging enough, but progressively more young scholars are using mixed methods to address multiple disciplines. They are also increasingly attempting to weigh in on topics of great importance to policymakers. Policymakers, generally speaking, prefer positivist tools, such as survey research. Other methods, such as ethnography, have generally been used by scholars to understand conflict situations on the ground.[30] While ethnography could help illuminate how citizens appropriate international law, and even the feelings of those excluded by it, the policy community may not embrace such a method because it relies on a small number of informants. Positivist approaches, nevertheless, have their limits, too. Survey research, for example, or qualitative surveys like those in this book, can do a better job of measuring disappointment than imparting the full range of the effects of international courts on local communities.

---

[28] See Jon Elster, *Closing the Books: Transitional Justice in Historical Perspective* (New York: Cambridge University Press, 2004); Ruti G. Teitel, "Transitional Justice Genealogy," *Harvard Human Rights Journal* 16 (2003): 69–94.

[29] Alan Bennett, *The History Boys: A Play* (London: Faber and Faber, 2006).

[30] See David Rohde, "Army Enlists Anthropology in War Zones," *New York Times*, October 5, 2007.

The role of international criminal law in transitional times should be returned to its rightful, rather modest place. The insights of the growing literature on international law and society, legal anthropology, and contentious politics must be integrated into what is, at present, a largely positivist research program to address the impact of international law. A law and society approach to international criminal law may yield a more complete understanding of the role of international tribunals in transitional societies than existing dominant frameworks. This literature has been overlooked because it does not employ the language of "impact" or "effects," or even contributions to democratization, but this strand of research has contributed to our understanding of each of these things. A number of insights from this literature should be incorporated into any discussion of the impact of international criminal tribunals.

Legal anthropologists such as Sally Engle Merry have addressed what they refer to as the "vernacularization of human rights discourse": the process by which social movements that have their origins in international law may use international legal language in combination with different forms of governance at the national and local levels simultaneously, recasting international law in more plural terms.[31] In other words, individuals adapt, appropriate, and expand international norms in ways that are different from their initial application. They would lack this basis for legitimate discourse if international law were not a resource which had been lent to them in the first place. These processes should be understood within the framework of the effects of international law.

Second, in a similar vein, there are, as one recent volume argues, multiple paths to and from international justice.[32] The work of international tribunals does not stop at the doors of the court. One representative of an NGO noted that the work of the ICTY "untied certain knots" in Bosnian society and facilitated the movement of different groups into Republika Srpska in the early years when movement was still limited.[33] Such contributions should be understood as one of the court's many positive effects.

Lastly, court proceedings are linked with other social processes, such as the distribution of benefits, the identification of missing persons, and processes of memorialization. It is at the nexus of international law and other social processes that research can be richest and most useful. This study has revealed that some of the court's most positive results were not necessarily those expected by policy makers, or even many scholars. The positive contributions identified in this book draw upon the research that looks at how international law is used in an everyday context. This study has not offered a definitive set of criteria with which to measure effects, but it has found that, by and large, Bosnians feel the ICTY has made

---

[31] Richard A. Wilson, "Conclusion: The Anthropology of Human Rights," in Mark Goodale and Sally Engle Merry, eds., *The Practice of Human Rights: Tracking Law Between the Global and the Local* (Cambridge: Cambridge University Press, 2007) 347–348. Wilson gives an overview of legal pluralism in the field of anthropology.

[32] See Marie Benedict Dembour and Tobias Kelly, eds., *Paths to International Justice: Social and Legal Perspectives* (Cambridge: Cambridge University Press, 2007).

[33] Interview with civil society organization representative, Tuzla, July 20, 2004.

progress in fulfilling the extended mandate that it set out for itself. The full impact of the ICTY extends far beyond the list of effects the court proffered on its web site. There is reason to be modest when anticipating what effects can be captured: social science theories of complexity have given us insight into why efforts to derive specific criteria and then measure those criteria will inevitably be frustrating.[34]

However, the narrowness of this study should be acknowledged too. The discussion about transitional justice and the Bosnian war is more far-reaching than the material presented here. The ICTY and the local trials in Bosnia that it helped produce were only a small part of the judicial processes for the mass atrocities of the Bosnian war. The International Court of Justice; courts in Germany, the Netherlands, Canada, and Australia; and courts in New York utilizing the Alien Tort Claims Act (ATCA) have all addressed Bosnia's crimes, to name a few. In many instances, they relied on the ICTY's decisions and documentation. Some, like the ICJ, inherited its institutional flaws by, for example, relying on documents submitted to the ICTY that had been redacted by the Serbian government which was eager to limit its culpability for the war in Bosnia. Each of these courts has addressed some aspects of the Bosnian war, but there is little cumulative understanding of the different findings and impact of these judicial solutions. These different cases and forums raise the issue of the ICTY in the global judicial landscape.[35] The general public is still insufficiently aware of the work done by these courts. This is partly a consequence of the fact that the trial records are extensive, not easily accessible, and sometimes just far away.

Generalizability?

How transferable is the Bosnian experience to other postwar states? Postwar Bosnia is a unique political animal by any standard, not likely to be replicated anywhere else in the near future. Still, some of the central insights of this study – the power courts have to facilitate political participation from below and the creation of local judicial capacity – are evident throughout Southeastern Europe and beyond. Even without coercive tools to remove politicians and impose laws, international justice has positively influenced developments in other countries in the region.

The value of educating people who are affected by international criminal trials emerges as one of the most important findings of this book. To anyone close to the work of the ICTY, the importance of outreach is an obvious observation. However, policymakers failed for a long time to appreciate the relationship between outreach and impact. Fifteen years after the founding of the court, the ICTY's Outreach Program is still supported by a trust fund into which donations are placed on an

---

[34] Robert Jervis, *System Effects: Complexity in Political and Social Life* (Princeton, NJ: Princeton University Press, 1998), 10.

[35] See Mark A. Drumbl, "Looking Up, Down, and Across: The ICTY's Place in the International Legal Order," *New England Law Review* 37 (2003): 1037.

ad hoc basis, rather than by a reliable line item in the court's budget; employees in this department must fight for resources on a project by project basis.[36] Most Bosnians, for instance, still do not know why and how the ICTY was formed, or what its mandate is; there remains much confusion about the court, its purpose, and its limitations. This and other uncertainties could have been minimized by more effective institutional design. Outreach must be funded. Courts' expressivist impact will always be limited if individuals do not know how they work. The data presented here illustrates that improved outreach and media coverage have led to more favorable attitudes about the court and have tempered unrealistic expectations in segments of the population it targeted. Favorable attitudes toward judicial institutions have been correlated to positive aspects of democratization in some studies. Still, there must be reasonable expectations of what the public will know even under the best circumstances.

Outreach, however, is not a panacea for the politically charged environments in which legal interventions in postconflict countries will inevitably be conducted. Political actors will interpret the work of the court for their constituencies with both personal and political aims in mind. Dissemination of factual, scrupulously collected information by the court about the nature and extent of atrocities can help overcome this problem, but even the best data collection efforts will not completely prevail over the strategic use of (mis)information.

International courts will also be more effective if foreigners working on the ground understand the court and its *raison d'être*. Outreach efforts must target internationals working inside the country, lest they unwittingly (or even deliberately) undermine its work. Mixed signals on the part of foreign representatives can confuse citizens, who often have more contact with foreign representatives of NGOs and international institutions in their country than with court representatives. The ICTY, for example, had local partner organizations, but often faced other obstacles on the ground, such as international institutions that felt its work was counterproductive to their own goals.

Looking Up: The Work of the Court

While the social setting in the region was a problem for the realization of the court's extended mandate, several problems with the transparency and accountability of the ICTY that have hindered its impact in the region also deserve mention. The lack of institutional oversight at international tribunals, more generally, will be one of the main institutional challenges for the effective development of international criminal law as a form of global governance.

First, the ad hoc international courts – the ICTY and ICTR – were created by the UN Security Council. In an anarchic international system, there is virtually no

---

[36] Discussions with ICTY employees, The Hague, December 5, 2008.

independent oversight of the day-to-day operations of such courts. International institutions, however, need to be subject to the same review processes as domestic institutions, so that there are checks and balances on internal processes and decision-making. A lack of oversight does not help improve the international legal system. The ICTY may uphold important universal principles and laws, but the individuals who staff them, as is the case in any institution, are subject to the same human frailties that impact work in other fields: corruption, vanity, greed, and sometimes, yes, incompetence. In the absence of oversight mechanisms, court procedures will remain far from "best practice."

The current climate at the court is untenable. As of 2009, a culture of silence affects many former employees, and constructive criticism of the court can be heard from only a small circle of them. There have been cases of court employees calling former staffers in attempts to sway conference presentations. Structural incentives to silence critics will only perpetuate weak and ineffective institutions. International courts should be subject to the same internal good governance that foreign civil servants hope for in the regions they address.

The current lack of transparency affects court output in a very real way and can have lasting consequences. To give but one example, Chief Prosecutor Carla del Ponte agreed to let the Serbian government redact documents of the Supreme Defense Council (SDC) of the Federal Republic of Yugoslavia (FRY) before they were transferred to The Hague.[37] Honoring Del Ponte's agreement, the judges in the trial chamber allowed the documents to be redacted under rule 54bis, accepting Serbia's argument of "vital national interest." This, however, former ICTY staffers argued, was not a provision provided for in the rule, which did allow protections under national security interests.[38] The redacted SDC minutes contained vital information about Serbia's involvement in all of the wars in the region, and especially in Bosnia. This decision thus hindered not only the work of the ICTY, but possibly future court decisions affecting the region.

At the ICJ case filed in 1993, in which Bosnia charged the FRY (which, because of the dissolution of the country, later became Serbia) with aggression and genocide in Bosnia, the court relied exclusively on the evidence provided by the ICTY. The full SDC minutes were not transferred to the ICJ for review in the case and many observers have argued that the outcome could have been more favorable to Bosnia were these crucial documents available to the judges.[39] The minutes, although not

---

[37] See "Case Concerning the Application of the Convention on the Prevention and Punishment of the Crime of Genocide," ICJ, February 26, 2007. The full 171 page judgment is <www.icj-cij.org/docket/files/91/13685.pdf#view=FitH&pagemode=none&search=%22Bosnia-Herzegovina%201993%22> (accessed July 1, 2009).

[38] Simon Jennings, "Secrecy and Justice at the ICTY," Institute of War and Peace Reporting (IWPR), *Tribunal Update*, No. 550, May 14, 2008, <www.iwpr.net/?p=tri&s=f&o=344616&apc_state=henh> (accessed July 1, 2009).

[39] Ibid. See also Merdijana Sadović, "Call for Serbia to Release Confidential Documents," IWPR, *Tribunal Update*, No. 527, November 23, 2007, <www.iwpr.net/index.php?apc_state=hen&s=o&o=l=EN&p=tri&s=f&o=340861> (accessed July 1, 2009).

a smoking gun for any of the crimes in the region, contained some crucial information. Former ICTY prosecutor Geoffrey Nice cautioned:

the documents do not provide in any sense a simple answer to any of the outstanding questions. They provide much more context, they provide much more detail, they provide more evidence about the states of mind of, not just Milošević, but other people sitting in that council, and would have enabled fact-finders and decision-makers to make better and deeper judgments about what was going on.[40]

The case of the redacted SDC documents was emblematic of larger issues within the Tribunal, such as the transparency of the court, the problem of obtaining documentation in the first place, and the ultimate consequences of poor decisions by Tribunal, staffers who were not held to account. As historian Marko Attila Hoare observed, "The whole [Tribunal] isn't really public, it's not transparent, and there's not much democracy involved."[41] This must change, not only at the ICTY but at international courts more generally.

This lack of court oversight also led to some poorly crafted cases that hurt the court's reputation. For example, the prosecution's case against former Kosovo Prime Minister Ramush Haradinaj was so poorly presented that the defense declined even to make a case before the court. The SENSE News Agency (created to cover events at the court), blamed the outcome on the fact that large chunks of evidence had come from the Serbian Ministry of Interior, investigators' mistakes during the identification process, and a "bungling prosecution team."[42] Effective oversight mechanisms could help ensure that cases such as this one are not repeated.

This case also highlighted the strategy of the longest serving Chief Prosecutor, Carla del Ponte (1999–2007), who was criticized for her policy of indicting representatives of all ethnic groups, called by some a "strategy of proportionality" or "equation of guilt." According to her approach, the impartiality of the tribunal would be shown by an effort to indict political and military leaders of every ethnic group, including the Bosniaks and Kosovar Albanians. The director of the Helsinki Committee for Human Rights in Serbia, Sonja Biserko, pointed out that: "This approach backfired as most of the indictees representing these two groups were either acquitted or got very mild sentences."[43]

[40] Merdijana Sadović, "Nice Assesses ICTY Prosecution Record," IWPR, *Tribunal Update*, No. 533, January 11, 2008, <www.iwpr.net/?p=tri&s=f&o=341910&apc_state=henftri341906> (accessed July 1, 2009).
[41] Jennings, "Secrecy and Justice at the ICTY."
[42] "Why Did the Prosecution Fail to Prove 'What Everybody Knows'?" Sense News Agency, April 7, 2008, <www.sense-agency.com/en/stream.php?sta=3&pid=11099&kat=3> (accessed on July 2, 2009).
[43] Interview with Sonja Biserko, Director, Helsinki Committee for Human Rights in Serbia, The Hague, December 6, 2008.

Short sentences and perceived inconsistencies in sentencing practices affected the court's impact in the region.[44] The outcome of the trial of the so-called Vukovar Three, three former JNA officers, was a source of great disappointment among victims in Croatia. Mile Mrkšić, Miroslav Radić, and Veselin Šljivančanin were charged with the 1991 murders of 260 Croatian prisoners at the Ovčara farm, outside of Vukovar, a city in Eastern Croatia. Mrkšić was sentenced to 20 years in prison, while Šljivančanin received only five, and Radić was found not guilty. Many Croatian citizens felt the results were far too lenient for what was considered the biggest crime in Croatia since World War II.[45] The relationship between sentencing and the extra-legal goals of international tribunals remains an important issue to follow.

Transparency also means being open to outside scrutiny. Most requests submitted to the court registrar to conduct basic social science research have been refused. The court, of course, has the right not to accept every graduate student who shows up at its doors, but the ICTY, and international courts more generally, should foster a climate in which scholarly inquiry is supported in the spirit of contributing to better institutional practices. With a few exceptions, even basic questions, not pertaining to any sensitive material, addressed to many ICTY staffers in The Hague throughout the course of this study were met with suspicion and even fear.

Furthermore, a scarcity of studies conducted at the court itself (with a few notable exceptions) means that there is a limited understanding about how those who work inside the court view the ICTY's extended mandate.[46] It seems there is still a lot of ambivalence in the minds of some international judges and prosecutors about the court's extended role and how much it should be considered a part of their job. Some Outreach employees have struggled to find staffers willing to visit the region for planned outreach events.[47] International legal professionals typically build their careers and gain prestige in their home countries, not at the foreign sites of mass atrocity. Is it also worth noting that outreach activities often add to their normal workload. Some legal professionals believe that outreach trips may

---

[44] See Drumbl, *Atrocity*. See also William Schabas, "Sentencing by International Tribunals: A Human Rights Approach," *Duke Journal of Comparative and International Law* 7 (1997): 461.

[45] Goran Jungvirth, "Croat Anger at 'Lenient' Sentences for Vukovar Three," IWPR, *Tribunal Update*, No. 519, September 28, 2007, <www.iwpr.net/?p=tri&s=f&o=339396&apc_state=henh> (accessed July 1, 2009).

[46] Some researchers independently solicit former ICTY staffers, but have received no institutional assistance. See, for example, "Judging History: The Uses of Historical and Background Contextual Evidence at the International Criminal Tribunal for the Former Yugoslavia," Call for Participants in Online Survey, Investigators Richard A. Wilson and Andrew Corin, <web2.uconn.edu/hri/research/ictyresearch.php> (accessed July 2, 2009). Eric Stover, however, obtained assistance from the court for his study about witnesses. See Stover, *The Witnesses*, xi.

[47] Interviews with ICTY staff, The Hague, December 2008.

negatively influence their own attitudes toward their cases.[48] However, if international courts hope to be able to fulfill extra-legal mandates, there must be institutional acceptance of their obligation to explain their findings to the societies they address. That institutional support must include not only appropriate funds, but time to participate in those activities.

The court has been very timid in its judgments regarding crimes in the region. There is anecdotal evidence from inside the courtroom that the judges have relied on additional criteria. For example, with the exception of the Krstić case, the ICTY's judges have been reluctant to find that genocide occurred in Bosnia. We know little about how the prejudices of the judges have affected the judgments overall. From inside the courtroom, the evidence is mostly anecdotal. For example, after the reading of a judgment of a low-level war criminal, one former court employee reported hearing an ICTY judge say, "We thought he was guilty of genocide but we wanted save that charge for the big fish!"[49] Some judges have been more outspoken in their views of genocide charges. ICTY judge Christoph Flügge argued in an interview that the term "genocide" could pertain only to the Holocaust, and he questioned the utility of the term to describe "such crimes" as the Srebrenica massacre, for which he preferred the term "mass murder."[50] These comments, predictably, provoked a strong reaction in Bosnia and in the Bosnian diaspora.

The Karadžić trial will be one of the court's last opportunities to assess whether genocide occurred during the Bosnian war outside of Srebrenica. However, some argue there is evidence for other convictions. Edina Bećirević's analysis of the war in Eastern Bosnia in 1992 and 1993 illustrates how a campaign to dehumanize Bosniaks was part of the preparation for genocide, which began at the beginning of the war.[51] Through a discussion of the ICTY's work, she illustrates how the atrocities in Eastern Bosnia have been generally treated as crimes against humanity.[52] The ICTY included charges of genocide in its cases against Slobodan Milošević, Radovan Karadžić, Ratko Mladić, Biljana Plavšić, Goran Jelisić, Momčilo Krajišnik, Duško Sikirica, Radislav Krstić, and others, but so far has not secured a genocide conviction against anyone except Krstić, or has eliminated the charge in plea agreements.

The paper trail the ICTY leaves will be crucial to addressing many aspects of the court's legacy, including how it understood the genocide in Bosnia. There is much discussion about where the court's archive will end up. Some observers have argued that, in the age of digitization, the physical location of the papers is not so important, while others argue that the original documents – or at least copies – are

[48] Ibid.
[49] Discussions with former ICTY staff, The Hague, December 2008.
[50] "'A Victory for Justice': UN Tribunal Judge on the Karadžić Trial," interview with Christoph Flügge, *Spiegel Online*, July 9, 2009, <www.spiegel.de/international/spiegel/0,1518,635205,00.html> (accessed July 12, 2009).
[51] See Edina Bećirević, *Na Drini genocid* (Genocide on the Drina River) (Sarajevo: Buybook, 2009), 97.
[52] Ibid., 15–16.

important in order to create a living memorial to the victims of violations of international law.[53] This debate will continue as the ICTY winds down, but local wishes should be canvassed before any final decision is made, in effort to avoid another insult to citizens in the region.

Even if international courts remain focused on perpetrators, the principle of "do no harm" to the individuals they are meant to serve should govern institutional practice. For example, reports that the court destroyed personal belongings of victims of the Srebrenica genocide is a shameful discovery for an international institution that aspires to respond to the needs of victims.[54] What was likely due to institutional carelessness conveys, understandably, a much different message in the region.

Regional Context: Serbia and Croatia

As in Bosnia, the ICTY's impact in other countries in Southeastern Europe has illustrated both the promise and the limitations of international law in challenging environments. In Serbia, in the absence of enforced compliance, the work of the court was viewed with more skepticism than in other countries in the region. There, in contrast to Bosnia, public attitudes toward the court over the years are publicly available, as a handful of organizations consistently provided data. Those numbers are not as encouraging as the ones presented in this study. Mirko Klarin, Director of the SENSE News Agency and one of the original proponents of an international tribunal in the region, argues, "If the impact of the ICTY in the countries of the former Yugoslavia is measured exclusively by the pervasive public perception of the Tribunal there, perhaps the best thing to do would be to shut it down and not wait for the end of its mandate."[55]

Christopher Lamont outlines these attitudes, using the work of the Belgrade Center for Human Rights. Beliefs about events during the war have changed over time. For example, the number of citizens in Serbia who believed that, "In Bijeljina during 1992 paramilitary formations from Serbia killed civilians," dropped from 30 percent of those surveyed in 2001, to 14 percent in 2004 and 2005. Similarly, the numbers of those who believed that "Sarajevo was under siege for around 1,000 days," declined from 53 percent in 2001 to 40 percent in 2004 and 2005.[56] Both of

---

[53] On the former position see: Robert Donia and Edina Bećirević, "ICTY Archive Must be Open to All," IWPR, *Tribunal Update*, No. 545, April 4, 2008, <www.iwpr.net/?p=tri&s=f&o=343812&apc_state=henh> (accessed on April 6, 2008). The latter position is from an interview with Mirsad Tokača, President, Research and Documentation Center, Sarajevo, June 9, 2008.

[54] "Srebrenica Artifacts Destroyed in The Hague," BIRN, *Justice Report*, July 16, 2009.

[55] Mirko Klarin, "The Impact of the ICTY Trials on Public Opinion in the Former Yugoslavia," *Journal of International Criminal Justice* 7, no. 1 (March 2009): 89–96.

[56] Christopher Kazumi Lamont, "Coercion, Norms and Atrocity: Explaining State Compliance with International Criminal Tribunal for the former Yugoslavia Arrest and Surrender Orders," Ph.D. diss., University of Glasgow, 2008, 243.

these events had been documented in ICTY prosecutions. What is more puzzling is that these changes in attitudes happened after the so-called October Revolution in 2000. Klarin argues that "in Milošević's time, the Tribunal had more support and a better image among part of the Serbian public. Things were simpler back then, black and white: being critical of the regime and 'against' Milošević almost automatically meant being 'for' the ICTY."[57] However, he notes, despite discouraging data, "it is quite possible, indeed probable that the situation would be even worse without ICTY trials and judgments."[58] In addition, as this study has pointed out, survey data is but one measure of impact.

The court has made some inroads in Serbia, nonetheless, argues Professor Diane Orentlichter, in a report for the Justice Initiative of the Open Society Institute. She outlines how cooperation with the court has proceeded as a result of threats and ultimatums presented by the international community: indictees are transferred when deadlines loom for foreign aid, and so on. Notwithstanding international arm twisting as a force for compliance, the court has also made some positive contributions.[59] The work of the ICTY has "shrunk the public space" of denial in Serbian society, she says. Others argue that the manipulation of information about atrocities is no longer as widespread as it used to be. Former Human Rights Watch researcher Bogdan Ivanišević observed that previously it was common to hear the numbers of victims of the Srebrenica massacre understated or that deaths there were caused by the Bosnian Army, but that is no longer as prevalent.[60] Now, he says, "There is incomparably less distortion of the past."[61] More importantly (and often overlooked), argues journalist Dejan Anastasijević, was the fact of "physically removing some of the worst criminals" from the region.[62]

Furthermore, as in Bosnia, it should be mentioned that the ICTY has bolstered local institutional capacity. Serbia would not have started to grapple with war crimes cases were it not for the ICTY. Many of the initial judgments, however, have yielded decisions disappointing to many, such as the April 2007 judgment in the trial of members of the Scorpions paramilitary unit, which was under the command of the Serbian Ministry of Interior (MUP). The trial addressed the execution of six Bosniak males captured on video after the fall of the Srebrenica enclave. This was the first trial in Serbia to deal with events in Srebrenica. Advocates argued that the judgment of the Belgrade District Court's War Crimes Chamber failed to acknowledge that the indictees were connected with state agents and, ultimately,

[57] Mirko Klarin, "Impact of the ICTY Trials."

[58] Ibid.

[59] Diane F. Orentlicher, "Shrinking the Space for Denial: The Impact of the ICTY in Serbia," Open Society Justice Initiative, Open Society Institute, May 2008, <www.soros.org/initiatives/osji/articles_publications/publications/serbia_20080520/serbia_20080501.pdf> (accessed July 4, 2009).

[60] Ibid, 19.

[61] Ibid, 19.

[62] Ibid, 17.

a state-sponsored plan of criminality.[63] In Serbia, there is much to be done: the number of trials overall has been low, and the lack of willingness to tie crimes to state institutions is a cause for concern.[64] Trials will not be effective in contributing to the rule of law if they do not address the difficult question of command responsibility, as in The Hague.

Perhaps most importantly, it should be emphasized that denial prevails in Serbia. The ICTY is often accused of causing political instability in the region, but Serbia's consistent strategy of denial fractures relations in the region even more. Despite the existence of judicial institutions to try war criminals, the political elite in Serbia have been entirely unwilling to deal directly with the violations of international humanitarian law and genocide with which the state is connected. The systematic relativization of war crimes by those at the highest levels in Serbia has left the public ignorant about the crimes of the recent past.[65] Consequently, although Orentlicher's report presented relatively positive conclusions, understanding of the role of the ICTY in Serbia must be expanded with further studies based on extensive field research.

Croatia, too, has had a fraught relationship with the court, but the positive contributions are perhaps clearer there. The country's greater overall desire to join Euro-Atlantic structures made ICTY cooperation a priority, even if those leading the country did not always think conditionality was a fair trade. The national conversation regarding what is widely referred to as the Homeland War opened up after the death of Franjo Tuđman in 1999. The handover to the ICTY of a series of Croatian generals, most notably, Ante Gotovina, Mirko Norac, and Rahim Ademi, raised the question of how the public in Croatia would react to war crimes accusations against individuals largely viewed as defending their nation from Serbian aggression. Vjeran Pavlaković argues that, for example, the rhetoric regarding national commemorations of Operation Storm, in which up to 250,000 Serbs in Croatia were displaced from their homes, now includes admissions by political elites that war crimes were committed against Serb victims, an admission that, he argued, "would have been unimaginable under Tuđman."[66] Leaders in Croatia largely had a two-track approach to the court, Pavlaković argues. "On the one hand, both [former Croatian Prime Minister Ivica] Račan and [former

---

[63] Igor Jovanović and Anes Alić, "Serbia Sentences its Scorpions," *ISN*, April 17, 2007, < www.isn. ethz.ch/isn/Current-Affairs/Security-Watch/Detail/?ots591=4888CAA0-B3DB-1461-98B9-E20E7B9C13D4&lng=en&id=53124> (accessed July 30, 2009).

[64] For a different view, see Patrice C. McMahon and David P. Forsythe, "The ICTY's Impact on Serbia: Judicial Romanticism Meets Network Politics," *Human Rights Quarterly* 30, no. 2 (May 2008): 412–435.

[65] "Srebrenica: Transitional (In)justice," *Helsinki Bulletin* 34, Helsinki Committee for Human Rights in Serbia, July 2009.

[66] Vjeran Pavlaković, "Eye of the Storm: The ICTY, Commemorations and Contested Histories of Croatia's Homeland War," Meeting Report, Woodrow Wilson International Center for Scholars, November 14, 2007, <www.wilsoncenter.org/index.cfm?topic_id=1422&fuseaction=topics. publications&doc_id=481710&group_id=7427> (accessed July 4, 2009).

Croatian Prime Minister Ivo] Sanader have promised full cooperation with The Hague, and have, for the most part, handed over suspects and documents when they have been requested. On the other hand, there has never been any systematic effort to demystify the Homeland War or challenge the glorification of [General] Gotovina, who has transcended the reality of soldier of fortune and bank robber to become a saintly embodiment of Croatia's struggle for freedom."[67] Consequently, it is not surprising that, not unlike in Serbia, citizens in Croatia have a pragmatic approach to the court. Surveys there show that Croatians believe cooperation with the ICTY will help facilitate accession to the European Union, a goal important to the Croatian public at large, although support has waned in recent years.

One thing stands out about the period during which the majority of the field research for this book was conducted. It may help explain variations in the ICTY's impact in the region. In Bosnia, the international community sent a strong signal that non-cooperation with the ICTY would not be tolerated and that non-compliance would be punished. Political candidates were disqualified and penalties imposed. As soon as that strategy changed under later High Representatives and it was clear there would be no consequences for the denial of war crimes, politicians such as Dodik quickly reverted to their old ways. While individuals continued to use the law as a resource and local prosecutions carried on, in the short term, attitudes toward the ICTY quite predictably took a turn for the worse since 2006. Elites play a significant role in indicating which norms should prevail. The ICTY made gains when it had allies on the ground supporting its work. This is an important lesson for other international courts.

Beyond Southeastern Europe, the proliferation of international and hybrid war crimes tribunals continues to make analysis of their impact an important endeavor. International and mixed tribunals in Sierra Leone, Cambodia, and Lebanon, not to mention the ongoing work of the International Criminal Court (including the recent indictment of Sudanese President Omar Al Bashir), highlight the unresolved questions of the ICTY and ICTR. These institutions face vastly different social settings in which to implement universal laws, however selectively, but citizens will adapt these universal principles in their own contexts. International tribunals, like at the ICTY, will face an uphill challenge in contexts where conflict has not yet come to an end.[68]

The Future of Bosnia

The future of Bosnia and Herzegovina, for many, is uncertain. The 2006 general elections kicked off a wave of renewed nationalism that rolled back some of the

---

[67] Vjeran Pavlaković, "Better the Grave than a Slave: Croatia and the International Criminal Tribunal for the former Yugoslavia," in Sabrina P. Ramet, Konrad Klewing, and Reneo Lukić, eds., *Croatia after Independence: Politics, Society, Foreign Relations* (Munich: Oldenbourg Wissenschaftsverlag, 2008), 16.

[68] I am grateful to Peter Juviler for emphasizing this point to me.

progress in the country. The most recent High Representatives there, Miroslav Lajčák and Valentin Inzko, did not seem to have a strategy for how to deal with it. The international community in Bosnia is in a difficult position: officially it is there to uphold and implement the Dayton Peace Agreement but, to move the country forward, it needs to facilitate constitutional reforms, strengthen state-level institutions, streamline government institutions, and make Dayton a piece of Bosnian history. This seems impossible in the current climate, and many analysts have argued that Bosnia is facing its "biggest political crisis since the end of the war."[69]

Trials for mass atrocities in Bosnia continue, however, as do the exhumations and investigations that are a part of international war crimes prosecutions. Sabaheta Fejzić was one of the survivors of the Srebrenica genocide who protested the closing of the ICTY on that cold and rainy March day in 2004, in the scene that opened this book. Her son Rijad had been just 17 when he was pulled from her arms and handed over to soldiers of the Army of Republika Srpska (VRS). Rijad was executed, and his body was later found in a mass grave. Fourteen years later, on a solemn July 11, 2009, Sabaheta buried her son at the Srebrenica-Potočari Memorial and Cemetery. He joined 533 other victims, including 44 who, like Rijad, were under 18 at the time of their tragic deaths. When Slobodan Milošević had died in his cell years earlier, Sabaheta had told the press she felt cheated by his death.[70] International justice was important to her. Her son's identification and burial were important as well. The lesson in her story is that international criminal law has its rightful place, but it can be only a small part of processes of postconflict social repair. While trials are important to survivors, they are often secondary to other more pressing needs in the aftermath of political violence.

There is much more to be studied on the impact of international criminal tribunals, especially in Bosnia. This book combined methods in an attempt to produce a general overview, but still it leaves much territory uncovered, notably Central Bosnia and Herzegovina. In addition, there is much we do not know about how the findings in the courtroom have enlightened conventional wisdom about the causes and events of the war.

This book follows the first early pioneering studies on the topic, and in a sense is a continuation of these; attitudes and institutional changes should continue to be measured with some regularity. Future projects ought to delve deeper into the processes with which criminal trials are intertwined: data collection, exhumations, the distribution of benefits, and refugee returns. These processes overlap, affecting developments that shape the relationship between citizens in nascent democracies well beyond the courtroom. Courts, be they international or local, are only a small part of this process, but they contribute to a liberalizing dynamic. Further "bottom up" research on the impact of and attitudes toward international

---

[69] Sabina Niksic, "Europe Remembers Srebrenica, but Not Bosnia," *Agence France Press*, July 12, 2009.

[70] Mike Corder, "Embittered by Aborted Milošević Trial, Bosnian Victims Look to Karadžić Case for Justice," *Associated Press*, July 28, 2008.

courts is needed, studies which recognize that even the terms of the discussion are still in their infancy.

In conclusion, this study has found a legacy of the ICTY not identified to date: that without the Tribunal, Srebrenica family associations might not have been as successful at organizing networks around the genocide of July 1995; the Bosnian government would not have grappled with the fact that crimes were committed under its leadership; and NGOs would have been more reluctant to work in other entities. Local trials for war crimes most certainly would not have been held. Still, the Dayton Peace Agreement has meant that trials have reverberated through a charged political environment that has sometimes made them look farcical.

While this study was completed at a time when public optimism was at an all-time postwar low, the communities in Bosnia who represent progressive, multi-ethnic political options – those who refused nationalist politics from day one – will continue to forge new political options. If the work of the court helps those political entrepreneurs articulate their desire for a lawful Bosnia in which the rights of all citizens are respected, the ICTY will have fulfilled at least part of its extended mandate, and will have enabled a country once engulfed by war to court democracy's promise.

Annex 1
Interview Questions for Chapter 5
Making Progress with Few Resources: Civil Society and the ICTY

The interviews for this chapter were conducted in-person with representatives of 53 Bosnian non-governmental organizations randomly sampled from all over the country. The interviews were conducted primarily in 2004. This chapter is a repetition of a study by Kristen Cibelli and Tamy Guberek, *Justice Unknown, Justice Unsatisfied?: Bosnian NGOs Speak about the International Criminal Tribunal for the Former Yugoslavia* (Boston, MA: Tufts University, 2000). Each interviewee signed and received a copy of the human subjects consent form required by the Institutional Review Board (IRB) of Columbia University.

International Criminal Tribunal for the former Yugoslavia (ICTY)

01. Does the Tribunal play a role in your NGO's activities?
02. Has the Tribunal inspired any of the work of your NGO?
03. If the Tribunal did not exist, would the work of your NGO be different? If so, how?
04. Do you feel comfortable with your level of knowledge about the Tribunal?
05. Do you know what criteria are used for indictments? Do you know what crimes individuals can be charged with?
06. What do you think of sealed indictments?
07. Are you aware of the process of plea agreements? How do you evaluate this strategy?
08. How do you feel about the strategy of the Tribunal – its use of plea agreements and its policy to search for so-called "big fish"?
09. Does your organization see the Tribunal as credible?
10. What do you think of the sentences given by the Tribunal?
11. Is the length of the sentence or the fact that the person was held accountable more important?
12. Has your organization or any of the members had any direct experience with the Tribunal?
13. How do you feel about the witness protection offered by the Tribunal? Would you be a witness for the Tribunal?
14. What do you think about the decision to prosecute rape as a war crime?
15. Do you feel the Tribunal has paid enough attention to this crime?
16. Do you know who has the responsibility to arrest war criminals?
17. If SFOR fails to arrest war criminals, does this jeopardize or affect the credibility of the Tribunal?
18. Does the way SFOR conducts arrests affect the credibility of the Tribunal?
19. Beyond holding individuals accountable for war crimes, do you think the Tribunal has broader goals?

20. Does the Tribunal advance democratization in Bosnia and Herzegovina?
21. Does the Tribunal serve as a deterrent?
22. Does it help advance the rule of law in Bosnia and Herzegovina?
23. Does individual criminal responsibility hinder or improve interethnic relations in Bosnia?
24. Does the Tribunal prevent individuals from taking revenge?
25. Do you think the Tribunal affects the return of refugees?
26. Does the Tribunal bring justice to Bosnia and Herzegovina?
27. Does the Tribunal bring reconciliation to Bosnia and Herzegovina?

Information Sources and Outreach Program

28. Where does the organization get information about the Tribunal?
29. Does the organization use the internet to access information about the Tribunal?
30. Is broadcasting of trials useful for your organization? Do you watch broadcasts?
31. Is the broadcasting of trials helpful now?
32. Does your organization know about the Outreach Program of the Tribunal?
33. Do you believe you have received adequate information from the Tribunal Outreach Program? If no, what information did you expect from this program that you did not get?
34. Have NGOs been used to the greatest extent possible to help the Tribunal with outreach? If not, what else should they be asked to do?
35. How can the Outreach Program best be made accessible to your organization and the local community?
36. Do you feel that information about the Tribunal is used or manipulated by the people in power?
37. Have you heard about the bounty program of the United States?[1]
38. Do you think it will encourage people to help the Tribunal?
39. Do you think the arrest of Radovan Karadžić and Ratko Mladić is an important goal for Bosnia and Herzegovina?

Truth and Reconciliation Commission (TRC)

40. Do you feel that there has been enough public discourse about the causes of the war?
41. Has your organization heard about the TRC proposed for Bosnia and Herzegovina?
42. Do you think a TRC could be helpful for Bosnia and Herzegovina?
43. What could a TRC do on a national level for reconciliation in Bosnia and Herzegovina?
44. Is a TRC realistic and feasible at this time?
45. What potential problems could you see for a TRC?
46. What suggestions do you have for the organizers of the TRC so that it works best?

International Court of Justice Case

47. Does your organization know about the ICJ case?
48. How does the organization feel about the case?

---

[1] In 1998, the U.S. Department of State set up a reward program, offering up to $5 million (USD) for information leading to the arrest of war crimes suspects, including Ratko Mladić and Radovan Karadžić.

49. Is the case important?
50. What are the possible implications of the case if it is won or lost?

Court of Bosnia and Herzegovina ("State Court")

51. Do you know about plans to create a War Crimes Chamber?
52. What do you think of this plan? Is Bosnia ready for a War Crimes Chamber?
53. What lessons can the work of the ICTY provide for the architects of the Chamber?

Reparations

54. Are you aware of a victim's right to reparations in international law?
55. Would you support a Bosnia-wide program to provide reparations to victims in Bosnia, regardless of their ethnicity?

Human Rights

56. Has the international community in Bosnia and Herzegovina paid enough attention to war crimes and the subject of the past more generally?
57. Does the promotion of human rights in Bosnia help the work of your non-governmental organization? Do you have contact with any international non-governmental organization?

Questions for Srebrenica-Related NGOs

58. Could you comment on the Tribunal's decision to arrest Naser Orić?
59. Will recent cases involving perpetrators of crimes in Srebrenica help facilitate returns?

Srebrenica Commission

60. What do you think about the Srebrenica Commission?

Conclusion

61. Are there any important issues that I have left out? Do you have any additional comments?

Annex 2

Survey Instrument for Chapter 7

From the Battlefield to the Barracks: The ICTY and the Armed Forces

This survey was administered in five Bosnian cities (Sarajevo, Tuzla, Mostar, Banja Luka, and Bijeljina) in the fall of 2005. 463 respondents filled out an anonymous questionnaire containing the questions listed below. The original survey instrument was translated into Bosnian, Croatian and Serbian and included background information on the study required by the Institutional Review Board (IRB) of Columbia University.

1. Location
☐ Federation of Bosnia and Herzegovina   ☐ Republika Srpska

2. Ethnicity
☐ Bosniak   ☐ Croat   ☐ Jew   ☐ Serb   ☐ Roma   ☐ Other _____

3. Age
☐ 18–22   ☐ 23–29   ☐ 30–39   ☐ 40–49   ☐ 50 or over

4. Do you live in the same municipality as you did before the war?
☐ Yes   ☐ No

5. What is your highest level of education?
☐ Primary school   ☐ High school   ☐ Associate degree   ☐ University degree
☐ Graduate school

6. What is the highest level of education of your father?
☐ Primary school   ☐ High school   ☐ Associate degree   ☐ University degree
☐ Graduate school

7. What is the highest level of education of your mother?
☐ Primary school   ☐ High school   ☐ Associate degree   ☐ University degree
☐ Graduate school

8. Did you lose an immediate member of your family (father, mother, brother, sister, children or grandparent) as a result of the war?
☐ Yes   ☐ No

9. Current rank
Federation:
☐ Private   ☐ Private First Class   ☐ Corporal   ☐ Sergeant   ☐ Staff Sergeant
☐ Master Sergeant   ☐ Sergeant Major   ☐ Lieutenant   ☐ Senior Lieutenant
☐ Captain   ☐ Major   ☐ Colonel   ☐ Brigadier   ☐ Other _____

RS:
☐ Private ☐ Private First Class ☐ Corporal ☐ Sergeant ☐ Staff Sergeant
☐ Sergeant First Class ☐ Master Sergeant ☐ Sergeant Major ☐ Lieutenant
☐ Senior Lieutenant ☐ Captain ☐ Major ☐ Colonel ☐ Brigadier ☐ Other _____

10. Did you serve in the armed forces during the war?
☐ Yes ☐ No

If you answered no, continue with question 13.

11. If yes, please indicate which one?
☐ Army of Republika Srpska ☐ Army of the Republic of Bosnia and Herzegovina
☐ Croat Defense Council ☐ Police of Republika Srpska
☐ Police of Bosnia and Herzegovina ☐ Police of Herceg Bosna
☐ Croatian Army ☐ Yugoslav People's Army ☐ Other _____

12. If so, why did you join the armed forces?
☐ Mobilization/draft ☐ Voluntarily
☐ I was already in the army, police, or territorial defense forces ☐ Other _____

Trust in Government

13. In your opinion, how much of the time do you think you can trust the Council of Ministers to do what is right?
☐ Almost always ☐ Most of the time ☐ Sometimes ☐ Never ☐ Don't know

14. In your opinion, how much of the time do you think you can trust the government in the Federation to do what is right?
☐ Almost always ☐ Most of the time ☐ Sometimes ☐ Never ☐ Don't know

15. In your opinion, how much of the time do you think you can trust the RS government to do what is right?
☐ Almost always ☐ Most of the time ☐ Sometimes ☐ Never ☐ Don't know

16. Do you think that the people running the government are corrupt?
☐ Very corrupt ☐ A little corrupt ☐ Almost no one is corrupt ☐ Don't know

17. Do you believe the government is accountable to its citizens?
☐ Almost always ☐ Most of the time ☐ Sometimes ☐ Never ☐ Don't know

18. Who or what do you think will help make the government more accountable to its citizens? Check all that apply.
☐ International community ☐ Non-governmental organizations
☐ Citizens ☐ Politicians ☐ Don't know ☐ Other _____

Political Participation

19. Did you vote in the last municipal elections in 2004?
☐ Yes ☐ No

20. Did you vote in the last general elections in 2002?
☐ Yes ☐ No

Political Views

21. Did you vote for the non-nationalist parties in the last elections (for example, the SDP, Liberal Party, etc.)?
□ Yes   □ No

Interethnic Relations

22. One always needs to be suspicious of members of other ethnic groups.
□ Agree   □ Slightly agree   □ Slightly disagree   □ Disagree   □ Don't know

23. How would you evaluate interethnic relations in your community?
□ Very good   □ Good   □ Bad   □ Very Bad
□ There are only members of my ethnic group in my community   □ Don't know

24. How would you evaluate interethnic relations in Bosnia and Herzegovina?
□ Very good   □ Good   □ Bad   □ Very Bad   □ Don't know

Armed Forces of Bosnia and Herzegovina, Views of Colleagues and Superiors

25. Would you say that your colleagues keep their promises?
□ Always   □ Most of the time   □ Sometimes   □ Rarely   □ Don't know

26. Would you say that your colleagues in the other entity keep their promises?
□ Always   □ Most of the time   □ Sometimes   □ Rarely   □ Don't know

27. I am confident that the new joint command of the Armed Forces of Bosnia and Herzegovina is qualified to lead the army towards NATO membership.
□ Agree   □ Slightly agree   □ Slightly disagree   □ Disagree   □ Don't know

International Community

28. In your opinion, does the international community work in the best interest of Bosnia and Herzegovina?
□ Always   □ Most of the time   □ Sometimes   □ Rarely   □ Don't know

29. In your opinion, does the International Criminal Tribunal for the former Yugoslavia (ICTY) work in the best interest of Bosnia and Herzegovina?
□ Always   □ Most of the time   □ Sometimes   □ Rarely   □ Don't know

30. Do you believe the international community is pushing defense reform in a positive direction?
□ Generally   □ Somewhat   □ Not at all   □ Don't know

31. If yes, what are the most important reforms in your opinion? Check all that apply.
□ Creation of a state level defense ministry   □ Demobilization
□ Creation of a joint chain of command   □ Reduction of arms
□ Implementation of NATO standards   □ Other _____

Dayton Peace Agreement

32. Do you believe the Dayton Peace Agreement should be changed to abolish the entity structure in Bosnia and Herzegovina?
☐ Yes ☐ No ☐ Don't know

33. Do you believe the Dayton Peace Agreement treated all parties in the war equally?
☐ Yes ☐ No ☐ Don't know

Please explain _____

International Humanitarian Law

34. Do the laws of conduct during wartime, such as the Geneva Conventions, affect your daily work?
☐ Yes ☐ No ☐ Somewhat ☐ Don't know

35. Do you feel you are adequately educated in international humanitarian law?
☐ Yes ☐ No ☐ Not adequately ☐ Don't know

36. Do you believe you could identify a violation of the Geneva Conventions in a conflict situation?
☐ Yes ☐ No ☐ Don't know

37. If international humanitarian law (e.g., the Geneva Conventions) did not exist, would your work be different if at all?
☐ Yes ☐ No ☐ Somewhat ☐ Don't know

38. Do you feel there have been enough criminal trials of violations of international humanitarian law committed during the war?
☐ Yes ☐ No ☐ Don't know

39. Were all parties equally guilty for violations of international humanitarian law during the war?
☐ Yes ☐ No ☐ Don't know

40. If not, on a scale from 1 to 6, please rank which party, in your opinion, you felt was most guilty using a 1 and the least guilty using 6.
☐ Army of the Republic of Bosnia and Herzegovina ☐ Croatian Army
☐ Croat Defense Council ☐ Yugoslav People's Army
☐ Paramilitary formations (which side?) _____ ☐ Army of Republika Srpska

If you served in the army during the war, please answer the following questions; if you did not, please skip to question 45.

41. Did soldiers in your unit take actions against civilians during the war that you think probably qualify as criminal violations of the laws of war?
☐ Yes ☐ No

42. Were soldiers in your unit punished by your commanders for those crimes against civilians during the war?
☐ Yes ☐ No

43. If not, should there have been proceedings against those soldiers?
☐ Yes ☐ No

44. Were you instructed on how to treat civilians and combatants during the war?
☐ Yes ☐ No

International Criminal Tribunal for the former Yugoslavia (ICTY)

45. Do you feel it was necessary for the ICTY to be formed?
☐ Yes ☐ No ☐ Don't know

46. Do you feel comfortable with your level of knowledge about the ICTY?
☐ Yes ☐ No ☐ Somewhat ☐ Don't know

47. Do you follow the trials at the ICTY?
☐ Yes ☐ No ☐ Sometimes

48. Where do you get information about the ICTY? Check all that apply.
☐ Press ☐ TV ☐ Internet ☐ Books and publications ☐ Other_____

49 Do you watch the broadcasts of trials from the ICTY?
☐ Yes ☐ No ☐ Sometimes

50. Is the ICTY a credible institution in your view?
☐ Yes ☐ No ☐ Somewhat ☐ Additional comments _____

51. Do you believe the indictments of the ICTY for violations of the norms of international humanitarian law are brought about in a fair and impartial manner?
☐ Yes ☐ No ☐ Sometimes ☐ Don't know

52. If not, why not?_____

53. Are you satisfied with the level of cooperation with the ICTY?
☐ Yes ☐ No ☐ Somewhat ☐ Don't know

54. Please name any of the individuals tried at the ICTY._____

55. Have you had any direct experience with the ICTY (e.g., as a witness, gave a statement, etc.)?
☐ Yes ☐ No

56. Can you name any of the specific crimes and individuals sentenced by the ICTY for those crimes?
_____

57. Does the topic of the ICTY come up in discussion with other military personnel during your workday?
☐ Yes ☐ No ☐ Sometimes

58. Does the ICTY contribute to a better understanding of the rules of conduct of military personnel during wartime?
☐ Yes ☐ No ☐ Somewhat ☐ Don't know

59. Does the work of the ICTY positively affect your relationship to international humanitarian law?
☐ Yes ☐ No ☐ Somewhat ☐ Don't know

60. Do you believe the judgments of the ICTY will prevent individuals from committing war crimes in the future?
☐ Yes ☐ No ☐ Somewhat ☐ Don't know

61. Does the ICTY contribute to justice in Bosnia and Herzegovina?
☐ Yes   ☐ No   ☐ Somewhat   ☐ Don't know

62. Does the ICTY contribute to reconciliation in Bosnia and Herzegovina?
☐ Yes   ☐ No   ☐ Somewhat   ☐ Don't know

63. Does the ICTY influence the rule of law in Bosnia and Herzegovina?
☐ Yes, it has positive effects   ☐ Yes, it has somewhat positive effects
☐ No, it has negative effects   ☐ No, it has somewhat negative effects

64. Does the ICTY contribute to the democratization of society in Bosnia and Herzegovina?
☐ Yes   ☐ No   ☐ Somewhat   ☐ Don't know

65. In your opinion, will domestic trials positively affect democratization, justice, reconciliation and the rule of law in Bosnia and Herzegovina?
☐ More than the ICTY   ☐ Less than the ICTY   ☐ About the same   ☐ Don't know

66. Has the ICTY's work affected your views about the following? Check all that apply.
☐ Who was responsible for starting the war   ☐ What happened during the war
☐ The current political structure of Bosnia and Herzegovina
☐ The future of Bosnia and Herzegovina   ☐ Other_____

67. Bosnia and Herzegovina should cooperate with the ICTY ONLY because if it does not it will be punished by the international community.
☐ Agree   ☐ Slightly agree   ☐ Slightly disagree   ☐ Disagree   ☐ Don't know

68. Politics influences developments at the ICTY in a way that inhibits its ability to dispense justice fairly.
☐ Agree   ☐ Slightly agree   ☐ Slightly disagree   ☐ Disagree   ☐ Don't know

69. International prosecutions will help Bosnia find out the facts about what happened during the war.
☐ Agree   ☐ Slightly agree   ☐ Slightly disagree   ☐ Disagree   ☐ Don't know

70. Bosnia and Herzegovina should cooperate with the ICTY because perpetrators of war crimes should be brought to justice.
☐ Agree   ☐ Slightly agree   ☐ Slightly disagree   ☐ Disagree   ☐ Don't know

71. The ICTY is biased against members of my ethnic group.
☐ Agree   ☐ Slightly agree   ☐ Slightly disagree   ☐ Disagree   ☐ Don't know

72. Members of ethnic groups other than mine exaggerate the extent of their suffering during the war for political purposes.
☐ Agree   ☐ Slightly agree   ☐ Slightly disagree   ☐ Disagree   ☐ Don't know

73. Politicians from my ethnic group misrepresented historical events in order to lead the country into war.
☐ Agree   ☐ Slightly agree   ☐ Slightly disagree   ☐ Disagree   ☐ Don't know

74. Politicians from other ethnic groups misrepresented historical events in order to lead the country into war.
☐ Agree   ☐ Slightly agree   ☐ Slightly disagree   ☐ Disagree   ☐ Don't know

75. Factual knowledge about wartime events has improved interethnic relations in Bosnia and Herzegovina.
□ Improved relations   □ Worsened relations   □ Did not affect relations
□ Not sure/Don't know

76. I trust the ICTY to provide accurate information about the war.
□ Agree   □ Slightly agree   □ Slightly disagree   □ Disagree   □ Don't know

77. The ICTY is a waste of money.
□ Agree   □ Slightly agree   □ Slightly disagree   □ Disagree   □ Don't know

78. If yes, where should this money have been invested?
□ Domestic trials   □ Schools and hospitals   □ Reparations for victims
□ All of above   □ Other_____

EUFOR/SFOR

79. Do SFOR/EUFOR's efforts to arrest war criminals negatively affect your work?
□ Yes   □ No   □ Somewhat

80. Do you believe conflict would result in Bosnia and Herzegovina if EUFOR leaves?
□ Yes   □ No   □ Maybe

NATO's Partnership for Peace (PfP)

81. Do you believe Bosnia and Herzegovina should have been admitted to PfP?
□ Yes   □ No

82. Do you believe the issue of non-cooperation with ICTY should continue to be a bar to PfP entry?
□ Yes   □ No   □ Don't know

Conclusion

83. Would you feel comfortable reporting what you believed was a war crime to your superior?
□ Yes   □ No   □ Don't know

84. If, NO, why?

_____

85. What is the best solution for addressing the war crimes committed during the war? Check all that apply.
□ Amnesty   □ Trials   □ Reparations   □ Other_____

86. I support the creation of a Truth and Reconciliation Commission (TRC) in Bosnia and Herzegovina.
□ Yes   □ No   □ Don't know   □ Not informed

87. A recent report of the Srebrenica Commission concluded that 19,473 individuals participated in the Srebrenica massacre of July 1995. How should the government respond to this new information? Check all that apply.
☐ Widespread amnesty   ☐ Partial amnesty excluding those most responsible
☐ Widespread prosecutions   ☐ Other_____

88. How would you characterize the war in Bosnia and Herzegovina?
☐ Civil war   ☐ Aggression   ☐ Combination of an aggression and civil war   ☐ Other _____

89. The arrest of Ratko Mladić and Radovan Karadžić is an important goal for the future of Bosnia and Herzegovina.
☐ Agree   ☐ Slightly agree   ☐ Slightly disagree   ☐ Disagree   ☐ Don't know

Do you have any additional comments?
_____

This is an anonymous questionnaire. Please do not write your name anywhere on this document.

Note: Once completed please fold in half.

Bibliography

With a few exceptions, this bibliography contains only books and scholarly articles. ICTY documents, reports, dissertations, press releases, newspaper and magazine articles, and audiovisual materials are in the footnotes only.

Akhavan, Payam. "Justice in the Hague, Peace in the Former Yugoslavia? A Commentary on the United Nations War Crimes Tribunal." *Human Rights Quarterly* 20, no. 4 (1998): 737–816.

Almond, Gabriel A., and Sidney Verba. *The Civic Culture: Political Attitudes and Democracy in Five Nations*. Newbury Park, CA: Sage Publications, 1989.

Alvarez, Jose E. "Rush to Closure: Lessons of the Tadić Judgment." *Michigan Law Review* 96, no. 7 (June 1998): 2031–112.

Anderson, Elizabeth, and Richard H. Pildes. "Expressive Theories of Law: A General Restatement." *University of Pennsylvania Law Review* 148, no. 5 (May 2000): 1503–75.

Andjelic, Neven. *Bosnia-Herzegovina: The End of a Legacy*. London: Frank Cass, 2003.

Andreas, Peter. *Blue Helmets and Black Markets: The Business of Survival in the Siege of Sarajevo*. Ithaca, NY: Cornell University Press, 2008.

"The Clandestine Political Economy of the War and Peace in Bosnia," *International Studies Quarterly* 48 (2004): 29–51.

Armatta, Judith. *Twilight of Impunity: The War Crimes Trial of Slobodan Milošević*. Durham, NC: Duke University Press, 2010.

Azinović, Vlado. *Al Kai'da u Bosni i Hercegovini: Mit ili stvarna opasnost* (Al Qaeda in Bosnia and Herzegovina: Myth or present danger?). Prague: Radio Slobodna Europa, 2007.

Bass, Gary Jonathan. *Stay the Hand of Vengeance: The Politics of War Crimes Tribunals*. Princeton, NJ: Princeton University Press, 2000.

Bassiouni, Cherif. "To Deter and Dissuade, and so Deny – Use of International Courts." *UN Chronicle* 36, no. 1 (Spring 1999): 63.

Bećirević, Edina. *Na Drini genocid* (Genocide on the Drina River). Sarajevo: Buybook, 2009.

Bennett, Alan. *The History Boys: A Play*. London: Faber and Faber, 2006.

Biro, Miklos, Dean Ajdukovic, Dinka Corkalo, Dino Djipa, Petar Milin, and Harvey M. Weinstein. "Attitudes toward Justice and Social Reconstruction in Bosnia and Herzegovina and Croatia." In *My Neighbor, My Enemy: Justice and Community in the Aftermath of Mass Atrocity*, edited by Eric Stover and Harvey M. Weinstein. Cambridge: Cambridge University Press, 2004.

Boas, Gideon. *The Milošević Trial: Lessons for the Conduct of Complex International Criminal Proceedings*. Cambridge: Cambridge University Press, 2007.

Bose, Sumantra. *Bosnia After Dayton: Nationalist Partition and International Intervention*. Oxford: Oxford University Press, 2002.

Bringa, Tone. "Averted Gaze: Genocide in Bosnia-Herzegovina." In *Annihilating Difference*, edited by A. L. Hinton. Berkeley: University of California Press, 2002.

Brooks, Peter, and Paul Gewirtz, eds. *Law's Stories: Narrative and Rhetoric in the Law*. New Haven, CT: Yale University Press, 1996.

Bunce, Valerie. *Subversive Institutions: The Design and the Destruction of Socialism and the State*. Cambridge: Cambridge University Press, 1999.

———. "Should Transitologists Be Grounded?" *Slavic Review* 54, no. 1 (Spring, 1995): 111–27.

Burg, Steven L., and Paul Shoup. *The War in Bosnia-Herzegovina*. Armonk, NY: M.E. Sharpe, 1999.

Carothers, Thomas. "The End of the Transition Paradigm." *Journal of Democracy* 13, no. 1 (2002): 5–21.

Chandler, David. *Bosnia: Faking Democracy after Dayton*. London: Pluto Press, 1999.

Chesterman, Simon. *You, the People: The United Nations, Transitional Administration, and State-Building*. New York: Oxford University Press, 2005.

Cibelli, Kristen, and Tamy Guberek, *Justice Unknown, Justice Unsatisfied?: Bosnian NGOs Speak about the International Criminal Tribunal for the former Yugoslavia*. Boston: Tufts University, 2000.

Cigar, Norman L., and Paul Williams. *Indictment at the Hague: The Milošević Regime and Crimes of the Balkan Wars*. New York: New York University Press, 2002.

Clark, Janine Natalya. "International War Crimes Tribunals and the Challenge of Outreach." *International Criminal Law Review* 9 (2009): 99–116.

Cobban, Helena. "Think Again: International Courts." *Foreign Policy* (March–April 2006): 22–28.

Cohen, Geoffrey L. "Party Over Policy: The Dominating Impact of Group Influence on Political Beliefs." *Journal of Personality and Social Psychology* 85, no. 5 (2003): 808–22.

Cohen, Lenard J. *Serpent in the Bosom: The Rise and Fall of Slobodan Milošević*. New York: Basic Books, 2002.

Cohen, Roger. *Hearts Grown Brutal: Sagas of Sarajevo*. New York: Random House, 1998.

Coles, Kimberley. *Democratic Designs: International Intervention and Electoral Practices in Postwar Bosnia-Herzegovina*. Ann Arbor: University of Michigan Press, 2007.

Congram, Derek, and Jon Sterenberg. "Grave Challenges in Iraq." In *Handbook of Forensic Anthropology and Archeology*, edited by S. Blau and D. Ubelaker. Walnut Creek, CA: Leftcoast Press, 2008.

Ćurak, Nerzuk. *Dejtonski nacionalizam* (Dayton's nationalism). Sarajevo: Buybook, 2004.

Del Ponte, Carla, with Chuck Sudetic. *Madame Prosecutor: Confrontations with Humanity's Worst Criminals and the Culture of Impunity*. New York: Other Press, 2009. Originally published as *La caccia: Io e i criminali di guerra* (The hunt: The war criminals and I) (Milan, Italy: Feltrinelli, 2008).

Dembour, Marie Benedict, and Tobias Kelly, eds. *Paths to International Justice: Social and Legal Perspectives*. Cambridge: Cambridge University Press, 2007.

Denich, Bette. "Dismembering Yugoslavia: Nationalist Ideologies and the Symbolic Revival of Genocide." *American Ethnologist* 21, no. 2 (1994): 367–90.

Donia, Robert J. *Sarajevo: A Biography*. Ann Arbor: University of Michigan Press, 2006.

———. "The New Bosniak History." *Nationalities Papers* 28, no. 2 (June 2000): 351–58.

———. "The Quest for Tolerance in Sarajevo's Textbooks." *Human Rights Review* 1, no. 2 (January–March 2000): 38–55.

Donia, Robert J. and Smail Čekić. *Milošević Guilty of Genocide: Decision on Motion of the Hague Tribunal of 16 June 2004* (Miloševiću dokazan genocid u Bosni). Sarajevo: Institute for Research of Crimes Against Humanity and International Law of the University of Sarajevo, 2007.

Donia, Robert J., and John V.A. Fine Jr. *Bosnia and Hercegovina: A Tradition Betrayed*. New York: Columbia University Press, 1994.

Doyle, Michael H. "Too Little, Too Late? Justice and Security Reform in Bosnia and Herzegovina." In *Constructing Justice and Security After War*, edited by Charles T. Call. Washington, D.C.: United States Institute for Peace, 2007.

Dragović-Soso, Jasna. *Saviours of the Nation: Serbia's Intellectual Opposition and the Revival of Nationalism*. London: Hurst & Company, 2002.

"Why did Yugoslavia Disintegrate? An Overview of Contending Explanations." In *State Collapse in South-Eastern Europe: New Perspectives on Yugoslavia's Disintegration*, edited by Lenard J. Cohen and Jasna Dragović-Soso. West Lafayette, IN: Purdue University Press, 2007.

Drakulić, Slavenka. *They Would Never Hurt a Fly: War Criminals on Trial in The Hague*. London: Viking, 2004.

Drumbl, Mark A. *Atrocity, Punishment, and International Law*. Cambridge: Cambridge University Press, 2007.

"Looking Up, Down and Across: The ICTY's Place in the International Legal Order." *New England Law Review* 37 (2003): 1037–1057.

"The Expressive Value of Prosecuting and Punishing Terrorists: Hamdan, the Geneva Conventions, and International Criminal Law." *George Washington Law Review* 75, no. 5/6 (2007): 1165–1199.

Ehrenfreund, Norbert. *The Nuremberg Legacy: How the Nazi War Crimes Trials Changed the Course of History*. New York: Palgrave Macmillan, 2007.

Elster, Jon. *Closing the Books: Transitional Justice in Historical Perspective*. New York: Cambridge University Press, 2004.

Evans, Peter B., Harold K. Jacobson, and Robert D. Putnam. *Double-Edged Diplomacy: International Bargaining and Domestic Politics*. Berkeley: University of California Press, 1993.

Falk, Richard, Jacqueline Stevens, and Balakrishnan Rajagopol, eds. *International Law and the Third World*. New York: Routledge, 2008.

Feinberg, Joel. "The Expressive Function of Punishment." In Joel Feinberg, *Doing and Deserving: Essays in the Theory of Responsibility*. Princeton, NJ: Princeton University Press, 1970.

Finnemore, Martha, and Kathryn Sikkink. "International Norm Dynamics and Political Change." *International Organization* 52, no. 4 (1998): 887–917.

Fletcher, Laurel E., and Harvey M. Weinstein. "Violence and Social Repair: Rethinking the Contribution of Justice to Reconciliation." *Human Rights Quarterly* 24, no. 3 (2002): 573–639.

Fletcher, Laurel E., and Harvey M. Weinstein. "A world unto itself? The application of international justice in the former Yugoslavia." In *My Neighbor, My Enemy: Justice and Community in the Aftermath of Mass Atrocity*, edited by Eric Stover and Harvey M. Weinstein. Cambridge: Cambridge University Press, 2004.

Franzosi, Roberto. "Narrative Analysis – Or Why (And How) Sociologists Should be Interested in Narrative." *Annual Review of Sociology* 24 (1998): 517–54.

Gagnon, V.P., Jr. *The Myth of Ethnic War: Serbia and Croatia in the 1990s*. Ithaca, NY: Cornell University Press, 2004.

Galligan, Denis J. *Law in Modern Society*. Oxford: Oxford University Press, 2007.

Garth, Bryant G., and Austin Sarat, eds. *How Does Law Matter?: Fundamental Issues in Law and Society*. Chicago: Northwestern University Press, 1998.

"Studying How Law Matters: An Introduction." In *How Does Law Matter?: Fundamental Issues in Law and Society*, edited by Bryant G. Garth and Austin Sarat. Chicago: Northwestern University Press, 1998.

Gibson, James L. *Overcoming Apartheid: Can Truth Reconcile A Divided Nation?* New York: Russell Sage Foundation, 2004.

Goldstone, Richard J. "Advancing the Cause for Human Rights: The Need for Justice and Accountability." In *Realizing Human Rights: Moving from Inspiration to Impact*, edited by Samantha Power and Graham Allison. New York: St. Martin's Press, 2000.

For Humanity: Reflections of a War Crimes Investigator. New Haven, CT: Yale University Press, 2000.

Gow, James. *The Serbian Project and its Adversaries: A Strategy of War Crimes.* London: Hurst and Company, 2003.

Triumph of the Lack of Will: International Diplomacy and the Yugolsav War. New York: Columbia University Press, 1997.

Gutman, Roy. *A Witness to Genocide: First Inside Account of the Horrors of Ethnic Cleansing in Bosnia.* Rockport, MA: Element Books, 1993.

Gutman, Roy, David Rieff, Anthony Dworkin, and Sheryl A. Mendez, eds. *Crimes of War 2.0: What the Public Should Know.* New York: W. W. Norton and Co., 2007.

Hafner-Burton, Emilie, and James Ron. "Human Rights Institutions: Rhetoric and Efficacy." *Journal of Peace Research* 44, no. 4 (2007): 379–84.

Hafner-Burton, Emilie M., and Kiyoteru Tsutsui. "Justice Lost! The Failure of International Human Rights Law to Matter Where Needed Most." *Journal of Peace Research* 44, no. 4 (2007): 407–25.

Hagan, John. *Justice in the Balkans: Prosecuting War Crimes in the Hague Tribunal.* Chicago: University of Chicago Press, 2003.

Hagan, John, and Sanja Kutnjak. "The Politics of Punishment and the Siege of Sarajevo: Toward a Conflict Theory of Perceived International (In)Justice." *Law and Society Review* 40, no. 2 (2006): 369–410.

Hagan, John, Ron Levi, and Gabrielle Ferrales. "Swaying the Hand of Justice: The Internal and External Dynamics of Regime Change at the International Criminal Tribunal for the Former Yugoslavia." *Law & Social Inquiry* 31, no. 3 (2006): 585–616.

Hampton, Jean. "The Moral Education Theory of Punishment." *Philosophy and Public Affairs* 13, no. 3 (Summer 1984): 208–38.

Harrell, Peter E. *Rwanda's Gamble: Gacaca and a New Model of Transitional Justice.* New York: Writers Club Press, 2003.

Hartmann, Florence. *Paix et châtiment: Les guerres secrètes de la politique et de la justice internationales* (Peace and punishment: The secret wars of politics and international justice). Paris: Flammarion, 2007.

Hayner, Priscilla B. *Unspeakable Truths: Confronting State Terror and Atrocity.* New York: Routledge, 2001.

Hilbink, Lisa. *Judges Beyond Politics in Democracy and Dictatorship: Lessons from Chile.* Cambridge: Cambridge University Press, 2007.

Hirschman, Albert O. *Exit, Voice and Loyalty: Responses to Decline in Firms, Organizations and States.* Cambridge, MA: Harvard University Press, 1970.

Hoare, Marko Attila. *How Bosnia Armed.* London: Saqi Books, 2004.

Hoare, Quintin, and Noel Malcolm, eds. *Books on Bosnia: A Critical Bibliography of Works Relating to Bosnia-Herzegovina Since 1990 in West European Languages.* London: The Bosnian Institute, 1999.

Human Rights Center and the International Human Rights Law Clinic, University of California, Berkeley, and the Human Rights Center, University of Sarajevo. "Justice, Accountability and Social Reconstruction in Bosnia and Herzegovina: An Interview Study of Bosnian Judges and Prosecutors." *Berkeley Journal of International Law* 18 (2000): 102–64.

Huntington, Samuel P. *The Third Wave: Democratization in the Late Twentieth Century.* London: University of Oklahoma Press, 1993.

Huyse, Luc. "On the Choices Successor Elites Make in Dealing With the Past." *Law and Social Inquiry* 20, no. 1 (1995): 51–78.

Jarvis, Michelle. "Gender Perspectives on ICTY Practice and Procedure." In *International Criminal Law Developments in the Case Law of the ICTY*, edited by Gideon Boas and William Schabas. Leiden, The Netherlands: Martinus Nijhoff Publishers, 2003.

Jervis, Robert. *System Effects: Complexity in Political and Social Life.* Princeton, NJ: Princeton University Press, 1998.

Jones, John R.W.D. and Steven Powles. *International Criminal Practice.* 3rd ed. Ardsley, NY and Oxford: Transnational Publishers/Oxford University Press, 2003.

Jouhanneau, Cécile. "'Si vous avez un problème que vous ne voulez pas régler, créez une Commission': Les commissions d'enquête locales dans la Bosnie-Herzégovine d'après-guerre" ('If you have a problem you do not wish to solve, create a commission': Local Inquiry Commissions in post-war Bosnia and Herzegovina). *Mouvements* 53 (March–May 2008): 166–74.

Kaplan, Richard. *Europe and the Recognition of New States in Yugoslavia.* Cambridge: Cambridge University Press, 2005.

Kaplan, Robert. *Balkan Ghosts: A Journey Through History.* New York: Picador, 2005.

Katzenstein, Peter J., ed. *The Culture of National Security: Norms and Identity in World Politics.* New York: Columbia University Press, 1996.

Keck, Margaret E., and Kathryn Sikkink. *Activists Beyond Borders: Advocacy Networks in International Politics.* Ithaca, NY: Cornell University Press, 1998.

Klarin, Mirko. "Nuremberg Now!" in *The Path to The Hague: Selected Documents on the Origins of the ICTY.* The Hague: United Nations Publications, 1995.

"The Impact of the ICTY Trials on Public Opinion in the Former Yugoslavia." *Journal of International Criminal Justice* 7, no. 1 (March 2009): 89–96.

Klotz, Audie. *Norms in International Relations: The Struggle Against Apartheid.* Ithaca, NY: Cornell University Press, 1999.

Kolind, Torsten. *Post-War Identification: Everyday Muslim Counterdiscourse in Bosnia Herzegovina.* Aarhus, Denmark: Aarhus University Press, 2008.

Kritz, Neil J., ed. *Transitional Justice: How Emerging Democracies Reckon With Former Regimes.* 3 vols. Washington, D.C.: United States Institute of Peace Press, 1995.

Lang, Anthony, Jr. "The United Nations and the Fall of Srebrenica: Meaningful Responsibility and International Society." In *Can Institutions Have Duties? Collective Moral Agency and International Relations*, edited by Toni Erskine. New York: Palgrave Macmillan, 2004.

LeBor, Adam. *Complicity with Evil: The United Nations in the Age of Modern Genocide.* New Haven, CT: Yale University Press, 2007.

Lempert, Richard O. "Mobilizing Private Law: An Introductory Essay." *Law and Society Review* 11 No. 2 (1976): 173–189.

Linz, Juan L., and Alfred Stepan. *Problems of Democratic Transition and Consolidation: Southern Europe, South America and Post-Communist Europe.* Baltimore: Johns Hopkins University Press, 1996.

Longman, Timothy, Phuong Pham, and Harvey M. Weinstein. "Connecting Justice to Human Experience: Attitudes Toward Accountability and Reconciliation in Rwanda." In *My Neighbor, My Enemy: Justice and Community in the Aftermath of Mass Atrocity*, edited by Eric Stover and Harvery Weinstein. Cambridge: Cambridge University Press, 2004.

Loyd, Anthony. *My War Gone By, I Miss it So.* New York: Penguin Books, 2001.

Lutz, Ellen, and Kathryn Sikkink. "The Justice Cascade: The Evolution and Impact of Foreign Human Rights Trials in Latin America." *Chicago Journal of International Law* 2, no. 1 (2001): 1–34.

Maass, Peter. *Love Thy Neighbor: A Story of War*. London: Papermac, 1996.

Maček, Ivana. *Sarajevo Under Siege: Anthropology in Wartime*. Philadelphia, PA: University of Pennsylvania Press, 2009.

Mamdani, Mahmood. *When Victims Become Killers: Colonialism, Nativism, and the Genocide in Rwanda*. Princeton, NJ: Princeton University Press, 2001.

Matton, Sylvie. *Un génocide annoncé*. (A genocide foretold) Paris: Flammarion, 2005.

McAdams, A. James, ed. *Transitional Justice and the Rule of Law in New Democracies*. Notre Dame, IN: University of Notre Dame Press, 1997.

McCann, Michael W., ed. *Law and Social Movements*. Aldershot, UK: Ashgate Publishing, 2006.

"Causal vs. Constitutive Explanations (Or on the Difficulty of being so Positive …)." In *Law and Social Movements, edited by Michael W. McCann*. Aldershot, UK: Ashgate Publishing, 2006.

Rights at Work: Pay Equity Reform and the Politics of Legal Mobilization. Chicago: University of Chicago Press, 1994.

McMahon, Patrice C., and David P. Forsythe. "The ICTY's Impact on Serbia: Judicial Romanticism meets Network Politics." *Human Rights Quarterly* 30, no. 2 (May 2008): 412–35.

Meernik, James. "Justice or Peace: How the International Criminal Tribunal Affects Societal Peace in Bosnia." *Journal of Peace Research* 42 (2005): 271–90.

Mégret, Frédéric, and Florian Hoffmann. "The UN as a Human Rights Violator? Some Reflections on the United Nations' Changing Human Rights Responsibilities." *Human Rights Quarterly* 25, no. 2 (2003): 314–42.

Meron, Theodor. "The Case for War Crimes Trials in Yugoslavia." *Foreign Affairs* 72, no. 3 (Summer 1993): 122–35.

Merry, Sally Engle. *Human Rights and Gender Violence: Translating International Law into Local Justice*. Chicago: University of Chicago Press, 2006.

Minow, Martha. *Between Vengeance and Forgiveness: Facing History After Genocide and Mass Violence*. Boston: Beacon Press, 1998.

"Stories in Law." In *Law's Stories: Narrative and Rhetoric in the Law*, edited by Peter Brooks and Paul Gewirtz. New Haven, CT: Yale University Press, 1996.

Moustafa, Tamir. *The Struggle for Constitutional Power: Law, Politics, and Economic Development in Egypt*. Cambridge: Cambridge University Press, 2007.

Moustafa, Tamir, and Tom Ginsberg. "Introduction: The Functions of Courts in Authoritarian Politics." In *Rule by Law: The Politics of Courts in Authoritarian Regimes*, edited by Tom Ginsberg and Tamir Moustafa. Cambridge: Cambridge University Press, 2008.

Mustafić, Ibran. *Planirani Haos 1990–1996* (Planned chaos 1990–1996). Sarajevo: UG Majke Srebrenice i Podrinja, 2008.

Nettelfield, Lara J. "Research and Repercussions of Death Tolls: The Case of the Bosnian Book of the Dead." In *Sex, Drugs and Body Counts: The Politics of Numbers in Global Crime and Conflict*, edited by Peter Andreas and Kelly M. Greenhill. Ithaca, NY: Cornell University Press, 2010.

Neuffer, Elizabeth. *The Key to My Neighbor's House: Seeking Justice in Bosnia and Rwanda*. New York: Picador, 2001.

Newton, Michael A., and Michael P. Scharf, *Enemy of the State: The Trial and Execution of Saddam Hussein*. New York: St. Martin's Press, 2008.

Nino, Carlos Santiago. *Radical Evil on Trial*. New Haven, CT: Yale University Press, 1996.

Nuhanović, Hasan. *Uloga međunarodnih elementa u Srebrenici "zaštićenoj zoni" – hronologia, analiza i komentari*. (Role of international elements in the Srebrenica "protected area" – chronology, analysis and commentary) Tuzla: 2003.

Pod zastavom UN-a: međunarodna zajednica i zločin u Srebrenici (Under the flag of the UN: the international community and crime in Srebrenica). Sarajevo: Preporod, 2005.

O'Donnell, Guillermo, and Phillipe C. Schmitter. *Transitions from Authoritarian Rule: Tentative Conclusions About Uncertain Democracies*. Baltimore: Johns Hopkins University Press, 1986.

Off, Carol. *The Lion, The Fox and The Eagle*. Toronto: Vintage Canada, 2001.

Osiel, Mark. *Mass Atrocity, Collective Memory and the Law*. New Brunswick, NJ: Transaction Publishers, 2000.

Paris, Roland. *At War's End: Building Peace after Civil Conflict*. New York: Cambridge University Press, 2004.

Pavlaković, Vjeran. "Better the Grave than a Slave: Croatia and the International Criminal Tribunal for the former Yugoslavia." In *Croatia after Independence: Politics, Society, Foreign Relations*, edited by Sabrina P. Ramet, Konrad Klewing, and Reneo Lukić. Munich: Oldenbourg Wissenschaftsverlag, 2008.

Peskin, Victor. *International Justice in Rwanda and the Balkans: Virtual Trials and the Struggle for State Cooperation*. Cambridge: Cambridge University Press, 2008.

"Courting Rwanda: The Promises and Pitfalls of the ICTR Outreach Programme." *Journal of International Criminal Justice* 3, no. 4 (2005): 950–61.

Pickering, Paula M. *Peacebuilding in the Balkans: The View from the Ground Floor*. Ithaca, NY: Cornell University Press, 2007.

Plavšić, Biljana. *Svedočim – knjiga pisana u zatvoru* (I testify – A book written in prison). Banja Luka: Trioprint, 2005.

Pouligny, Beatrice. *Peace Operations Seen from Below: UN Missions and Local People*. Bloomfield, CT: Kumarian Press, 2006.

Power, Samantha, and Graham Allison, eds. *Realizing Human Rights: Moving from Inspiration to Impact*. New York: St. Martin's Press, 2000.

Price, Richard. "Moral Limit and Possibility in World Politics." In *Moral Limit and Possibility in World Politics*, edited by Richard Price. Cambridge: Cambridge University Press, 2008.

Putnam, Robert. "Diplomacy and Domestic Politics: The Logic of Two-Level Games." *International Organization* 42, no. 3 (1988): 427–60.

Putnam, Tonya. "Human Rights and Sustainable Peace." In *Ending Civil Wars: The Implementation of Peace Agreements*, edited by Stephen J. Stedman et al. Boulder, CO: Lynne Rienner Publishers, 2002.

Rajagopal, Balakrishnan. *International Law from Below: Development, Social Movements and Third World Resistance*. Cambridge: Cambridge University Press, 2003.

Ramet, Sabrina P. *Balkan Babel: The Disintegration of Yugoslavia from the Death of Tito to Ethnic War*. Boulder, CO: Westview Press, 1996.

Nationalism and Federalism in Yugoslavia, 1962–1991. Bloomington: Indiana University Press, 1992.

Riedlmayer, András J. "From the Ashes: The Past and the Future of Bosnia's Cultural Heritage." In *Islam and Bosnia: Conflict Resolution and Foreign Policy in Multi-Ethnic States*, edited by Maya Shatzmiller. Montreal: McGill-Queen's University Press, 2002.

"Crimes of War, Crimes of Peace: Destruction of Libraries During and After the Balkan Wars of the 1990s." *Library Trends* 56, no. 1 (Summer 2007): 107–32.

Risse, Thomas, Stephen C. Ropp, and Kathryn Sikkink, eds. *The Power of Human Rights: International Norms and Domestic Change*. Cambridge: Cambridge University Press, 1999.

Rockoff, Jennifer M. "Prosecutor v. Zejnil Delalić (The Čelebići Case)." *Military Law Review* 166 (2000): 172–198.

Rohde, David. *Endgame: The Betrayal and Fall of Srebrenica, Europe's Worst Massacre Since World War II*. New York: Farrar, Straus and Giroux, 1997.

Roht-Arriaza, Naomi, and Javier Mariezcurrena, eds. *Transitional Justice in the Twenty-First Century: Beyond Truth versus Justice*. Cambridge: Cambridge University Press, 2006.

Rosenberg, Gerald N. *The Hollow Hope: Can Courts Bring About Social Change?* Chicago: University of Chicago Press, 1991.

"Positivism, Interpretivism and the Study of the Law." In *Law and Social Movements, edited by Michael W. McCann*. Aldershot, UK: Ashgate Publishing, 2006.

Rupnik, Jacques. "The Post-Communist Divide." *Journal of Democracy* 10, no. 1 (1999): 57–62.

Rustow, Dankwart. "Transitions to Democracy: Toward a Dynamic Model." *Comparitive Politics* 2, no. 3 (1970): 337–63.

Schabas, William. "Sentencing by International Tribunals: A Human Rights Approach." *Duke Journal of Comparative and International Law* 7 (1997): 461–517.

Scharf, Michael P. *Balkan Justice: The Story Behind the First International War Crimes Trial Since Nuremberg*. Durham, NC: Carolina Academic Press, 1997.

Schimmelfennig, Frank. "Strategic Calculation and International Socialization: Membership Incentives, Party Constellations, and Sustained Compliance in Central and Eastern Europe." *International Organization* 59, no. 4 (2005): 827–860.

Schirmer, Jennifer. *The Guatemalan Military Project: A Violence Called Democracy*. Philadelphia, PA: University of Pennsylvania Press, 2004.

"Whose Testimony? Whose Truth? Where are the Armed Actors in the Stoll-Menchú Controversy?" *Human Rights Quarterly* 25, no. 1 (2003): 60–73.

Schmitter, Phillipe C. "The Conceptual Travels of Transitologists and Consolidationists: How Far to the East Should They Attempt to Go?" *Slavic Review* 53, no. 1 (Spring 1994): 173–85.

Scott, James C. *Seeing Like a State: How Certain Schemes to Improve the Human Condition Have Failed*. New Haven, CT: Yale University Press, 1998.

Sekulic, Dusko, Garth Massey, and Randy Hodson. "Who Were the Yugoslavs? Failed Sources of a Common Identity in the Former Yugoslavia." *American Sociological Review* 59, no. 1 (February 1994): 83–97.

Sikkink, Kathryn. "The Role of Consequences, Comparison and Counterfactuals in Constructivist Ethical Thought." In *Moral Limit and Possibility in World Politics*, edited by Richard Price. Cambridge: Cambridge University Press, 2008.

Sikkink, Kathryn, and Carrie Booth Walling. "The Impact of Human Rights Trials in Latin America." *Journal of Peace Research* 44, no. 4 (2007): 427–45.

Silber, Laura, and Alan Little. *Yugoslavia: Death of a Nation*. New York: Penguin Books, 1997.

Skinner, Mark, and Jon Sterenberg. "Turf Wars: Authority and Responsibility for the Investigation of Mass Graves." *Forensic Science Journal* 151, nos. 2–3 (2005): 221–32.

Sloane, Robert D. "The Expressive Capacity of International Punishment: The Limits of the National Law Analogy and the Potential of International Criminal Law." *Stanford Journal of International Law* 43, no. 1 (2007).

Sniderman, Paul, and Edward Carmines. *Reaching Beyond Race*. Cambridge, MA: Harvard University Press, 1997.

Snyder, Jack L., and Leslie Vinjamuri. "Trials and Errors: Principle and Pragmatism in Strategies of International Justice." *International Security* 28, no. 3 (2003/4): 5–44.

Sriram, Chandra Lekha. *Confronting Past Human Rights Violations: Justice vs. Peace in Times of Transition*. London: Frank Cass, 2004.

Stewart, Christopher S. *Hunting the Tiger: The Fast Life and Violent Death of the Balkans' Most Dangerous Man*. New York: Thomas Dunne Books, 2008.

Stiglmayer, Alexandra, ed. *Mass Rape: The War Against Women in Bosnia-Herzegovina*. Lincoln: University of Nebraska Press, 1994.

Stover, Eric. *The Witnesses: War Crimes and the Promise of Justice in The Hague*. Philadelphia, PA: University of Pennsylvania Press, 2007.

Stover, Eric, and Gilles Peress. *The Graves: Srebrenica and Vukovar*. Zurich: Scalo Publishers, 1998.

Stover, Eric, and Harvey M. Weinstein, "Conclusion: A common objective, a universe of alternatives." In *My Neighbor, My Enemy: Justice and Community in the Aftermath of Mass Atrocity*, edited by Eric Stover and Harvey M. Weinstein. Cambridge: Cambridge University Press, 2004.

eds., *My Neighbor, My Enemy: Justice and Community in the Aftermath of Mass Atrocity*. Cambridge: Cambridge University Press, 2004.

Stover, Eric, and Rachel Shigekane. "The Missing in the Aftermath of War: When Do the Needs of Victims' Families and International War Crimes Tribunals Clash?" *International Review of the Red Cross*, no. 848 (2002): 845–66.

Subotić, Jelena. *Hijacked Justice: Dealing with the Past in the Balkans*. Ithaca, NY: Cornell University Press, 2009.

Tabeau, Ewa. *Rat u brojkama: demografski gubici u ratovima na teritoriji bivše Jugoslavije 1991–1999 (War in figures: Demographic losses in the wars on the territory of the former Yugoslavia 1991–1999)*. Belgrade: Helsinki Committee for Human Rights in Serbia, 2009.

Tabeau, Ewa, and Jakub Bijak, "War-related Deaths in the 1992–1995 Armed Conflicts in Bosnia and Herzegovina: A Critique of Previous Estimates and Recent Results." *European Journal of Population/Revue Européenne de Démographie* 21, nos. 2–3 (June 2005): 187–215.

Tarrow, Sidney G. *Power in Movement: Social Movements, Collective Action, and Politics*. Cambridge: Cambridge University Press, 1994.

Teitel, Ruti. *Transitional Justice*. Oxford: Oxford University Press, 2002.

"Transitional Justice Genealogy," *Harvard Human Rights Journal* 16 (2003): 69–94.

Tetlock, Philip, and Aaron Belkin, eds. *Counterfactual Thought Experiments in World Politics: Logical, Methodological, and Psychological Perspectives*. Princeton, NJ: Princeton University Press, 1996.

Thompson, Mark. *Forging War: The Media in Serbia, Croatia, Bosnia and Hercegovina*. Luton, UK: University of Luton Press / Article 19, 1999.

Tilly, Charles. *Contentious Performances*. Cambridge: Cambridge University Press, 2008.

Democracy. Cambridge: Cambridge University Press, 2007.

Social Movements, 1768–2004. Boulder, CO: Paradigm Publishers, 2008.

Tilly, Charles, and Sidney Tarrow. *Contentious Politics*. Boulder, CO: Paradigm Publishers, 2007.

Treves, Tullio, Marco Frigessi di Rattalma, Attila Tanzi, Alessandro Fodella, Cesar Pitea, and Chiara Ragni. *Civil Society, International Courts and Compliance Bodies*. The Hague: TMC Asser Press, 2005.

Urusaro Karekezi, Alice, Alphonse Nshimiyimana, and Beth Mutamba. "Localizing Justice: Gacaca Courts in Post-Genocide Rwanda." In *My Neighbor, My Enemy: Justice and Community in the Aftermath of Mass Atrocity*, edited by Eric Stover and Harvey M. Weinstein. Cambridge: Cambridge University Press, 2004.

Verdery, Katherine. *What Was Socialism and What Comes Next*. Princeton, NJ: Princeton University Press, 1996.

Vinjamuri, Leslie, and Jack L. Snyder. "Advocacy and Scholarship in the Study of International War Crimes Tribunals and Transitional Justice." *Annual Review of Political Science* 7, no. 1 (2004): 345–62.

Vulliamy, Ed. *Seasons in Hell: Slaughter and Betrayal in Bosnia*. New York: Simon and Schuster, 1994.

Wagner, Sarah E. *To Know Where He Lies: DNA Technology and the Search for Srebrenica's Missing.* Berkeley: University of California Press, 2008.

Wesselingh, Isabelle, and Arnaud Vaulerin. *Raw Memory: Prijedor, Laboratory of Ethnic Cleansing.* London: Saqi Books, 2005.

Wiebes, Cees. *Intelligence and the War in Bosnia 1992-1995.* Munster, Germany: Lit Verlag, 2003.

Williams, Erin D., and John D. Crews. "From Dust to Dust: Ethical and Practical Issues Involved in the Location, Exhumation, and Identification of Bodies from Mass Graves." *Croatian Medical Journal* 44, no. 3 (2003): 251-58.

Williams, Paul R., and Michael P. Scharf. *Peace with Justice?: War Crimes and Accountability in the Former Yugoslavia.* Lanham, MD: Rowman and Littlefield Publishers, 2002.

Wilson, Richard A. "Conclusion: The Anthropology of Human Rights." In *The Practice of Human Rights: Tracking Law Between the Global and the Local*, edited by Mark Goodale and Sally Engle Merry. Cambridge: Cambridge University Press, 2007.

The *Politics of Truth and Reconciliation in South Africa: Legitimizing the Post-Apartheid State.* Cambridge: Cambridge University Press, 2001.

Woodward, Susan L. *Balkan Tragedy: Chaos and Dissolution After the Cold War.* Washington D.C.: The Brookings Institution Press, 1995.

Zacklin, Ralph. "The Failings of Ad Hoc International Tribunals." *Journal of International Criminal Justice* 2, no. 2 (2004): 541-45.

Zakaria, Fareed. "The Rise of Illiberal Democracy." *Foreign Affairs* 76, no. 6 (November/December 1997): 22-43.

Zemans, Frances Kahn. "Legal Mobilization: The Neglected Role of Law in the Political System." *American Political Science Review* 77 No. 3 (1983): 690-703.

Index

victim mobilization and, 27–28, 144
victims' needs addressed by, 278–81
war in Bosnia as civil war, 180
Women of Srebrenica and, 107
International Crisis Group, 39
International Herald Tribune, 119
international humanitarian law.
    See humanitarian law, international
*International Justice in Rwanda and the
    Balkans: Virtual Trials and the Struggle
    for State Cooperation* (Peskin), 47
international law, society and, 49–51
    constitutive branch of, 26, 49
    international courts and, influence of,
        25–26
    origins of, 50
    SFRY and, 33–34
    social movements and, 17
    Third World and, development barriers in,
        50
International Police Task Force (IPTF), 164,
    259
    reform of, 240
International Research and Exchange Board
    (IREX), 157
International Strategic Studies Association
    (ISSA), 141
Internet, Čelebići trial on, 185–86
Inzko, Valentin, 291
IPTF. *See* International Police Task Force
IREX. *See* International Research and
    Exchange Board
ISSA. *See* International Strategic Studies
    Association
Ivanišević, Bogdan, 288
IWPR. *See* Institute for War and Peace
    Reporting
Izetbegović, Alija, 73, 189–90
    square, 270
Izetbegović, Bakir, 73, 189–90

Jagger, Bianca, 108
Jakovljević, Ranko, 259
Janvier, Bernard, 80, 120
Jelavić, Ante, 248
Jelisić, Goran, 154, 286
JMC. *See* Joint Military Commission
JNA. *See* Yugoslav People's Army
Johnson, Michael, 253
Johnstone, Diana, 141, 142
Joint Military Commission (JMC), 214
Jokić, Dragan, 130

Jovanović, Vladislav, 83
Jurčević, Marinko, 241
justice cascade, 34–35
    in Bosnia, 35–36
    ICTY and, 35
Justice in the Balkans (Hagan), 43
*Justice Unknown, Justice Unsatisfied?:
    Bosnian NGOs Speak about the
    International Criminal Tribunal for the
    former Yugoslavia* (Cibelli/Guberek), 22,
    148–49

Kambanda, Jean, 187
Karadžić, Radovan, 66, 91, 164 166, 286
    arrest of, 269–70
    criminal indictments against, for
        Srebrenica massacre, 83, 115, 134, 182
    prosecution of, 90, 93
    public opinion on arrest of, 166–67, 230
    Srebrenica enclave and, militarized
        separation of under, 79
    as war hero, 139
Kertes, Mihalj, 61
The Key to My Neighbor's House (Neuffer),
    43
Klarin, Mirko, 287
KM. *See* convertible mark
Konjic municipality, 176. *See also* Bradina,
    attacks on
    attacks on Bradina in, 194–99
    Bosniak views on Čelebići prison camp,
        199
    church repair throughout, political
        symbolism of, 205–06
    Croat return to, 206
    ethnic demography of, postwar, 205,
        206
    ethnic demography of, prewar, 176
    ICTY Outreach Program in, 207–08
    national elections and, as factor for war,
        192–93
    postwar developments in, 204–07
    refugee return to, 205
    Serb views on Čelebići prison camp,
        199–200
    wartime deaths in, 176
    wartime narratives within, 192–200
Kopanja, Željko, 183, 190
Kordić, Dario, 74
Kosovo, international war crimes in, 60
Kovač, Radomir, 153
Kovač, Slobodan, 252

as "opinion-shaper", 160, 162
for Srebrenica massacre, 82
Medica Zenica, 149
Médecins Sans Frontières (MSF), 120
Mégret, Frédéric, 30
Mehmedović, Hatidža, 104
Memišević, Fadila, 103
Memorandum of the Serbian Academy of
    Sciences and Arts (SANU), 63
Merry, Sally Engle, 280
Mikerević, Dragan, 111, 128
military forces, in "transitional justice"
    formal procedures for, 215–16
    reconstruction of, democracy and, 212
    scholarly analysis of, 211–13
Milošević, Dragomir, 68
Milošević, Slobodan, 6, 24, 154, 286, 291
    in "Kula camp video", 61
    as media focus, 63, 157–58
    multinational crimes of, 60–61
    rise to power of, 60
    Srebrenica massacre and, 60–64, 83, 116,
        130–31, 132, 140, 182
    use of Red Berets by, 61
Milošević trial, 60–64, 130–31
    "Kula camp video" in, 61
    media coverage of, 157–58
    multinational crimes as basis of, 60–61
Milovanović, Manojlo, 85
Ministry of Internal Affairs (MUP), 72, 165,
    189, 288
Minow, Martha, 175
    on power of narrative, 175
Missing Persons Institute (MPI), 107, 125
Mitrović, Petar, 265
Mladić, Ratko, 69, 83, 166, 286
    criminal indictments against, for
        Srebrenica massacre, 134, 182
    as fugitive, 271
    public opinion on, 166–67, 230
    Srebrenica massacre under, 115, 116, 120
    as war hero, 139
moral education theory, punishment in, 11,
    276
Mothers of the Enclaves of Srebrenica and
    Žepa, 21, 22, 99, 103, 124, 263
    ICTY support for, 107
    main goals of, 103
    Potočari Memorial and, 108–09
Mothers of Srebrenica and Podrinje, 104
    demands for accountability by, 112–13
MPI. See Missing Persons Institute

Mrkšić, Mile, 62, 285
MSF. See Médecins Sans Frontières
Mucić, Zdravko, 177–178, 186
    criminal charges against, 178
    sentencing for, 188
Munich questionnaire, 217
MUP. See Ministry of Internal Affairs
Muslims. See Bosniaks
Mustafić, Ibran, 104, 119
Mustafić, Rizo, 101, 119
My Neighbor, My Enemy (Stover/Weinstein),
    45, 46

narratives, legal, role in social sciences,
    174–76
    academic support for, 175
    Čelebići trial and, 192–200
    DPA and, 179
    ICTY and, lack of, 179–81
Nations in Transit (Freedom House), 39
NATO. See North Atlantic Treaty Organization
Nechle, Mohammed, 245
The Netherlands
    family associations' demands for
        reparations, 118–19
    financial donations to Bosnia, 117
    ICMP and, financial support for, 117
    IKV in, 116–17
    Potočari Memorial and, financial support
        for, 117
    Srebrenica massacre and, responsibility for,
        114–16, 117, 119
Netherlands Institute for War Documentation
    (NIOD), 114, 116–17
Neuffer, Elizabeth, 43
New York Times, 182, 196–97, 248
newspapers. See media coverage, of ICTY
Nezavsine Novine, 183, 190
NGO Development Foundation, 149
Nice, Geoffrey, 61, 132, 139, 180, 284
    ICTY Outreach program and, 154, 155
NIOD. See Netherlands Institute for War
    Documentation
non-governmental organizations (NGOs)
    Amnesty International, 35, 123
    Freedom House, 39–40
    Human Rights Watch, 4, 35
    International Crisis Group, 39
    Mothers of the Enclaves of Srebrenica and
        Žepa, 22, 99, 103
    War Crimes Chamber and, 254–55
Noor (Queen), 108